unwins

book of bulbs

Andrew McIndoe

First published in the UK in 2007 by
Westland Horticulture Ltd

Unwins Ltd is a registered trademark of
Westland Horticulture Ltd
Alconbury Hill
Huntingdon
Cambridgeshire PE28 4HY

British Library Cataloguing in Publication Data
A catalogue record for this book is available from the British Library

ISBN 978-0-9556222-0-5

Produced for Westland Horticulture Ltd by
OutHouse Publishing
Winchester, Hampshire SO22 5DS

Project Editor Sue Gordon
Art Editor Robin Whitecross
Proof reader Lesley Riley
Indexer June Wilkins

Repro by Altaimage Ltd
Printed by Printer Trento Srl, Italy

contents

there's always a place for flowerbulbs

Flowerbulbs are are little bits of magic that can transform your garden in many ways. You can plant groups of bulbs in the border to add splashes of colour before later-flowering shrubs and perennials come into their own. You can plant them in containers for the patio, either on their own or mixed with seasonal bedding plants. You can use them in the house, in pots or as cut flowers, to bring spring and summer a little closer. You can sprinkle them lightly or plant them in big, bold drifts to bring fresh, bright colours to the dull green spaces beneath trees, hedges and mature shrubs.

Above: *Allium cristophii* becomes even more bewitching as the flowers fade. Right: Just a few tulips in a pot is all it takes …

history and holland

Left: The flat fields of the Netherlands have become the home of the flowerbulb.

Think of flowerbulbs and we immediately think of Holland: tulips from Amsterdam, windmills, clogs full of crocus, Dutch girls in national costume holding armfuls of flowers. In fact, although Holland is steeped in bulb history, no flowerbulbs are native to the Netherlands. All have found their way there from far afield.

Compared to most other plants, those that produce bulbs of some description are easy to dig up and transport and have a good chance of survival when replanted somewhere else sometime later. For this reason, it was often the early explorers, merchants and travellers who were responsible for carrying bulbous plants from one country or continent to another, then introducing them into cultivation or, perhaps, the wild.

So, the flora of a country located on a sea route had the greatest chance of distribution. For example, agapanthus found their way from South Africa to Madeira and the Scilly Isles; crocosmia to the shores of southwest England, Scotland and southern Ireland. Tulips, on the other hand, gradually made their way overland from Central Asia to their more well-known home in Holland.

the rise of the tulip

The tulip is the national flower of Turkey and has been cultivated by the Turks for over a thousand years. Tulips were associated with the wealth and power of the great Ottoman empire and feature in the art and culture of the day. Tulips have always been flowers of passion, exciting the attention of botanists and plant collectors, but it was when the Europeans began to travel and collect plants in the 16th century that the interest in tulips really began in earnest. Carolus Clusius, an eminent botanist working at the University of Leiden, brought the tulip to Holland. The Dutch had already seen pictures of these wonderful flowers, and the introduction of the real thing fanned the flames of the famous 'tulipomania' that consumed Holland in the early 17th century.

By 1625 a single tulip bulb of a scarce variety could fetch as much as the price of a house. Fortunes were made, and were then lost as quickly when the tulip market crashed in 1637. Tulipomania might have been over but the foundations of the Dutch bulb industry were well and truly laid. Today the Netherlands produces around nine billion bulbs each year, of which seven billion are exported; the USA is the largest importer.

Above: The Keukenhof: always inspiring, imaginative and breathtaking in spring. Right: *Tulipa* 'Estella Rijnveld'.

the Keukenhof garden

Keukenhof is the world-famous showcase of the Dutch bulb industry. It was landscaped as a park in the English style in the 1830s and has been used as an open-air exhibition of flowerbulbs since 1949. Attracting over one million visitors every year, it is one of the most photographed sights in the world. Growers invest time and money to produce imaginative and stunning displays, demonstrating how bulbs can be used and showing myriad varieties, old and new. Every year all seven million bulbs are renewed, the planting schemes are changed and even the grass is replaced.

A host of golden daffodils revelling in the sunshine: a scene that is the very essence of spring.

daffodils, from market to garden

The daffodil is one of the few flowerbulbs that Holland has not made her own. More daffodils and narcissi are produced in the UK, notably in Cornwall and Lincolnshire, than in the Netherlands. Our native daffodil, *Narcissus pseudonarcissus* subsp. *pseudonarcissus*, is the dainty, delicate creature that inspired Wordsworth's famous poem. Most cultivated yellow-trumpet daffodils are descended from the larger and bolder Spanish daffodil, *Narcissus pseudonarcissus* subsp. *major*, which was introduced to Britain by the Romans.

Daffodils have long been grown in Cornwall for early cut flowers, brought into bud and bloom by the mild climate two months or more before the rest of the country and sent by train to the London markets. With milder winters, the season is now shorter and, with the development of air transport, the range and availability of flowers is greater – but there is still nothing to beat an early daffodil as a harbinger of spring.

Today there is an infinite variety of types of daffodils and it is these, rather than just the basic yellow daffodil, that are in great demand for use in gardens. Dwarf varieties are increasingly grown for their weather resistance and suitability for containers; fragrant narcissi and those of delicate and unusual colouring are favoured for their ability to mix easily with other plants.

From the left: *Lilium speciosum* var. *rubrum*, *Hyacinthus orientalis* 'King Codro', *Fritillaria imperialis*, *Narcissus pseudonarcissus* 'Lobularis'.

Flowerbulb facts and fables

The lily The lily has been cultivated since the earliest times. Lilies appear in paintings attributed to the Minoan civilisation, on the island of Crete. The Assyrians regarded the lily as a holy flower, attributing it with medicinal qualities. The petals of lilies were used with honey to make a cosmetic that removed facial wrinkles, and the crushed bulbs were thought to cure infections.

The hyacinth The hyacinth was prized by the Dutch nearly as highly as the tulip. Hyacinths are tricky to grow and propagate, and the Dutch growers were masters of their trade. In Dutch gardens, hyacinths and auriculas were grown between low box hedges, where the flowers could be protected and admired. In France, in the mid-18th century, Madame de Pompadour, mistress of Louis XV, planted hyacinths in the Dutch style in the gardens at Versailles. The French aristocracy quickly adopted the fashion, and the passion for hyacinths in France grew apace. These wonderful fragrant blooms are still French favourites today.

The crown imperial The crown imperial, *Fritillaria imperialis*, is a stately bloom with a tall, straight stem and a ruff of emerald-green leaves above its hanging bell-shaped flowers. Legend has it that the crown imperial was originally white with upturned blooms. The story goes that, when all other flowers bowed their heads as a mark of respect for Jesus on his way to Golgotha, the crown imperial, so proud of her green ruff, did not. When Jesus looked her way she blushed and bowed her blooms, and to this day you will find tears in the heart of every *Fritillaria imperialis* flower.

The daffodil The national flower of Wales was originally the leek, but the Victorians did not consider a vegetable glamorous enough to pin on their lapels on St David's day, so the daffodil, which flowers around the patron saint's birthday, was adopted as the country's national flower instead. The Tenby daffodil, *Narcissus obvallaris*, was common in the Tenby area of Pembrokeshire at the time. Trainloads of the bulbs in bud and flower were dug up each year and sent to London's Covent Garden for St David's day, resulting in the disappearance of the plant from the wild. The bulbs are still found in many gardens in the local area.

what is a bulb?

Lily bulbs: powerhouses of energy, with food and water ready and waiting to produce strong stems, healthy leaves and luscious blooms.

Choosing the right bulbs for your garden

You can grow practically any flowerbulbs in your garden if you choose the right situation for them. Some bulbs are easy, growing and flowering no matter where or how you plant them. Others are more discerning and have preferences of soil and aspect. By growing some in pots and containers, you have more control over soil type. Gardeners in cold, exposed areas, or with very sunny or shady gardens, must choose carefully.

Good choices for well-drained, sunny situations
Tulip, allium, hyacinth, iris, canna, crocosmia, gladiolus, nerine

Good choices for shady situations
Narcissus, chionodoxa, *Anemone blanda* 🏆, bluebell, begonia, cyclamen

Good choices for moist soils
Narcissus, fritillaria, snowdrop, calla, bluebell

Good choices for cold gardens
Snowdrop, crocus, narcissus, *Scilla siberica* 🏆, chionodoxa

Horticulturalists use various terms when describing different types of bulb. They talk about gladiolus corms, dahlia tubers, canna rhizomes and tulip bulbs but, as far as the gardener is concerned, all fall into the category of flowerbulbs.

what do bulbs do?

Although these various types of 'bulb' are different in structure, all have the same purpose: the storage of food and water. Usually this is to enable the plant to survive from season to season through a period of dormancy. Possibly because the soil and weather during this dormant period are not warm or wet enough for growth, the plant rests beneath the surface as a bulb. Then, when conditions are right, it is ready, with its store of food and water, to grow, flower and set seed before things take a turn for the worse.

bulbs – born survivors

Bulbs are an adaptation to environment. Think of bluebells growing in a beech wood. The bulbs rest beneath the surface of the soil during the cold days of winter. As the days lengthen and temperatures rise, the bulbs produce leaves and then flower just as the leaves of the beech trees begin to unfurl. The bluebells set seed, and the foliage starts to wither and die down as the leaf canopy of the trees thickens, robbing the bluebells of light and water. The bluebells retreat beneath the surface until the following spring, leaving their flower stalks to dry and distribute seed. Without the bulb to supply food, the bluebell could not grow quickly enough to flower and set seed before competition from the beech trees becomes too much.

Cyclamen tubers store food and water, enabling the plants to survive periods of adverse conditions.

Building bulbs for the following season

For a bulb to store food for the following season, it has first to manufacture it. As with any plant, a bulb will draw nutrients from the soil, but the majority of the stored food is manufactured in the leaves and passed down to the bulb. So it is essential that the leaves of flowerbulbs are allowed to remain on the plant for as long as possible and are left to die down naturally. If the leaves are cut off prematurely, the bulb will not have stored enough food for next year's flowers.

A bulb is a living thing

It is important to remember that a bulb is a living thing. Even when dormant, it is respiring slowly. It requires air and will produce heat and water vapour. If exposed to high temperatures and sunlight, it will dry out. If suffocated in a plastic bag, it will become damp and warm and will rot.

In its dormant state, it allows you to handle it carefully and transplant it in the desired position ready to grow and bloom the following season. It has to complete its annual life cycle: you cannot miss a year by storing bulbs through the growing season to plant in a year's time. In other words, when you have bought them, do not forget to plant them!

Different types of bulb

True bulbs *For example narcissus, tulip, allium, amaryllis*

Onions are true bulbs. They consist of swollen leaf bases attached to a basal plate: a flattened, compressed stem. In the heart of the bulb, the embryo shoot and flowerbuds wait to emerge. Lilies too are true bulbs, made up of waxy leaf scales.

Corms *For example crocus, gladiolus, crocosmia, freesia*

These are flattened, compressed stems surrounded by fibrous papery leaves. The shoots are at the top of the corm and also on the sides, beneath the protective leaves.

It is important not to damage the shoot or shoots at the top of the corm, as these contain next season's flowers.

Tubers *For example begonia, cyclamen, anemone, dahlia*

There are two types of tubers: stem tubers and tuberous roots. The former are swollen stems that sit just below the ground or on the soil surface. They are usually fleshy and may have roots over much of the surface. They have dormant shoots on the upper surface and, sometimes, the sides. A potato, usually thought of as a root vegetable, is actually a stem tuber.

A tuberous root is a swollen root that stores food and water. It can be divided, as long as there is a shoot on each piece of the tuberous root. A dahlia is a classic example.

Rhizomes *For example canna, calla, flag iris*

Rhizomes are swollen stems that store food and water for the plant. They grow horizontally on, or just below, the soil surface with the main growing point at the leading end but with other side shoots that can develop into side branches. These can be removed from the parent plant and, as long as they have some roots and a shoot, they will grow independently.

From the left: True bulbs, corms, tubers and a rhizome.

buying flowerbulbs

Bulbs, bulbs and more bulbs in a Dutch flower market.

Buying a few flowerbulbs each year is one of the great pleasures of gardening, and the cost of buying them is small in relation to the rewards they bring. Some flowerbulbs can be regarded as perennial plants; others are best replaced on an annual basis. Although most gardeners plant their bulbs with the intention that they will be there for years to come, in reality many varieties are best renewed annually, especially those that are grown in pots and containers.

Store your bulbs in a cool, airy place. Never leave them in polythene bags, where the damp conditions will make them 'sweat' and cause deterioration.

when to buy

Spring-flowering bulbs are bought in late summer and autumn. Some, such as tulips and narcissi, may still be available in early winter and, if planted immediately, will still perform well the following spring.

Popular spring-flowering bulbs to buy in autumn: daffodils, narcissi, hyacinths, tulips, crocus, snowdrops, muscari, fritillarias

Summer-flowering bulbs are bought in late winter and spring. Many, such as begonias and dahlias, are not hardy, so they should be stored or planted indoors before they are planted outside in the garden.

Popular summer-flowering bulbs to buy in early spring: dahlias, lilies, begonias, gladioli, cannas, callas

Tips on buying flowerbulbs

- Buy early in the season: the range will be greater and the choice wider.
- Look for firm bulbs, with their outer coats intact. Spots of green mould and sunken patches on the bulbs are a bad sign. Leave them in the shop.
- Gently feel the bulbs: they should be firm and not shrivelled. Towards the end of the buying season, look out for deterioration of bulbs sold in prepacks.
- Handle bulbs gently: rough treatment can cause bruising and damage.
- Buy top-quality, top-size bulbs. Cheap bulbs may be of a smaller, inferior grade and their performance and flower size can also be inferior.

bulb size

The size of a flowerbulb is expressed as the girth measured in centimetres around the bulb at its widest point. This is shown on the packaging or, for loose bulbs, on the display case. Some bulbs are graded exactly within a size range, for example the bulbs of *Hyacinthus* 'Delft Blue' labelled as '16/17' are between 16 and 17cm in girth. Other bulbs may be graded to a minimum size, for example the bulbs of *Tulipa* 'Ballerina' labelled as '7up' are at least 7cm in girth and may be larger. Bulb size varies according to type and variety. However, if, when you are buying one variety, there is a choice of size, buy the larger bulbs as these normally give better results.

If you are not sure what the growing conditions are like in your garden choose good, reliable, well-established varieties such as ***Tulipa 'Prinses Irene'*** 🏆, ***Tulipa 'Red Riding Hood'*** 🏆, ***Narcissus 'February Gold'*** 🏆, ***Narcissus 'Ice Follies'*** 🏆, ***Muscari armeniacum*** 🏆, ***Lilium regale*** 🏆 *and* ***large-flowered Dutch crocus****. These are foolproof and will perform in any situation. Once you have succeeded with these, you can be more adventurous with more unusual and exotic varieties.*

The RHS Award of Garden Merit 🏆

Many of the plants in this book have the symbol 🏆 after their names. This denotes that they have been given the Award of Garden Merit (AGM) by the Royal Horticultural Society. To qualify, a plant has to be easy to grow, of sound constitution and, most importantly, a good all-round garden plant. This is not to say that a plant without an AGM is not worth growing. It means that, to date, the Royal Horticultural Society has not trialled it or the plant does not meet all these criteria.

loose or prepacks?

In garden centres, flowerbulbs are sold loose and in prepacks. Loose bulbs can offer better value, and you can choose each bulb individually. This is a good way to buy larger bulbs that handle easily, including tulips, narcissi, gladioli and hyacinths.

Prepacks protect the bulbs, and the package shows you what to expect from the bulbs and gives cultural information. This is the best way to buy specialist varieties and smaller bulbs such as iris, crocus, muscari and fritillarias.

Left: The size of a lily bulb is the girth, in centimetres, at the widest point. Below: Shiny specie tulip bulbs – full of promise of flowers.

buying flowerbulbs

Above: For a mass display like this, plant tulip bulbs in autumn. Below: Pot-grown flowerbulbs are a great way to add near-instant colour.

buying bulbs already growing in pots

Many flowerbulbs are available pot-grown, in leaf and bud, ready either for immediate planting in containers in the garden or for temporary decoration in the house on the window sill. Gardeners on heavy soil often prefer this way of planting more delicate bulbs, such as dwarf iris. As pot-grown plants, they have already developed healthy root systems and should establish easily if planted directly into the open ground. Those used in pots and containers can be transplanted to a more permanent position after flowering.

More robust subjects, such as tulips and narcissi, are also available as pot-grown stock. They are a great way of adding almost instant colour to areas where bulbs were not planted in advance. Some summer-flowering bulbs, especially dahlias and lilies, are available pot-grown from late spring and are ideal to fill gaps and provide instant colour in the summer garden.

Tips on buying some of the most popular varieties of flowerbulbs

Buying daffodil and narcissus bulbs – *buy in late summer and autumn*

Daffodils and narcissi are robust bulbs that withstand handling. Bulb size varies greatly according to variety. Bulk packs of large-flowered varieties are readily available in garden centres. These are ideal for naturalising. Larger bulbs usually produce more flower stems in the first year. Smaller bulbs will still perform and multiply in seasons to come. Dwarf narcissi and specialist varieties are usually offered, and are best bought, in prepacks.

Buying tulip bulbs – *buy in autumn and early winter*

Some varieties of tulip produce smaller bulbs than others. However, where large-grade bulbs (sized 8up and above) of tall varieties are available, choose these for best performance. Delay planting until late autumn (see page16).

Buying hyacinths – *buy in autumn*

If you want them to flower by Christmas, buy prepared hyacinths in September and plant immediately. Larger bulbs produce larger flowers and, often, second blooms on each bulb. Smaller bulbs are ideal for beds and pots outdoors.

Take care when handling hyacinth bulbs as they can cause skin irritation. Wear gloves and wash your hands afterwards.

Buying crocus – *buy in autumn*

The bulbs of specie crocus are always smaller than those of the large-flowering, Dutch crocus. They all give good results. Buy crocus bulbs in large quantities: you generally need many more than you think you do to make any sort of an impact in the garden. After purchase, store the bulbs in a cold place and plant them any time up until early December.

Even autumn-flowering crocus bulbs are sold during the autumn.

Buying snowdrops – *buy in autumn (or 'in the green' in early spring – see page 72)*

Buy snowdrop bulbs in early autumn and plant them immediately. They dry out easily so, if you have to store them for a few days, keep them cool and dark. They are rarely at their best in the first year after planting: be patient.

Buying begonias – *buy in late winter or early spring*

Begonia tubers are dry and fibrous on the outside. They should feel firm when bought. When stored in a warm room or shop for several weeks, the tubers can dry out and deteriorate; an occasional light spraying with water, as well as storing them in wood shavings or dry peat substitute, will help to prevent this. Lightly scratch the skin of the tuber with a fingernail and the skin should lift to reveal a fleshy pink or gold interior. If the inside is dry, brown and fibrous, the tuber is dead and will not grow. Begonia tubers are easily damaged by frost, so always store them in a frost-free place.

Buying dahlias – *buy in late winter or early spring*

The size of a dahlia tuber varies with the variety: large tubers do not necessarily mean larger plants, and vice versa. Dahlia tubers are remarkably resilient: even shrivelled tubers produced late in the season often give excellent results. Dahlia tubers also need protection from frost. Store them in a cool, airy place until you plant them.

Buying lilies – *buy in autumn, winter or early spring*

Buy lilies as soon as they appear in the shops. Keep them cold until you plant them and do this as soon as possible to prevent them from drying out. Bulb size varies with variety, but choose large-grade bulbs, where they are available, for the best display.

planting flowerbulbs

Nearly all bulbs are easy to grow, from exotics such as *Zantedeschia aethiopica* (left) to the native bluebell, *Hyacinthoides non-scripta* (below).

Bulbs are the easiest of plants to plant. They are clean, compact and light to handle. They will not go into immediate decline if planting is postponed for a short while or if you forget to water them straightaway. Most bulbs are forgiving plants and will still perform if you do not get the planting depth or situation quite right.

planting depth

Tips on planting and suggested depths are given throughout the book. However, if in doubt, plant bulbs at three times their depth below the surface of the soil or compost.

planting distance

Usually the information on the packet recommends planting too far apart for a display with impact. Spacing the bulbs one bulb's width apart will give a dense clump. Double or treble the space will allow for the flowers to open and the bulbs to multiply if they are left in the ground for the following year.

when to plant

Most spring-flowering bulbs can be planted any time in the autumn. Crocus and narcissi can be planted at any point until early December. Small bulbs, such as snowdrops, are best planted straight after purchase – the earlier the better, as this prevents drying out. Do not plant tulip bulbs before the end of October. Early planting will result in soft growth, which is susceptible to tulip fire (an incurable fungal disease that causes damage to flowers and foliage).

Summer-flowering bulbs need more consideration. Plant lilies in early spring before the bulbs dry out. Dahlias, cannas and begonias are not frost-hardy: if you want to plant early in the year, start them off in pots and give them protection indoors.

soil conditions

Nearly all bulbs like good drainage, even those that tolerate moist conditions. On heavy soils, especially clay, add sharp sand or horticultural grit to the ground. Dig in a generous amount around and below the bulbs. On very heavy clay, a 2cm layer of sharp sand immediately below the bulbs prevents rotting.

where to plant

Most flowerbulbs prefer a sunny position, but will do equally well in light shade. The flowers of spring bulbs such as crocus and daffodil last longer in light shade than they do in full sun.

Above: *Tulipa* 'Black Parrot' against *Philadelphus coronarius* 'Aureus'. Right: Alliums with foliage of different textures: *Allium* 'Mount Everest' with *Cercis canadensis* 'Forest Pansy' and (far right) *Allium* 'Globemaster' with fennel.

Flowerbulbs can so easily transform a garden into something special. Exciting planting combinations with shrubs and perennials can be hard to achieve without know-how and careful planning, but spring- and summer-flowering bulbs are a magic ingredient that will, with just a little imagination, add a designer touch to any scheme.

Put a little thought into the effects you can achieve by planting flowerbulbs with different flowers and foliage. For example, you can accentuate the colour of a gold-variegated evergreen by adding yellow daffodils or tulips. Try contrasting deep plum tulips against a yellow-foliage shrub, or blend them with one that has wine-red leaves. Pink tulips are wonderful with silver-blue foliage, as are purple and blue crocus.

Top: A stunning planting of tulips in pots provides a dramatic focal point in this generously planted garden. Above: The green-streaked, salmon-orange flowers of *Tulipa* 'Groenland' rise through blue forget-me-nots. Right: *Tulipa* 'Blueberry Ripple' is deliciously blended with purple sage and *Erysimum* 'Bowles' Mauve'.

A few tips for effective planting

- Plant in informal groups of more than five bulbs: there are few bulbs that look impressive individually. Possible exceptions are lilies, large alliums and crown imperials *(Fritillaria imperialis)*.
- In large beds and borders, repeat groups of the same variety through the planting: this amplifies the effect and gives continuity.
- Avoid planting in straight lines: usually this works only in large-scale, formal schemes.
- A colour scheme is easy to achieve with flowerbulbs. Limiting the number of colours and restricting the palette creates a sophisticated effect.
- Blue is a useful link between other colours: adding blue flowers can make just about any other colours work together.

bulbs for fragrance and colour indoors

Growing bulbs indoors is often our first introduction to this wonderful group of plants, and more often than not our first gardening experience. As children, perhaps we grew a hyacinth in a glass? Maybe we planted a few crocus bulbs in one of those pots with holes in the sides? These ways of growing bulbs never seem to wane in popularity. However, Continental influence has established a more innovative approach to the use of flowerbulbs, and has provided a greater variety of material for indoor decoration. You can be just as creative and imaginative with bulbs in the house as you can in the garden. However you use them, there is no denying the delight you will find in bringing a little seasonal colour and scent indoors.

Above: The delicate flowers of *Iris* 'Joyce' bring spring to the winter window sill. Right: The waxy flowers of a bowl of hyacinths fill a room with their sweet perfume.

Paperwhite narcissus and hyacinths can be grown among damp stones in a glass container such as this.

will all bulbs grow indoors?

Not all bulbs lend themselves to growing indoors. Some are too tall and ungainly for indoor containers. Many cannot cope with the warmer temperature and faster growth rate that this brings. Those that object often produce weak leaves and no flowers. Hyacinths, large-flowered crocus, certain narcissi and a few tulips are the most successful subjects for forcing. Other hardy bulbs, such as muscari, dwarf iris and snowdrops, can be lifted from the garden and gently coaxed into flowering a little earlier indoors than they would outside.

Any hardy bulbs grown indoors need a cool period to produce roots and become established before they set about throwing up leaves and flowers. Impatience produces poor results.

what does forcing mean?

Forcing means encouraging bulbs to bloom a little earlier than they would naturally. By growing the bulbs indoors for all or part of their growing season, in a warmer environment than they are used to in the garden, they will grow more quickly and come into flower earlier than when they are grown outdoors. However, if they are made to perform too quickly, some flowerbulbs may fail.

can I use any type of container?

Because indoor bulbs are grown in containers for a relatively short period of time, they can cope without drainage – as long as care is taken with watering. Traditionally glazed ceramic, terracotta or plastic bowls are often used for flowerbulbs. However, any type of pot, box, trough, glass tank or vessel can be used, provided it holds a sufficient amount of compost and will look good when filled with bulbs in flower. A layer of gravel or broken crocks in the bottom of the container helps with drainage.

do I have to use bulb fibre?

You can use any multi-purpose compost for bulbs, but bulb fibre has been specially formulated for bulbs growing in containers that have no drainage holes. It is an open compost, with plenty of air space, and usually contains added charcoal, which should keep the compost 'sweet' if it becomes too moist.

Never use garden soil in pots. It contains all sorts of living things that are harmless in the open ground but will multiply and become a problem in the confined environment of a pot or container.

Hyacinths are the most popular bulbs for growing indoors. Their heavy spikes of waxy flowers are deliciously scented and will fill a room with their fragrance. Hyacinth bulbs go on sale at the beginning of September, just as we return from the holidays and it seems that summer is over. A few prepared hyacinths planted in mid-September will flower in midwinter and are a great way of bringing next spring a little closer.

Planted in early autumn, prepared hyacinth bulbs will bloom in midwinter.

what are prepared hyacinths?

Prepared hyacinth bulbs have been given several weeks of cold treatment prior to sale; this makes the bulbs think that they have been through winter. When planted, they quickly develop roots and set about producing leaves and flowers. The cold treatment needs to be long enough to be successful, so bulbs should not appear in the shops before the end of August; professional growers keep bulbs in cold storage until early September.

Watch out!

Always wear gloves when handling hyacinth bulbs; they can cause irritation of the skin. Avoid putting your hands to your face and wash your hands when you have finished planting them. Once the bulbs are planted and the outer skin of the bulb is moist, this problem does not normally occur.

can I grow unprepared hyacinths indoors?

You can grow unprepared hyacinths indoors; they will simply flower later than prepared bulbs, depending on when they are planted. As a rule, they can be gently forced into flowering about three weeks before they would if they were in the garden. Some varieties are more successful than others: pink, blue and white hyacinths always work; yellow and salmon varieties can sometimes be tricky.

Buy early – as soon as you see them. Prepared hyacinths kept in a warm shop for several weeks lose the effect of their cold treatment.

how to grow a bowl of prepared hyacinths

- Buy your bulbs in early September and plant by the middle of the month if you want flowers before or at Christmas. Bulbs planted later in the month will bloom by New Year.

Always choose bulbs of the same variety for each container. Mixed varieties will grow at different rates and flower at different times.

- Before you plant your bulbs, store them in a cool, dark place. Always use bulb-planting compost in bowls or pots that have no drainage holes.

- Put a layer of compost in the bowl to a depth of at least 6cm. Sit the bulbs on the top of the compost. The bulbs can be almost touching, but ideally you should leave a gap of a centimetre or so between them. Do not firm the compost or press down on the bulbs; if you do, they will push themselves out of the compost as they produce roots.

- Fill the bowl to just below the rim with compost, firming it very gently between the bulbs. The nose of the bulb should be poking out of the compost by a centimetre or two.

- Water the compost lightly; do not saturate it.

- Place the bowl in a cool dark place. It will probably need to remain here for ten to 14 weeks. Inspect regularly and moisten the compost if necessary. If you cannot find a suitable place, sit the bowl in a large cardboard box and close the lid. Keep the box in the coolest place you can find.

Never try to hurry your hyacinths. Extra heat early on, or insufficient time in the dark, will result in premature leaf growth, stunted flowers or total failure. This applies whether you are growing prepared or unprepared bulbs.

- When the leaf shoots are 5cm high, and flame-shaped, the bowl can be moved into a cool, light room. The flame-shaped shoots indicate that the flowerbuds have emerged from the bulb. If you move them earlier than this, the leaves will probably grow ahead of the flowers and the flowers will open low down in the foliage.

- If you want to delay flowering, stand the bowl outside in a sheltered position. The flowers will continue to develop slowly. Move the bowl inside two or three weeks before you want the flowers to open.

Hyacinth flowers are big and heavy, especially some of the blue varieties. Once the flowers are fully open and the spikes are at their maximum height, they have a habit of flopping over. Be prepared for this and stake them with thin green canes and twine or support them with twigs. If flowers flop irretrievably, cut them and put them in water. The flowers last just as long when cut as they do on the bulbs.

- If you are growing a large number of hyacinths, it is worth growing them individually in 9cm flowerpots. You can then pot them up or group them in containers nearer to flowering time. By growing them in this way, you can group the bulbs that are at the same stage of development and you can use them more creatively. They look great knocked out of their pots and put in a glass container with moss or gravel.

crocus

The cheerful, striped blooms of *Crocus vernus* subsp. *albiflorus* 'Pickwick' open early indoors.

Large-flowered, Dutch crocus are easy to grow in pots and bowls indoors. The flat brown corms soon develop fat creamy shoots; these are often showing when the bulbs are sold. If you cannot plant them immediately, store the corms in a cool, dark place and they will remain in this state for several weeks.

Crocus can be planted in shallow bowls provided there is at least 4cm of compost below the bulbs. The fine roots form a fibrous mat and rarely push the bulbs out of the compost. In bowls without drainage holes, use bulb fibre and plant the corms so that they are immediately below the surface. Ideally the emerging shoots should only just be covered.

Lightly water the compost. Place the bowl of bulbs in a cool, dark place until spiky leaves are emerging from the shoots and the papery sheath that covers the flowerbuds can be seen in the middle of the leaves. By now the shoots will be about 5cm high.

Move the bowl into a cool, and light position until the flowerbuds have emerged and are clearly showing colour. At this stage the bulbs can be brought into a warmer room to flower. The blooms last much longer in cool temperatures, so a light kitchen or bathroom window sill is the ideal place for crocus.

Crocus bulbs can be grown in any type of pot. You can grow a few bulbs in a plastic 10cm pot and use it to add colour to a planted arrangement of foliage plants and early primroses.

growing crocus in crocus pots

Crocus are often grown in pots with holes in the sides – miniature versions of those used for growing strawberries and herbs. These pots can be tricky to pot up and maintain. Fill the pot to just below the holes in the sides. Position the bulbs from the inside, with the shoots pointing out through the holes. Continue filling and planting until the pot is full, then plant three or four bulbs in the top so that the shoots are just peeping through the surface. Keep in the dark until the leaves and buds have emerged.

Good varieties to grow

Blue, purple and white crocus seem to be most successful indoors. Yellow crocus sometimes fail to produce flowers, particularly when temperatures are too warm. All flowers have orange stigmas at their centre.

***Crocus vernus* subsp. *albiflorus* 'Jeanne d'Arc'**: pure white

***Crocus vernus* subsp. *albiflorus* 'Pickwick'** (left): white veined with purple

***Crocus vernus* subsp. *albiflorus* 'Purpureus Grandiflorus'**: rich purple

***Crocus vernus* subsp. *albiflorus* 'Queen of the Blues'**: mauve-blue flowers

***Crocus vernus* subsp. *albiflorus* 'Remembrance'** (below): a favourite, with large, open goblet-shaped flowers of violet-blue

You will find planting in crocus pots much easier if you moisten the compost thoroughly before you start; it will then stay in position more easily.

fragrant paperwhites and other narcissi

Some narcissi, particularly those with several small, scented flowers on each stem, are suitable for growing in pots for the house (the larger-flowered daffodils and narcissi are more challenging). Most originate from cool regions of the world and need a cold period to initiate roots and flowers and for the leaves to develop properly. Without this, they will fail. Some are given a cold preparation prior to sale, in the same way as prepared hyacinths.

Paperwhite narcissus

The most popular narcissus for growing indoors is ***Narcissus* 'Paper White Grandiflorus'**. It hails from warmer regions and does not require a period of cold or slow initial growth. The shiny, rich brown bulbs are sold in early autumn and can be planted any time from then on. If they are stored as dry bulbs in a cool, dark place, growth can be delayed; when planted and watered, they quickly start to grow.

The bulbs contain all the nutrients the plant needs to grow and flower, so this bulb is often grown in pebbles, shells or glass nuggets with just a little water (see page 29). Once roots have been produced, the leaves and flowerbuds grow quickly. The porcelain white and wonderfully fragrant blooms open on 30–40cm stems.

Buy paperwhite bulbs as soon as you see them. Store them in a cold, dark place. Plant a few bulbs every couple of weeks from mid-September onwards and you can have a succession of blooms from November through until late January.

The blooms of *Narcissus* 'Paper White Grandiflorus' are deliciously fragrant.

The selection sold today is more compact in habit than that available a few years ago and has longer-lasting flowers.

fragrant paperwhites and other narcissi

The charming *Narcissus* 'Tête à Tête' is one of the best for early flowering indoors.

narcissi in pots and bowls

All narcissi, other than paperwhites, need about 17 weeks of cold before they can be brought into flower successfully indoors. You can plant them as you would hyacinths (see pages 24–25), with the bulbs poking out of the compost surface, or you can pot them with the bulbs completely covered. Either way, once you have planted them, keep them in a cold, dark place until the roots have developed and the leaves and buds have grown at least 10cm out of the bulbs or the surface of the compost.

Once you have brought them into the light, you should still keep them as cool as possible, forcing them gently into flower with more warmth only when the flowers are about to open.

Rather than growing them indoors throughout their development, you may find you have more success if you pot them up in containers outdoors. Keep these close to the walls of the house through autumn and early winter; then move them into a cool place indoors when the leaves and flower buds are 10cm high. This is the ideal way to achieve early flowers in a conservatory or cool sunroom.

what do I do with the bulbs afterwards?

A pot of narcissi, or a bowl of hyacinths, that has grown and bloomed indoors will have given you great pleasure. Not only will you have had the rewarding experience of seeing the bulbs grow and develop, but the flowers, once they have opened, will have lasted longer than a bunch of cut flowers. After flowering, they can be planted out in the garden, but it is important to plant them as deep as you would plant dry bulbs – in other words, the soil above them must be at least three times the depth of the bulb. If you cannot put them in the garden, throw them away; they have done their job and you can buy new ones next year. If you plant the same bulbs again in pots they will most probably disappoint.

Good varieties to grow

Narcissus 'Grand Soleil d'Or' Traditionally popular for growing indoors, this narcissus has clusters of golden yellow flowers with orange centres; the fragrance is fresh and delicious. As it grows to 45cm, it can be ungainly in pots or bowls and today is more frequently used as a cut flower.

Narcissus 'Tête à Tête' 🏆 This is a compact variety, with one, two or three tiny yellow daffodil heads on short stems above short, upright leaves. It is a favourite for growing indoors, outdoors in pots and in the open ground. Indoors, it gets drawn up and spindly in warm conditions away from daylight.

Narcissus 'Bridal Crown' 🏆 Strong and compact, with scented, ivory white double flowers, this is good for growing indoors and as a cut flower (see page 53).

Narcissus 'Golden Harvest' This is one of the best yellow-trumpet daffodils for forcing. 'Dutch Master' 🏆 is similar.

Growing paperwhites in a glass cylinder

- Choose a wide glass cylinder or cube about 20–25cm tall.
- Place a thin layer of stones or pebbles in the base of the cylinder and sit three paperwhite bulbs on them. (Pieces of slate are used in the container pictured here.)
- Fill between the bulbs with small pieces of stone.
- Sit another three bulbs between the noses of the lower bulbs and fill between them with stones, to hold the bulbs firmly in place.
- Add enough water to moisten all the stones but leave the water level just below the lower layer of bulbs.
- Keep the cylinder of bulbs in a cool, light place. A cold conservatory or a window sill is ideal.
- The bulbs will start to root immediately and shoots will develop. The bulbs should bloom in about 8–10 weeks, sometimes sooner.

Warm temperatures will encourage softer, more spindly growth and your flowers will not last as long.

Tulips indoors

Despite Mediterranean origins, tulips are not easy bulbs to grow indoors. Most are not worth the effort, but some single early tulips can succeed if, like narcissi, they have a period of cold treatment before forcing.

Plant tulip bulbs in a loam-based compost, such as John Innes No.2, rather than bulb fibre. They do not need a great depth of compost, but they are relatively tall, so pots are more in proportion than shallow bowls. Pot them in October, with the tips of the bulbs just above the surface. Keep them cool and dark until the shoots are 6cm high or more; then move them into a cool, light position. Do not move them into a warmer room until the buds are clearly visible.

Good varieties to try are ***Tulipa* 'Attila'** (left), with light purple blooms on strong stems, and ***Tulipa* 'Apricot Beauty'** 🏆, with soft salmon-orange flowers (see page 56). Two short, single varieties sometimes sold for forcing for the earliest flowers are ***Tulipa* 'Brilliant Star'**, with bright scarlet flowers, and ***Tulipa* 'Christmas Marvel'**, which has rose-pink or red flowers. Both flower reliably, but the blooms are unremarkable.

If you particularly want potted tulips flowering in the house a little earlier than those in the garden, pot your bulbs as if you were growing them for the patio (see page 54). Leave them in a sheltered spot near the house until the shoots are 8–10cm high. Then put them indoors in a dark or heavily shaded place, perhaps a garage or shed. Once the stems and leaves have grown, move them to a warmer location. This is the ideal way to grow pots of tulips for a conservatory. Most varieties of tulip can be coaxed into flower when treated this way.

Tulips grown indoors are usually exhausted after flowering. There is little point in saving the bulbs or planting them in the garden for another year.

bringing early bulbs from the garden indoors

Perhaps you have a wealth of spring bulbs in the garden? You can lift some when they are in growth and bring them indoors for earlier flowering. Many dwarf bulbs lend themselves to this and can be used to create imaginative and naturalistic decorations for the house.

Snowdrop

Bulbs of the common snowdrop, ***Galanthus nivalis*** 🏆, rarely produce a satisfactory display indoors when planted as dry bulbs in pots in the autumn. However, once snowdrops are established in the garden, you can dig up a clump in early January and bring it indoors for flowering. Lift them when they have just emerged and the buds are pointing upwards. Use a small spade or trowel, digging deep beneath the bulbs. Pot them in a container that is deep enough to take the bulbs and roots comfortably and surround them with moist multi-purpose compost. A little moss and a few leaves on the surface of the pot will complete the picture.

As soon as the flowers fade, plant the snowdrops back in the garden, with the bulbs at the same depth as they were growing when you lifted them.

Snowdrops (above) and muscari (below) can be lifted from the garden and brought into the house for early flowers.

Grape hyacinth

Muscari armeniacum 🏆 seeds freely in the garden. A few unwanted clumps are ideal for indoor decoration. Muscari produce their leaves in winter, so it is easy to locate them well before the flowers emerge. The early foliage can become untidy and you may need to remove some or all of this when you lift them for indoors. The bulbs are often on or near the surface of the soil; this makes them particularly useful to use in shallow containers. Dig them up when you can just see the buds emerging: little green or blue knobbly spikes in the middle of each rosette of grassy leaves. Put them in containers with a little compost and moss

Grape hyacinths also look attractive surrounded by small seashells. Maybe you have some lying around from a trip to the beach last summer?

Crocus look particularly effective when potted up in small terracotta pots: plant several and line them up on the window sill to show off the beauty of the individual shining flowers as they open.

on the top and keep moist. A cool, light position keeps the flower stems strong and upright. When the blooms open, they are wonderfully fragrant and very long lasting. When the flowers fade, you can plant the bulbs back in the garden.

Crocus

Clumps of large-flowered, **Dutch crocus** and small, delicate **specie crocus** can also be lifted from the garden, potted up, and brought into the house for early flowers. Yellow crocus often fail in the house when grown from dry bulbs, so this is a good way of getting them to flower indoors. Lift the bulbs from the garden when the shoots are well developed, the leaves have emerged and the flowerbuds are clearly visible in the centre of each shoot.

Dwarf narcissus

Most dwarf narcissi open successfully indoors when lifted in bud from the garden. The bulbs can be deep in the soil, so use a long sturdy trowel or a border spade, digging down well beneath the roots. Dig the bulbs up when the buds and leaves are well above the ground. Pot them in deep containers and fill with compost to at least the depth they were growing in the soil. If you do not, the leaves may open up and flop, spoiling the effect.

Taller varieties of narcissi can be supported with twigs of birch or hazel. These often open their catkins and fresh green leaves if the cut ends are plunged well into the compost. Put the cut twigs in place when you pot the bulbs.

A pot of *Anemone blanda* brings spring to the window sill indoors before being planted in the garden for future years.

Cyclamen

The bright, beautifully formed blooms of ***Cyclamen coum*** 🏆 start to open in late winter, gradually emerging through the rounded dark green and silver-marbled leaves. These little gems are a treat to dig up and bring into a cool room or conservatory to take over from their larger, flamboyant cousins, which by this time are fading. Lift them carefully and surround with potting compost and moss and keep moist. They should be returned to the garden after a few days to set seed and multiply for future years.

Display Cyclamen coum in shallow bowls or large terracotta saucers, perhaps with twigs and lichen and small fir cones.

no bulbs in the garden?

You can buy pots of early-flowering bulbs in garden centres and nurseries; these are usually available from late December onwards. Snowdrops, dwarf iris, crocus, dwarf narcissi, *Cyclamen coum*, *Anenome blanda* 🏆 (see page 48) and grape hyacinths are just some of the little treasures you can buy, all ready to flower, for a couple of pounds a pot. You may need to keep the pots outside until the shoots develop a little more before you bring them into the house. Moved directly into a warm room, some will throw up lots of long, weak leaves rather than concentrating on producing their flowers.

amazing amaryllis

Three or five amaryllis bulbs can be grown in a large pot. The bulbs can be planted close together, with only a couple of centimetres between them. Amaryllis bulbs are not cheap, but they are spectacular and worth every penny!

Left: The stunning double-flowering *Amaryllis* 'Aphrodite'.

The spectacular amaryllis has become one of our most popular indoor plants. Millions of bulbs are bought and given as gifts every year. They are easy to grow and quick to reward with their extravagant, exotic blooms. A few years ago the choice was simply red, white, pink or striped. Today numerous named varieties can easily be found, offering a wider choice of colour and flower form, including fantastic doubles.

Amaryllis bulbs are usually offered for sale in the late autumn and early winter, and are popular as Christmas gifts. Those sold as loose bulbs are usually of larger size and better quality than those sold as a boxed gift complete with a pot and compost. However, these will still flower reliably.

The large-flowered, single amaryllis have the biggest bulbs and, as a rule, the bigger the bulb, the more flowers it will produce. Some of the double and butterfly-flowered varieties produce much smaller bulbs, and are usually more expensive to buy.

Plant amaryllis bulbs as soon as you buy them. Use a multi-purpose compost, ideally with added John Innes. The flowers on tall stems tend to make the plants top heavy, so use a big clay pot or a plastic pot inside a heavier pot. When planting single bulbs, choose a pot 5–6cm larger than the bulb in diameter. Spread the fleshy roots down into the pot and fill between them with the compost. Position the bulb so that the top third, the neck and shoulders, is above the compost. Water thoroughly, but make sure the pot is not standing in water. Place the pot in a light position; a window sill above a radiator is the ideal place to start the bulb into growth provided you move the pot away from the heat as soon as the bud starts to emerge.

The flowerbud should emerge before the leaves, but do not panic if the leaves

The bulbs sold as indoor amaryllis are really hippeastrums, members of the amaryllis family, but amaryllis is an easier, more attractive name. Derived from species native to South Africa, these are only suitable for growing indoors.

How do I get my amaryllis to bloom again next year?

- Once the flowers have faded, keep the bulb in a light position. Remove the flower head but leave the stalk for a week or two; this will continue to manufacture food and pass it down to the bulb. Remove the stem when it starts to look unsightly.
- Keep watering and feeding with a general liquid fertiliser while the leaves grow and develop.
- Once the danger of frost has passed, stand the plant outside, in a sunny position. You can plunge it in the ground to stop it being blown over.
- By late summer the leaves should be starting to yellow; if they are not, bring the plant indoors and withhold water. Once the leaves start to deteriorate, cut them off at the top of the bulb – just like it was when you bought it. Stop watering.
- Now is the time to re-pot your plant, particularly if it has been plunged outside and there could be worms in the pot: you need to get rid of them. Once you have shaken off the soil, re-pot immediately.
- Stand the pot in a light position indoors and do not water until the flowerbud starts to emerge from the bulb. If you water, the leaves will appear and the flower may not.

If you follow these instructions, your amaryllis should flower every year. If it does not, just follow the procedure as if it had flowered normally and keep fingers crossed for the next season.

appear first. Amaryllis usually bloom 6–8 weeks after planting. In a cool, light situation the flower stem will be strong and needs no support. In warmer conditions the stem may be taller and weaker and may need staking with a fine green cane or a stiff wire support. Larger grade bulbs usually produce two or three flower stems.

Some amaryllis such as 'Red Peacock' (top right) are sold by name, others are just sold by colour, such as salmon (top left) and white (above).

summer bulbs indoors

Far left: *Zantedeschia* 'Anneke' can be grown in a cool room or conservatory or in a pot outside. Indoors, calla lilies normally flower in winter and early spring; outside, they flower in summer. Left: a red gloxinia. Below left: *Eucharis amazonica*.

There are some summer-blooming bulbous plants that can be grown as houseplants. As we live outdoors more and more, and make greater use of the patio and garden in summer, indoor plants become less important. These indoor summer bulbs have become less popular than they were, but they are fun to try.

Begonia

Tuberous begonias (see pages 61–62) can be kept indoors in a shaded conservatory or in a light position in the house instead of moving them into outdoor containers. Their large, flamboyant flowers are less prone to weather damage when grown in the house, and you may achieve blooms of prize-winning proportions. The large-flowered, upright doubles are the best for the house: pendulous varieties are somewhat untidy for use indoors.

Gloxinia

Gloxinias have faded in popularity now, but a few years ago their fibrous corms were always to be found on sale in early spring alongside begonias. They cannot be grown outside, but work well as houseplants, producing large velvety leaves and showy trumpet-shaped flowers in white, red, blue and pink, in a variety of combinations.

They are fairly easy to grow. The corms should be planted individually in 13cm pots in spring. Nestle them into the surface of multi-purpose compost and lightly water around the edge of the pot. Keep them in a warm, light position but out of direct sunlight as the shoots develop and produce leaves and buds. If the plant becomes unstable and wobbly (they are prone to this!), secure it with a short green cane and avoid moving it around too much.

Gloxinias produce an abundance of flowers over a long period. A good one is a spectacular sight. A poor one is unattractive, to say the least.

Amazon lily

Eucharis amazonica 🏆 (*grandiflora*) is a spectacular tropical bulb that is becoming increasingly popular as a houseplant. It has large glossy, dark green leaves reminiscent of an aspidistra. Tall stems carry waxy white, green-tinged flowers, rather like narcissi; their fragrance is sweet, spicy and exotic. The bulbs are not always readily available but are worth seeking out.

Pot them in spring in loam-based compost, leaving the top third of the bulb above the surface, as you would do with an amaryllis (see page 32). Keep them warm and light, but out of direct sunlight. They like humidity, so a light misting helps. The flowerbuds should appear in late summer or autumn. When the flowers are over, keep the plant on the dry side; growth usually continues slowly throughout the year.

Glory lily

Also called the climbing lily, ***Gloriosa superba* 'Rothschildiana'** is often sold as a dormant 'bulb'. It is a long, fleshy tuber and should be planted vertically in a deep pot of multi-purpose compost. It needs warmth and humidity to succeed. Strong shoots carry shining green leaves with tendrils at their tips; that is how the plant climbs. The exotic flowers have reflexed petals of red and yellow, and prominent stamens. This is a fabulous flower – never easy, but well worth a go.

Tuberose

Polianthes tuberosa 🏆 is used in the commercial production of perfume. The double form, **'The Pearl'**, is the one most frequently grown. It has tall spikes of double, cream flowers usually flushed with pink. The scent is heavy and exotic. Plant the bulbs in pots of loam-based compost in spring. Do not water until the shoots appear and then grow on in a warm conservatory or a sunny room. The flowers appear in late summer and need plenty of light and warm temperatures before they open. Tuberose is increasingly used as a cut flower.

Aztec lily

Sprekelia formosissima, sometimes known as the Jacobean lily, is a stunning red, orchid-like flower from Mexico. It makes an attractive pot plant if the bulbs are potted like amaryllis (see page 32), in early spring in loam-based compost. Narrow leaves, similar to those of agapanthus, soon appear, followed by the alluring flowers in summer. Keep the bulbs in the same pot for several years; they resent disturbance.

Calla lily

The calla lily, or arum lily, crosses the boundaries between indoor plant and patio plant. They are popular as cut flowers, and are increasingly used as houseplants.

The white arum lily, ***Zantedeschia aethiopica*** 🏆, is a vigorous plant with large green leaves and white flowers on thick, fleshy stems (see page 64). Planted indoors as a dry rhizome in early spring, it produces leaves and flowers within a couple of months.

Hybrid zantedeschias come in a wide range of luscious colours (see also page 64). They are shorter in stature, growing to around 60cm, with narrow green or white-spotted leaves with the familiar slim, waxy flowers sold in florists. A single rhizome will produce a substantial clump of leaves and several flowers. Plant each rhizome in a 15–20cm pot of multi-purpose compost; water sparingly until the shoots emerge, then keep moist. They are superb plants for the conservatory or a patio but can be equally successful in the house.

Top: *Polianthes tuberosa*, tuberose. Middle: *Gloriosa superba* 'Rothschildiana', the glory or climbing lily. Bottom: *Sprekelia formosissima*, the Aztec lily.

bulb flowers as cut flowers

In an arrangement tulip flowers always turn upwards after a few hours. The only way to keep them in place is to use a soft florist wire inserted into the stem just behind the head of the flower and wound gently back down the stem.

Tulips are at their best in a tall vase that supports the stems.

Flowerbulbs provide us with a wealth of material for indoor decoration. Even before the last autumn leaves have fallen, florists are selling spring flowers: early tulips, daffodils and hyacinths. Freesias and lilies are available all year, and summer brings dahlias and gladioli, ideal for arranging.

buying bulb flowers

Good-quality cut flowers are widely available from florists, supermarkets and garden centres. Avoid those that have been hanging around for long periods on garage forecourts and in convenience stores. Take a look at the stems and leaves: if these look fresh and green, the flowers should be fresh.

Bulb flowers should be bought in bud if possible. As a general rule, buds should be showing some colour. Tight green buds often open to weaker, short-lived flowers.

arranging bulb flowers

When putting bulb flowers in an arrangement, use floral foam (oasis) as a base, to secure the flowers in position. It is important to soak the foam thoroughly at the outset. Float a block on a bowl of water (with the brand name uppermost) and leave it to absorb water and sink; it will then be fully saturated.

Cut the stems of the flowers and put them in a bucket of water in a cool place for a few hours before you arrange them. A solution of flower food added to the water (in the vase and in the bowl used to soak the foam) will prolong the life of the flowers.

Care of cut flowers

- Strip the lower leaves off the stems if these are going to be completely submerged when the flowers are in water. Remove any damaged or yellowing foliage.
- Cut at least the bottom 2–3cm off stems, then put them into water immediately.
- Ideally add cut-flower food to the water before the flowers. This not only provides nutrients that would come from the bulb, it also kills the bacteria that multiply in the water and shorten the life of the flowers. Do not change the water if you are using flower food.
- Some bulb flowers, such as narcissi and hyacinths, contain a lot of sticky sap in their stems. In a vase of mixed flowers, this sap can shorten the life of the other blooms. Either cut the stems and put them in a bucket of water for several hours before arranging them or put them in a vase on their own.

tulips as cut flowers

Tulips sold today for cut flowers have been selected and bred for their sturdy stems and long-lasting blooms. They are not as prone to flopping in water as tulips used to be. Cut off the bottom few centimetres of the stem, removing the white part if this is still in place. Put them in a vase containing only a few centimetres of water with added cut-flower food. Keep the water topped up to this level as required. The flowers will continue to grow as they develop; a taller vase is useful as it will support the stems as they get longer.

When purchased in tight bud, tulips can be stored out of water for several days to delay the opening of the flowers. Wrap the flowers in newspaper, covering the buds carefully. Lay them in a cool dark place. When you put them in water, cut the stems and leave the flowers wrapped in water for several hours before removing the paper.

Other bulb flowers to look out for

Triteleia Sometimes known as *Brodiaea laxa* and often sold as Californian bluebell, this appears in the shops in early summer. Fine stems carry starry blue flowers. It is very long lasting and good value: worth growing in the garden for cutting. See page 105.

Gladioli Small-flowered gladioli are popular for flower arranging. See page 104. Large-flowered gladioli are available in late summer. All are good value and useful where tall flowers are needed. In arrangements, break off the tips of the spikes; these deteriorate before the rest of the flower and look untidy.

Ornithogalum Sometimes known as chinchincheree, this South African bulb has long stems carrying dense spikes of greenish-white flowers. It is a good mixer in arrangements, remarkably long lasting and available most of the year.

Amaryllis Increasingly popular as a cut flower in winter, amaryllis is long lasting and dramatic and suits Continental-style arrangements. They are expensive, but just one or two stems have great impact. See pages 32–33.

The flowers of some bulbs need nothing more than a plain, simple vase.

Bulb flowers with soft stems can be difficult to arrange in floral foam (oasis). Use a stick of the same diameter as the stem to make holes prior to pushing in the bulb flower stem. This technique is useful for all narcissi and for hyacinths.

lilies as cut flowers

Lilies are available as cut flowers all the year round. They are long lasting and good value. They offer a wide range of glorious colours, both pale and intense, and many oriental varieties are wonderfully fragrant. A few lilies make a big impact and they lend themselves to a simple arrangement of a few stems in a tall glass vase.

Buy lilies a few days ahead of when you want them to look their best, to allow the buds to open. Strip the foliage off the bottom of the stem and cut at least 6cm off the stem. Place them in a vase at least half full of water to which you have added flower food.

Lily pollen can be a problem. The anthers are usually brown capsules carried on long filaments and are revealed as the buds open. The anthers soon split to reveal sticky orange pollen. This stains very badly if it gets on clothing, furnishing fabrics and carpets, so great care is needed. To prevent this happening, pick off the brown pollen sacs as the flowers open: wear gloves and hold a bag or saucer under the flowers to catch any that fall.

Lily pollen can be harmful to cats if it gets on their fur and they lick it off when grooming. Keep flowers well away from your pets and remove stamens as the flowers open.

growing your own bulb flowers for cutting

The vegetable plot is a great place to grow flowers for cutting. Plant some at the back of the plot, or round the edges. If you have narcissi in pots for the patio, plant the bulbs here after flowering and use them for cut flowers next year.

Left: If you have room in your garden or on your allotment, plant some bulbs for cutting. Below from left: *Narcissus* 'Winston Churchill', *Narcissus* 'Salome', *Narcissus* 'Orangery', *Tulipa* 'Black Parrot', *Tulipa* 'West Point'.

There is great satisfaction in cutting a few flowers from the garden for the house. Like home-grown vegetables, the flowers are fresher and have a much longer life than those bought in shops. It also means you can have the varieties you like, rather than ones that suit commercial production.

spring

Daffodils and narcissi picked when the flowers are in advanced bud or just open will last in water for a week or more. They have a lovely spring fragrance that bought flowers often lack. *Narcissus* **'Pink Charm'**, with its ivory-white petals and salmon-pink trumpet, is a good choice, as is the similar **'Salome'** 🏆. **'Sir Winston Churchill'** 🏆 has semi-double flowers with white petals interspersed with shorter orange and gold segments. It is fragrant and reliable. *Narcissus* **'Apricot Whirl'** and **'Orangery'** have a split and flared apricot trumpet, forming a ruffled layer in front of the white petals – exotic and striking. All of these are easy to grow among shrubs and perennials, adding colour and providing a flowers for the house.

Tulips are never in short supply in the shops in winter and early spring, but are few and far between by the time they are in bloom in the garden. Why not grow a few just for cutting? Tall, elegant lily-flowering tulips such as ***Tulipa* 'White Triumphator'** 🏆, the golden yellow **'West Point'** 🏆 and tangerine **'Ballerina'** 🏆 make excellent cut flowers: half a dozen stems in a glass vase are all you need. Parrot tulips such as **'Black Parrot'** 🏆 and the flamboyant **'Flaming Parrot'** make exotic cut flowers. Plant an extra ten bulbs in an out-of-the-way place and cut five stems at a time.

A spring-flowering bulb such as a tulip or narcissus costs about the same as a single flower bought as a cut flower. Consider which is better value … a little planning is worthwhile!

summer and autumn

Lilies are a worthwhile addition to any garden for cutting, particularly garden lilies such as ***Lilium regale*** 🏆, which are not readily available as a cut flower. A large bulb costs a little over £1 and will produce a magnificent stem of scented trumpets. A single stem may well be all you need in a room for visual impact and scent.

Dahlias offer perhaps the largest variety of colour and flower form of any plant in the summer garden. They flower prolifically and last well when cut. Because the blooms bruise easily in transit, they are also much longer lasting when cut from the garden than when bought from a florist. They are becoming increasingly fashionable as cut flowers, particularly those with unique flower forms, such as the cactus and pom-pom varieties. Again, a tuber costing a little over £1 will provide a wealth of flowers over a long period.

Large-flowered gladioli are difficult to accommodate as garden plants. Their strong, upright form and stature does not mix well with other plants. However, they are dramatic cut flowers and are worth growing for this purpose. Ten big corms cost about £2 and, if given a sunny, well-drained spot, will produce ten fantastic flower spikes. If you have an allotment, plant a generous row to keep the house in flowers for several weeks. In smaller gardens they are useful in that narrow border along the fence that is so often useless for anything except climbing plants.

Nerines make wonderful cut flowers later in the autumn. The long, naked stems of ***Nerine bowdenii*** 🏆 carry fine starry, sugar-pink blooms with delicately curled petals. They are long lasting both in the garden and in water in the house. They look superb on their own in a simple vase or in an arrangement with autumn berries and Michaelmas daisies.

Above: The richly fragrant blooms of *Lilium regale* are superb for cutting. Below: Dahlias such as cactus *Dahlia* 'Nuit d'Eté' provide plenty of blooms for cutting in late summer.

Freesia plants are far from decorative, but the delicate, scented flowers are great favourites. The dainty blooms on sale in the florist give little clue to the habit of the plant: freesias produce tall, branched stems up to 90cm or more, with several flower heads over a number of weeks. If you feel adventurous and have a cold greenhouse or conservatory, they are worth a try, particularly if you are going to cut the flowers for the house.

Buy the corms in autumn and plant them half way down a deep 30cm pot in loam-based compost. Push a network of birch twigs into the pot at this stage, for support – the twigs need to reach a height of 45cm or more. Keep them in a cool, light spot and the flowers will appear in late winter. Alternatively, plant in spring in pots outside in a sunny, sheltered position.

bulbs in pots

Growing flowerbulbs in pots is the ideal way to add colour to areas of your garden where planting in the open ground is impossible, or where an extra seasonal injection of colour is needed. Even if you do not have a garden, you can grow bulbs in pots on a balcony or window sill or in window boxes, bringing colour and fragrance closer to your home. Pots are ideal for bulbs: they provide the well-drained conditions that bulbs love, and you have control over the compost in which you plant them. Containers can be grouped, rearranged, brought into view and removed as the fancy takes you. Growing in pots is just another way to get creative with flowerbulbs …

Above: Dwarf *Iris* 'George' emerges between purple heuchera leaves. Right: The soft orange flowers of *Tulipa* 'Prinses Irene' glow in the early morning spring sunshine.

pots and containers

As long as a container has drainage holes and will hold a reasonable amount of compost, it can be used to grow bulbs outdoors. You may choose a traditional flowerpot, a sophisticated contemporary aluminium container, an imitation lead planter, a wooden beer crate or even an old pair of boots. The depth of compost required in the container depends on the bulbs. Ideally the compost below the bulb should be at least three times as deep as the bulb itself, and you should have the same amount above the bulb too.

choosing the compost

You do not have to use bulb fibre for bulbs in pots outdoors; any good-quality multi-purpose compost will do. Bulbs are already packed with an adequate supply of food to grow and flower, so a high level

Terracotta pots come in all shapes and sizes. At Whichford Pottery, Warwickshire, these wonderful large pots contain an exotic cocktail of crown imperials, tulips and narcissi garnished with euphorbias, grasses and wallflowers.

If you use fresh compost in containers for flowerbulbs in the autumn, you can re-use it the following year for summer-flowering seasonal bedding plants, as long as you add controlled-release fertiliser and some additional fresh John Innes loam-based potting compost.

of plant nutrients is not required. It is essential that the compost is well drained, however, and it is important not to compact it by pressing it down too firmly into the container when planting.

care of pots from planting to flowering

Pots planted in autumn with spring-flowering bulbs can be moved close to the wall of the house in severe winter weather; here they will be protected from chilling winds and sheltered by the eaves from excess wet. They can be moved into flowering position when the shoots have emerged and the days are warmer.

Once the bulbs are in full leaf growth, pots should be watered periodically, when the compost feels dry. This is particularly important once the flowers start to open and the leaves are fully developed; at this stage a pot full of bulbs can dry out quickly on a warm breezy day.

combining containers

By grouping pots together, not only can you achieve exciting colour combinations, you can prolong the season of interest by planting for continuity. Pots of spring-flowering bulbs grouped with foliage plants such as euonymus, heucheras, grasses and ferns can create a pleasing picture over many weeks. When the spring-flowering bulbs fade, they can be replaced by lilies, dahlias or other summer-flowering bulbs or bedding plants.

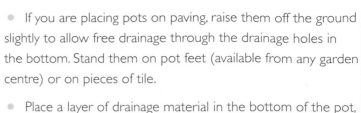

Planting bulbs in a container

- If you are placing pots on paving, raise them off the ground slightly to allow free drainage through the drainage holes in the bottom. Stand them on pot feet (available from any garden centre) or on pieces of tile.
- Place a layer of drainage material in the bottom of the pot, to a depth of at least 2–3cm. This can be broken pieces of pot, stones or gravel.
- Partially fill the pot with compost. How much you use depends on the size of the bulbs and how many layers you are planting. If you are planting a single layer, fill to within four to five times the depth of the bulb from the top of the pot.
- Position the bulbs, nestling them into the surface of the compost. In a pot they can be almost touching, leaving only 1cm between the bulbs, but it is important to think about how large the flowers will be when fully open and space the bulbs accordingly.
- Fill the pot lightly with compost to within 1 or 2cm of the rim of the pot.
- Water thoroughly after planting to settle the compost.

Tulips, hyacinths and larger-flowered narcissi make a really good display in a container, but if you plant these with winter bedding plants you will find that they can interfere with, and swamp, the bedding plants. On the other hand, without that top layer of planting, pots can look bare and forlorn in winter until the bulbs emerge. For a fresh, green topping for the pots, sow grass seed over the surface of the compost once the bulbs have been planted. This will provide an emerald sward in the pots and a lovely backdrop for your bulbs as they grow (here Tulipa 'Red Impression').

Remember: you can grow dwarf bulbs in deep pots, but tall bulbs in shallow containers rarely succeed.

spring-flowering bulbs for pots

A pot of flowerbulbs will bring spring to your patio or doorstep. Spring flowers are a welcome sight from indoors, and by growing bulbs and bedding plants in pots, you can bring them closer to the window. There is virtually no limit to what you can grow and the planting combinations you can create.

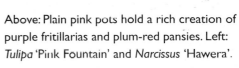

Above: Plain pink pots hold a rich creation of purple fritillarias and plum-red pansies. Left: *Tulipa* 'Pink Fountain' and *Narcissus* 'Hawera'.

The tendency when choosing bulbs for pots and containers is to select dwarf and compact varieties. This is not essential. It is the situation that should determine the choice. For exposed and windy sites, for pots or the open ground, the best option, may be short, compact varieties. In sheltered situations, taller varieties can be grown in containers as long as there is sufficient depth of compost. Above all else, choose varieties that do not need support, as this can spoil the effect.

planting partners

Spring-flowering bulbs in pots combine well with winter bedding plants such as pansies, evergreens, grasses and heathers. If you are growing bulbs with other subjects, you need to plant them at a depth that allows room for the other plants above them. It is a good idea to group taller bulbs in the centre of the pot and use seasonal bedding plants nearer the sides, with dwarf bulbs tucked between them.

a succession of flowers

It is possible to achieve a succession of flowers in one big pot by planting in layers. Early-blooming bulbs are planted near the surface of the soil and those that flower later are planted progressively deeper. This will provide several weeks of flowers.

how you do it

Choose a large pot, 35cm or more in diameter and of regular flowerpot depth. Select varieties of bulbs that will give a succession of blooms from early spring to late spring. On the top layer use dwarf, early-flowering bulbs. Beneath these, plant early-flowering tulips or narcissi. On the lowest layer, plant late-flowering tulips.

Can bulbs be kept in the same pot from year to year? *Some can be. Lilies, for example, will succeed for several seasons if the compost is topped up and some controlled-release fertiliser is added when the plants are in full leaf growth to build the bulbs for the following year. However, most spring-flowering bulbs, including tulips and narcissi, are never as good in pots the following season, if they perform at all. Flowerbulbs are inexpensive to buy, and it is never worth compromising your precious spring display for the sake of buying new bulbs on an annual basis.*

Flowering times vary from year to year. Although we plan for continuity, sometimes more than one variety will flower at the same time. Never mind: more flowers and more spring colour!

bulb recipes for beautiful spring pots

Left: An elegant urn opulently planted with *Tulipa* 'Barbados', *Narcissus* 'Sun Disc', carex and pansies.

Layering bulbs

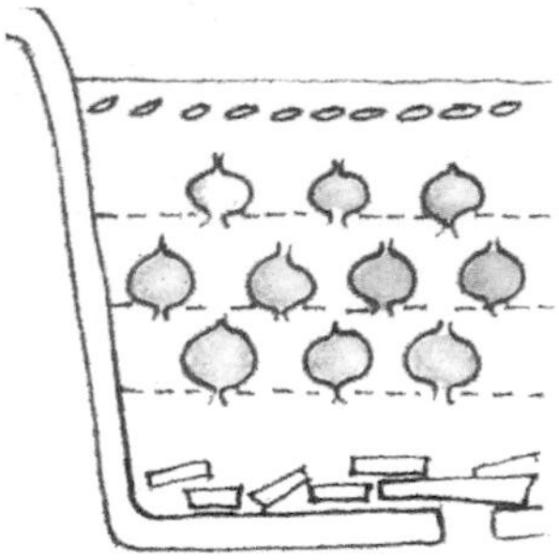

- Place broken crocks or stones in the bottom of the pot.
- Add 15–20cm of multi-purpose compost with added John Innes or bulb fibre.
- Nestle late-flowering tulip bulbs into the surface of the compost leaving 1–2cm between bulbs.
- Add compost to just cover the bulbs, ideally leaving the tips showing.
- Place the next layer of bulbs on the compost, avoiding the noses of bulbs in the lower layer.
- Cover the bulbs with compost and fill the pot to within 15cm of the top.
- Add small bulbs for the top layer and fill the pot with compost to within 2cm of the rim.
- If you wish, you can sprinkle the surface with grass seed and cover it lightly with compost.
- Water thoroughly.
- Wait for spring.

Suggested recipes

1 Top layer: *Scilla siberica* 🏆. Middle layer: *Narcissus* 'Tête à Tête' 🏆. Bottom layer: *Tulipa* 'Golden Apeldoorn'.

2 Top layer: *Muscari armeniacum* 🏆. Middle layer: *Tulipa* 'Red Riding Hood' 🏆. Bottom layer: *Tulipa* 'Queen of Night'.

3 Top layer: *Crocus tommasinianus* 'Whitewell Purple'. Middle layer: *Narcissus* 'Jetfire' 🏆 or *Tulipa* 'Orange Princess' 🏆. Bottom layer: *Tulipa* 'Prinses Irene' 🏆.

4 Top layer: *Iris reticulata* 🏆. Middle layer: *Tulipa saxatilis* Bakeri Group 'Lilac Wonder' 🏆. Bottom layer: *Tulipa* 'Passionale'.

5 Top layer: *Crocus chrysanthus* 'Romance'. Middle layer: *Narcissus* 'Geranium' 🏆. Bottom layer: *Tulipa* 'Ballerina' 🏆.

6 Top layer: *Chionodoxa luciliae* 🏆. Middle layer: *Narcissus* 'Jack Snipe' 🏆. Bottom layer: *Tulipa* 'Purissima' 🏆.

In smaller pots, omit the bottom or middle layer of bulbs – the combinations will still work.

spring-flowering bulbs for pots

Allium

Most alliums are unsuitable for pots because their foliage starts to die down as the flowers develop and can be unsightly. ***Allium karataviense* 'Ivory Queen'** is an exception. It has broad, grey-green leaves that look splendid from the time they emerge in mid-spring. The blooms are carried on short stems, up to 20cm in height, and open to fluffy spheres of creamy-white flowers; these fade to green, but remain attractive for a month or so.

The bulbs of this allium can be left in the pots and will perform again for several seasons. This variety also looks effective grown in a scree bed covered with gravel but, being short-stemmed, it is lost in a bed or border,

Anemone

Anemone blanda 🏆 looks wonderful planted extravagantly in a shallow bowl. Soak the corms overnight before planting them 2–3cm deep, and the same distance apart for best effect. The prettily divided foliage emerges at the same time as the narrow-petalled blue, white or pink blooms, and remains after they have faded.

Left: *Allium karataviense* 'Ivory Queen'. Top: *Anemone blanda*. Above: *Anemone coronaria* De Caen Group.

After Anemone blanda has finished flowering, you can remove the bulbs from the bowl, divide them into clumps and transplant them under trees or shrubs to add colour for years to come. Left in the ground undisturbed, they will naturalise and spread freely.

Anemone coronaria, ordinary anemones, are not always easy to grow. They hail from the Mediterranean, so they like well-drained soil and a good bake in the summer sun. You may have more success growing them in pots than in the open ground, and they make an attractive container subject in their first season. Soak the corms overnight before planting them 5–6cm deep (pointed end down), and a similar distance apart, in a John Innes compost with added horticultural grit. For best results, use unglazed terracotta containers. Place them in a sunny sheltered position, ideally near a wall. The foliage resembles that of parsley and will fill the pot before the pink, red, blue or white buttercup-like blooms emerge on 20–30cm stems.

After flowering, the bulbs can be taken out of the pot and planted in the open ground in a sunny, well-drained spot.

Crocus

The large-flowered, **Dutch crocus, *Crocus vernus* subsp. *albiflorus***, are reliable and easy to grow. Their stout, grass-like leaves are dark green with a silver-green central stripe; their shining goblet-like blooms can be white, mauve, blue, purple, yellow or striped. When open, the flowers display orange stigmas – the very essence of spring. They are inexpensive bulbs to buy, and a pot or bowl generously filled with crocus all of one colour, or in a blend of colours, is a real early-spring fillip on the patio or doorstep. Plant the bulbs 2cm apart and 4cm deep.

Dutch crocus are ideal for planting in a container above other, later-flowering bulbs such as tall tulips. They are also attractive planting partners for some of the early-flowering dwarf specie tulips, such as Tulipa humilis Violacea Group.

Smaller-flowered, **specie crocus**, including ***Crocus chrysanthus*** varieties, are useful for early colour in pots planted with other bulbs and seasonal bedding plants. Because the corms are small, they can be planted above other, later-flowering bulbs and will not interfere with the emerging shoots

Specie crocus bulbs can be poked into the compost around the edge of pots between winter bedding plants, providing cheery early colour.

of the bulbs below them. Their leaves are narrow, and fading flowers die down quickly, so they do not spoil the display that follows. Plant 2cm apart and 3cm deep.

Crown imperial

Fritillaria imperialis (see page 95) makes a wonderfully dramatic subject for a large pot or container. The flower stems grow up to 1m, carrying the crown of exotic bell-shaped blooms. These can be golden yellow, orange or deep orange-red, under a ruff of emerald-green leaves.

Plant the bulbs with at least 12cm of compost above the bulbs and the same beneath them. Shallow planting can result in short, distorted flower stems. Place the bulbs on their sides, to prevent water from settling in the growing tip, as this can cause the emerging shoot to rot.

Try three bulbs in a large, deep terracotta pot for a traditional setting or in a stylish metal container for a contemporary scheme. Crown imperials grown in pots are an excellent choice alongside trimmed box and other architectural subjects.

Above left: *Crocus vernus* subsp. *albiflorus*.
Above right: *Crocus chrysanthus* 'E.P. Bowles'.

Snake's head fritillary

Fritillaria meleagris (see page 85) is an exquisite flower with hanging, bell-shaped blooms of white or purple intricately marked with a chequerboard of shaded squares. The flowers can be seen to great advantage when grown in a pot, especially when the containers are raised on a low wall or table.

Plant the bulbs immediately after purchase to prevent them drying out and shrivelling. The snake's head fritillary likes moist soil, so a loam-based, moisture-retentive compost is ideal. Plant the bulbs 6cm deep and 3–4cm apart.

Snake's head fritillaries look good in groups in the centre of small containers. They can also be combined with dwarf narcissi, chionodoxa and specie crocus in shallow pans or bowls oversown with grass to create a miniature naturalistic meadow in a bowl.

spring-flowering bulbs for pots

Top: A contemporary bowl simply planted with *Hyacinthus orientalis* 'Blue Jacket'. Above, from left: 'Koh-i-noor', a pretty blend of lilac and white hyacinths, 'Pink Pearl'.

Hyacinth

Hyacinthus orientalis are unbeatable for fragrance. Their scent is especially good on cool spring mornings, so they are a good choice for pots near the house, where they can be enjoyed daily. The heavy flower spikes of some varieties can become unstable and flop, but this is less likely to happen when the bulbs are grown outside than when they are indoors. Hyacinths produce large shoots and take up space in pots; either plant them on their own, 2–3cm apart, or space them out with room for other plants between. For a mass effect, choose smaller-grade bulbs and plant densely, leaving only 1cm between the bulbs. It is always better to choose all one colour or perhaps a blend of two shades. Varieties do not necessarily flower at the same time and the impact can be disappointing if only one or two flowers are out at once.

Hyacinths can be grown in pots of any depth as long as the bulbs are covered by 3–4cm of compost and there is at least 6cm of compost beneath the bulbs. In very shallow pots, the strong roots can push the bulbs out of the compost.

Hyacinths come in a wide range of stunning colours: think about the containers you plant them in to create interesting colour combinations. Try rich blue hyacinths, such as 'Blue Jacket' 🏆, in traditional orange-brown terracotta, or perhaps rich plum-purple ones, such as 'Woodstock', in zinc or imitation lead.

Ipheion

***Ipheion* 'Rolf Fiedler'** 🏆 is a charming dwarf bulb that has become popular in recent years. The foliage is low and grass-like; it smells of onions when crushed, hinting at the plant's relationship with the allium family. The leaves appear in autumn and winter, and the star-shaped, bright sky-blue flowers in early to mid-spring. Blue

Ipheion 'Rolf Fiedler' 🏆 is a delightful companion for the jewel-like Primula wanda 🏆 (above). In shades of violet, magenta and cerise, these dark-leaved primulas cry out for a pure blue, brighter planting partner.

flowers are always popular, and this is a heavenly blue that is bound to please. Plant in groups of three or five bulbs around the edge of larger pots; the tiny bulbs can be just poked into the compost.

Dwarf iris

The dwarf irises are wonderful early-flowering bulbs that can easily get lost in beds and borders but are shown to advantage in pots. The shoots emerge early, full of promise. The vertical, reed-like foliage grows to 20cm, and the flowers open around 15cm up the stem. ***Iris reticulata*** 🏆 is deep violet marked with golden yellow. However, there are many varieties, with flowers ranging from palest blue to deep purple. ***Iris* 'Harmony'** is rich blue, ***Iris* 'George'** 🏆 velvet purple and ***Iris* 'Katharine Hodgkin'** 🏆 pale blue veined and marked with darker blue and yellow.

Plant the bulbs as soon as you buy them, in early autumn. They seem to shrivel and deteriorate in storage, despite liking warm, dry conditions once they are planted. They should feel firm and plump beneath their papery outer coats; if the outer coats are loose and the bulbs are shrivelled, do not buy them.

Plant *Iris reticulata* varieties with at least 6cm of compost covering the bulbs. An unglazed terracotta pot is an ideal container. If you are growing the bulbs on their own, cover the surface of the compost with alpine grit to show the flowers to greatest advantage.

Dwarf irises make perfect planting partners for early dwarf narcissi such as Narcissus canaliculatus or Narcissus 'Peeping Tom' 🏆*. In a mild early spring they will flower together; in a cold one, the narcissi will follow the irises.*

Above left: *Iris reticulata*. Above right: *Muscari macrocarpum* 'Golden Fragrance'.

Grape hyacinth

Muscari armeniacum 🏆 are inexpensive bulbs to buy and can be relied on to produce a display of deep blue, fragrant flowers in mid-spring. The blooms are long lasting, and the fresh green, grass-like foliage emerges soon after the bulbs have been planted in autumn, making a welcome contribution to pots in the winter months.

Grape hyacinths are ideal to use in large pots above tulips or narcissi. Plant the bulbs with the tips 5cm below the surface and 4–5cm apart to leave space for the shoots of the bulbs underneath to push through. Alternatively, fill pots with just grape hyacinths; the bulbs can be placed so that they are not quite touching. This will result in a pot overflowing with green foliage and sapphire flowers.

A pot of grape hyacinths is a useful addition to a group of pots containing other bulbs and spring-flowering pansies and primulas. Blue is an excellent mixer, providing a link between any other colours and enabling them to sit happily together.

***Muscari macrocarpum* 'Golden Fragrance'** are lovely for a pot in a warm, sheltered location. The blue-green, grass-like foliage appears early. The flowerbuds emerge purple-brown, opening to soft yellow, and reach 15–20cm in height. Their gentle colouring may be lost in the border, but in pots they can be seen to advantage, and, if sited near the house, their unusual fruity fragrance can be enjoyed daily.

Muscari armeniacum make lively planting partners for *Tulipa* 'Red Riding Hood'.

narcissi for pots

Daffodils come in a great variety of shapes and sizes. Many are excellent for bright early colour in pots, and their hardy constitution means they perform regardless of cold weather. Varieties with heavy double blooms often flop and break when grown in pots; those with stout stems and long-lasting blooms are ideal.

Narcissi grow well in any type of container and are a good choice for cooler, shadier situations, where their cheerful flowers last longer than they do in full sun. Plant them in a loam-based compost and watch that they do not dry out in winter or early spring as this will damage their performance. Plant the bulbs about half way down an average flowerpot, covered with compost by at least three times the depth of the bulb. They are normally planted in early or mid-autumn to allow them to produce plenty of roots before the shoots start to grow. If you plant them late, plant at the

Narcissus 'Tête à Tête': early, reliable, compact – and widely grown in pots indoors and out.

Daffodil and narcissus foliage usually takes a long time to die down in the garden. By growing them in pots you can put them out of the way after flowering until the leaves have withered.

Favourite daffodils and narcissi for pots

***Narcissus* 'Bell Song'** This dainty narcissus has 20cm stems carrying two or three delicate blooms with ivory-white petals and short, soft salmon trumpets. It makes a pretty planting partner for purple heucheras.

***Narcissus* 'Bridal Crown'** 🏆 This multi-headed narcissus has double ivory-white blooms with orange and gold centres and a rich fragrance. The strong, upright foliage and flower stems reach 30cm. It is lovely in a large tub with deep red wallflowers.

***Narcissus* 'Geranium'** 🏆 Similar in habit to 'Bridal Crown', this sweetly fragrant narcissus has single, white-petalled blooms with orange-red centres (see page 95). 'Geranium' is a vibrant planting partner for the lily-flowering *Tulipa* 'Ballerina'.

***Narcissus* 'Jack Snipe'** 🏆 The elegantly held, long-lasting flowers have white petals and sharp yellow trumpets on 20cm stems. They make a fresh combination rising above pale yellow primroses.

***Narcissus* 'Jetfire'** 🏆 A bright, cheerful dwarf daffodil with golden yellow petals and orange trumpets (see pages 78, 79), 'Jetfire' is early-flowering, weather-resistant and a good companion for blue crocus. It grows to 20–30cm in height.

***Narcissus* 'Minnow'** 🏆 This multi-headed narcissus, with two or three flowers on each stem, blooms in mid-spring. Its lemon-yellow, short-trumpeted flowers are sweetly scented. It reaches 30cm in height and is delightful with blue forget-me-nots.

***Narcissus* 'Pipit'** 🏆 This excellent variety has one or two long-lasting, acid yellow flowers on each stem. The short, broad trumpets quickly fade from bright yellow to rich cream, creating a most pleasing effect, especially with the sharp green flowers of euphorbias. It grows to 30cm in height,

***Narcissus* 'Tête à Tête'** 🏆 This is probably the most popular dwarf narcissus for pots, indoors and out. Clumps of short green leaves surround 15–20cm tall stems, each of which carries one, two or three small bright yellow flowers (see opposite page). It flowers in early spring and combines well with *Anemone blanda.*

Clumps of narcissi are ideal to add colour towards the back of a border among shrubs or along the base of a hedge. If you have filled all available space in the flower borders, transplant a few to the back of the vegetable patch or alongside the compost heap: the flowers will come in handy for cutting in future years.

same depth: shallow planting can result in stunted plants and short flower stems.

When you grow a single variety of narcissus in a pot, you can transplant the whole clump straight from the pot into the open ground once flowering is over. Plant the clump deeper than it was in the pot, positioned so that the soil covers about four times the depth of the bulb.

Above, from the top: *Narcissus* 'Bell Song', *Narcissus* 'Bridal Crown', *Narcissus* 'Jack Snipe', *Narcissus* 'Pipit'.

tulips for pots

Avoid varieties that have weak stems, very heavy flowers and a tendency to flop. Choose those that are long lasting, in colours that suit your taste and style of garden and of a height that suits your container. For shallow containers, choose short-stemmed tulips. For deep pots, you can choose either tall or short varieties, depending on the effect you want.

Using multi-purpose compost, plant tulip bulbs with at least three to four times the depth of the bulb covering them. They can be planted close together to achieve a massed effect, but remember to allow room for their blooms to open. Space them at least the width of a bulb apart, and more in the case of large, open-flowered varieties.

Hybridisation and selection produces a constant stream of new varieties, so it is always worth experimenting with anything that appeals. However, there are also a number of well-established favourites that continue to prove their worth. Here are a few that can be recommended for pots.

***Tulipa* 'Ballerina', sensational against the bold leaves of *Cynara cardunculus*, the cardoon.**

Sleek, elegant, frilly, flamboyant, bright, bewitching, subtle, sensational: all these words could describe tulips. However, they are normally classified as tall or dwarf, early-, mid- or late-flowering, or in one of a multitude of categories that describe the flower form. There are masses of tulips to choose from, and the majority are excellent in pots.

The size of tulip bulbs depends on the variety, but always buy top-size, top-quality bulbs to ensure a good display in your pots. Buy early for the greatest choice of variety, then store the bulbs in a cool, dry place and plant them in late autumn or early winter. Planting too early can result in premature growth, frost damage and susceptibility to tulip fire (see page 101).

dwarf and specie tulips

Dwarf varieties are ideal for shallow containers and in more exposed situations in the garden. Specie tulips and their hybrids are normally seen in areas of gravel or the rock garden but make wonderful subjects for pots too. All like good drainage, so use loam-based compost with added grit.

***Tulipa* 'Red Riding Hood'** is one of the best known dwarf varieties. The leaves emerge grey-green, delicately patterned with chocolate brown. The pointed buds open to large, bright scarlet flowers with black centres, on 25cm stems (see page 47). The blooms are long lasting and weather-resistant. There is also a form of 'Red Riding Hood' with double flowers.

***Tulipa* 'Shakespeare'** is one of a group of *Tulipa kaufmanniana* hybrids known as 'Waterlily' tulips, characterised by large, wide-opening blooms on short stems. 'Shakespeare' reaches about 15cm in height with deep yellow, red-flushed flowers.

The early dwarf tulips combine well with brightly coloured winter- and spring-flowering pansies and violas, which are usually producing their finest flush of flowers as the tulips bloom.

Clockwise from top left: *Tulipa* 'Für Elise', *Tulipa clusiana* 'Lady Jane', *Tulipa saxatilis* Bakeri Group 'Lilac Wonder', *Tulipa* 'Pirand'.

***Tulipa* 'Pirand'** is a new dwarf variety, with showy flowers of a bright red edged in creamy white.

***Tulipa* 'Für Elise'** is a lovely variety with blue-green foliage and champagne-coloured blooms with pointed petals.

***Tulipa clusiana* 'Lady Jane'** is a delicate, fine-boned beauty of a specie tulip, with narrow grey-green leaves and flower stems reaching 20cm. The pencil-thin flowerbuds open to narrow-petalled blooms, deep pink outside and white within. This is a delightful bulb to grow in pots and containers along with the blue grass *Festuca glauca*.

***Tulipa humilis* Violacea Group** is a short specie tulip, 20cm tall. Shiny green foliage is the backdrop for purple-pink blooms with purple-black markings at the base of the petals. It flowers early and works well with large-flowered crocus in shallow pots.

***Tulipa saxatilis* Bakeri Group 'Lilac Wonder'** is tall and vigorous for a specie tulip, with shiny green foliage and stems growing to 30cm in height. The anemone-like flowers have satin petals of lilac-pink with yellow centres. It looks pretty with silver-foliage plants and blue violas.

tulips for pots

single early tulips

Single early tulips are mostly shorter than their later-flowering relatives, with slightly smaller blooms. They work well in pots and are useful to combine with single late varieties to give continuity of blooms.

Tulipa **'Apricot Beauty'** 🏆 is popular for its dreamy salmon-orange flowers, which combine beautifully with the grey-green leaves. It looks lovely in terracotta containers and against brick walls. It grows to 40cm and is sleek and delicate in habit. It is not a good choice for cold gardens.

Tulipa **'Generaal de Wet'** is a graceful, glowing orange variety, at its best with the light shining through its silky petals.

These single early varieties work well with purple-foliage plants. Try them with purple heucheras and ajugas. These look good all winter and make an ideal backdrop for the tulip flowers in spring.

Above left: *Tulipa* 'Prinses Irene'. Above right: *Tulipa* 'Gavota'. Below left: A generously planted pot of *Tulipa* 'Apricot Beauty'.

triumph tulips

Flowering in late spring, the triumph tulips have rounded blooms of robust constitution. The stems grow up to 40cm in height, and the flowers are long lasting and reliable.

Tulipa **'Gavota'** has flowers of deep red-brown with broad, creamy-yellow margins. Sleek and sophisticated, it makes a striking contrast to other 'pretty' spring flowers.

Tulipa **'Passionale'** is commercially grown for cut flowers. It has good mid-green foliage and soft purple-pink flowers that combine well with the pinks, blues and yellows of the spring garden.

Tulipa **'Prinses Irene'** 🏆 is a strong tulip with blue-green leaves and glowing orange blooms flamed with purple, on stems 30cm tall. The flowers are long lasting and stand up to any weather. **'Orange Princess'** 🏆 is a double form of 'Prinses Irene' and has all the excellent qualities of the single form.

Single late and Darwin tulips are large enough and bold enough to grow with wallflowers, whose rich colours and sweet fragrance are always pleasing in large containers.

single late and Darwin tulips

These are tall varieties, reaching 50–60cm, with elegant blooms in mid- to late spring. Their flowers are exactly what we all imagine a tulip should be.

Tulipa 'Queen of Night' is a favourite that fits into any situation and is a certain winner in a pot. Tall, strong stems carry silky, purple-black flowers – seductive and sensuous. If you grow only one tulip in your garden, grow this one.

Tulipa 'World's Favourite' flowers slightly earlier than 'Queen of Night'. This is a hot tulip. Large blooms of glowing orange-red delicately edged with gold are carried on strong stems. In flower, this tulip outshines anything else in the garden and brightens the dullest of days.

Below: *Tulipa* 'Queen of Night'. Right: A pot of *Tulipa* 'World's Favourite' heralds spring.

tulips for pots

Left: A mixed planting of early double tulips.
Below left: *Tulipa* 'Lucybelle'.

double tulips

Double-flowered tulips bloom early or late in the season. The early varieties are usually quite short in stature with strong stems and open blooms of muddled tissue-paper petals. They are pleasing flowers with a comparatively strong fragrance.

***Tulipa* 'Peach Blossom'** is the best known early-flowering double, with pink papery blooms flushed with white-green and yellow at the base. It grows to 20cm in height, with attractive grey-green leaves.

The double early tulips work well planted as a mixture, particularly when combined with grape hyacinths – the blue forms the link between the contrasting colours of the tulips.

***Tulipa* 'Oranje Nassau'** 🏆 has large double blooms of orange flushed with red.

The later-flowering double tulips are flamboyant and showy. Their heavy flowers can be damaged by wind and rain, but they are a lovely choice for a sheltered spot.

***Tulipa* 'Angélique'** 🏆 has dreamy pale pink, cream-flushed blooms on 40cm stems. ***Tulipa* 'Mount Tacoma'** has pure white, paeony-like flowers.

***Tulipa* 'Black Hero'** (see page 98) is a double form of 'Queen of Night' (see page 57). Its shining, purple-black petals are lovely even as they fade, hanging on to the 50cm stems until the last moment.

***Tulipa* 'Lucybelle'** is a wonderful new double tulip with soft orange, many-petalled flowers cradled in excellent foliage. It is long lasting and weather-resistant.

Try planting double late tulips under double early tulips in deep pots for a continuous display of frilly, informal flowers; ideal for a cottage garden look.

Sky-blue forget-me-nots (shown here with Tulipa 'Monte Beau') are at their best during the flowering time of the early double tulips. Their colour successfully partners a tulip of any colour, and the light airy habit of the forget-me-nots is a pleasing contrast to the strong form of the tulips.

lily-flowered tulips

Although they are mostly tall in stature, these tulips are ideal for pots. Elegant blooms with pointed petals are carried on tall stems way above the foliage and any other planting there is in the same container. Groups of lily-flowered tulips work well in the centre of large pots, adding that essential height that other spring-flowering subjects fail to provide.

***Tulipa* 'West Point'** 🏆 is golden yellow, weather-resistant and long lasting, reaching 50cm in height. ***Tulipa* 'Ballerina'** 🏆 (see page 54) is similar in stature, but has glowing orange blooms. Fully open flowers are a glorious sight on a sunny day.

***Tulipa* 'Lily Chic'** is shorter and therefore ideal for a pot in a more exposed position. The cherry-red flowers are faintly streaked with pale grey and are carried on stout stems near the leaves.

***Tulipa* 'White Triumphator'** 🏆 is a tall, elegant tulip, with long-lasting blooms of pure white. It looks particularly pleasing with *Narcissus* 'Thalia' and blue violas.

Right: *Tulipa* 'West Point'. Below left: *Tulipa* 'Lily Chic'. Below right: *Tulipa* 'White Triumphator'.

To accentuate the tall, sleek form of lily-flowering tulips, grow them with low foliage plants such as thymes, helichrysum, santolina and dwarf hebes. All of these plants are widely available in the seasonal bedding plant selection, on sale at the same time as the tulip bulbs.

summer-flowering bulbs for pots

Flowerbulbs in pots are not confined to the spring season. There are a number of bulbs, corms and tubers that grow well in containers and, if planted in spring, will provide many weeks of interest and colour from early summer through to late autumn. Most are sun lovers so are ideal for patio pots, enjoying a good bake in a sunny spot. Some are not frost hardy, so need to be started indoors on a window sill, or in a greenhouse, before being moved outside after any danger of frost has passed.

A pot of dahlias with orange flowers and bronze leaves makes a strong focal point against a tropical-looking background of bold foliage and brightly coloured flowers.

Begonia

There are few plants that can rival the begonia for the flamboyance of its flowers. There are large-flowered varieties with frilled and flounced, many-petalled blooms, pendulous varieties ideal for hanging baskets and tall containers, and small-flowered forms that produce a long succession of blooms. These last are ideal in mixed containers. Colours include red, white, yellow, orange, pink and salmon.

Growing tuberous begonias

- Plant the tubers indoors in early spring, individually in 15cm pots filled with multi-purpose compost. Nestle the tubers into the surface and lightly water, avoiding the centre of the tuber.
- Keep the pots in a frost-free greenhouse or on a light, cool window sill. If conditions are too warm, or there is insufficient light, growth will be leggy and weak. Protect from strong sunshine, which could scorch the foliage.
- The plants can be moved outside in late spring once danger of frost has passed. Plant them into bigger pots, window boxes or hanging baskets. They like to be sheltered from wind, in partial shade. Foliage can scorch in full sun.
- Feed regularly with a high-potash, soluble fertiliser. They start to bloom in midsummer: remove dead flowers as they fade, if they do not fall off naturally.
- Use thin canes to support upright plants during the growing season. Stems may become heavy under the weight of flowers and foliage and may break off.

There are many superb named varieties of begonia; these are normally available only from specialist importers and growers and are for the adventurous gardener. Most begonias for garden use are sold by colour rather than variety.

how do you keep begonias for next year?

Tuberous begonias can be kept from season to season but must be stored in a frost-free place over winter. As the plants finish flowering and the foliage starts to deteriorate, gradually withhold water. The foliage and stems will die down. Stems normally fall away from the tuber; if not, cut them down, allowing the lower part of the stems to shrivel and fall away later. Keep the pots dry, on their sides in a cool, airy place, or take the tubers out and store them in dry compost until next spring. Sulphur powder on the corms before storage helps prevent fungal diseases.

types of tuberous begonia

Giant double begonias have large, double blooms, 15cm or more across, and usually smaller, single female flowers (recognised by the green seed capsule behind the flower). If the small flowers are removed, the plants can be encouraged to produce even larger blooms. In the past, these were considered to be plants that could be damaged by bad weather and needed a sheltered position; however, more resistant varieties have now been selected that stand up to wind and rain.

Top: Double trumpet *Begonia* 'Amber Giant'. Above: Primadonna *Begonia* 'Candy Frills'.

Giant double-trumpet begonias have more petals and an elegantly pointed centre of coiled petals, intensifying the colour in the heart of the bloom. *Fimbriata* or carnation-flowered begonias have cut edges to the petals, giving a more shaggy effect. Primadonna begonias are an improved form with more petals, with elegantly ruffled edges. Picotee varieties have petals edged in a different colour, creating an interesting layered effect.

summer-flowering bulbs for pots

Sensation begonias A strain of free-flowering begonias with arching stems and drooping clusters of double flowers. They are smaller in flower than the large-flowered hybrids but more floriferous, in bright colours, some with picotee blooms. They are easy to grow, reliable and great for pots and hanging baskets.

Tuberous begonias are bought in early spring as dry tubers often called corms. These are odd-looking, fibrous structures: always challenging the gardener to decide which way up to plant them. Some show tiny pink or yellow shoots: this is the top of the tuber. If there are no clues, look for the concave surface, with a shallow hollow left by last season's stems. This is the top of the tuber. The base of the tuber is the rounded, convex surface.

Non-stop begonias have smaller corms and produce plenty of smaller flowers over a long period. They are reliable, weather-resistant and are suited to general container planting. Use them in window boxes, hanging baskets and patio pots in partially shaded situations. They can also be bought as plants in late spring.

Pendula begonias produce a number of lax stems that hang down over the edge of pots or hanging baskets. The small to medium-sized flowers are freely produced and hang on pendulous stalks, giving a cascade effect on fully grown plants.

Canna

Cannas, or Indian shot, are spectacular, exotic plants with superb leaves and spikes of vibrant flowers from early summer until mid-autumn. They grow from thick, fleshy rhizomes that can be bought when dormant in early spring.

There are varieties with deep bronze-purple foliage; others have attractively veined leaves. Some grow to about 1m in height; others grow much taller. Canna flowers come in shades of yellow, orange, red and pink.

Ideally start the plants indoors in early spring. This may mean planting them initially in 20cm pots and potting on into larger containers when they are moved outside.

Cannas like plenty of water during the growing season and a rich fertile soil, so grow them in large pots (30cm or more in diameter) in John Innes No.3 compost. Small pots are useless: as the plants attain height, they will blow over.

Plant the rhizomes about 10cm deep, laying them horizontally on the compost with any shoots pointing upwards. Position them so that the main shoots will grow in the middle of the pot: if you place the rhizome in the centre of the pot, the shoots may be too close to the side of the container.

Left: Pendula begonias are ideal for tall containers and hanging baskets, especially in shade. Below: *Canna* 'Mozart'.

Good varieties include

Canna **'Black Knight'**: deep wine-purple foliage and spikes of large, rich red flowers

Canna **'Lucifer'**: short and bushy with ribbed leaves and spikes of red, yellow-edged flowers

Canna **'Mozart'** (below left): spectacular plum-purple leaves striped with salmon and orange; large, bright orange flowers on 1.5m stems

Canna **'Phasion'** 🏆: spectacular plum-purple leaves striped with salmon and orange; large, bright orange flowers on 1.5m stems

Canna **'Striata'** 🏆: large green leaves, herringbone striped with yellow; bright orange flowers on tall stems

Canna **'Striped Beauty'** (right): similarly striped leaves and spikes of orange buds opening to clear yellow flowers

Position cannas with striped foliage where the sun can shine through the leaves for a stunning effect.

Many cannas, including *Canna* 'Striped Beauty' (above), have wonderful foliage as well as showy flowers.

Keep the pots in a cool, light room or, better still, in a greenhouse or conservatory with some heat. Growth should be advanced by the time you move the pots outdoors, once any danger of frost is over.

Alternatively, canna rhizomes can be planted directly into their final pots outside in mid-spring. Position the pots in the sunniest, warmest spot you can find. Covering the pots with heavy-gauge horticultural fleece helps to keep them warm at night. Cannas are knocked back by frost, so take care!

Once outside, cannas need full sun to flower well and to develop good leaf colour. Occasional dead heading and removal of faded flower spikes and damaged leaves is all the care they need, apart from regular watering and feeding with a high-potash liquid or soluble fertiliser.

Watch out for slugs and snails. These pests love the emerging shoots of cannas and can cause serious damage to the leaves; this becomes more of a problem as the foliage matures.

When the weather turns colder, pots can be moved into a greenhouse or conservatory and cannas will continue to flourish for a few more weeks. Alternatively, allow the first frost to knock back the foliage, cut back the plants, and move pots into a frost-free shed or garage. Stop watering and keep them dry until the spring.

Far left: *Zantedeschia* 'Captain Tendens'. Left: *Zantedeschia* 'Galaxy'.

Calla lily

Calla or **arum lilies** are really hybrids of *Zantedeschia*. They first became popular as cut flowers. Their sleek, waxy, long-lasting blooms come in a range of deep and vibrant colours. The lush foliage is as much a feature as the flowers; some varieties have attractively spotted and splashed leaves. They suit simple modern arrangements but are also a welcome contrast to more familiar English flowers, such as roses. Once they had become established as cut flowers, callas began to appear as houseplants (see page 35).

Some of the earlier varieties were shy to produce flowers, but breeding and selection has changed this dramatically. Modern hybrid callas are easy to grow, suit outdoor conditions in summer and produce a long succession of luscious flowers in pots on the patio.

Calla lilies require the same treatment as cannas (see pages 62–63). Buy the rhizomes in spring. They are very compact and may appear small in proportion to the size of the plant and the flowers they promise. If you are starting them indoors, plant one rhizome in a 15–20cm pot with the top 4cm below the surface.

Water lightly and keep the soil just moist. Place the pot in a light, frost-free position. As soon as the leaves start to emerge, increase watering. When in full leaf, callas can be thirsty.

Move the plants outside when danger of frost is past. These colourful hybrid callas like sun or semi-shade to flower well. They grow to around 40cm in height, and blooms start to appear in midsummer.

Alternatively, you can plant the corms outside in late spring, directly into pots on the patio. Like cannas, the foliage is knocked back by frost, so do not start them too early.

Exciting callas to grow

Zantedeschia **'Anneke'**: deep maroon flowers and spotted leaves (see page 34)

Zantedeschia **'Black Magic'**: beautiful greenish-yellow flowers with black throats and leaves spotted with silver

Zantedeschia **'Captain Tendens'** (above left): broad blooms of mango and gold

Zantedeschia **'Galaxy'** (above right): cerise-pink flowers on dark stems

The white arum lily, ***Zantedeschia aethiopica*** ♕*, is larger in stature than the hybrid zantedeschias, with broad, spear-shaped green leaves and large white flowers on 1m stems. This too can be grown as a patio plant. Buy dry rhizomes in early spring.*

Dahlia

Some dahlias make excellent bushy, free-flowering plants for summer pots. Plant them as tubers in early spring indoors or in late spring outside. Some varieties have bulky tubers, needing large containers.

Growing dahlias in pots

- Plant the tubers with the remains of last year's stems uppermost and just below the surface of the compost.
- Use either multi-purpose compost with added John Innes or John Innes No.3 loam-based compost.
- Either start them in 10–15cm pots and pot on into their final containers or plant them directly into their final pots. Eventually most varieties need a pot at least 30cm in diameter.
- If you are planting indoors, keep the pots in a light, cool but frost-free place.
- As the shoots reach 10–12cm, pinch the tops out to encourage bushy growth. Repeat as necessary, allowing them to develop naturally from early summer on.
- Dahlias produce a long succession of flowers. Remove blooms as they fade to keep the plants looking good and prolong flowering.

Dahlias are knocked back by the first frost. Once the top growth has gone, tubers can be removed from the pots, dried and stored in dry compost in a frost-free place until spring. But as most dahlia tubers cost about £1, it may be easier to start with new ones each year.

Good dahlia varieties

There are many new dahlia varieties every year; choose compact ones for pots. Those with purple or dark green foliage are particularly decorative and look good with other patio foliage plants, especially cannas and exotics. These varieties grow to less than 60cm tall.

gallery dahlias *have rounded flowers made of many-shaded petals. They are free flowering and easy to grow.*

Dahlia **'Gallery Art Deco'** 🏆: elegant apricot-orange flowers

Dahlia **'Gallery Art Nouveau'** 🏆: similar to 'Art Deco' but with rich cerise-purple blooms (top right)

Dahlia **'Gallery Rembrandt'** 🏆: rounded flowers of pale and deep lilac-mauve

melody dahlias *are compact with excellent dark green foliage and a long succession of many-petalled flowers.*

Dahlia **'Melody Dora'**: pointed petals, pink outside, deep cream within

Dahlia **'Melody Lisa'**: sugar-pink petals, white at the centre of the flower (middle right)

single-flowering dahlias *have great charm and attract pollinating insects.*

Dahlia **'Sneezy'**: clear yellow flowers with golden yellow eyes

Dahlia **'Red Riding Hood'**: scarlet flowers with yellow centres (bottom right)

Dahlia **'Roxy'**: bright cerise-purple flowers and deep wine-coloured foliage (bottom right)

lilies

Lilium **'Lollypop'** has cheerful, white-centred blooms; the end of each petal is deep cerise-pink. *Lilium* **'Vermeer'** has soft pink flowers, paler in the centres.

oriental hybrids

Oriental hybrids are vigorous lilies, often growing to over 1.2m in height. Strong stems with broad, deep green leaves carry large, well-spaced open blooms. The petals

Left: *Lilium* **'Mona Lisa', a compact grower and ideal for pots and containers. Below:** *Lilium* 'Vermeer'.

Pots of lilies add a touch of extravagance to any summer garden, whether you choose compact and colourful varieties or tall, elegant and exotic ones. Many have deliciously scented blooms that fill summer evenings with a magical fragrance. It is not surprising that they have been voted Britain's favourite flowers – ahead of roses, sweet peas and delphiniums.

Lily bulbs vary in size, according to variety. A small bulb does not necessarily mean that the plant too will be small and compact. Likewise, some large-growing lilies, especially the oriental varieties, have comparatively small bulbs, but produce tall flower stems and very large flowers.

dwarf patio lilies

These are mostly Asiatic and oriental hybrids that have short, stout stems with fresh green foliage. Their flowers are open and upward-facing with broad petals.

Lilium **'Mona Lisa'** is a favourite, a scented oriental lily reaching 40cm in height, with open blooms of pink and white flushed deep pink towards the centre.

Also popular is *Lilium* **'Peach Pixie'**, with upward-facing blooms of peachy orange on strong 40cm stems; **'Butter Pixie'** is yellow and **'Crimson Pixie'** is orange-red.

Asiatic hybrids

These are useful for early colour. Often brightly coloured with strong stems, about 90cm tall, carrying upward-facing blooms, these lilies grow and bloom quickly.

Lilium **'Latvia'** has starry, pale yellow flowers with cinnamon-orange centres.

Some lilies, especially the Asiatic hybrids, produce prolific roots from the base of the stem, above the bulb. In smaller pots it is an advantage to cover the bulbs with just 3–4cm of compost, wait for the shoots to emerge, and then top the pot up with compost as the shoots grow. This encourages more root production between the bulb and the surface of the compost at the top of the pot.

are pointed and reflexed, and the flowers are usually very fragrant. Many oriental lilies are familiar florist flowers.

One of the best known is ***Lilium* 'Star Gazer'**, with white petals deeply streaked and spotted with cerise.

***Lilium* 'Casa Blanca'** 🏆 has tall, strong stems carrying large pure white, richly fragrant blooms. ***Lilium* 'Kiss Proof'** is a striking lily with open, cerise flowers, paler at the edges of the petals.

trumpet lilies

Older varieties of trumpet lilies are favourite border plants. Some grow very tall and are unsuitable for pots, but some of the shorter ones, at about 1m in height, make excellent subjects for large containers. The white trumpet lily *Lilium longiflorum* is the one sold as cut flowers.

The favourite, ***Lilium regale*** 🏆, grows to over 1m in height, with richly scented, white blooms flushed purple-pink on the outside of the petals.

***Lilium* 'Red Dutch'** is a richly coloured lily growing to over 1m in height, with open trumpet blooms of mahogany red edged with creamy yellow.

***Lilium* 'White Sheen'** is a dwarf longiflorum lily, with 40cm stems bearing pure white, scented trumpet blooms.

Lily bulbs do not like to be out of the soil for too long as this causes them to dry out. The waxy scales shrivel and the bulb opens up, allowing soil water to penetrate. Plant them as soon as you get them, or store them in a cool place, in wood shavings or dry compost.

Planting lilies in pots

- For smaller pots, less than 30cm in diameter, choose three bulbs of a shorter-growing variety, such as *Lilium* 'Peach Pixie'.
- For larger, deep pots, over 45cm in diameter, choose five bulbs of a short- or taller-growing variety, such as *Lilium* 'Casa Blanca'.
- Lilies like a rich compost with plenty of nutrients, so use John Innes No.3 compost or a 50:50 mixture of this with a multi-purpose, soil-less compost.
- Place a layer of broken crocks or large stones in the bottom of the pot for drainage, then half fill the pot with compost, leaving at least 20cm to the top of the pot.
- Lay the lily bulbs on their sides, nose to tail, on the surface of the compost, spreading their roots behind them. Planting on the side prevents water from lodging between the fleshy scales, which can cause the bulbs to rot.
- Top up the pot with compost, then water.
- When the shoots have emerged and are growing freely, lilies benefit from an occasional liquid feed with a high-potash fertiliser.

Top: The opulent *Lilium* 'Casa Blanca' is deliciously scented. Above: *Lilium regale*, a classic beauty with a wonderful fragrance.

After the flowers fade

Once the blooms have faded, cut off the flower heads, removing the developing seed capsules, but leave the stems. Keep watering and feeding, to build the bulbs up for the next year. Either use a liquid feed or apply a controlled-release granular fertiliser. The stems will die naturally in late summer or autumn. The bulbs can be left in the pots for three or four seasons. After this, you can plant the whole clump in the border or re-pot the bulbs straightaway in fresh compost.

naturalising flowerbulbs

Natural drifts of bulbs in bloom are one of the most evocative images of spring: a sight that sings in celebration of fresh, crisp colour. In the dappled shade under trees and against the emerald backdrop of new grass, bulb flowers shine from early spring until early summer; some even perform in autumn. In late winter early aconites open their golden blooms in the dry shade between tree roots, and pink and white cyclamen carpet slopes and rocky banks. The first snowdrops bloom, pure and white, often with pale blue crocus, which open to reveal orange stamens. Primrose-yellow and golden daffodils follow in a brash display before sapphire bluebells spread a shimmering carpet under the trees. Camassias and fritillaries are meadow gems of late spring that add sparkle to lengthening grass. Towards the end of the year, pink cyclamen, autumn crocus and colchicums flower beneath the trees as the canopy starts to thin with the autumn leaf fall.

Above: Gleaming flowers of *Crocus* 'Whitewell Purple' peep through spring grass. Right: *Narcissus* 'Jack Snipe', with white petals and a yellow trumpet, and the fragrant double *Narcissus* 'Pencrebar' bask in the sunshine under birch trees.

what is naturalising?

Naturalising bulbs means growing them as they grow in nature: never in straight rows or regular clumps, but as if they have seeded naturally, gradually spreading and expanding their colonies.

A sapphire carpet of English bluebells in the dappled light beneath beech trees: an effect to aim for in the garden by naturalising bulbs.

is naturalising only for large gardens?

No, certainly not. A natural effect can be achieved in a small space under a tree, at the base of a wall or fence, or beneath a mature shrub. It is simply a matter of selecting suitable bulbs for the purpose and planting them informally.

choosing the right bulbs

Many bulbs, both species (those that occur in the wild) and garden hybrids (those that have been bred and selected in gardens), can be used for naturalising. However, to achieve that wildflower look, it is always better to choose varieties that have small, graceful flowers. Avoid all double-flowered, highly coloured daffodils and anything that looks as if it belongs in a highly manicured garden.

Naturalised bulbs suit the edge of grassed areas, around large shrubs or under trees. This is how bulbs grow in the wild. The reason plants produce bulbs is to give them a competitive edge early in the year. The bulb contains a water and food reserve, so the plant is able to grow, flower and set seed before the tree canopy starts to compete for nourishment.

Plants in the wild distribute seeds around themselves, producing colonies of the same type. The effect is usually lost when we plant mixed bulbs in a mish-mash of shapes, colours and heights. The other problem with mixed bulbs is that they do not all flower together, so in a clump of ten bulbs we may be very disappointed to see just two or three flowers at any one time.

Planting bulbs in grass

- At the time of planting, do bear in mind the foliage that will remain after flowering is over. Leaves need to die down naturally, returning food to the bulb ready for next year's performance. Site bulbs where you can live with long grass throughout the spring. Leave enough space between the plantings to allow mower access if needed.

- Make sure you plant the bulbs deep enough. Plant them at least three times the depth of the bulb, and space them at least the same distance apart as twice the diameter of the bulb. Remember to allow room for the bulbs to multiply without the clumps becoming overcrowded.

- The best way to plant bulbs in grass is to lift squares of turf the size of your spade blade and dig out a sensible hole four times the depth of the bulb. Loosen the soil in the base of the hole and position the bulbs in the hole before backfilling and replacing the turf. A hole like this will accommodate about ten narcissus bulbs or 20 crocus bulbs.

- Group at least five of these plantings together to create a colony with impact. Placing a few clumps close together and scattering others a little distance from the main colony gives a natural effect.

- Where the ground is soft and the grass is thin, you can use a bulb planter. If you are planting a lot of bulbs, it is worth investing in a long-handled bulb planter that can be pushed into the ground with your foot.

Top: *Crocus tommasinianus* multiplies by seeding itself freely in short grass. Above: Flowerbulbs are easily planted in grass by lifting a square of turf, planting the bulbs and replacing the grass. Any damage to the turf is soon repaired by autumn rainfall.

Tips for that natural look

- Plant in irregular clumps or drifts, not neat round ones.

- Avoid spacing the bulbs regularly: create a scattered effect over the planting area.

- Where several groups of bulbs are clustered together, vary the size of the clumps.

- Plant in drifts of one type except in the case of large-flowered or specie crocus, where mixing bulbs can be effective.

The famous gardener and plantswoman Gertrude Jekyll had a clever technique for naturalising bulbs. She used potatoes, which she scattered across the ground in handfuls. Wherever a potato came to rest, she planted a bulb.
You can scatter large bulbs directly in this way, but do not drop them from a great height as this will bruise and damage the bulbs.

snowdrops

Snowdrops can be relied on to appear whatever the weather.

When we catch sight of the first snowdrops, we know that winter days are numbered and spring is on the way. We wonder at their bravery: delicate, dainty white and green blossoms emerge from the cold, wet ground at what can be an inhospitable time of year. It is no wonder that gardeners get hooked on these fragile beauties.

Snowdrop bulbs are sold and planted in early autumn. They are small and delicate and dry out easily; it is important that you plant them as soon as you have bought them. They like semi-shade and, ideally, a moist soil rich in organic matter.

You need to plant a huge number of snowdrops to achieve a naturalised effect quickly. One hundred snowdrop bulbs might sound a lot, but it goes nowhere – even in a small garden. Probably the best approach is to build your snowdrop colony gradually, planting a few more clumps each year.

Plant in groups of ten or more bulbs, spacing them 4cm apart and 6–7cm deep. This will result in a thin planting in the first year, but leaves enough space for the bulbs to multiply and spread in subsequent seasons. They usually reach their potential after two or three years.

Snowdrops are also sold in late winter and early spring as pot-grown stock, in leaf and flower. This is a reliable way of establishing them. Some specialist growers supply snowdrop bulbs 'in the green' in spring. These are lifted in clumps from the open ground in full leaf, as the flowers are fading, and may be despatched by mail order. Plant them as soon as possible in small clumps of three or five bulbs, grouping several clumps together. Plant to the same depth as they were growing: to the base of the green part of the leaves. Water thoroughly after planting.

Snowdrops can be naturalised in grass successfully, but for them to produce extensive colonies they need to be allowed to set seed before the grass is cut. The foliage and flower stems must have died back completely before you mow. Do not cut the grass too short at first. Avoid using chemical lawn treatments in

Look out for

Galanthus **'S. Arnott'** 🏆 (above): tall and vigorous with large, fragrant flowers

Galanthus **'Magnet'** 🏆: large, shining white flowers on long, arching stems

Galanthus **'Atkinsii'** 🏆: a tall snowdrop with simple, open flowers on long stems

Over the years snowdrops will spread a spring carpet in light shade under trees.

spring where snowdrops are planted; lawn weed killers are best avoided in these areas at all times.

snowdrop varieties

There are numerous named varieties available from specialist growers. Many are choice and expensive, and price tags of several pounds for a single bulb are not uncommon. The following are recommended for naturalising.

Snowdrops grow well at the base of rural hedges where the soil is rich in organic matter. Often the dark green leaves of common ivy provide the perfect background for their dainty white flowers.

Left: *Galanthus nivalis*. Above: *Galanthus elwesii.*

Galanthus nivalis 🏆, the common snowdrop, is probably the best, with narrow green leaves and dainty white and green, scented flowers. It is perhaps the hardiest and easiest snowdrop to grow.

Galanthus nivalis f. *pleniflorus* **'Flore Pleno'** 🏆, the double snowdrop, has irregular double flowers. It is a strong, hardy plant and usually appears shorter in stature than the single variety. It is shown to greatest advantage at the edge of paths or at the base of walls.

Galanthus elwesii 🏆 has broader, grey-green leaves and larger flowers than *Galanthus nivalis*. It also flowers earlier in the season, often before Christmas. A native of Turkey, it tolerates drier conditions and more sunshine than most snowdrops. It is an excellent choice for rockeries and paved areas.

crocus

Crocus are brilliant bulbs for naturalising. Most are cheap to buy, so you can plant plenty for little outlay. They have narrow, dark green leaves that blend well with grass. Their seedheads are carried low in the foliage rather than on tall stems. Once the leaves start to wither, mowing will do no harm as long as the grass is not cropped too short. The smaller-flowered, specie crocus create the most naturalistic effect, but the large-flowered, Dutch crocus still work wonderfully when planted en masse in short grass.

Crocus corms are resilient and can be planted at any time in autumn or early winter provided they have been stored in a cool, dark place. Plant either in clumps of 20 or so bulbs or in much larger drifts. To plant in drifts, lift several areas of turf, perhaps 90cm x 60cm, scrape away 10cm of soil, then space the bulbs irregularly across the area, approximately 3cm apart, before backfilling with soil and replacing the turf. This is easier in beds and borders, where crocus bulbs can be naturalised under large deciduous shrubs.

Left: Delicate crocus flowers open wide in the sunshine to invite pollinating insects.

specie crocus

Crocus tommasinianus 🏆 is one of the loveliest, with slender, pale lilac-blue flowers with orange stigmas. It flowers early, often opening in the late-winter sunshine. It is an excellent choice under apple trees and can spread rapidly and freely if it likes the situation. It is especially successful on poor, free-draining soil, particularly chalk.

There are a number of cultivars. To name a few: ***Crocus tommasinianus* 'Barr's Purple'**, with purple flowers, silvery on the outside; **'Ruby Giant'**, vigorous, with red-purple flowers; **'Whitewell Purple'**, with purple-blue, wide-opening flowers.

Crocus can be planted in drifts of one variety, but they also work well in large drifts of mixed colours. An attractive effect can be created by planting neighbouring drifts of varieties whose flowers are in shades of the same colour. Try the pale lavender-blue Crocus tommasinianus 🏆 *(near right) with the stronger purple Crocus tommasinianus 'Whitewell Purple' (middle right) and the red-purple Crocus tommasinianus 'Ruby Giant' (far right).*

From the left: *Crocus chrysanthus* 'Gipsy Girl', *Crocus chrysanthus* 'Ladykiller', *Crocus sieberi* subsp. *sublimis* 'Tricolor', *Crocus sieberi* 'Albus'.

Crocus chrysanthus has short, spiky foliage and tiny goblet-shaped flowers reaching 6–8cm in height. The petals are often delicately patterned on the outside. It succeeds in the same conditions as *Crocus tommasinianus*. There are many cultivars: ***Crocus chrysanthus* 'Gipsy Girl'** has golden yellow petals with purple-brown, feathered stripes on the outside. **'Ladykiller'** 🏆 has cream blooms heavily marked with purple on the outside. **'Cream Beauty'** 🏆 has rich cream flowers, greenish brown at the base and yellow inside. **'Snow Bunting'** 🏆 is white. **'Blue Bird'** is pale blue. **'E.P. Bowles'** is deep yellow with purple feathering on the outside.

Crocus sieberi 🏆 has very short leaves and short flower stems carrying wide-opening, brightly coloured blooms. It is rarely more than 8cm in height, but it makes up for this with its cheery appearance. **'Albus'** 🏆 is white with yellow centres and blooms exceptionally early. The flowers of **'Firefly'** are violet-blue. ***Crocus sieberi* subsp. *sublimis* 'Tricolor'** 🏆 is the showiest variety, with sparkling lilac petals, turning white and then vivid yellow towards the throat of the flower; the stigma and anthers are bright orange.

Dutch crocus

The large-flowered, **Dutch crocus**, or ***Crocus vernus* subsp. *albiflorus***, also work well naturalised in grass or gravel. They have larger corms than specie crocus, but are planted the same way. They are often sold by colour, not named variety, but there are a number of favourites that have been offered for many years (see right).

Large-flowered crocus can be susceptible to weather damage, especially when the blooms are fully open, and they may be vandalised by birds. Some say that blue crocus are left alone by the birds, claiming that the yellow ones are the most susceptible to attack. Others dispute this, pointing out that some birds seem to be either colour-blind or indiscriminate!

In manicured gardens, without any informal areas of grass, Dutch crocus can be used to add colour to the planting circles around trees in lawns. If these are kept free of grass, they can be planted with ground-cover plants such as Vinca minor, the lesser periwinkle. The large-flowered crocus will grow through the vinca, displaying their blooms against its evergreen foliage.

Favourite Dutch crocus

***Crocus* × *luteus* 'Golden Yellow'** 🏆 (above): orange-yellow

***Crocus vernus* subsp. *albiflorus* 'Jeanne d'Arc'**: pure white flowers with orange stigmas

***Crocus vernus* subsp. *albiflorus* 'Pickwick'**: white flowers striped with deep lilac-purple (see page 26)

***Crocus vernus* subsp. *albiflorus* 'Purpureus Grandiflorus**: rich purple

***Crocus vernus* subsp. *albiflorus* 'Queen of the Blues'**: mauve-blue flowers

***Crocus vernus* subsp. *albiflorus* 'Remembrance'**: shining flowers of violet-blue (see page 26)

daffodils and narcissi for naturalising

Daffodils and narcissi are the flowerbulbs most widely chosen for naturalising in gardens. Bulbs are readily available, inexpensive to buy and easy to plant. The majority succeed on most soils, and they are suited to the damp winter climate of the British Isles. Their cheerful shades of white, yellow and orange brighten the dullest of days and glow supreme in sunshine.

What's the difference between daffodils and narcissi? *Nothing. All daffodils are narcissi: Narcissus is the botanical term. In everyday gardeners' language, the term daffodil is usually used for those with a distinct trumpet, whereas narcissus is used for those with a flattened flower and a short trumpet.*

A massed planting of golden yellow daffodils rejoices in the low spring sunshine.

The main drawback with daffodils and narcissi naturalised in grass is their leaves: they take longer than any other flowerbulb to die down. In the case of the larger hybrid daffodils, it can be at least six weeks from the time the flowers fade. If you have a fairly small number of daffodils growing in grass, remove the flower stalks soon after flowering. The stalk is the part of the plant that tends to remain sticking up from the grass once the leaves start to fade; remove it, leaving the fading leaves to blend unobtrusively into the long grass.

specie narcissi

Most true specie daffodils have special soil requirements. These are plants for the keen gardener with patience and the right soil. Seed or bulbs are usually sourced through specialist growers. In the long term, sowing seed is often more successful than planting bulbs. Small specie daffodils spread successfully if allowed to seed. Never remove the flower stems or seedheads after flowering and leave for at least eight weeks before mowing. Examine the plants carefully: look for parchment capsules that have split and shed their seed before you mow.

Narcissus pseudonarcissus 🏆, the wild daffodil, is a British native and enjoys well-drained soil that is not too dry. It is often found on banks under the dappled shade of trees, at the edge of woodlands, or at the base of hedges where well-drained soil is rich in organic matter. It flowers early, with dainty flowers on 20cm stems; the petals are pale primrose, the trumpet a stronger yellow. When happy, it will seed freely and spread to form large, well-spaced colonies.

Avoid planting large-flowered hybrid daffodils and narcissi near Narcissus pseudonarcissus. They will hybridise with the species to produce plants with coarser flowers than the wild daffodil, thus spoiling the effect.

Narcissus obvallaris 🏆, the Tenby daffodil, is reputedly one of the easiest species to establish in the garden. Unfussy and vigorous, it has bright yellow blooms.

Narcissus cyclamineus 🏆 needs damp, acid soil. It thrives on raised banks near water, where the soil is moist but not waterlogged. It grows best among ferns and leaf litter, rather than in grass. It flowers very early, usually in late winter. Fine, bright green stems up to 15cm high carry tiny, bright yellow blooms with reflexed petals.

Narcissus bulbocodium 🏆, the hoop petticoat daffodil, has tiny yellow, long-lasting flowers with broad, bold trumpets and small spiky petals. It prefers an acid soil and good drainage. A native of the Iberian peninsula and North Africa, it likes a dry summer and plenty of sunshine and is frequently seen on rocky banks and in gravel. It can be successfully naturalised in a meadow if the grass is not too lush.

Above: *Narcissus pseudonarcissus* brings early colour to the base of a hedge. Below: *Narcissus cyclamineus* enjoys a shady spot.

small hybrid narcissi

Narcissus **'February Gold'** 🏆 takes some beating for its dainty early flowers. Bright green leaves and flower stems set off the fine, golden yellow trumpet daffodil flowers. It grows to around 30cm in height, which means it is tall enough to compete with longer grass.

Narcissus **'Hawera'** 🏆 is one of the latest of the dwarf narcissi to bloom. It has pale yellow flowers with short trumpets, carried in twos and threes on fine green stems. The thin, grassy foliage presents few problems as it dies down. It grows to 20cm in height, so is a bulb for shorter grass at the edge of a lawn.

Narcissus **'Jetfire'** 🏆 is similar in stature to 'February Gold', but differs in having a wonderful orange trumpet. The flowers, carried on 20cm stems, are long lasting and weather-resistant. It is a good choice for shadier areas, where the colour will lift

Above: *Narcissus* 'February Gold' is one of the earliest small narcissi to flower, while *Narcissus* 'Hawera' (right) is one of the latest.

Most dwarf narcissi are suitable for naturalising in grass or among low ground-cover plants. It is most important to bear in mind the length of the grass or the height of any associated planting, as this could conceal shorter varieties. As grass now keeps growing through the winter, this can be a problem: a cut mid-winter, before the bulbs emerge, helps.

the planting and the flowers will not fade as they do in full sun.

Narcissus **'Peeping Tom'** is a taller variety, growing to 30cm or more. It has golden yellow blooms with downward-pointing trumpets and upwardly swept petals. It is graceful and elegant, and has emerald-green leaves and flower stalks.

Narcissus **'Rip van Winkle'**, with its double starry flowers on 15cm stems, naturalises well in short grass at the base of trees. Its bright yellow blooms brighten a shady spot, and it is a delightful partner for chionodoxa and blue pulmonarias.

Narcissus **'Tête à Tête'** is usually considered a narcissus for pots and containers (see pages 28, 52), but its vigorous habit makes it suitable for naturalising in short grass and gravel. Short, upright leaves are the backdrop to golden yellow flowers, often in twos, on 15–20cm stems. It can look too cultivated for country gardens, but is an ideal choice for small town gardens. This is a good bulb to grow in pots for one season, then use for naturalising the following year.

Narcissus **'Jack Snipe'** is a lovely dwarf daffodil with graceful flowers (see pages 53, 68). The white petals are swept back from clear yellow trumpets. Growing to 20cm or so, it is the perfect choice to plant in clumps under trees, perhaps to grow through dark green ivy. It flowers later than 'Jetfire' and 'February Gold'; planted with them, it maintains continuity.

Top: *Narcissus* 'Jetfire'. Above: *Narcissus* 'Peeping Tom'. Right: *Narcissus* 'Rip van Winkle'.

All the hybrid narcissi increase their numbers by producing offsets. This means that the bulbs need room to spread. Remember this when planting. Space the bulbs at least the width of a bulb apart and ideally double or treble this, to allow for multiplication over the years. Once colonies become overcrowded, flowering performance is likely to deteriorate.

daffodils and narcissi for naturalising

The early flowers of *Narcissus* 'Ice Follies' shine when lit by the low spring sunshine.

Most large narcissi naturalise well in grass, and millions are sold for this purpose every year. Sacks of yellow daffodils for naturalising contain whichever variety or varieties are in plentiful supply that season. These will give good results, provided the bulbs are of good quality. Mixed daffodils and narcissi can work if planted in large numbers and big drifts. In the average garden they are best avoided: select single varieties instead.

larger hybrid narcissi

The following grow to about 40cm in height and flower in early to mid-spring.

***Narcissus* 'Actaea'** 🏆 is a lovely pheasant's-eye narcissus with flattened flowers of broad white petals and a shortened, golden and dark red trumpet forming the eye. 'Actaea' is graceful and elegant when planted sparsely as individual bulbs in drifts in longer grass under trees.

***Narcissus* 'Golden Harvest'** is a good, reliable favourite trumpet daffodil with golden yellow blooms early in the season. It naturalises well in grass and spreads quickly. It is a good choice to draw the eye to a focal point: the bright flowers shine in the garden, whatever the weather.

***Narcissus* 'Ice Follies'** 🏆 is one of the most popular narcissi for naturalising. It flowers early, with prolific weather-resistant blooms. The petals are white, and the broad,

Clumps and drifts of daffodils and narcissi in bloom are a dominant feature in any garden. Bear this in mind when selecting varieties and positioning the bulbs. Yellow always draws the eye more than any other colour. Never use it in areas of the garden where you would rather not attract attention.

flattened and pleated trumpet is pale yellow, fading to cream. 'Ice Follies' is very reliable, but perhaps heavy in appearance.

Narcissus 'Mount Hood' 🏆 is a trumpet daffodil with white petals and a pale yellow trumpet that fades to white as the blooms age. 'Mount Hood' is striking but subtle when naturalised in grass and is a good choice for those trying to avoid the clashing yellows and pinks so common in spring gardens. *Narcissus* **'Finland'** is a newer variety that is similar in colouring.

Narcissus **'Sempre Avanti'** is an early-flowering narcissus with creamy petals and a short orange trumpet. It can look very effective naturalised in grass under trees that have dark brown bark and among evergreen ground cover such as periwinkle or ivy.

Narcissus 'Saint Keverne' 🏆 is a reliable yellow trumpet daffodil with medium-sized, well-proportioned flowers on strong stems. It is hardy, performs year after year and resists basal-rot, a disease that can affect some larger daffodils and narcissi.

Narcissus 'Thalia' is one of the most beautiful of all narcissi. Fine 30cm stems carry two or three pure white blooms with starry petals and short white trumpets. It naturalises well in grass and is stunning among blue forget-me-nots under a white-flowered cherry such as *Prunus* 'Shirotae'.

Above left: *Narcissus* 'Mount Hood'. Above right: *Narcissus* 'Actaea'. Below: The delicate *Narcissus* 'Thalia' blooms open in mid-spring.

Tulips for naturalising

Most tulips do not lend themselves to naturalising in grass. Shorter varieties become swamped and taller ones fail to compete, especially on heavy soil. The taller single tulips can be planted in grass to give a naturalistic effect for just one season. The red *Tulipa* **'Apeldoorn'** gives the effect of early poppies. Single purple tulips, such as *Tulipa* **'Queen of Night'** (above left) and **'Purple Flag'** (above right), are effective naturalised together as a mix of shades of one colour. They will usually need replacing every year.

bluebells and camassias

Plant the small, round bulbs in autumn, 4–6cm deep in informal clumps of 20 or more, leaving 3–4cm between the bulbs. You can lift patches of turf and plant the bulbs as you would do with narcissi or, on soft ground, you can use a large dibber. Alternatively, for large areas tended by patient gardeners, the bulbs can be planted up to 20cm apart. The idea is that the ripe seed will be scattered around each plant and will have room to grow and develop over the following two or three years until the seedlings reach flowering size. This technique works best in thin grass. The seed must be allowed to ripen naturally (the seedhead becomes parchment-like and the capsules split to release coarse black seeds). At this stage, some manual help with scattering the seeds will ensure they are spread evenly.

English bluebell

Nothing can compare with the sapphire hue and gentle fragrance of Britain's wild bluebell.

The wild bluebell, ***Hyacinthoides non-scripta***, is the very essence of the English countryside in spring. Carpeting beech woods, just as the fresh green foliage of the trees is opening, and colouring banks and hedgerows, the delicate, scented sapphire bells nod gently on slender stems that arch at the tips. Bluebells will create a naturalistic effect in any garden where there is a little dappled shade provided by trees or large shrubs.

Bluebells look particularly effective in the grass under trees that have white or grey bark, such as the British native birch, Betula pendula.

Bluebells are protected wildflowers and bulbs cannot legally be collected from natural habitats. Reputable suppliers always state that the bulbs are from a cultivated source and have been grown specifically for sale.

An alternative to bluebells for naturalising in grass are ***grape hyacinths (Muscari armeniacum)****. They seem to succeed in any situation and spread freely. As with bluebells, you should let the green seedheads turn to parchment, split and shed their black seeds before mowing the grass.* *See also page 91.*

English bluebells prefer light soils and thin grass; they do not compete well with coarse, lush grass. Most rabbits and deer leave them alone, but Muntjak deer seek them out and devour them.

Spanish bluebell

The Spanish bluebell, ***Hyacinthoides hispanica***, is larger and coarser than its English cousin. The individual bells are bigger and more open, and the flower stem does not bend so gracefully at the tip. The bulbs are large and round, spreading prolifically by offsets and seed.

The Spanish bluebell has always been maligned for its tendency to breed with the English bluebell, thereby invading native populations. Because the Spanish bluebell is stronger, it quickly takes over. None the less Spanish bluebells deliver a fine show in mid-spring and can be used in gardens if they are well away from native bluebell populations. Some of the pink, white and lilac forms are particularly decorative.

Spanish bluebells will successfully compete with coarser grass and normally thrive on any soil.

Above: Sunshine spotlights the blue spires of *Camassia leichtlinii* as they open against the white bark of *Betula utilis* var. *jacquemontii*. Left: *Hyacinthoides hispanica*, the Spanish bluebell.

Camassia

Just when the bluebell flowers begin to fade, camassias start to bloom. These lovely prairie bulbs are easy to grow and succeed on any soil that is not too dry or waterlogged. They grow well in grass, in sun or partial shade. Their pure blue flowers look particularly lovely against the white bark of Himalayan birches.

Camassia leichtlinii has starry blue flowers carried on strong spikes that rise 60cm or more above the upright, silvery green leaves. The large bulbs should be planted in autumn, 15cm deep and a similar distance apart. The common name, quamash, is of Native American origin.

Camassia cusickii has pale, steel-blue, more delicate flowers and longer, more untidy foliage than *leichtlinii*.

other little gems for naturalising

Above: The dainty *Chionodoxa luciliae*, glory of the snow, is a good choice to plant in groups around trees, where it enjoys the dappled shade. Below: *Anemone blanda* blue shades.

Anemone blanda

Growing best on a well-drained soil rich in organic matter, ***Anemone blanda*** ♕ succeeds in sun or partial shade in short, thin grass, on banks or at the edge of the tree canopy. In spring the short stems uncurl to spread fern-like leaves and the narrow buds open into single starry, many-petalled flowers with pale yellow stamens. The semi-double variety ***Anemone blanda* 'White Splendour'** ♕ is a vigorous plant that spreads successfully into drifts; it makes a delightful companion for the sapphire-blue *Scilla siberica* ♕. The lovely ***Anemone blanda* blue shades** is always popular, with long-lasting flowers in shades of sky blue.

For best results soak Anemone blanda corms for 24 hours prior to planting 6cm deep and 3cm apart in groups of 10–20 corms.

Glory of the snow

Chionodoxa luciliae ♕ is a charming early-spring flowerbulb with narrow green leaves and fine, 15cm stems carrying sapphire-blue, white-centred starry flowers. It grows well in the dappled shade of trees or beneath deciduous shrubs. If allowed to seed, it spreads prolifically. Initially, plant the bulbs 10cm deep and only 2–3cm apart, in clumps of 10–20 bulbs.

Chionodoxa luciliae is pretty planted beneath an early-flowering cherry such as Prunus cerasifera 'Nigra' ♕. It also adds early colour to beds planted with roses, which can be very bare at this time of the year. The bulbs will enjoy the summer shade provided by the roses when they are in leaf and flower.

Winter aconite

Eranthis hyemalis 🏆 is a cheerful sight when it opens its buttercup-yellow, green-frilled flowers just 6cm above the ground in late winter. It is often the first of the spring bulbs to flower, continuing to accompany the snowdrops while screaming at the sugar-pink *Cyclamen coum*. Opinions vary on its requirements: some say it likes dry conditions, others that it likes moist soil that must never dry out. It does seem to do best close to the trunks of deciduous trees, where it enjoys plenty of light when in flower and the shade of the tree canopy in summer. It also seems successful between hellebores, where, again, it has

light in winter and shade from the leaves in summer. Plant the corms 5cm deep and 3cm apart, in small clumps, and hope for the best. If it likes you, it will flourish!

Winter aconites look lovely in pockets between mossy stones and flagstones, perhaps grouped around the base of a birdbath or stone ornament.

If you have trouble establishing fritillaries, try starting them in pots: plant five bulbs to a 12cm pot and transplant without disturbing the roots once the stems are 10–15cm high.

Snake's head fritillary

Also known as the snake's head lily, ***Fritillaria meleagris*** is a beautiful British native wildflower that used to be widespread in watermeadows. The delicate chequerboard-patterned, bell shaped flowers hang from 30cm stems, which also carry narrow grey-green leaves. Sadly, colonies are today few and far between, but it is widely grown in gardens. To naturalise, it needs full sun and a damp site that does not dry out in summer. It will tolerate quite heavy soil. Plant the small waxy bulbs as soon as you have bought them; dry shrivelled bulbs rarely grow. Plant 10cm deep and 5cm apart in the open ground or in thin grass.

Far left: Winter aconite, *Eranthis hyemalis*, nestled against a tree trunk. Left: *Fritillaria meleagris*. Above: *Hermodactylus tuberosus*.

Widow iris

Hermodactylus tuberosus is a member of the iris family from North Africa and Turkey, so it is an excellent choice to naturalise in dry, sunny situations where the bulbs will get a good baking in summer. Gravel areas, along the base of walls, and borders alongside paving are ideal. The blue-green, grass-like foliage grows to 30cm; the curious green and black iris flowers are usually shorter and appear in mid-spring. Plant the bulbs in autumn, in groups of 10–20, 6–8cm deep and 4cm apart.

Plant Hermodactylus tuberosus with the starry white Ipheion uniflorum (left): both like to be left undisturbed to multiply, ideally in a sunny area of thin gravel.

hardy cyclamen

Cyclamen hederifolium **spreads a sugar-pink autumn carpet beneath this beech tree.**

Cyclamen are members of the primula family. In the wild, some grow in woodland conditions, others in open scrub, some in lowland areas, others in the mountains. They develop tubers, usually called corms, which enable them to survive times of the year when there is little water. These vary in size, according to species and age, from 2–3cm across to 15cm or more.

Corms should be planted in moist soil, with the flat or concave side of the corm upwards and just below the soil surface. Old, large corms can be difficult to stimulate into growth. Alternatively, buy pot-grown plants in flower and leaf. This way, you see the colour of the flowers and can judge the plant's maturity and flower power.

Cyclamen are efficient when it comes to sowing their own seeds. As the flowers fade, the delicate stems gradually coil up and form fleshy springs that draw the seed capsules down under the leaves and into contact with the soil. When it germinates, each seed develops a single, tiny leaf and a miniature corm. From this stage onwards you can transplant the corms, to spread the colony.

Cyclamen hederifolium

This cyclamen appears in early autumn. Fine 10cm stems emerge from the soil carrying delicate hanging buds that open to the characteristic flowers with reflexed, gently twisted petals in shades of white, pink, cerise and magenta. The first blooms appear before the leaves and the later ones are shown above the newly emerged, ivy-like leaves of dark green variously patterned with grey, silver and sage.

Cyclamen hederifolium 🏆 prefers a slightly shaded position. While it copes with summer drought, it thrives best when there is adequate moisture from autumn through to spring, without the soil becoming waterlogged. It loves a situation under a mature shrub or at the base of a shady wall. It grows well through fallen leaves or a mulch of gravel or scree; any of these help to prevent soil from splashing on to the delicate flowers. They also provide the ideal medium for germinating seeds, enabling the plants to multiply.

Cyclamen are ideal for an undisturbed corner. They do not suit highly cultivated conditions, where the hoe will behead emerging seedlings. They resent overfeeding, but enjoy an organic compost mulch, which will help hold moisture. Left undisturbed, they multiply, brightening autumn and early spring year after year. They have a place in every garden and make wonderful partners for hellebores and heucheras.

autumn crocus for naturalising

Above, from the left: *Cyclamen coum*, *Crocus speciosus*, *Colchicum autumnale*.

Cyclamen coum

Cyclamen coum 🏆 does things the other way round, displaying its more rounded, marbled leaves in autumn and following on with its squatter, more rounded flowers through winter and early spring. The colours are often stronger than those of *Cyclamen hederifolium*, and some varieties display very silver foliage. *Cyclamen coum* prefers some moisture in the soil throughout the year. It is a very hardy species and well suited to English gardens. Plant *Cyclamen coum* with snowdrops for the ultimate spring picture.

The autumn-flowering saffron crocus, Crocus sativus, is an interesting plant to grow, but both climate and cultivation are against its use for naturalising. Each flower produces three orange stigmas. These are collected and dried to produce saffron, the world's most expensive spice. Originally a native of Greece, saffron is grown commercially in southern Europe and parts of Asia. The flowers produce no fertile seeds, so bulbs spread only by offsets and need transplanting if they are to colonise.

There are some spring-like flowers that bloom in autumn. In addition to the hardy cyclamen, certain crocus and colchicums excel in this season, as if to remind us that it is time to be thinking about, and planting, spring-flowering bulbs.

Crocus speciosus

This makes a surprising sight in autumn, when its fragile, elegant goblet-shaped blooms emerge from thin grass or bare ground in full sun. The mauve-to-blue flowers may look unseasonal at first sight, but they echo the colour of Michaelmas daisies and shine against the orange, flame and gold shades of autumn. ***Crocus speciosus*** 🏆 likes poor soil and good drainage, seeding freely when content.

Colchicum autumnale

Often called naked ladies, or meadow saffron, ***Colchicum autumnale*** has flowers like large crocus blooms. They emerge mauve-pink, fragile and leafless from the grass or border soil. *Colchicum autumnale* likes fertile ground in full sun and is tolerant of quite heavy clay. The flowers grow to 12cm or so in height. The leaves that follow in spring are a surprise: lush and exotic, they emerge like cos lettuces, growing to 20cm or more in height and persisting until early summer. They are certainly a problem in the lawn when it comes to mowing and must be confined to unimportant areas of rough grass.

All autumn-flowering crocus and colchicum bulbs are sold in early autumn for immediate planting and they flower for the first time shortly afterwards. The large bulbs of colchicums will bloom as dry bulbs. Sit one on a saucer filled with sand on a sunny window sill and its naked blooms will soon emerge and flower – a delight for adults and young children alike, and a reminder of just what it is that bulbs are all about.

adding colour to beds and borders

Flowerbulbs are indispensable when it comes to adding seasonal colour and variety to flower beds and borders. They are not greedy for space and will fit into spaces between roses, shrubs and perennials where other plants would not. Throughout spring, flowerbulbs deliver a colourful performance while other plants are still waking up. In summer and autumn, dahlias, lilies, gladioli and other colourful bulbs continue the display started by early-flowering shrubs and roses, and add strength to the spectacle provided by later-flowering perennials.

Above: The increasingly popular *Scilla peruviana*. Right: The cherry-red flowers of *Tulipa* 'Lily Chic' echo the colour of the grevillea behind it.

early-spring bloomers

Snowdrops and snowflakes

Clumps of snowdrops can be grown between shade-loving perennials such as hostas. ***Galanthus nivalis*** 🏆, the common snowdrop (see page 73), is the best choice. It flowers before the hostas even consider venturing forth and, if the fading leaves of the snowdrops persist, they are smothered when the hosta leaves unfurl; these provide welcome shade, keeping the ground cool for the snowdrops in summer.

Leucojum aestivum, summer snowflake, produces its dainty white bells towards the end of the snowdrop season. It grows in sun or shade, to a height of 40cm or more, producing a clump of emerald-

Left: The bright blooms of *Iris bucharica* will appear every spring. Below: The tall slender stems of snowflake carry delicate flowers.

Beds of roses and perennials can look dull and lifeless in winter and early spring. Plant dwarf bulbs to add welcome life and colour in spots where they can be avoided when any cultivation takes place. Some will seed and naturalise, creating quite a different picture from that which unfolds as the permanent planting comes into leaf and bloom.

White plant labels look unsightly in the border, so use either black labels, scratching the name on, or copper labels, which weather nicely. Anchor the labels securely, using stout wire or a short bamboo cane.

Other early bloomers

These early-flowering bulbs are all suitable for adding to beds and borders between perennials and under roses and deciduous shrubs. Take care to avoid damaging them when cultivating the soil. Plant in groups of several bulbs and mark the planting positions clearly.

Chionodoxa luciliae 🏆: starry blue and white flowers

Eranthis hyemalis 🏆: buttercup-like flowers with green ruffs on short stems

Ipheion uniflorum: ice-blue flowers

Puschkinia scilloides: pale blue flowers delicately striped with darker blue

Scilla siberica 🏆: sapphire-blue flowers on short stems

Scilla mischtschenkoana 🏆: blue-white flowers in short spikes

green, narcissus-like leaves. The white flowers, delicately marked with green, are carried on fine stems above the foliage. An excellent choice to add early interest to the border, it is particularly effective with low-growing, variegated evergreens such as euonymus or among the spotted leaves and bright blue flowers of pulmonarias.

To control the spread of grape hyacinths, remove the seedheads while still green – before they dry, split and release their black seeds across the border.

The deep blue spikes of *Muscari latifolium*.

Grape hyacinth

The well-known ***Muscari armeniacum*** 🏆 grows anywhere and quickly forms clumps or drifts of sapphire-blue flowers between deciduous shrubs. In some situations it can become invasive, but on the whole its fragrant flower spikes make a welcome addition to the border.

***Muscari armeniacum* 'Dark Eyes'** is a choice variety with stout spikes of deep blue flowers, each tiny bell delicately edged in white. More expensive to buy than *Muscari armeniacum*, it is one to give pride of place at the front of the border.

Muscari latifolium 🏆 is another refined subject, with spikes of dark blue flowers and broader leaves. Plant in groups of ten or more bulbs, spacing the bulbs 3cm apart. Grow it at the edge of paving, in sun or semi-shade, in among purple-leaved heucheras or ajugas.

Hyacinth

The bulbs of bedding hyacinths are of a smaller grade than those grown indoors and they produce lighter flower spikes. They are useful for early colour and fragrance in beds near the house. Plant the bulbs 6cm apart in groups of three or five and repeat several clumps in a bed. They are ideal between perennials that will grow up and smother their fading leaves. They prefer well-drained soil and will perform year after year if left undisturbed.

Hyacinths that have been grown in the house can be used for this purpose. When the flowers have faded, cut off the stems, leave the leaves intact and water thoroughly. Plant the whole clump of bulbs so that the bulbs are at least 10cm below the surface and let the foliage die down naturally. The following year, the flowers will be smaller and lighter, but just as fragrant and effective.

Iris bucharica

By mid-spring the early dwarf irises have faded and the later Dutch varieties are just beginning to emerge. ***Iris bucharica* 'Foster'** 🏆 produces a clump of shining green leaves and stems growing to 30cm. Each stem carries several bright yellow and creamy-white flowers that open in succession. It grows in both sun and semi-shade and on any soil, but it favours chalk. It is easy to grow and reliably performs year after year.

daffodils and narcissi for beds and borders

Before choosing daffodils to plant in a border bear in mind the following

- The foliage takes a long time to die down and can look unsightly: position the bulbs where the fading leaves will be hidden by neighbouring plants.
- The eye will naturally be drawn to yellow wherever it is used in the garden. Do not use bright yellow daffodils in areas that you do not want to be the focus of attention: choose a more subtle colour instead.

The delicate flowers of *Narcissus* 'Barrett Browning' add gentle colour to a border.

Daffodils and narcissi take some beating when it comes to reliability. They succeed on practically any soil and perform year after year, usually multiplying at the same time. Plant them in clumps of five or more bulbs, and their long-lasting flowers will brighten the dullest of situations. The choice of varieties and range of colours have never been wider.

choosing daffodils and narcissi

Because of the wide variety of flower forms in daffodils and narcissi, there is a detailed classification system. However, for simplicity, this is not followed in this book.

Botanically, all daffodils and narcissi belong to the genus *Narcissus*. In gardens, those with obvious trumpets are regarded as daffodils and those with very short or split trumpets or cups are regarded as narcissi. Those with several heads on a stem are always thought of as narcissi.

Double forms are confusing, but usually those with large, single heads are regarded as double daffodils and those with smaller flowers, or several on a stem, are referred to as double narcissi.

If possible, remove the flower heads of daffodils and narcissi as the flowers fade. This stops the plant wasting energy on seed formation. The stems manufacture food for the bulb, but they are often the last part of the plant to die down and removing them after flowering makes the plants less obtrusive as the season progresses.

There are several narcissus varieties with salmon-pink cups, including **'Pink Charm'**, *'Salome'* 🏆, *'Easter Bonnet'* *and* **'Rosy Sunrise'** *(below). These are a lovely addition to the garden, looking best with blue planting partners. Although described as pink, the cups are orange-pink, so they clash with sugar-pink tulips and hyacinths.*

yellow-trumpet daffodils

Classic yellow daffodils make a bright and bold addition to any planting scheme. They look good against a backdrop of gold-variegated evergreens and are useful to brighten shady areas. Avoid planting these varieties alongside bright pink blossom: bright yellow and pink is rarely pleasing.

The classic *Narcissus* 'King Alfred' is rarely grown now. **'King Midas'** is a superb, robust variety with tall stems and weather-resistant, rounded yellow flowers. It is also resistant to disease and performs well in sun or shade. **'Rijnveld's Early Sensation'** 🏆 starts to flower in late winter, well before 'February Gold' (see page 78).

Also good are **'Carlton'** 🏆, **'Golden Harvest'** and **'Saint Keverne'** 🏆.

paler daffodils

White and pale yellow daffodils are a softer alternative to the bright golden yellow generally associated with the flower. They are less obtrusive in the garden and fit easily into any colour scheme.

Narcissus **'Mount Hood'** 🏆 is the best known, with white petals and creamy-yellow trumpets that fade as the flowers mature (see page 81). **'Finland'** is similar.

Narcissus **'Bravoure'** 🏆 has white petals and an elegant, pale yellow trumpet.

Most large-growing daffodils and narcissi grow to 35–40cm in height. The smaller narcissi, and other tall varieties recommended for naturalising, can also be used in beds and borders (see pages 76–81).

'Topolino' 🏆 is similar, but much shorter, at only 20cm. ***Narcissus*** **'Neon'** and **'Daydream'** 🏆 are yellow, but a white circle at the base of the petals gives a lighter effect. **'Saint Patrick's Day'** is a pleasing pale yellow-green with a creamy trumpet edged in lime.

yellow-petalled narcissi

Narcissi with yellow petals and orange cups are widely planted for their cheerful flowers that brighten the dullest day.

Narcissus **'Fortune'** is the classic variety, with a broad orange cup, longer and more daffodil-like than most.

'Sempre Avanti' is early-flowering, with creamy-yellow petals and an orange cup. **'Scarlett O'Hara'** is similar, but flowers a little later. **'Edward Buxton'** is pale yellow with a fringed orange cup.

'Altruist' is a new, fragrant variety, with rounded yellow petals and a short, deep orange-red cup.

white-petalled narcissi

Narcissi with predominantly white flowers are fresh and charming. They are light and pretty, and mix well with tulips and early spring-flowering shrubs.

Narcissus **'Barrett Browning'** has rounded flowers with creamy-white petals and small red-orange cups. ***Narcissus*** **'High Society'** 🏆 is a fragrant variety with white petals and yellow, orange-fringed cups. ***Narcissus*** **'Professor Einstein'** is one of the less subtle varieties, with white petals and broad, fringed orange cups.

From the top: *Narcissus* 'King Midas', *Narcissus* 'Bravoure', *Narcissus* 'Altruist'. All these varieties are weather-resistant and have long-lasting flowers carried on strong stems.

daffodils and narcissi for beds and borders

Clockwise from far left: *Narcissus* 'Cheerfulness', *Narcissus* 'Golden Ducat', *Narcissus* 'Texas', *Narcissus* 'White Lion'.

double-flowered daffodils and narcissi

The larger double daffodils and narcissi are magnificent flowers, but in some cases the heads are too heavy for the stems. They are not for windy, exposed situations. Varieties with smaller blooms offer a different flower form in the spring garden. Both large and small are often fragrant.

Narcissus **'Golden Ducat'** is the best-known golden yellow, double daffodil. It has large, rounded flowers crammed with petals. They are long lasting and weather-resistant.

Narcissus **'White Lion'** 🏆 has ivory petals with segments of a deeper creamy yellow nestled between them. This is a wonderfully fragrant narcissus.

Narcissus **'Texas'** is the double form of 'Fortune' (see page 93), with golden yellow petals and short orange segments deep in the flower. *Narcissus* **'Ball of Fire'** and **'Tahiti'** 🏆 are similar in flower form and colouring.

Narcissus **'Pencrebar'** (see pages 68–69) is much smaller than other double-flowered daffodils and narcissi, with fine grassy foliage and fragrant, starry, double yellow flowers. It is an excellent choice to add golden highlights to the front of a border. It is also good for naturalising.

multi-headed narcissi

There are single- and double-flowering, multi-headed narcissi. Because of their smaller flowers, they are more subtle than large-bloomed varieties and mix easily with other border plants. Most are very fragrant and are also ideal for cutting.

There are both yellow and white forms of *Narcissus* **'Cheerfulness'** 🏆, the popular double-flowering, multi-headed narcissus that blooms later in the season. The yellow form has flowers the colour of clotted cream – lovely with blue forget-me-nots.

Narcissus **'Martinette'** and **'Golden Dawn'** 🏆 both have tall stems carrying

Sometimes the performance of daffodils declines after a few years: the bulbs produce leaves, but few flowers. This may be due to overcrowding of the bulbs. You could lift them when they are in leaf and replant, spacing the bulbs 5cm apart. However, daffodils are inexpensive to buy, and it is generally better to throw them away and buy new stock the next autumn.

Above: *Narcissus* 'Golden Dawn'. Below: *Narcissus* 'Geranium'.

several golden-petalled, fragrant blooms with deep orange cups.

Narcissus 'Geranium' 🏆 has rounded flowers with white petals and deep orange cups on stout stems.

Narcissus 'Avalanche' 🏆 has white-petalled flowers with lemon-yellow cups.

fritillarias

The larger fritillarias are magnificent accent plants for any border. Their exotic flowers and foliage are a dramatic contrast to other soft and pretty spring flowers. They are more expensive than many other flowerbulbs, but you do not need many. Often a group of three bulbs is enough to create a focal point in a mid-spring bed or border.

Fritillaria imperialis, crown imperial, is a stately subject. Its strong stems, clothed with bright green leaves on the lower part, rise to 1m before carrying a circle of bell-shaped flowers, from yellow to deep red, crowned in a ruff of green foliage.

Plant the large bulbs singly or in small groups, 25–30cm apart and 20cm deep, in well-drained, fertile soil in sun or partial shade. Like lilies, the waxy bulbs hate rough treatment and do not like to be dried out; plant as soon as you get them. They can be left undisturbed for years and will gradually multiply by producing offsets. Plant them to rise above lower planting – they look particularly effective amid the rich colours of wallflowers. Crown imperials can also be grown in pots (see page 49).

Lily beetle (see page 111) can attack fritillarias in the same way that it can damage lilies. Look out for the small, scarlet beetles in late spring and early summer. Although the fritillarias may have finished flowering, the beetle can damage the foliage, affecting the plant's performance the following year.

Above: The majestic *Fritillaria imperialis*. Below: The bewitching blooms of *Fritillaria persica*.

Fritillaria persica is a beautiful plant with elegant, tapering 80cm stems carrying blue-green leaves and terminating in a spike of deep plum-purple, bell-shaped flowers. Singly or in groups of three, it looks good with silver or purple foliage. Plant the bulbs 15cm deep, as for *Fritillaria imperialis*.

tulips for beds and borders

Groups of tulips can add splashes of contrasting colour to beds and borders. Here *Tulipa* 'Menton' and forget-me-nots are lively partners between emerging perennials.

To avoid fading flowerbulb foliage in the border, grow your tulips in heavy earthenware pots. These can be kept in a sheltered location during the worst of the winter and moved into position for flowering in spring. Once flowering is over, the pots can be moved out of sight; the gaps left in the border will quickly be covered by the surrounding plants. Discard the bulbs after flowering or plant them in the open ground; they rarely perform well in pots the next year.

Tulips are best planted in groups of at least three. Plant the bulbs a few centimetres apart, depending on the size of the bulb. If planted too sparsely, they will lack impact. When positioning the bulbs, envisage the size of the individual flowers when they open. Often the instructions on the packet recommend planting farther apart than is actually necessary; this weakens the impact when the tulips are in flower. Where possible, intensify the effect by repeating several clumps of the same variety through the border.

The upright form and sleek flowers of tulips are an eye-catching addition to the spring border. The soft mounds of herbaceous perennial foliage and the fresh, light leaves of deciduous shrubs contrast with the bold forms and bright colours of the tulip blooms.

Tulips offer a wider colour palette and variety of flower form than any other flowerbulb. Plain, striped, flamed, fringed, single, double: whatever combination you can conjure up in your imagination, the tulip is always one step ahead.

The tall Darwin, triumph and lily-flowering tulips are especially useful with herbaceous perennials, where their blooms rise above the emerging leaves. Tulip foliage is ugly as it dies down, but it does so quickly – usually within a month after flowering.

Good tulip varieties to grow for early flowers

All the tulips listed below grow to about 50cm in height unless stated otherwise

***Red tulips** make a strong statement in the garden. They look good against dark evergreens, but clash with pink blossom and yellow daffodils.*

Tulipa **'Apeldoorn'** is the classic red tulip. Tall stems carry big scarlet, black-eyed flowers that resemble large poppies when open.
'Red Impression' 🏆 is a newer variety, with elegant ruby-red flowers on strong stems with excellent foliage.

***Yellow tulips** are bright and cheerful, but disappear among yellow daffodils. Use them with gold-variegated evergreens and early blue flowers such as forget-me-nots and pulmonaria.*

Tulipa **'Golden Apeldoorn'** is the golden yellow form of 'Apeldoorn'. Equally reliable, it is still the best choice for a tall yellow tulip.
'Big Smile' is shorter, at only 30cm, with large, very early yellow flowers.
'Yellow Spider' has interestingly shaped, semi-double flowers with pointed petals. It grows to 40cm in height and fits well in the mixed border.

'Twister' is a very showy tulip, with clear yellow flowers lavishly flamed and streaked with deep red. **'World Expression'** is similar, but has creamy petals streaked red.

***Orange tulips** sit well with the blue flowers of spring, especially forget-me-nots and grape hyacinths. They make a strong statement in the garden and are not for the faint-hearted gardener.*

Tulipa **'World's Favourite'** is glowing orange-red with a fine gold edge to the petals. It is an outstanding tulip for any situation. See also page 57.
'Orange Emperor' 🏆 has more elongated blooms of glowing orange on 40cm stems. The flowers open wide in sunshine, looking like large, orange magnolias.
'Heart's Delight' is shorter, with golden yellow blooms that change to clear tangerine as the flowers mature.
'Ballerina' 🏆 is a soft orange, lily-flowering tulip with pointed petals on fine upright stems.

***Red and yellow tulips**, with flamed and streaked flowers, make an exciting contribution to the spring garden. Plant a few on their own or mix them with clear yellows and reds for a really lively cocktail.*

Tulipa **'Keizerskroon'** 🏆 has been popular since the 18th century. It has rounded flowers on 30cm stems; the red petals are broadly edged with yellow.
'Davenport' is taller, with broader yellow-fringed margins to the orange-red petals.

***White tulips** are clean and cool and ideal to plant with evergreen shrubs, especially those with green and white variegated foliage. They also work well with blue flowers.*

Tulipa **'Purissima'** ('White Emperor') 🏆 has long, creamy-green buds that open to huge, shining white flowers on 40cm stems.
'Schoonoord' is a good early double white tulip. Growing to only 30cm, it is ideal at the front of the border.

Top left: *Tulipa* 'Red Impression'. Top right: *Tulipa* 'Golden Apeldoorn'. Middle: *Tulipa* 'Keizerskroon'. Bottom left: *Tulipa* 'World's Favourite'. Bottom right: *Tulipa* 'Purissima'.

A selection of favourite later-flowering tulips

As a general rule, the colour palette becomes deeper and softer as the season progresses

***Pastel tulips** of soft pink, lilac and purple are welcome relief from the screaming yellows of early spring. They look heavenly when mixed with blue and lime green and create a lively look with early purple foliage.*

Tulipa **'Pink Diamond'** has ice-pink flowers on 40cm stems.
'Douglas Bader' is taller, with elegant blooms of palest pink.
'Pink Impression' 🏆 has deeper pink blooms on very strong stems; it is reliable and weather-resistant.
'China Pink' 🏆 is highly regarded, with softly pointed petals turning outwards at the tips.
'New Design' is apricot in bud, opening to pink, and has the bonus of pink-white margins to the leaves.
'Shirley' has white flowers delicately edged with lilac-purple.
'Passionale', with its light purple flowers on strong 40cm stems, is a good mixer with all of the above.

***White tulips** that flower later in the season sit easily in the border as the volume of green foliage increases with the lengthening days. They can be planted on their own or mixed with soft pink and purple tulips.*

Tulipa **'Maureen'** 🏆 is a classic white tulip, with elegant long-lasting blooms.
'Cheers' is shorter and earlier, with an attractive green tinge to the petals.

'White Triumphator' 🏆 (see page 59) is a tall, elegant lily-flowering tulip, with exceptionally long-lasting flowers.
'Snow Parrot' has exotic ruched and pleated petals of creamy white.

A mixed planting of black and white tulips is dramatic and sophisticated. Plant 'Queen of Night' with 'Maureen' or 'Cheers', or try 'Black Hero' with 'Mount Tacoma' (see page 58) for a double black and white delight.

***Dark tulips**, like plum-purple foliage, add depth and drama to any planting. They intensify any other colour and stand out boldly against the pale lime-green foliage of spring.*

Tulipa **'Queen of Night'** is the ultimate 'black' tulip (see page 57). Deep purple-black flowers with silky petals are carried on tall stems. It performs reliably for several years in the border.
'Black Hero' is the double form of 'Queen of Night' with layered petals; the overall effect is reminiscent of the plumage of a sleek bird.
'Black Parrot' 🏆 (see page 101) has dark, twisted and fringed petals and makes a dramatic statement against lime-green or yellow foliage.

Clockwise from top left: *Tulipa* 'Pink Impression', *Tulipa* 'White Triumphator', *Tulipa* 'Black Hero'.

multi-headed tulips

Multi-headed tulips have a number of smaller flowers on a single stem. They lack the elegance of single-headed tulips, but they have a long flowering period as the blooms do not all open at once. They are usually about 30cm in height.

Tulipa praestans **'Fusilier'** 🏆 is an old favourite. It has bright red flowers with pointed petals.

Tulipa **'Antoinette'** is an interesting tulip with pale yellow and cream buds maturing to apricot-pink. This is pleasing, as both colours appear on a stem at once.

'Candy Club', as the name suggests, has sugar-pink flowers edged with white.

Top left: *Tulipa* 'Antoinette'. Top right: *Tulipa* 'Blushing Lady'. Right: *Tulipa* 'Burning Heart'.

big tulips

Some tulips produce mammoth blooms.

Tulipa **'Blushing Lady'** is one of the tallest, growing to 60cm or more in height, with large, elegant buds of deep coral edged with gold. When mature, the open flowers are more than 20cm across.

'Burning Heart' produces glorious soft creamy-yellow, cup-shaped blooms flamed with scarlet. When mature, each flower is more than 15cm across.

exotic tulips

Above: *Tulipa* 'Virichic'. Left: *Tulipa* 'Deidre'.

Ever since the cultivation of tulips began, people have been captivated by the variety of form and colour of the tulip flower. Breeders have striven to produce blooms with ever wilder and more exotic shapes and colour combinations. A few well-positioned bulbs can have great impact among other spring flowers.

Tulipa **'Deidre'** has elegant, lily-like green and white blooms. **'Spring Green'** 🏆 is similar, but the petals are shorter.

'Virichic' and **'Groenland'** (see page 18) are viridiflora tulips, with green at the base of the petals melting into glorious swathes of deep pink and gold nearer the edges.

Plant tulips with the base of the bulbs at four times their depth below the surface: this means covering the bulbs with about 10cm of soil. Choose a spot in full sun and avoid wet conditions; on heavy soils, add grit. Most tulips do not grow well in grass.

parrot tulips

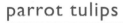

Tulipa **'Flaming Parrot'** is one of the showiest of the parrot tulips, with golden yellow petals streaked with scarlet.

Tulipa **'Black Parrot'** 🏆 is another dramatic tulip, with petals like twisted purple-black feathers. The blooms are held on 50cm stems. ***Tulipa* 'Estella Rijnveld'** has twisted cut petals of white lavishly streaked with deep red (see page 7).

Tulipa **'Rococo'** is a shorter tulip, with green, reptile-like buds that open to crimped and curled scarlet-orange petals. ***Tulipa* 'Yellow Snow Parrot'** is also comparatively short, with lemon-sorbet coloured blooms.

After buying tulip bulbs, store them in a cool, dark place and delay planting until late October or November. Early planting can lead to tulip fire, a disease that causes papery brown patches on the stems and foliage, and spotting or withering of the flowers. If tulip fire occurs, lift and dispose of the bulbs immediately. Tulip fire persists in the soil for several years, so grow your tulips in pots for the next few seasons.

Clockwise from top left: *Tulipa* 'Flaming Parrot', *Tulipa* 'Black Parrot', *Tulipa* 'Yellow Snow Parrot', *Tulipa* 'Rococo'.

alliums

Alliums, ornamental onions, are popular for their unique flower forms: soft, sparkling balls that bounce across the border, floating above the mounded forms of perennials and low shrubs. Mostly in shades of lilac and purple, and sometimes white, they mix easily with most other colours. Blooming after the last of the tulips have faded, they fill a gap in the flowerbulb year, before the lilies and dahlias start to flower in midsummer.

growing alliums

Plant alliums in small groups – those that have large bulbs in threes, and those with smaller bulbs in fives and sevens. Space the bulbs of larger-blooming varieties at least 15cm apart to show off the individual form of the flowers. In big borders, the bulbs can be planted singly, positioned randomly through the planting; this works well with aquilegias and poppies. Plant the bulbs at three to four times their depth in the soil.

Alliums grow on any well-drained soil in a sunny position. They can be left undisturbed after flowering and will continue to bloom year after year. Most alliums have leaves that start to shrivel and fade early in the season, as soon as the blooms start to open, so they leave no unsightly foliage to disfigure the border after the flowers are over.

varieties of allium

Allium azureum is one of the smaller varieties, with 2cm flower heads of pale sapphire blue on fine stems and grass-like foliage. It is a bulb for the front of a sunny border among plants like helianthemums and dianthus.

Allium hollandicum 🏆 and ***Allium hollandicum* 'Purple Sensation'** 🏆 both have medium-sized flowers on straight stems reaching 45cm in height. 'Purple Sensation' is darker in colour, opening rich red-purple. The flowers fade to develop into attractive seedheads that persist in the border until late summer. These alliums are effective planted with day lilies and *Iris sibirica* 🏆 and the light, airy flowers and foliage of *Nepeta* × *faassenii* 🏆.

Left: *Allium hollandicum* 'Purple Sensation'.
Above: *Allium cristophii*.

Allium cristophii 🏆 and ***Allium schubertii*** have large, more explosive flower heads on shorter stems. Both are superb plants to add near the front of a border. *Allium cristophii* has 15cm heads of sparkling silver-lilac, which turn green then dry to parchment and persist in the border for several weeks. *Allium schubertii* has even larger heads of tiny flowers on long

For best effect, plant alliums where the lower part of the stem and the leaves, will be hidden by other subjects. They work well among herbaceous geraniums and Alchemilla mollis, and they make excellent planting partners for low, silver-foliage shrubs such as artemisia, helichrysum and santolina.

stalks, creating a bigger globe of intricate design. After the flowers have faded, the seedheads persist well into winter and are superb to gather for floral decoration in the house.

Allium 'Globemaster' 🏆 is a magnificent plant, with larger solid heads of deep lilac flowers on 90cm stems. The flower heads get bigger as more tiny flowers crowd the spheres, a magnet for bees and other pollinating insects. The blooms have enough impact to be planted individually, and a few bulbs spaced 30cm apart in a bed will be the showpiece of the season.

Allium stipitatum 'Mount Everest' is one of the few white alliums, producing large heads of greenish-white flowers on stems up to 1m tall. The flowers are not as long-lived as some other varieties, but are just as attractive when they turn into green seedheads. It is lovely in a green and white border and lightens dark evergreen shrubs when planted in the foreground.

Allium 'Globemaster' produces large dense heads of sparkling mauve flowers.

Allium sphaerocephalon is often called drumsticks because that is exactly what it resembles. The small tight, purple flower heads are carried on 60–90cm fine stems that wave above lower planting. Plant it in clumps of seven or more bulbs among perennials or tall border annuals.

Nectaroscordum siculum, the honey garlic, is closely related and was originally classified as an allium. It has tall, slender stems, with a shower of small bell-shaped flowers of cream-green marked with deep red. As the flowers fade, they turn upwards to form neat conical seedheads. It is a lovely subject to mix with perennials and grasses in prairie-style planting, and can even be naturalised in long grass.

Clockwise from top left: *Allium stipitatum* **'Mount Everest',** *Allium schubertii, Nectaroscordum siculum, Allium sphaerocephalon.*

Alliums are left untouched by deer and rabbits because of the pungent nature of their onion foliage and flowers. This smell is not, however, apparent until the leaves or flowers are crushed.

some early summer-flowering bulbs

Left, from the top: *Babiana stricta*, *Calochortus superbus*, *Gladiolus communis* subsp. *byzantinus*. All are colourful plants for sunny situations.

As the stars of spring fade for another year, a cast of less familiar but no less beautiful flowerbulbs takes their place. These add variety and additional colour to the roses and perennials that come into their own in the middle of the year.

Babiana

Babiana stricta 🏆, or the baboon flower, is a colourful South African native, with short, sword-shaped leaves and clusters of bright pink, purple, blue or white flowers in late spring or early summer. The common name relates to the corms, which are gathered in the wild and eaten by baboons. *Babiana stricta* needs a sunny position on well-drained soil; it is not for cold situations. Plant the corms at least 15cm deep to protect them from frost.

Babiana is useful to plant at the front of the border among herbaceous geraniums, helianthemums, dianthus and other sun-lovers.

Calochortus

Calochortus superbus, or peacock flower, is another prairie native flowering in early summer. The tiny bulbs produce tall, thin stems reaching 60cm or more, with delicate foliage and fine, pointed flowerbuds. These open into rounded cone-shaped, exquisitely marked flowers.

Calochortus is useful among later-blooming perennials and looks effective rising above the delicate flower stems of heucheras.

Gladiolus

The large-flowering gladioli can be difficult plants to incorporate in mixed plantings as their heavy spikes can look awkward and ungainly. However, the smaller species and species hybrids are lighter and prettier and mix well with other plants.

Gladiolus communis* subsp. *byzantinus 🏆 is the earliest to flower and is a reliable cottage-garden favourite. Tall, 90cm spikes carry bright magenta flowers well above the sword-shaped leaves. Left undisturbed, it spreads to form large clumps; these are easily lifted and divided. It needs full sun to flower well.

Gladiolus* × *colvillii* 'The Bride'** 🏆 is also an early bloomer, with 60cm stems carrying elegant, ivory-white flowers; these are wonderful for cutting. ***Gladiolus **'Prins Claus'** is a little larger, with soft red-pink markings on the petals.

Gladioli such as 'The Bride' and 'Prins Claus' are often sold in a mix of ***Gladiolus nanus*** varieties. In pale pinks and whites, combined with stronger red-pink and cerise varieties, they look good in groups of ten or more at the front of the border.

Iris

The tall Dutch irises come into their own in late spring and early summer. Most familiar as cut flowers, they also make excellent subjects for the border with their stylish blooms in shades of blue, yellow-bronze and white. Plant the bulbs in autumn, in groups of five or more, with 8cm of soil covering the bulbs. They like well-drained soil and a sunny position.

Iris **'Professor Blaauw'** 🏆 has royal-blue flowers marked with gold on the falls (lower petals) on 60cm stems. **'Wedgwood'** is a popular old variety with mid-blue flowers. Dutch irises are often sold as a mix of blue, white and yellow shades: a refreshing addition to the border.

Scilla peruviana

This spectacular Mediterranean bulb produces large flower heads resembling something between an allium and an agapanthus (see page 88). ***Scilla peruviana*** needs a sunny situation, where it produces a rosette of green, hyacinth-like leaves before the large sapphire-blue flower heads appear in early summer.

Triteleia

Triteleia laxa *(Brodiaea laxa)* is a real early-summer gem. Fine stems carry sparkling heads of starry sapphire flowers 30cm or so above the ground. Plant the bulbs in autumn or early spring, 10cm or so apart, in loose groups. In full sun, the buds and slender leaves will easily make their way through thin ground-cover plants.

Triteleia laxa **'Koningin Fabiola'**, with its purple-blue flowers, looks wonderful in association with silver-foliage plants such as *Convolvulus cneorum*.

Scilla peruviana is ideal to grow through gravel with aromatics such as thyme, rosemary and lavender.

The herbaceous flag irises (see right) are often sold as semi-dormant rhizomes in the autumn. These establish easily if planted in fertile soil in full sun. The rhizomes need to be on the soil surface and unshaded to ripen enough to produce blooms. If you have bought them as dry rhizomes, you may need to anchor them on to the soil by tying each one to a short length of bamboo cane pushed firmly into the soil. The cane needs to remain in place until the rhizome has rooted. They take a year to establish and then perform reliably.

Both *Triteleia laxa* (right) and Dutch irises (above right) make excellent cut flowers, as well as adding colour to the border.

midsummer flowerbulbs

Eremurus

The foxtail lily is one of the most spectacular border plants. The tubers are curious structures with long, curved appendages and central eyes. Plant them 10cm or so below the surface in well-drained soil in a sunny position. Shuttlecocks of grey-green leaves appear in spring, followed by the flower spikes, which gather height until they open in long bottlebrushes of flowers in midsummer. Eremurus vary in height from 1 to 2m, but all are impressive creatures, commanding attention in any border.

Popular varieties include ***Eremurus* × *isabellinus* 'Cleopatra'**, with copper-yellow flowers, and the ***Eremurus* × *isabellinus* Ruiter Hybrids**, in a range of colours. All grow to about 1.5m.

Left: *Eremurus* × *isabellinus* 'Cleopatra', queen of the midsummer border. Below: *Dichelostemma ida-maia* 'Pink Diamond'.

Foxtail lilies are long-lived border plants that will deliver a spectacular performance year after year. They are particularly striking amid plantings of grasses and light, airy perennials such as Verbena bonariensis.

By midsummer the garden is often running out of steam. Perennials and seasonal bedding plants that excel in mid- to late summer are worth their weight in gold when it comes to maintaining the display. Often overlooked, summer-flowering bulbs are star performers at this time of the year and offer exceptional value if they are purchased early, in their dormant state.

Dichelostemma

The Californian firecracker, ***Dichelostemma ida-maia***, like eremurus, enjoys a sunny position and good drainage. Plant bulbs 10cm deep in autumn, adding grit underneath to improve drainage on heavy soils. In summer, fine stems carry tubular, green and yellow flowers tipped crimson. **'Pink Diamond'** has sugar-pink blooms.

Growing to only 30cm in height, Californian firecracker is effective when planted in gravel or scree and at the edge of sunny paved areas.

Summer-flowering bulbs that enjoy a hot, sunny situation and dry conditions after flowering are an ideal choice for drought-tolerant planting. However, remember that our winters can be very wet, even if summers are dry, so give these bulbs good drainage by preparing the ground well before planting and adding plenty of sharp grit to improve drainage. The more favourable the growing conditions, the better chance you have of the bulbs coming up again next year.

Ranunculus

Known as Persian buttercups, ***Ranunculus asiaticus*** are popular for the large, colourful double flowers. Finely cut foliage emerges first, followed by spherical green buds that open into the familiar rounded blooms that resemble layers of silky tissue paper. The small tubers, which look like tiny bunches of brown bananas, are usually planted in spring in a sunny, sheltered position. The flowers dislike wet weather, so a position near a sunny wall or fence is ideal.

Ranunculus make wonderful cut flowers, but the stems are sometimes too weak to support the blooms in a vase. Cut the ranunculus when the flowers are fully open and either change the water regularly or use a cut-flower food.

Tigridia

The tiger flower, ***Tigridia pavonia***, is another bulb that likes a hot, sunny situation and will thrive in drought conditions. It can grow to well over 1m in height, producing its showy open blooms in late summer. Each flower is short-lived, but there are plenty of buds, which open in succession. In colder areas, it is worth planting five bulbs 10cm deep in a 20cm pot in a greenhouse or conservatory. They can then be planted out in the border when growth is under way in early summer.

Try planting tigridia in a sunny border either among late-flowering perennials or to take over from earlier-blooming delphiniums and lupins.

Above: *Ranunculus asiaticus*. Above right: Mixed *Tigridia pavonia*. Right: *Sparaxis tricolor*. Below right: *Scadoxus multiflorus*.

Sparaxis

Sparaxis tricolor, the harlequin flower, is a little gem from South Africa. It grows like a small crocosmia or freesia, with a narrow fan of grass-like foliage. Fine stems carry bright, yellow-eyed starry flowers in a wide range of cheerful colours. It likes sun and good drainage and it will survive outside from year to year only in the very mildest areas. But it is worth planting, even for a single season. Try starting several bulbs in a pot and plant them out when growth is under way in early summer.

Sparaxis makes a lively contrast to grey-foliage plants and aromatics such as thymes and lavenders, which also enjoy hot, dry conditions.

Scadoxus

Scadoxus multiflorus, also called *Haemanthus multiflorus* or blood flower, is a very showy bulb from South Africa, with large allium-like heads of orange-red flowers in midsummer. The large bulbs should be planted out in the sunniest, most sheltered position in the garden. This is not the hardiest of subjects, but it is worth experimenting with and in a hot summer will make a stunning display.

Try planting scadoxus with blue agapanthus or exotic cannas for a striking, tropical display.

dahlias

Dahlia 'David Howard', a classic variety with glowing flowers and superb chocolate leaves.

Supremos of the village flower show? Gaudy allotment plants of yesteryear? Contemporary designer plants of the modern garden? However you classify them, there is no question that dahlias deliver rich and vibrant colour for many weeks from midsummer through autumn. Inexpensive to buy, easy to grow and offering a great variety of colour and flower form, there is a dahlia for every garden.

growing dahlias

A dahlia tuber costs less than a couple of pounds. It will produce a substantial plant by midsummer and a mass of flowers. Here's what you do.

Planning ahead pays off. In early spring, dormant dahlia tubers cost a quarter of the price of the same tuber grown on in a pot and ready to plant in the garden in midsummer. So buy early and you can afford four times as many.

Either ... Wait until early April, choose a position, ideally in full sun, and prepare the ground by forking it over and adding plenty of organic compost or well-rotted manure. Dahlias love a rich but well-drained soil. On heavy soils, add grit.

Plant the tuber so that the top is 6–8cm below the surface. All taller varieties need staking. Add stout canes, a wooden stake or a substantial grow-through support at the time of planting. Support the stems as the plant grows taller, using soft twine if necessary.

When the shoots have grown to a height of 15–20cm, pinch out the tips to encourage branching; the bushier the plant, the more flowers it will produce.

Remove the blooms as they fade to encourage more flowers.

Or ... Pot up dahlia tubers in March indoors. Plant them individually in 20cm pots using multi-purpose compost. The top of the tubers can be just below the compost surface.

Keep them in a frost-free greenhouse or conservatory or on the window sill of a cool room in the house. Pinch out the tips when the shoots are 20cm high. Repeat this as necessary until you plant them out in the garden in mid-May. Plant them as you would any other container-grown plant but slightly deeper, so that the tuber is 6–8cm below the soil surface.

At the end of the year ... Dahlias will grow and bloom until the first frosts. When frost blackens the foliage, cut them down. You can either lift the tubers and store them in a frost-free place or leave them in the ground and let them take their chances. As tubers are not expensive, the latter is perhaps the better plan.

Slugs love young dahlia shoots. Protect young dahlias with environmentally friendly slug pellets or mulch the surface of the ground around the plants with sharp grit.

Dahlias to look out for

There are hundreds of dahlia varieties, old and new, offering an incredible choice of flower forms and almost every colour apart from clear blue. Show dahlias, producing exceptionally large blooms, do not lend themselves to mixed plantings, but those with more modest flowers and interesting foliage mix superbly with shrubs and perennials and are wonderful for cutting. Here are a few enduring favourites.

'Bishop of Llandaff' 🏆 is the most widely planted dahlia, treasured for its deep red-brown foliage and brilliant scarlet flowers with dark eyes and gold stamens. It grows to 1.2m in height and is of light, open habit.
'Bishop of Llandaff' makes the perfect planting partner for summer-flowering perennials: crocosmia, achillea, rudbeckia and the light airy Verbena bonariensis, with its vivid purple, orange-eyed flowers.

'Rosamunde' is similar in habit and leaf colour, but has purple-pink, semi-double flowers.

'David Howard' 🏆 (see opposite page) has glorious double flowers of apricot-amber against deep chocolate foliage. It grows to 1.2m.

'Moonfire' 🏆 is similar in colour to 'David Howard', but has charming single flowers with orange centres on shorter plants – perfect for the front of a border.
Dahlias with bright flowers and dark foliage look good with cannas, phormiums, cordylines and other subjects planted for exotic effect.

'Arabian Night' is a tall, decorative dahlia with rounded blooms consisting of several layers of petals. The flowers are deep burgundy red and make a dramatic statement in any garden.

'Nuit d'Eté' is similar in colour to 'Arabian Night', but has elegant, spiky cactus blooms (see page 39).

'Ruskin Marigold' produces a mass of elegant, spiky cactus blooms of medium size in a warm shade of apricot-orange.

'Park Princess' is a short cactus dahlia, growing to less than 90cm in height. The bushy plants produce plenty of large, spiky-petalled pink flowers with a paler centre.
'Park Princess' is ideal with pink and white shrub roses, to prolong the season, or with blue nepeta, nigella or salvias for a soft, summery effect.

From the top: *Dahlia* 'Bishop of Llandaff', *Dahlia* 'Moonfire', *Dahlia* 'Ruskin Marigold': easy-to-grow varieties that mix well with shrubs and perennials.

lilies

> *Buy lily bulbs in early spring and they will probably be the best value plants you buy for your garden all year. At only £1 or £2 a bulb, what else can deliver such a splendid display? Look for the tall, oriental and trumpet varieties with strong stems and large, fragrant flowers.*

Lilies are one of the most potent tonics to prevent the garden from running out of steam in midsummer. As earlier flowers exhaust themselves, lilies open their exotic blooms, filling the garden with flamboyant colour and perfume. You can buy lilies pot-grown in late spring and early summer, ready for immediate planting. This is a useful way to fill gaps, but choice will be restricted to the more compact, shorter-stemmed varieties.

trumpet lilies

Of the old trumpet lilies, ***Lilium regale*** 🏆 reigns supreme. Gently arching, 1m stems carry narrow, dark green leaves and large trumpet blooms. Each richly fragrant flower is pure white, flushed gold in the throat and purple-pink on the reverse of the petals.

***Lilium* Pink Perfection Group** 🏆 is taller and can easily reach 1.5m. The large trumpet flowers with turned-back petals are deep dusky pink. It looks particularly effective when grown against the purple foliage of *Prunus cerasifera* 'Nigra' 🏆 or *Physocarpus opulifolius* 'Diabolo' 🏆.

***Lilium* Golden Splendor Group** 🏆, with soft gold flowers, and **African Queen Group** 🏆, coppery amber, tend to flower later, well into July. They work well with some of the hotter colours that grace our gardens at this time. Try it with achilleas or crocosmias: the lighter flower forms of these are a good contrast to the bold blooms of the lily.

Top: *Lilium regale* lights up a summer border. Far left: *Lilium* Pink Perfection Group. Left: *Lilium* Golden Splendor Group.

The Madonna lily

Lilium candidum 🏆 is the classic white lily with scented trumpet flowers gracefully arranged at the top of 1.2m, pale green stems. A symbol of purity, this is the lily that is depicted in art in the hand of the Virgin Mary. It can be difficult to establish because it resents disturbance but, once settled, it is a long-lived garden plant. It likes well-drained fertile soil in full sun.

turk's cap or tiger lilies

These have downward-facing flowers with rolled-back petals and prominently displayed stamens adding to the flowers' grace and movement. The true turk's cap lily is ***Lilium martagon*** 🏆, a beautiful species with small pinkish-purple flowers that suit a naturalistic setting in dappled shade.

Lilium lancifolium var. *splendens* 🏆 (*Lilium tigrinum*) produces stems up to 1.2m tall. The orange flowers are spotted purple-black and are carried on side branches, well spaced at the top of the stem. ***Lilium henryi*** 🏆 can be even taller, with lighter orange flowers finely spotted with black.

Plant lily bulbs 15–20cm apart, burying them at at least three times their depth. Lay the bulbs on their sides when you plant them. This prevents water from becoming lodged between the fleshy scales, which can cause damage at the base of the bulb. Lily bulbs hate to dry out, so plant them as soon as you purchase them. Unlike many summer-flowering bulbs, lilies are quite hardy and will not be worried by cold weather.

Left: *Lilium speciosum* var. *rubrum* is a lily to partner late-summer perennials. Right: *Lilium henryi* bursts through a cloud of fennel.

Both ***Lilium lancifolium*** and ***Lilium henryi*** flower in mid- to late summer, mixing well with the hot-coloured perennials that flower at this time, including dahlias, achilleas, crocosmias and cannas. They are also effective with the cloudy foliage of bronze fennel.

Lilium speciosum* var. *rubrum has reflexed petals of white flushed pink and spotted with deep carmine. It combines beautifully with the flat, fluffy flower heads of *Sedum spectabile*.

oriental lilies

Any of the oriental hybrids recommended for pots (see pages 66–67) make splendid border subjects. In the open ground, in fertile soil, many grow to 1.5m, producing magnificent open, scented flowers.

Lilium **'Acapulco'** has blooms of deep shocking pink. **'Lombardia'** is clear pink and **'Manissa'** soft banana yellow. Site them farther back in the border, to follow the spikes of delphiniums and foxgloves.

Lilies are effective planted singly between other plants, but are at their best in threes or fives of the same variety, planted where their stems rise above other subjects.

Lily beetle

Lilies are easy to grow and the only pest to watch for is lily beetle. This appears in late spring and early summer just as the lilies are growing well and producing buds. Look out for scarlet beetles up to 1cm long on the leaves. The damage is caused by the larvae: slimy green grubs that are easily missed until the leaves disappear into a mass of green sludge. The beetles are easily spotted against the foliage: pick them off and squash them or use a suitable systemic insecticide (available at garden centres).

late-summer sun-lovers

Left: The fiery flowers of *Crocosmia* 'Lucifer' add spark to the late-summer border. Below: *Galtonia candicans*.

These late-summer, sun-loving bulbs are planted in spring for late-summer and early-autumn flowering. They are a useful addition to give the garden a new lease of life when earlier-blooming plants have retired for the season.

Crocosmia

Crocosmia, or montbretia, is usually thought of as an herbaceous perennial. Most are sold as pot-grown plants when the shoots are emerging in late spring or early summer. Crocosmia grows from a small gladiolus-like corm and can be planted in the dormant state in early spring. Plant corms with 10–15cm of soil over them, in well-drained soil and a sunny position. They will not flower in shade.

> *The seedheads of crocosmias are as valuable as the flowers. Rounded, shining seed pods follow the vivid blooms and create an interesting effect on the arching wiry stems. They are wonderful for cutting and usually last well into autumn.*

***Crocosmia* 'Lucifer'** 🏆 is a superb variety. It has strong, sword-shaped leaves and arching spikes of fiery scarlet-orange flowers. It grows to 1m in height and is wonderful with heleniums, achilleas and day lilies. It flowers from midsummer.

A shorter variety, with dark stems and large open, orange flowers marked with red-brown, ***Crocosmia* × *crocosmiiflora* 'Emily McKenzie'** is not as hardy as some varieties, so needs a sheltered spot.

The montbretia of cottage gardens is ***Crocosmia masoniorum*** 🏆. This has orange and gold flowers. Easy to grow and hardy, it has naturalised widely in milder areas.

Galtonia

Galtonia candicans 🏆, the summer hyacinth, is a wonderful plant, producing 90cm stems carrying bell-shaped, lightly scented white flowers that open in succession from the bottom of the spike. The bulbs are usually planted in spring in a warm, sunny position; they like a moisture-retentive soil and will produce poor foliage if too dry.

Eucomis

Often called the pineapple flower, ***Eucomis bicolor*** 🏆 is a plant of exotic character but subtle colouring. It forms a rosette of succulent, pointed leaves from the centre of which the flower spike emerges like an

> *Protect slightly tender bulbs such as galtonia by spreading a deep layer of bark chips over the soil surface in winter. This will prevent frost from damaging the bulbs and will conserve moisture during the summer months.*

elongated pineapple. The spike is clustered with starry flowers, cream edged with purple, beneath a topknot of bright green leaves. It likes well-drained soil and should be planted 20cm deep to protect the bulbs from frost.

Nerine

A group of nerines in full bloom at the base of a sunny wall is one of the most uplifting sights in the autumn garden. The sugar-pink blooms of ***Nerine bowdenii*** 🏆, the hardiest nerine, are a dramatic contrast to the warm orange and flame tints of autumn and a pleasing companion for the purples and blues of Michaelmas daisies.

Plant the bulbs in autumn or early spring, leaving the neck of the bulb just above the soil surface. They want full sun and excellent drainage. Plant the bulbs 15cm apart to allow them room to produce offsets in years to come. They usually produce leaves in early winter; then these die down in spring and there will be no signs of life until mid-autumn, when the flower heads appear, carried on leafless stalks that reach 60cm before the delicate, long-lasting blooms unfurl.

Deer and rabbits

Many flowerbulbs are attractive to deer, rabbits and squirrels. In gardens where wildlife is prevalent, narcissi and alliums are a good choice as they are unpalatable to deer and rabbits. Most animal pests leave hyacinths, bluebells and scillas alone, but tulips need protection as deer love them and rabbits nibble the emerging shoots.

Plant eucomis individually or in groups in spring, to rise out of gravel or grit at the front of the border. It is effective with cream and green variegated hostas and purple heucheras.

Top: *Eucomis bicolor* loves to grow through gravel in a scree bed. Middle: *Nerine bowdenii*. Bottom: *Amaryllis belladonna*.

Amaryllis

The belladonna lily, ***Amaryllis belladonna*** 🏆, flowers a little earlier than the nerine. It is usually planted in early spring and then produces a few leaves that die down in early summer. The flowers appear on naked stems in late summer or early autumn. They are clear pink, lighter in the throat, and very beautiful. Plant the large bulbs with the tips just below the surface in a warm, sunny position, as nerines.

Crinum

Crinum* × *powellii 🏆, the elephant flower, has similar flowers to those of *Amaryllis belladonna*, but they appear earlier, along with the leaves. Also like the amaryllis, the huge bulb is planted with its neck above the ground in full sun, but crinum differs in that it needs moisture. Also known as swamp lily, it requires plenty of water during the growing season.

Nerine, Amaryllis belladonna and crinum all resent disturbance. They may take a season or two to settle down after planting before they perform properly: be patient.

almost bulbs

Agapanthus are good subjects to grow in pots. Use a loam-based compost with added grit in a large terracotta pot. Do not re-pot too frequently: agapanthus produce more flowers when pot-bound.

Top left: *Agapanthus campanulatus*, lily of the Nile. Top right: *Convallaria majalis*, lily of the valley. Above: *Alstroemeria*, the Peruvian lily.

There are a number of plants with fleshy roots or rhizomes that are sold in their dormant state alongside flowerbulbs in late winter and spring, and sometimes in autumn. They are liable to dry out more easily than bulbs and corms, so they are usually packed in peat or wood shavings. They should be kept in a cool place after purchase and planted as soon as possible.

Agapanthus

Agapanthus, lily of the Nile, are often offered for sale by colour rather than variety. Those labelled blue or white are usually ***Agapanthus campanulatus***, with strap-like leaves and large heads of flowers on 90cm stems.

Natives of South Africa, agapanthus need a hot, sunny situation to flower. They also need a reasonable amount of moisture during the growing season. Careful examination of the fleshy roots should reveal growth shoots; plant with these pointing upwards, just below the surface of the soil. Spread the roots out when you plant and on heavy soil add coarse grit to aid drainage.

Alstroemeria

The Peruvian lily is a wonderful border plant for a sunny position, where its fleshy tuberous roots will spread to form large clumps producing colourful, long-lasting flowers in summer. The beautifully marked blooms make excellent cut flowers, and many gardeners first know them this way. The roots are a puzzle when planting and break up easily, but this does not affect performance. Simply dig a broad hole, 40cm across, in well-prepared soil and plant them 10–15cm deep. Spread coarse grit on the surface of the soil to protect the fleshy shoots from slugs.

The tall fleshy stems of alstroemeria blow over easily. Place a grow-through plant support over the planting position or push birch or hazel twigs into the soil, to support the stems as they grow.

Lily of the valley

Lily of the valley, **Convallaria majalis** 🏆, is a favourite cottage-garden plant for a shady spot. Some gardeners struggle to

Lily of the valley is wonderfully fragrant and lovely to cut for the house: it blooms in early May. The foliage is also very attractive and makes effective ground cover; it lasts well into summer before it begins to die down.

grow it, whereas others find it vigorous and invasive. It likes a fertile soil, with some moisture in the growing season, and a position in semi-shade.

Dig a shallow hole in well-prepared ground and lay the long, stringy rhizomes across the bottom of the hole, 3cm below the surface of the soil. The fat pinkish 'pips' are the growth shoots, so these should be positioned pointing upwards.

Dicentra spectabilis

Dicentra spectabilis 🏆, bleeding heart or Dutchman's breeches, is a lovely early-flowering perennial with succulent stems, fernlike foliage and exquisite flowers that hang from the stems like pink and white hearts. A woodland plant by origin, it is easy to grow in shade or semi-shade, but needs a sheltered position where it can be protected from frosts, which can damage the emerging foliage.

Plant the fleshy roots as for alstroemeria; it will establish easily on well-drained soil rich in organic matter.

Dicentra dies down soon after flowering in dry conditions: keep the soil moist to maintain the beautiful foliage for several weeks in summer.

Gypsophila

Gypsophila paniculata, baby's breath, is a delightful perennial that produces clouds of tiny flowers on very fine wiry stems. It is a popular cut flower, traditionally grown as an accompaniment for sweet peas, which

Other perennials sold alongside bulbs include: iris (top), oriental poppies (middle), hostas (bottom), peonies and phlox. Some subjects establish quickly and easily, whereas others, such as peonies, take a year or two to settle down and produce flowers. For more reliable results, these are also sold as pot-grown plants, in growth, later in spring and summer.

Top: *Dicentra spectabilis*, bleeding heart. Above: *Gypsophila paniculata*, perfect for cutting to accompany sweet peas.

flower at the same time in early summer. There are pink and white forms.

The root of gypsophila is like a hard, brown carrot and should be planted vertically in the soil with the shoot-bearing tip 2–3cm below the surface. It likes a well-drained sunny position and grows best on chalk soils. The plant needs no support, despite its fine stems and mass of flowers.

Gypsophila is useful to plant in the border alongside oriental poppies, which flower early and then disappear. The gypsophila takes over and fills the gaps.

Tulipa 'Fantasy': exotic, beautiful and easy to grow.

Suffix 'i' to page references refers to illustrations.

index

acknowledgements

All photographs were taken by Andrew McIndoe, with the exception of:
Flora Pix: 113a
Kevin Hobbs 65c
Charlotte Strutt: 86
Terry Underhill: 34c, 35b, 112b
Westland Horticulture Ltd: 61a, 61b, 62a, 63, 64a, 64b, 65b, 65c, 66b, 106b, 107b, 107d

Computer Programming in the BASIC Language

Neal Golden / Second Edition

Harcourt Brace Jovanovich
New York Chicago San Francisco Atlanta Dallas *and* London

About the Author

Brother Neal Golden, S.C.
Chairman, Department of Mathematics
and Computer Science
Brother Martin High School
New Orleans, Louisiana

Editorial Advisors

Paul E. Dahnke
Mathematics Department Chairman
Sandusky High School
Sandusky, Ohio

Dr. Antonio M. Lopez, Jr.
Associate Professor
Mathematical Sciences
Loyola University
New Orleans, Louisiana

Bonnie Turrentine
Mathematics Teacher
Dedham High School
Dedham, Massachusetts

Patricia L. Zaiontz
Mathematics Teacher
L. B. J. High School
Austin, Texas

PICTURE CREDITS

Page viii, courtesy of International Business Machines Corporation; page 1, Hewlett-Packard Corporation; 66, courtesy of International Business Machines Corporation; 67, The Laboratory for Computer Graphics and Spatial Analysis, Harvard University; 110, Honeywell Corporation; 158, Social Security Administration; 202, Bunker Ramo Corporation; 250, United Press International; 286, courtesy of International Business Machines Corporation.

Printed in the United States of America

ISBN 0-15-359090-4

PREFACE

The input provided by teachers and students has played a major role in preparing the second edition of Computer Programming in the BASIC Language. For example, there are now two elements at the end of each chapter that will help the students to review: Chapter Summary and Chapter Objectives and Review.

These two items will help the student with the exercises that comprise the Rounds in each chapter. To make assignments easier, the exercises in the Rounds for Chapters One through Six are categorized by subject matter. In addition to those exercises that are categorized according to the mathematical background required (algebra one, geometry, etc.), each of the first six chapters contains exercises related to business and to the physical sciences. The Round exercises categorized as "Algebra One" show that the first four chapters can be used with students who have only a background in first-year algebra.

In addition to the numerous applications in the Rounds, each chapter contains a two-page topic (with exercises) that illustrates the use of computers in a career area, such as banking, insurance, sports, and so on.

The technological advances in computer programming have also played a major role in preparing the second edition. The growing use of microcomputers has been of particular import. Many of the programming techniques once classified as "additional features of BASIC" have become more common and new aspects of BASIC are now of the "additional features" class. The development of a new format for printouts of long programs has also had an impact on the second edition.

Additional comments regarding the text and its use can be found in the Teacher's Manual/Chapter Tests/Solution Key.

CONTENTS

INTRODUCTION

A Brief History of Computers

Perhaps no invention in history has made as rapid an impact on people's lives as the computer. According to one writer, if manned flight had developed as quickly as has computer technology, "an astronaut could have orbited the earth nine years after Orville Wright wobbled aloft at Kitty Hawk."

Some simple calculating machines were invented in the eighteenth century and even earlier. Then in the early nineteenth century, Charles Babbage (1792-1871) conceived the idea of a more practical calculating machine and even constructed an incomplete model. Later in the century, Herman Hollerith (1860-1929) created a mechanical device based on punched cards that was used to tabulate the results of the United States census of 1890. For the next fifty or sixty years the technology of computational machines grew steadily.

However, it was not until the period of scientific activity created by World War II that a truly explosive advance in computer technology began. The first electronic computer was completed in 1945 at the University of Pennsylvania by a team headed by Dr. John W. Mauchly and J. Presper Eckert. Their machine was called ENIAC ("Electrical-Numerical Integrator and Computer") and was built for the U.S. Army to solve ballistic problems. In 1951, they developed the UNIVAC I, the first commercially-produced computer. The first UNIVAC was delivered to the Census Bureau in Washington, where it was used almost continuously until 1963, when it was replaced by a newer model. Since that time the first UNIVAC has been on display at the Smithsonian Institute.

Compared to yesterday's computers, today's computers are smaller, faster, cheaper, and easier to use. However, what is meant by smaller, faster, cheaper, and easier to use?

1. Smaller. ENIAC weighed almost thirty tons and occupied the entire basement of a building. Contributing to the enormous size of this computer was its large number of heat-generating vacuum tubes—16,000. In the late 1950's, the vacuum tubes were replaced by transistors and other "solid-state" elements. Because of the small size of these solid-state elements, the computers that used them took up considerably less space. The 1960's and 1970's saw the continuation of the trend to miniaturization. More and more electronic components were packed into smaller and smaller integrated circuits. In the late 1960's, as a result of this trend, minicomputers were developed that were about the size of an office desk. Then in the late '70's came microcomputers, which could sit on a desk and yet had the computing power of a room full of equipment from a decade earlier.

2. Faster. The same trend that packed more electronic hardware into less space also created faster computers. ENIAC could do 5000 additions in one second. Its cycle times were measured in **milliseconds** (one thousandth of a second). The transistorized computers operated in **microseconds** (one millionth of a second). But as miniaturization increased, **nanoseconds** (one billionth of a second) were used. This was followed by **picoseconds** (one trillionth of a second).

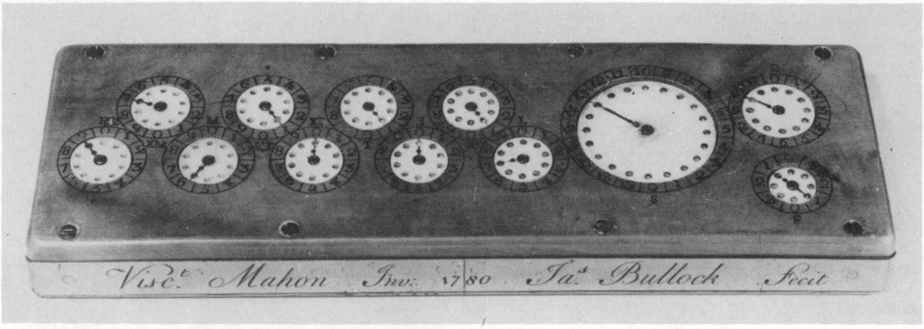

An Eighteenth Century "Calculating Engine"

3. Cheaper. Through the 1960's computers were large systems that cost hundreds of thousands of dollars. Only a governmental agency or a large company or university could afford this cost. Fortunately, the increased speeds of the machines allowed some companies to offer time-sharing service. In this setup many users (such as small businesses or high schools) connect to a large central computer system by means of telephone lines. Because this central computer system is so fast, it can execute the programs of dozens of users almost simultaneously. In this way, each user shares the cost of the machine by paying only for the time the user is connected to it. As time went by, the cost of a computer dropped sharply. A minicomputer of the 1970's could do the work of the large computers of earlier years at considerably lower costs. The advent of comparable microcomputers further reduced the costs. These developments have made it possible for a growing number of businesses, schools, and individuals to obtain their own computers. Some experts have predicted that by the end of the century, computers will be as common in homes as telephones are today.

4. Easier to Use. Along with the advancement in hardware there has also been advancement in software. "Software" refers to the programs that tell a computer what to do. During the first decade of computer design, each computer system had its own language. But in the late 1950's committees developed the FORTRAN and COBOL languages. FORTRAN (FORmula TRANslator) was designed for scientific use and COBOL (COmmon Business-Oriented Language) for business use. Now a person who learned either of these languages could program many different computers. In the middle 1960's the BASIC language (Beginners' All-purpose Symbolic Instruction Code) was created at Dartmouth College as a language intended expressly for students. It quickly became the primary computer language for time-sharing systems and, later, for the mini- and microcomputers. In the mid-1970's the language Pascal, named for a famous mathematician, gained widespread popularity.

The application of computers in business, industry, and education continues to grow at a rapid rate. It is no exaggeration to say that every person now comes in contact with computers in some way. Because today's students live in a computerized world, they must learn to deal with the machines that have created the "Second Industrial Revolution."

1

COMPUTER SYSTEMS; FLOWCHARTING

1-1 COMPONENTS OF A COMPUTER SYSTEM

In order to do the job that you expect of it, a computer must first be properly *programmed.* A **program** is a planned sequence of instructions that tells a computer system what steps to perform in order to produce a desired result or *output.*

Output is one of the four functions that any computer system must encompass. The complete list of functions is as follows:

(**a**) Input (**b**) Storage (**c**) Processing (**d**) Output

Each function may be handled by a different piece of machinery or, as with the mini- and microcomputers of recent years, combined into a single console.

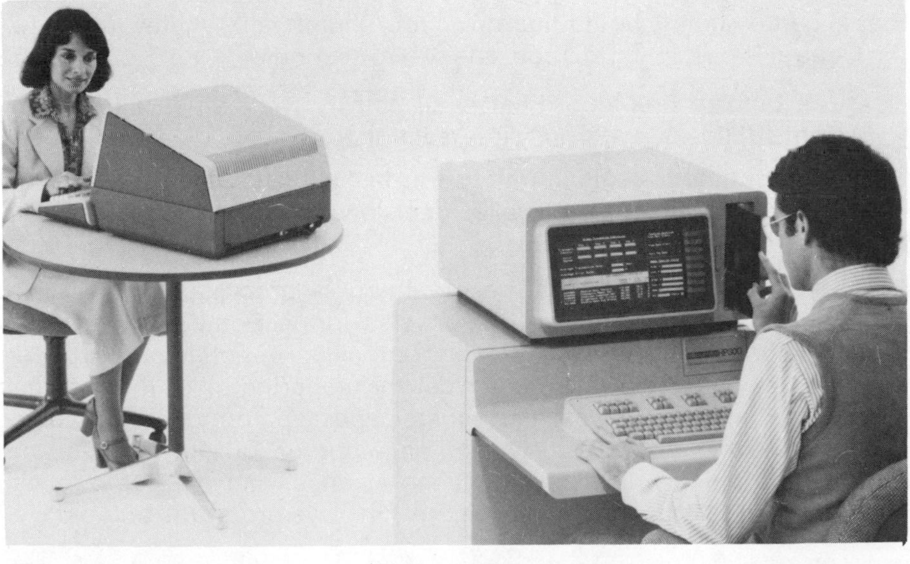

Here is a brief discussion of the four functions just listed.

(**a**) INPUT: This is the process of feeding a computer program (or data for the program) into the computer system. You start the process by typing at a computer keyboard. If the information you are typing flows directly into the computer's *memory* (see below) then the input function is complete. Otherwise the process continues through an intermediate stage during which the information is recorded in some way, for example onto a magnetic tape, paper tape, or set of punched cards. The tape or set of cards can then be read into the computer's memory using an input device, such as a magnetic tape drive, paper tape reader, or card reader.

(**b**) STORAGE: A program that is fed into a computer must be stored, as must the data that will be used in the computations. Also, intermediate results that are obtained during the course of a computer run must be held for use later in the procedure. There are two kinds of storage.

> **Memory** or **main storage** is used for temporary storage of programs, input data, intermediate results, and output results.
>
> **Auxiliary storage** is used for permanent data files and for programs that are used often. Such files and programs are usually recorded magnetically on *tapes* or *disks.*

(**c**) PROCESSING: The heart of a computer system is the **Central Processing Unit,** or **CPU.** For many years the CPU was a fairly large unit, sometimes sharing space with the memory unit. By the 1970's, technology had developed the "processor on a chip," an electronic element that is so tiny that it would not cover your thumbnail. Whatever its size, the Central Processing Unit consists of two sections.

> The **control unit** coordinates all activity, very much like a traffic policeman at a busy intersection.
>
> The **arithmetic-logical unit** performs all calculations and, under program control, makes decisions based on the results of its computations.

(**d**) OUTPUT: This refers to the obtaining of processed information from the computer in any of several physical forms. Some of these forms are the same as those used in the input process: punched cards, paper tape, and magnetic tape. Devices exist for preparing all of these forms of output. These include card punches, paper tape punches, and magnetic tape drives. There are two other important output devices, the *line-printer,* which prints an entire line at once, and the *cathode ray tube* (CRT), a television-like screen that displays programs and data.

Note: Throughout this text the word **terminal** will be used to refer to an input/output device that consists of a keyboard and either a CRT or a printer. A terminal can function either as an integral part of a self-contained computer system or as a separate unit that is connected, by telephone lines for example, to a time-sharing computer system.

EXERCISES 1-1

A

1. The four functions that any computer system must perform are __?__, __?__, __?__, and __?__.
2. __?__ or __?__ is used for temporary storage of programs and data.
3. __?__ is used for permanent files and programs.
4. CPU stands for C__?__ P__?__ U__?__.
5. The CPU consists of the __?__ unit and the __?__ unit.
6. Three common input devices are __?__, __?__, and __?__.
7. Auxiliary storage usually consists of __?__.
8. In addition to the three devices of Exercise 6, two other output devices are __?__ and __?__.
9. In addition to performing calculations, the CPU can also make __?__ based on the results of computations.

1-2 THE SYMBOLS OF FLOWCHARTING

Before writing a program, a programmer usually prepares a flowchart for the problem to be solved. A **flowchart** is a step-by-step outline of the procedure to be followed by the computer. These are the symbols.

SYMBOL	MEANING
	INPUT/OUTPUT
	ASSIGNMENT
 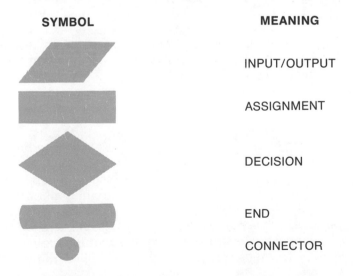	DECISION
	END
	CONNECTOR

Example: Compute the average of three numbers.

Solution:

Flowchart 1-1

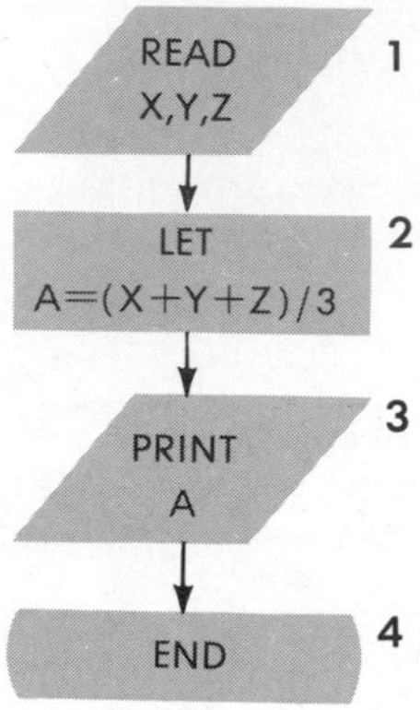

Comments:

The programmer chooses three letters (X, Y, and Z) to represent the numbers to be averaged.

The computing step uses the standard formula for finding an average, the programmer electing to call the answer "A." The computer can perform the usual operations of addition, subtraction, multiplication, division, raising to a power, and taking a root.

Since most terminals and other input equipment print only capital letters, letters are usually capitalized in flowcharts.

Note that in a flowchart it is customary to chart the steps either downward or from left to right. Arrows connect the symbols to show the flow of steps.

Inside each flowchart symbol there is a command to the computer.

1. For INPUT use the READ command.
2. For ASSIGNMENT use the LET command.
3. For OUTPUT use the PRINT command.
4. For END use the END command.

Example: Compute an employee's weekly wage, given his rate-per-hour and number of hours worked. Assume that there is no overtime pay.

Solution: *Flowchart 1-2*

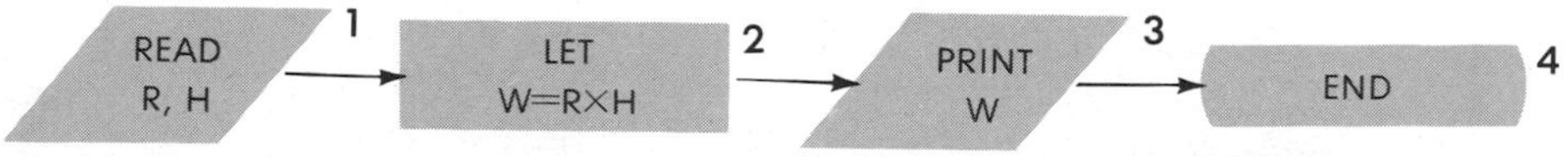

Comment:

The flowchart uses the variable R for rate, H for hours, and W for weekly wage. The flowchart boxes are numbered so that the explanation that follows can refer to them easily.

It is important to understand how variables are used in programming. A variable is the name of a particular location in the memory of the computer. In Flowchart 1-2 on page 4 the command in box 1, "READ R,H," causes two values to be obtained from a data list. In the BASIC language, which we shall study in this book, the data are usually listed in a DATA statement in the program itself and entered via a terminal keyboard. But for the flowchart it is sufficient to understand that the two values are read and stored, respectively, in memory locations designated "R" and "H." Storage positions have numerical addresses within the machine but in languages such as BASIC and FORTRAN the programmer needs only to use variables such as R and H. When the computer moves to box 2, it obtains the values stored in locations R and H, multiplies them and stores the product in a location named "W." Box 3 causes the value in W to be printed on an output device (printer, cathode ray tube, magnetic tape drive, and so on).

The rectangle (see Box 2) is called an **assignment box** because it causes the value obtained from the right side of "=" to be *assigned* to the storage location named by the variable on the left side. Thus, "=" should be thought of as a left-pointing arrow. For example,

$$\text{LET } W = R \times H$$

has the effect

$$W \leftarrow R \times H$$

that is, "let the value obtained by multiplying R and H be *assigned* to the location W." Some books actually use "←" in place of "=" in assignment boxes of flowcharts, but since the BASIC language uses "=," we use "=" in flowcharts in this text. In view of the above discussion, it is clear that "=" does not have the same meaning in BASIC as it does in an algebraic equation.

EXERCISES 1-2

A Write the letter that corresponds to each symbol.

1.
2.
3.
4.

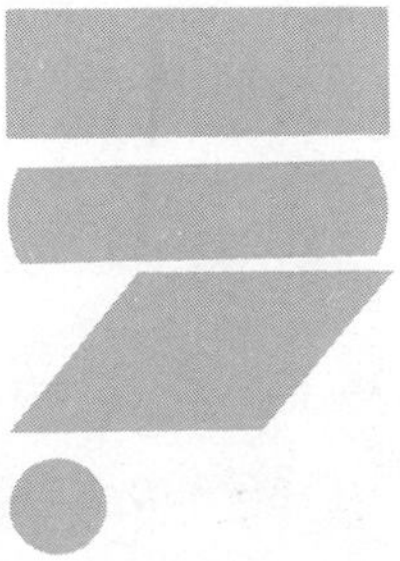

(a) Connector
(b) Decision
(c) Input/Output
(d) Assignment
(e) End

In Exercises 5 through 7 a flowcharting problem is stated and part of the flowchart shown. Complete the flowchart.

Example:

Compute a baseball player's batting average, given his number of at-bats and number of hits.

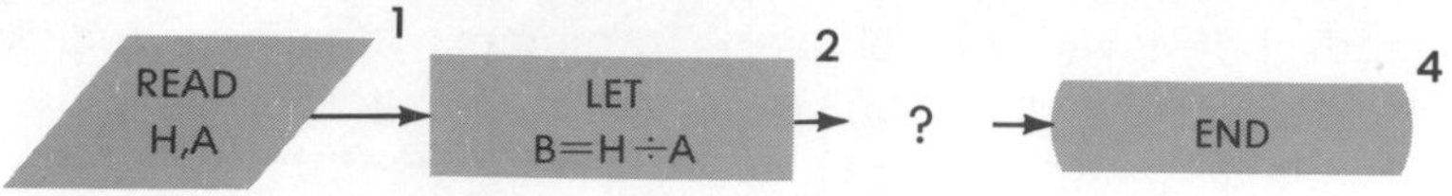

Answer:

5. Compute the geometric mean of two positive numbers.

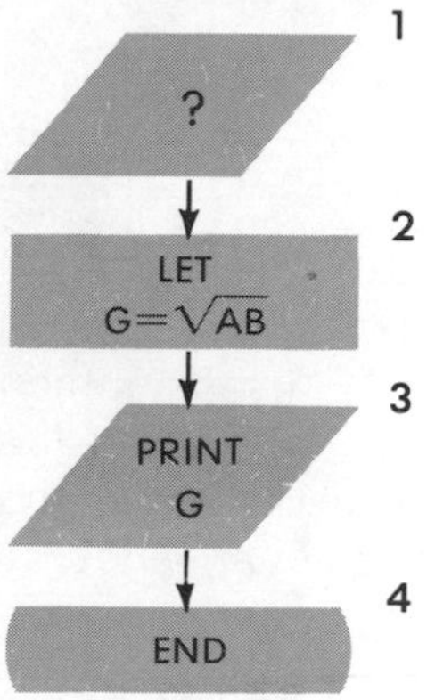

6. Read two real numbers; multiply them and divide the result by two.

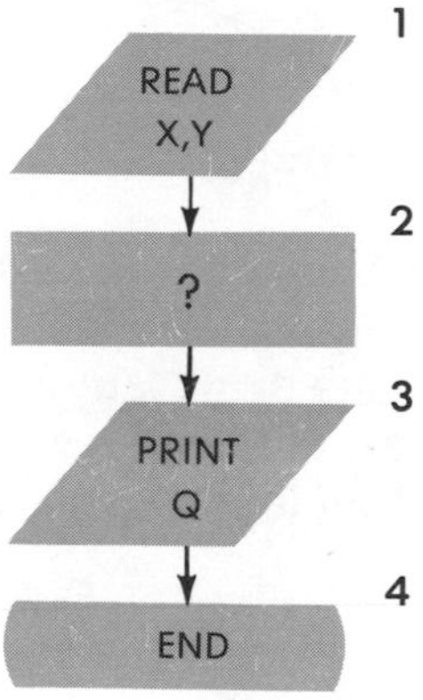

7. Compute the annual simple interest on a given investment if the rate is 6%.

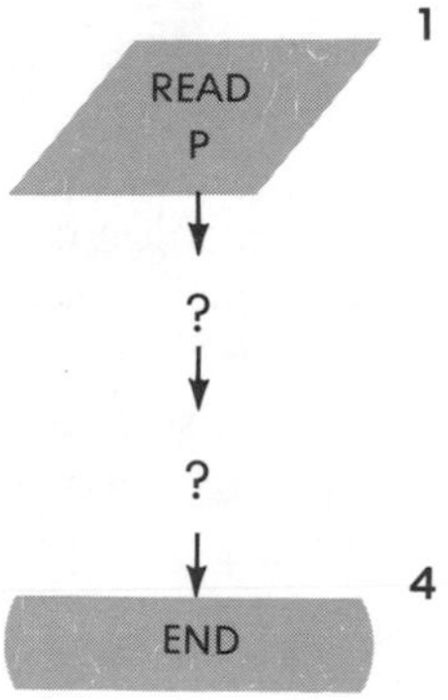

What is wrong in each of the following flowchart boxes?

8.

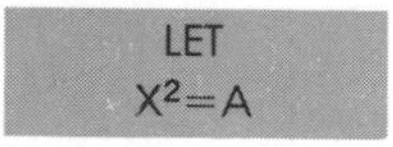

9.

10.

B Flowchart each of the following problems.

11. Compute the perimeter of a rectangle, given the length and width.

12. Compute the area of a circle, given the radius. (Note: use an approximation for π, such as 3.14159.)

1-3 FLOWCHARTS INVOLVING DECISIONS

Example: Read a real number x. If x is nonnegative, give its square root. If x is negative, print "NO REAL SQUARE ROOT."

Solution:

Flowchart 1-3

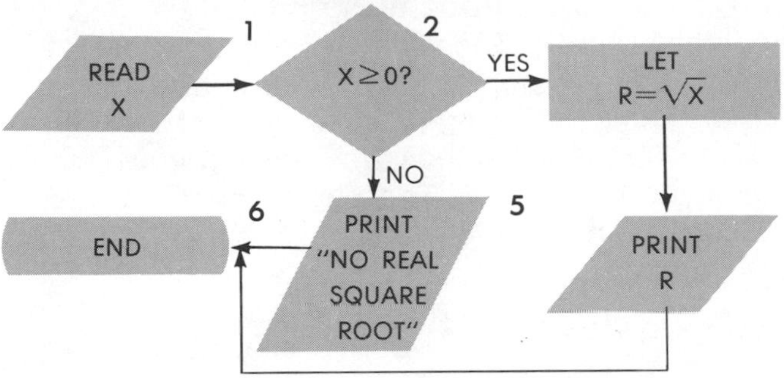

Comment:

A computer can compare two numbers and answer questions such as "$x = 0$?", "$x \neq 0$?", "$x < 0$?", "$x > 0$?", "$x \leq 0$?", and "$x \geq 0$?".

It must always be clear which direction to take when executing the steps of a flowchart. The answer to the decision box must be *yes* or *no*.

The logic of a flowchart can be followed by using a **trace**. In Table 1-1 below we follow the flowchart of the square root problem twice, first using $x = 16$ and then using $x = -5$.

Table 1-1 Trace 1: Assume 16 input as x.

Step Number	Flowchart Box Number	Values of Variables		Test	Yes or No?	Output
		X	R			
1	1	16				
2	2			$16 \geq 0$?	Yes	
3	3		4			
4	4					4
5	END					

Trace 2: Assume −5 input as x.

Step Number	Flowchart Box Number	Values of Variables		Test	Yes or No?	Output
		X	R			
1	1	−5				
2	2			$-5 \geq 0$?	No	
3	5					NO REAL SQUARE ROOT
4	END					

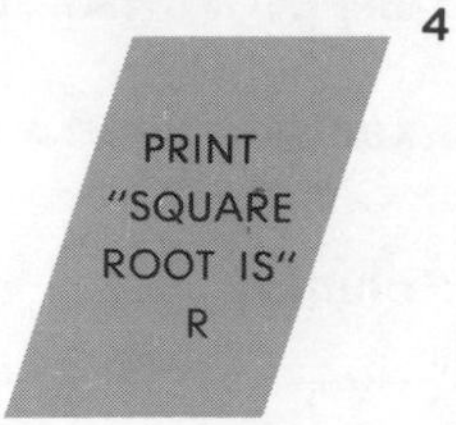

Note the difference between the two PRINT steps of Flowchart 1-3 on page 7 (box 4 and box 5). PRINT R causes the current *value* in the memory location named R to be printed on an output device. PRINT "NO REAL SQUARE ROOT" results in the *message* NO REAL SQUARE ROOT being printed as the output of the program. The two types of output can be combined. For example, box 4 in the square root flowchart could be changed to the one shown above. If, as in Trace 1 on page 7, x = 16, then box 4, as revised, would result in the output SQUARE ROOT IS 4 . The quotation marks are used in the program to begin and end the message. They are not actually printed as part of the output.

The PRINT boxes in Flowcharts 1-1 and 1-2 on page 4 could be similarly changed to those shown at the right.

Example:

Read a real number; print whether it is positive, negative, or zero.

Solution:

Flowchart 1-4

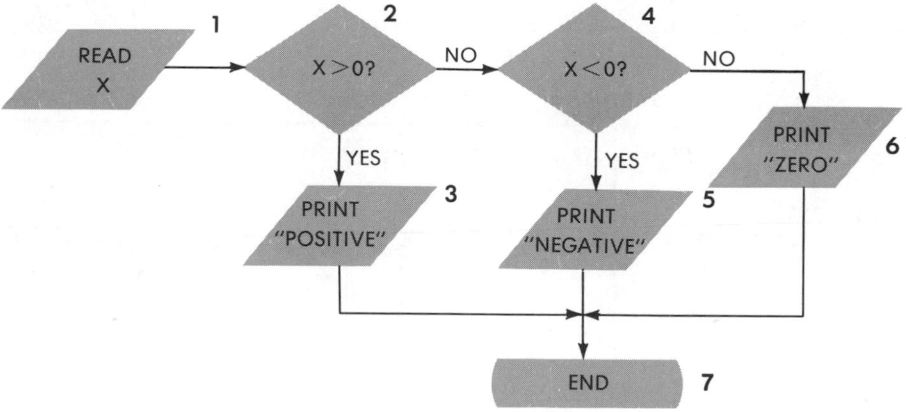

Note that the program does not require three decisions. If x is not greater than zero and not less than zero, the computer can automatically print ZERO since there is no other possibility left.

The decisions of the program could have been stated differently or in a different order. As long as the yes and no branches of the two decisions lead to the correct print statements, the program will work.

Let us now trace Flowchart 1-4 using the data list 7, −5, 0.

Table 1-2 Trace of Flowchart 1-4

Trace 1: Input 7 for x.

Step Number	Flowchart Box Number	Value of Variable x	Test	Yes or No?	Output
1	1	7			
2	2		$7 > 0$?	Yes	
3	3				POSITIVE
4	END				

Trace 2: Input −5 for x.

Step Number	Flowchart Box Number	Value of Variable x	Test	Yes or No?	Output
1	1	−5			
2	2		$-5 > 0$?	No	
3	4		$-5 < 0$?	Yes	
4	5				NEGATIVE
5	END				

Trace 3: Input 0 for x.

Step Number	Flowchart Box Number	Value of Variable x	Test	Yes or No?	Output
1	1	0			
2	2		$0 > 0$?	No	
3	4		$0 < 0$?	No	
4	6				ZERO
5	END				

EXERCISES 1-3

A Trace each flowchart for the data values listed. Refer to Table 1-1 on page 7.

1. DATA 10, −5

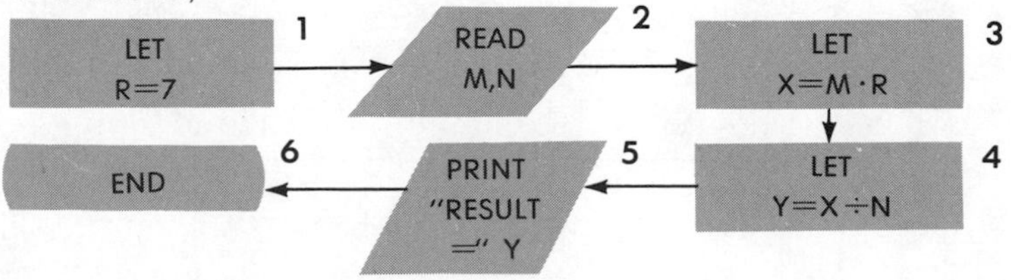

Trace each flowchart for the data values listed above the flowchart. Refer to Table 1-1 on page 7.

2. DATA 10, 4

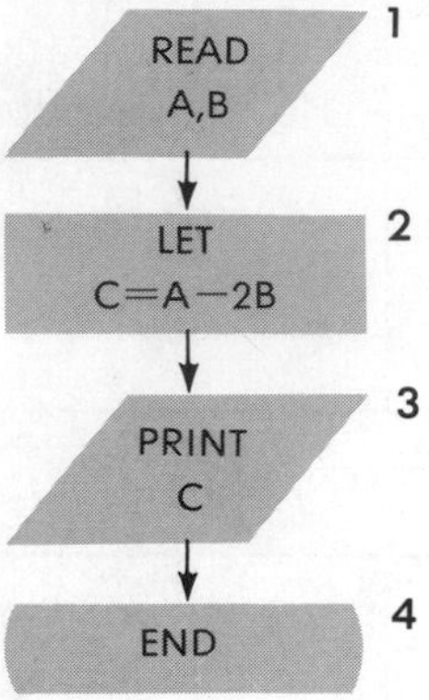

3. DATA 5

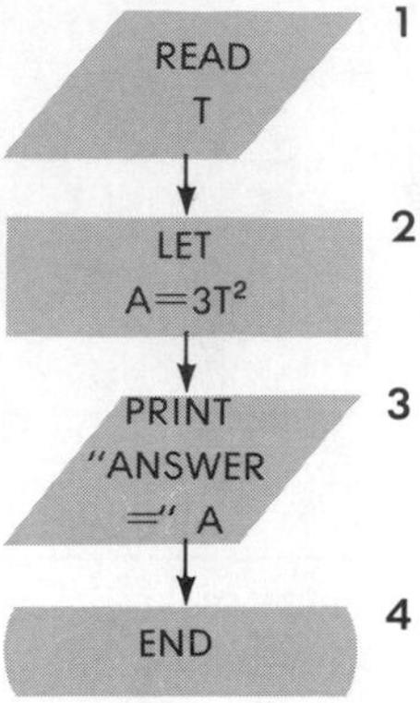

4. DATA −2

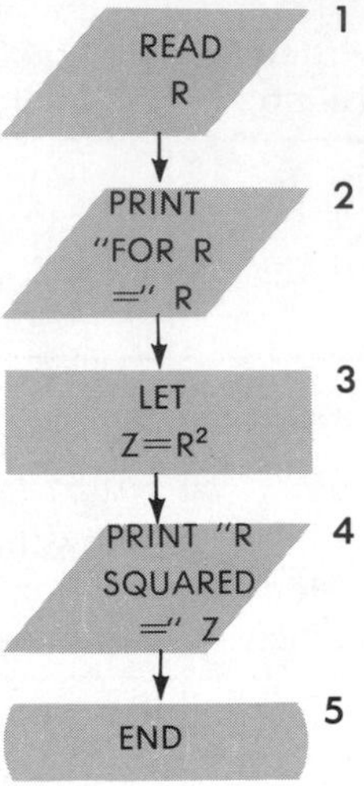

5. DATA 8, 2

6. DATA −5, 0

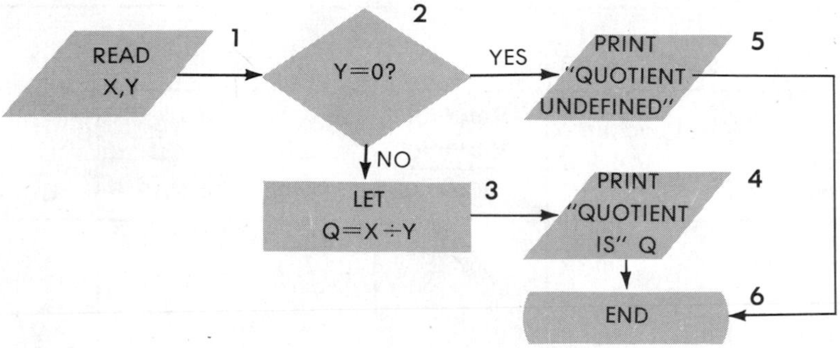

7. DATA 7, −3

8. DATA −4, −5

9. DATA −1, 6

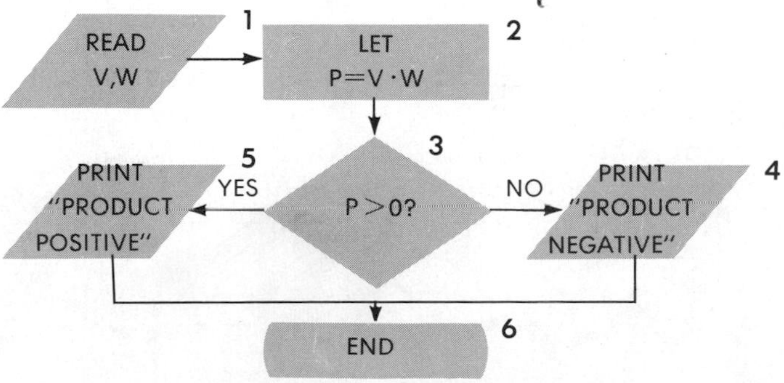

In Exercises 10 through 13 draw a portion of a flowchart that does what is stated.

Example: If X > 10, then print X; otherwise, assign X to Y.

Solution:

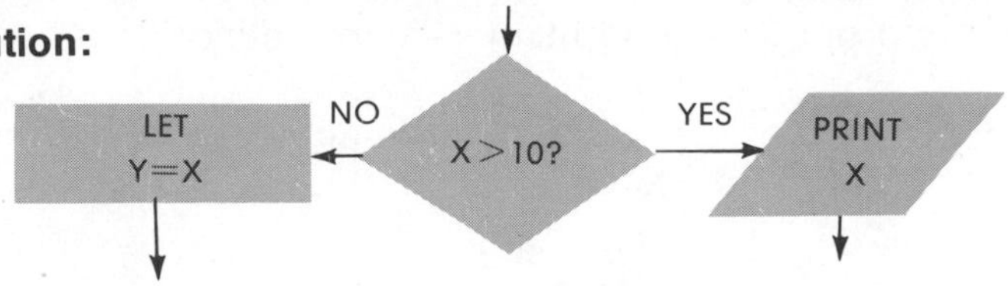

10. If $A^2 = S$, then print "SQUARE ROOT IS" A; otherwise, print "NO SQUARE ROOT."
11. Read M; if M = 100, then END; otherwise, let Y = 2M.
12. If D > 0, print "YES"; if D ≤ 0, print "NO".
13. Check whether X = 0. If it does, print "ZERO". If it does not, test whether Y = 0.

In Exercises 14 and 15, use the relationship that Galileo discovered between the distance an object falls and the time it takes to fall, specifically, $d = 16t^2$, where t is given in seconds and d in feet.

14. Complete the flowchart below which reads a value for t, computes d, and prints t and d.

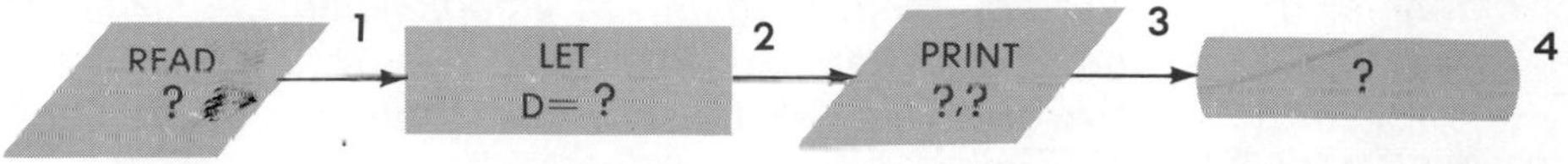

15. Trace the completed flowchart for these data values: 1, 2, 3, 4.

B Draw a flowchart for each of the following exercises.

16. Read two unequal real numbers X and Y. Print either "X < Y" or "Y < X."
17. Read real numbers A and B. Then print "A < B," "A = B," or "A > B."
18. Read three real numbers. Determine which is the largest. (Note: A computer can compare only *two* numbers at a time.)
19. Read three positive real numbers. Decide whether these three numbers could be the lengths of the sides of a triangle.
20. Read three numbers A, B, and C, representing the lengths of the sides of a triangle. Determine whether the triangle is ISOSCELES, EQUILATERAL, or SCALENE.
21. Change the wage problem of Flowchart 1-2 on page 4 as follows: input an employee's hourly rate and the number of hours worked the past week. Assume that any hours worked beyond forty are overtime hours for which he is paid double his regular rate.

1-4 PROCESSING MORE THAN ONE SET OF DATA

Rarely is a program written to process only one set of data. Computers are most often used for simple tasks that are performed many times. For that reason we take a second look at some of the programs already flowcharted in order to extend them to many sets of data.

Example: Find the average of sets of three numbers, where the number of sets is not known in advance.

Solution: *Flowchart 1-5*

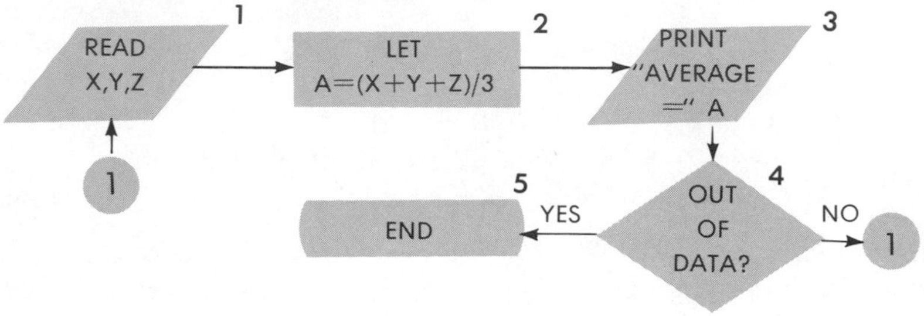

Comment:

The OUT OF DATA *decision is performed internally within the machine. In the program itself the data are listed. When the string of values for* X, Y, *and* Z *is exhausted, the computer receives a* "YES" *answer to the* OUT OF DATA? *question and ends the program.*

Here is a trace using data values 10, 8, 12, −2, 5, 7, 88, 90, 92.

Table 1-3 Trace of Flowchart 1-5

Step Number	Flowchart Box Number	Values of Variables				Test	Yes or No?	Output
		X	Y	Z	A			
1	1	10	8	12				
2	2				10			
3	3							AVERAGE = 10
4	4					Out of Data?	No	
5	1	−2	5	7				
6	2				3.33333			
7	3							AVERAGE = 3.33333
8	4					Out of Data?	No	
9	1	88	90	92				
10	2				90			
11	3							AVERAGE = 90
12	4					Out of Data?	Yes	
13	END							

A variable in a flowchart (that is, a memory location) can have only one value at a time. Whenever a new value is assigned to the variable, the previous value is lost.

Here are the general principles governing flowchart construction.

1. INPUT: Examples of correct **READ** boxes are shown below. You can see that the general form consists of the word **READ** followed by a list of variables.

READ X | READ A,B | READ R,Z,Q

When a **READ** box is executed, one or more values are obtained from a data list and entered into the location(s) named by the variable(s) in the list following the word **READ**. The previous contents of the locations are destroyed. A **READ** step has the same effect as an assignment box except that one or more variables are assigned values taken from a data list.

As the trace in Table 1-3 on page 12 implies, the first execution of the **READ** instruction causes the required number of values to be taken from the beginning of the data list and stored in the memory locations specified by the variables in the **READ** list. A "pointer" inside the computer keeps track of the position of the first unused value in the data list so that the next time a **READ** box is executed, the next data values in sequence are selected. If there are no more items in the data list or if there are not enough for all the variables in the **READ** command, the **OUT OF DATA**? question yields a "**YES**" answer and the program is terminated. For example, if the input list for the program on the previous page was 10, 8, 12, −2, 5, 7, 88, 90, 92, 46, 73, the number triplets (10, 8, 12), (−2, 5, 7), and (88, 90, 92) would be processed as in the trace. But since only the values 46 and 73 are left in the data list, there are not enough items for the three variables in the **READ** box; the **OUT OF DATA**? test would produce a "**YES**" result and end the program.

Arithmetic expressions may never appear in a **READ** box.

2. ASSIGNMENT: The general form of the assignment box is shown at the right. Other examples are shown below.

LET VARIABLE = EXPRESSION

LET X=4 | LET Y=2M−6 | LET S=(G+6)/(2L) | LET T=Z

It has already been pointed out that the = in an assignment box has the effect of ← so that the general form can be thought of as variable ← expression. As the examples illustrate, "expression" could be a constant, a variable, or a combination of constants, variables, and operations.

Carrying out an assignment command involves three steps.

(a) The current values of any variables appearing in the expression to the right of = are obtained from memory.
(b) If the right-hand expression is more complicated than a simple constant or a single variable, then this expression is evaluated, that is, all operations performed and one value obtained for the expression.
(c) The value of the expression is then assigned to the variable (i.e., stored in the memory location) on the left-hand side of the = .

An assignment step, like a READ, is destructive; that is, each time a new value is assigned to a variable, the previous value of that variable is lost and no longer available in memory. (If for some reason that value will be needed later in the program, a new variable should be introduced and the value "copied" into the new location where it can be held until needed.)

Using a variable in the expression to the right of = in a LET step does not harm the value of that variable. For example, if the statement W = R × H is executed, W receives a new value but (for the moment at least) the values in R and H remain the same.

3. OUTPUT: The general forms of the output command are illustrated at the right. The two forms may also occur in combination.

Examples of legitimate PRINT boxes follow.

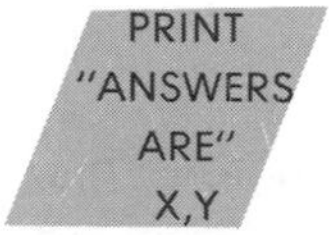

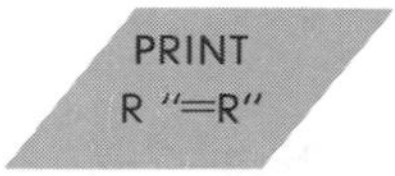

When variables are listed in the PRINT box, the current values of the variables are obtained from memory and printed on an output device in the order listed. Printing is nondestructive since no variables have their values changed in the process.

4. DECISIONS: The general form of the decision symbol is

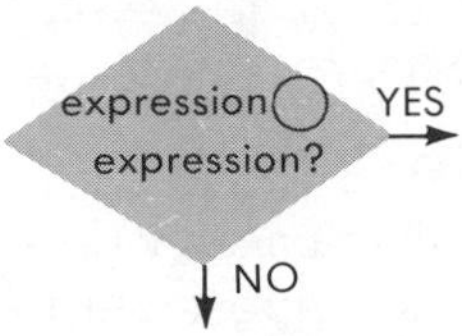

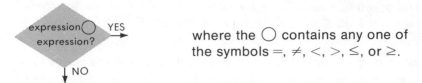

where the ○ contains any one of the symbols $=$, $\neq$, $<$, $>$, $\leq$, or $\geq$.

The YES and NO branches may exit from any two of the four points of the diamond. As in the assignment box, "expression" means a constant, a variable, or a combination of constants, variables, and operations. Here are further examples of valid decision boxes.

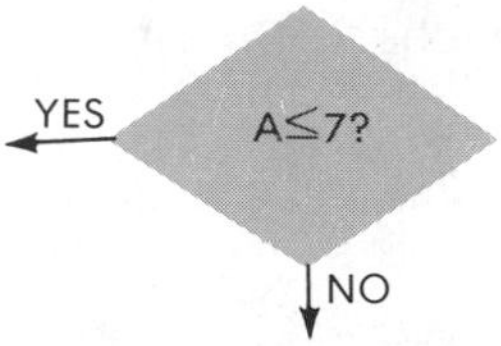

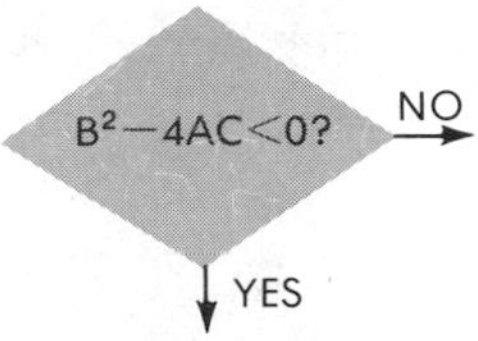

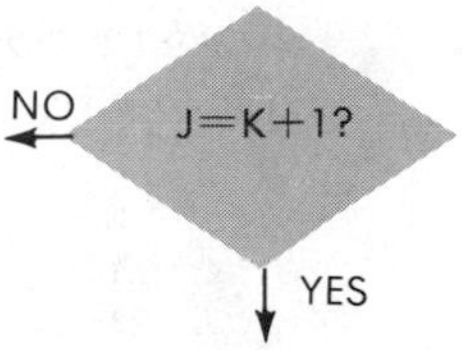

Execution of the decision box involves these steps.

(a) Obtain from memory the current values of any variables in the box.
(b) Evaluate (if necessary) the expressions on either side or both sides of the relation using the values of the variables found in (a).
(c) Test the truth or falsity of the statement appearing in front of the question mark in the decision box.
(d) Choose the appropriate exit path depending on the result of the test in (c).

Note, first, that no variables change their values as a result of the execution of a decision box. Second, expressions are permitted on both sides of the relation symbol in a decision box, whereas in an assignment command, an expression is permitted only on the right side of $=$. Third, the statement in the decision box may be an inequality but the statement in an assignment box always uses $=$.

5. END: The general form of the end symbol is shown at the right. The effect of this box is to halt execution of the program.

There may be no "dead ends" in a flowchart. Regardless of the number of decisions and the number of possible paths through the flowchart, every branch must ultimately connect to the END statement (often through the OUT OF DATA? step, though not necessarily). If the program is logically sound, END will always be the last statement executed.

6. CONNECTOR: This symbol is always used in pairs. The general form is shown by the pair →⊖ and ←⊖ where — represents a numeral or letter. Flowchart 1-5 on page 12 used ①. Ⓐ is another good choice. If additional connectors are needed, ②, ③, ④, etc., or Ⓑ, Ⓒ, Ⓓ, etc., can be used.

The purpose of the connector is to link flowchart boxes in cases where it would be inconvenient or (in complicated programs) impossible to draw a connecting arrow segment. If a lengthy flowchart must be continued on a second page, connectors are needed at the end of the first page and the beginning of the second to show the linkage.

EXERCISES 1-4

A For each box state whether it is a valid flowchart box. If not, explain why.

1.

2.

3.

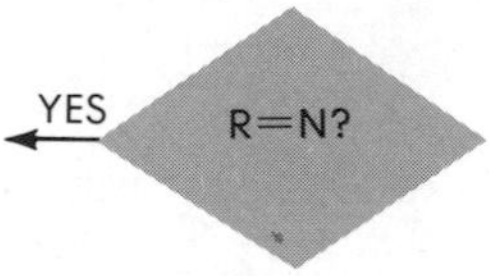

4.

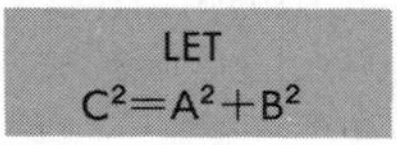

5.

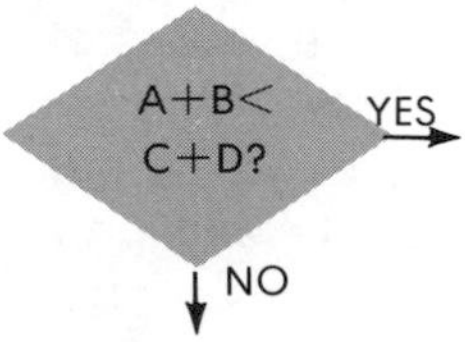

6.

7.

8.

9.

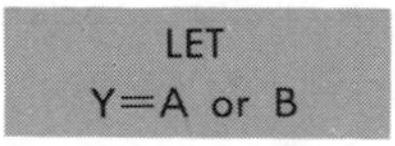

10.

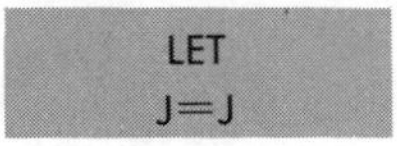

11.

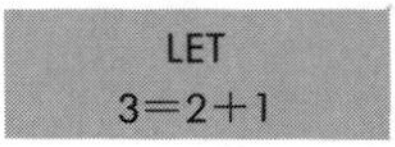

12.

13. Do the assignment boxes below accomplish the same result? If not, explain the differences in the execution of the two boxes.

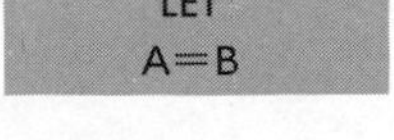

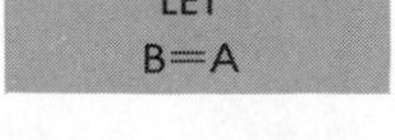

Write *Yes* or *No* to show whether each flowchart box below would change the value in Y.

14.

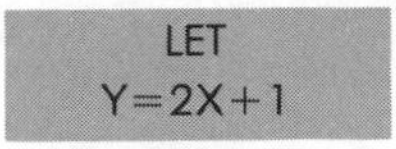

15.

16.

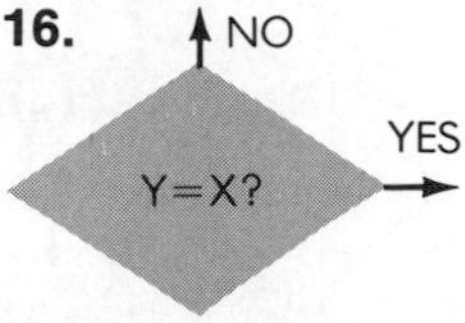

17.

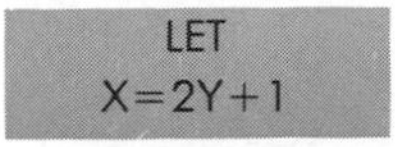

18.

19.

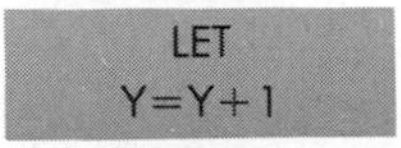

Trace each flowchart for the data listed. See Table 1-3 on page 12.

20. DATA 10, 20, 5, −2, 0, 11

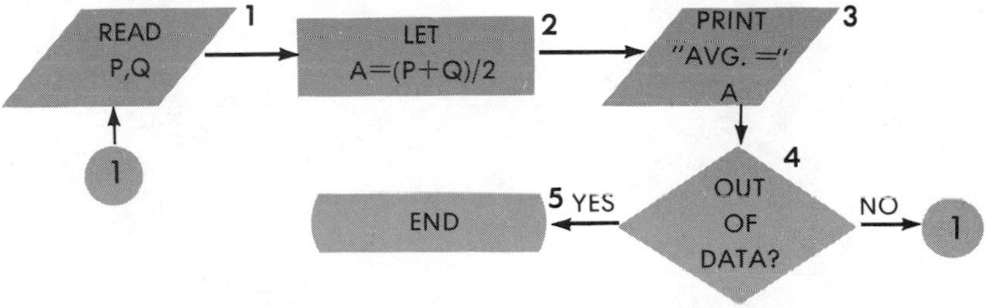

21. DATA 7, 4, 4, 8, 5, 5

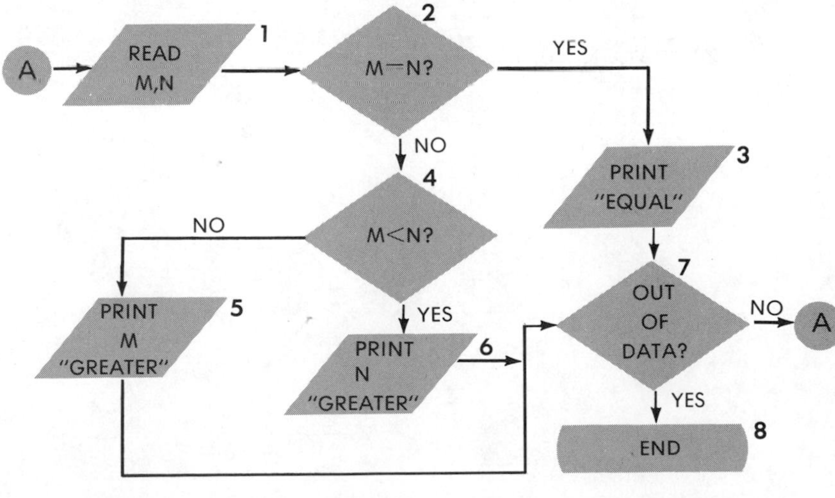

Trace each flowchart for the data listed. See Table 1-3 on page 12.

22. DATA 2, 7, 5, −4

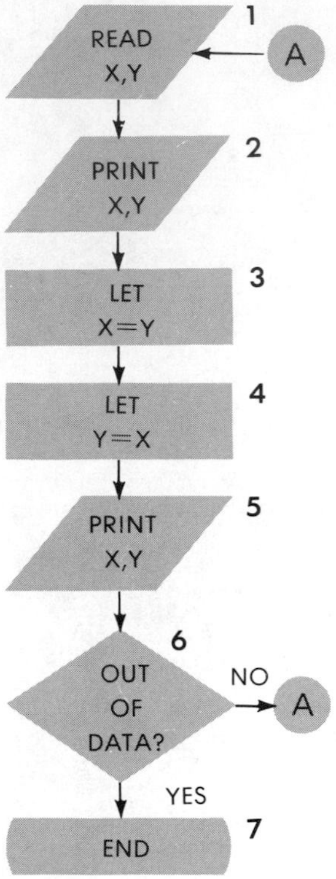

23. DATA 2, 7, 5, −4

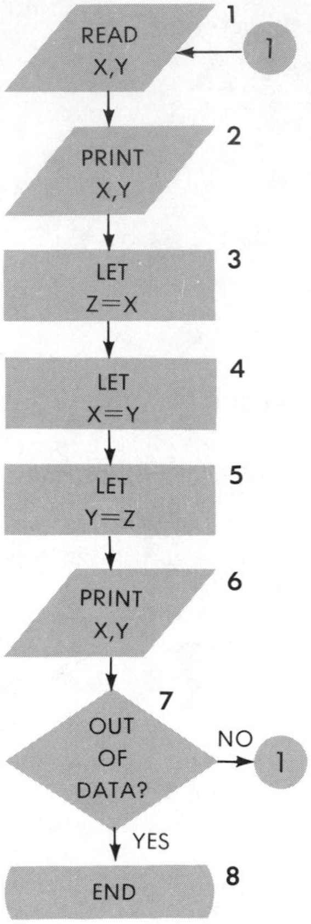

24. DATA 4, −3, 10, 0

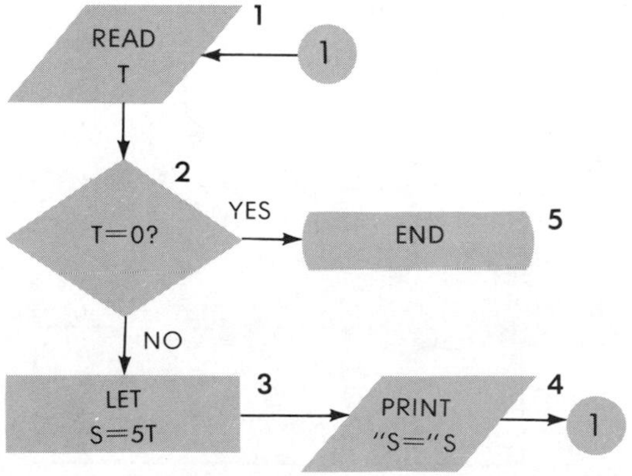

Suppose that you are given two rational numbers A and B (with A < B) and a third rational number C. Decide whether C is "between" A and B; that is, determine whether A < C < B.

25. Complete the flowchart below for this problem.

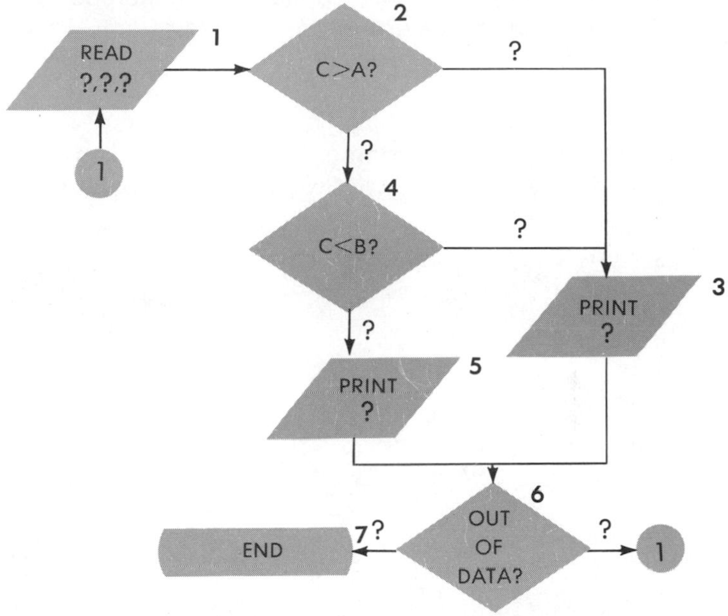

26. Trace the completed flowchart for these data values: 1, 2, 1.3, .7, .8, .9, 2.02, 2.07, 2.01.

27. Copy the flowchart symbols given and fill in the boxes for the following problem. "Accept any two nonzero real numbers and print the quotient of the greater divided by the smaller."

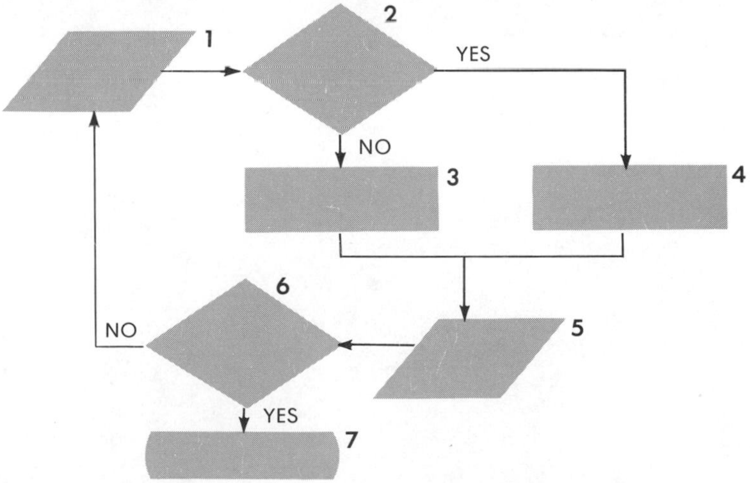

Flowchart each of these problems to handle as many sets of data as needed.

28. Compute the area of each of a set of rectangles.

29. Compute the area of each member of a set of triangles.

30. Compute the circumference of each member of a set of circles.

31. Compute the pay of each of a set of employees. (See Ex. 21, p. 11.)

C Do the following assignment boxes make sense? If not, explain why. If they are valid, what would be the result of each?

32.

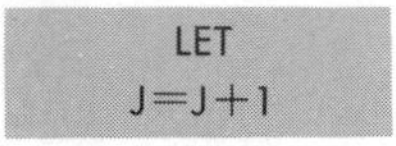

33.

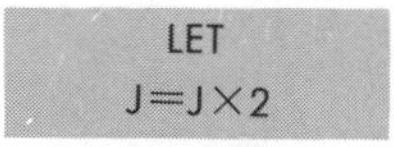

Trace each flowchart for the data listed.

34. DATA 4, −2, 7, 6, 0

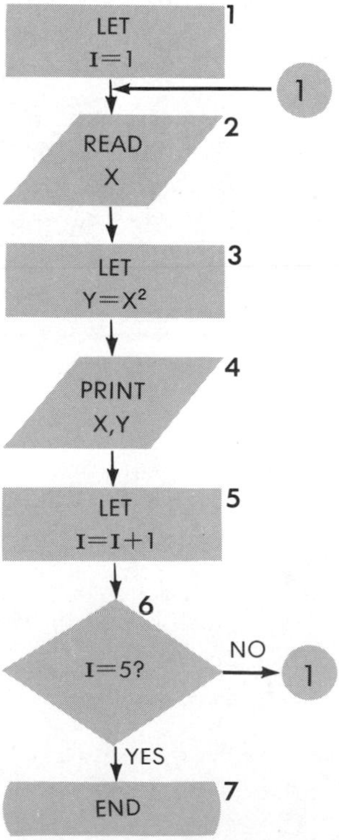

35. DATA 7, 6, 6, 7, 9, −7, −8, 3, 0, 14, 10, 5

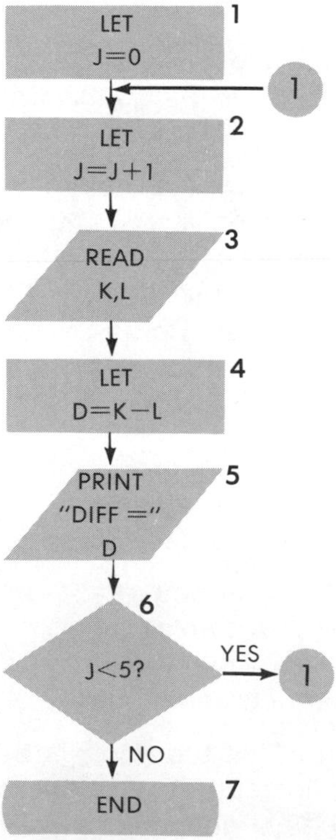

1-5 ADDITIONAL FLOWCHART PROBLEMS

Example: Read the coordinates of a point in the *xy*-plane. Decide the number of the quadrant in which the point lies. Assume that the point is not on an axis.

Solution: *Flowchart 1-6*

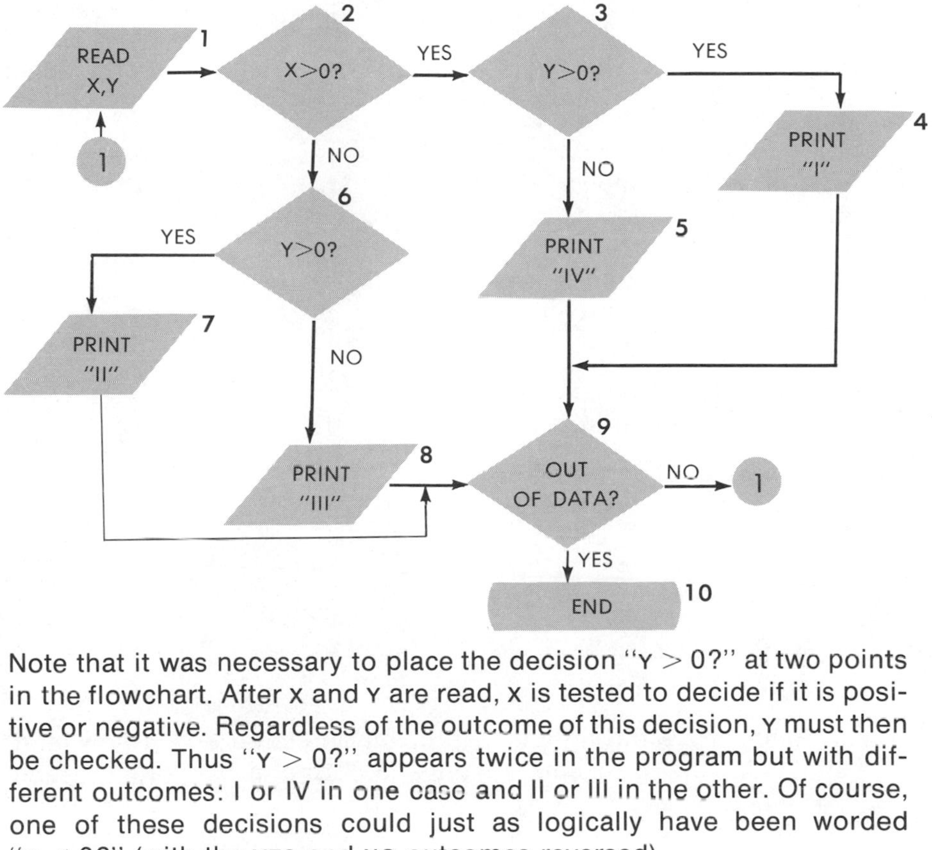

Note that it was necessary to place the decision "Y > 0?" at two points in the flowchart. After X and Y are read, X is tested to decide if it is positive or negative. Regardless of the outcome of this decision, Y must then be checked. Thus "Y > 0?" appears twice in the program but with different outcomes: I or IV in one case and II or III in the other. Of course, one of these decisions could just as logically have been worded "Y < 0?" (with the YES and NO outcomes reversed).

CAUTION: In algebra, coordinates are written as an ordered pair, in parentheses, as in (*x*, *y*). The computer does not have to *know* that X and Y form an ordered pair. To the machine X and Y are just numbers.

An ordered pair could be printed with a PRINT box like the one shown at the right. The left parenthesis, comma, and right parenthesis are dictated to the computer between quotation marks.

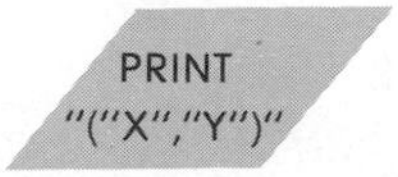

Make sure that the number of quotation marks in a PRINT box is *even*. In complicated output boxes such as the one just shown, it is easy to omit a left or right parenthesis.

EXERCISES 1-5

A **1.** Trace Flowchart 1-6 on page 21 for this list of data values: 2, 4, −1, −6, 10, −5, −5, 32.

What erroneous output will result from Flowchart 1-6 from each data pair below? (The output is erroneous since Flowchart 1-6 is not meant to handle zero coordinates.)

2. 0, 6 **3.** −2, 0 **4.** 0, 0 **5.** 0, −9 **6.** 7, 0

Consider $y - 6 < 7x + 3$ and a replacement set $\{(1, 15), (-2, 6), (1, 30), (-5, -20)\}$. The flowchart shown at the right should use each pair from the replacement set as data and determine which pairs are solutions of the inequality.

7. Complete the flowchart shown on the right.

8. Trace the completed flowchart for the given replacement set.

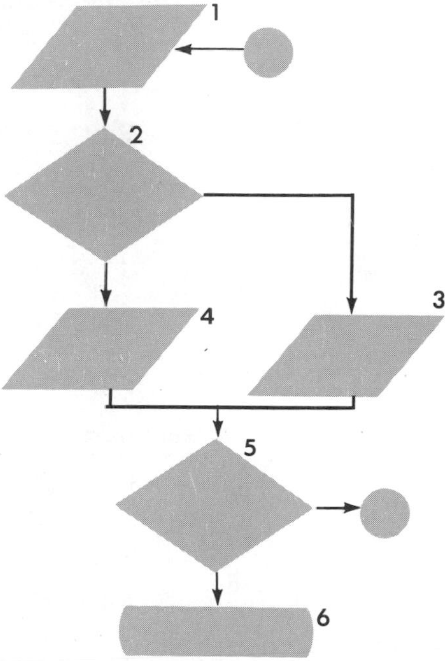

In Exercises 9 through 11 a problem is stated and a flowchart shown for that problem. Identify and correct any error(s) in each flowchart.

9. Read two numbers; double the larger and print the result.

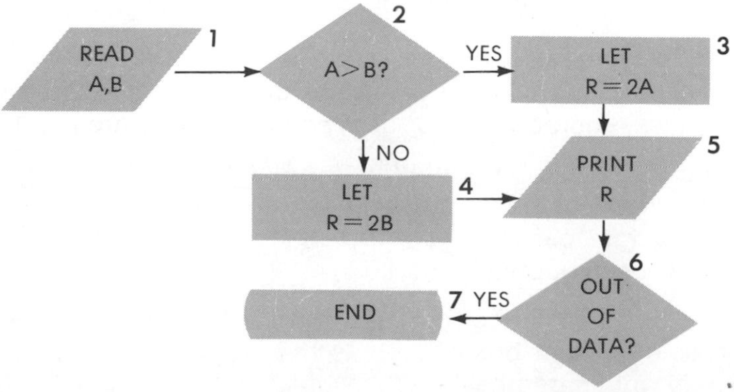

10. Given a real number, determine whether it is positive, negative, or zero.

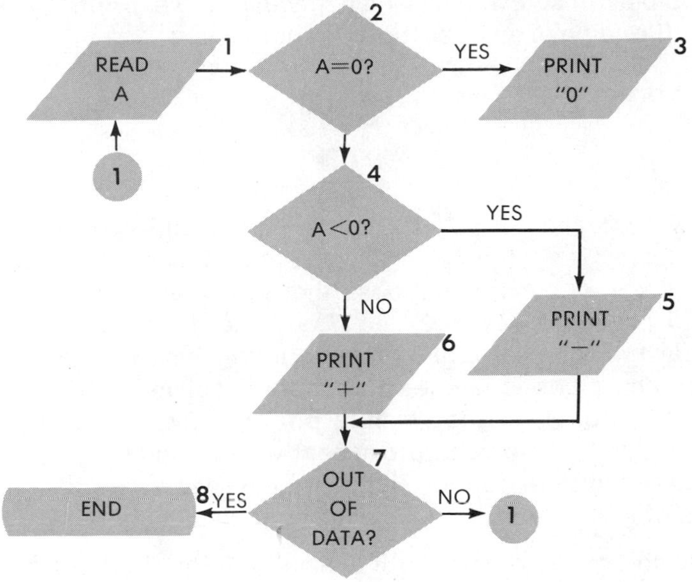

11. Read a real number. If it is not zero, print its reciprocal.

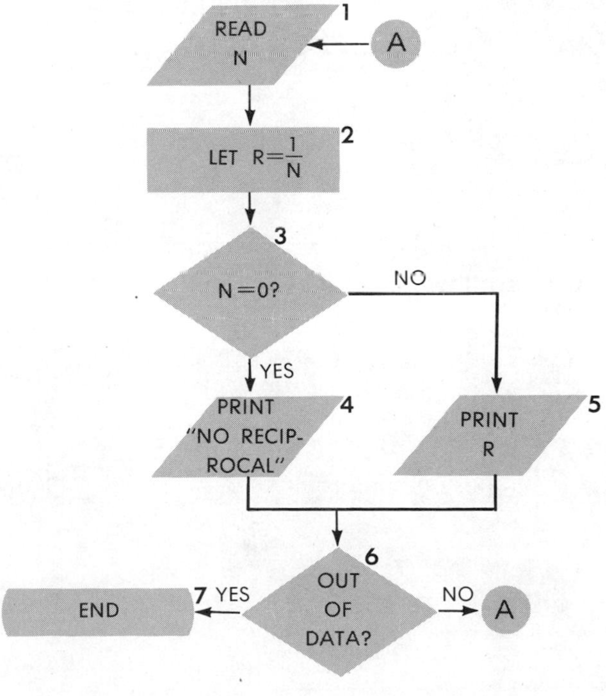

B **12.** The "slope-intercept form" of a linear equation is $y = \text{M}x + \text{B}$ where M is the slope and B, the y-intercept. Suppose you are to design a flowchart which, given M and B, prints the equation of the line. Consider the print box below.

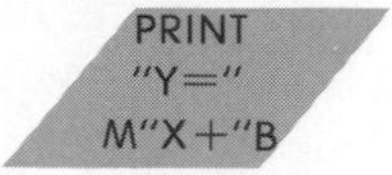

For M = 2 and B = 7, this print box would give as its output Y = 2X + 7. For M = −2 and B = 7, the output would be Y = −2X + 7. Now suppose that M = 2 and B = −7. The step would produce Y = 2X + −7. The double sign before the 7 is awkward. We would prefer printing just Y = 2X − 7. A different PRINT box is needed to handle negative values for B. Similarly if B = 0, we do not wish to print Y = 2X + 0 but instead just Y = 2X. Design a flowchart to accept M and B and print the equation "neatly" without double signs or needless zeros. (Is there any value of M that should be specially handled?)

For each box state whether it is a valid output box. If not, explain why.

13.

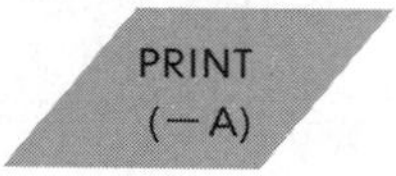

14.

15.

16.

17.

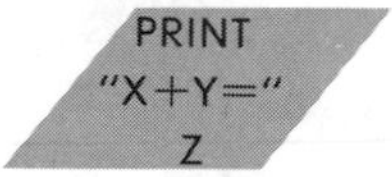

18.

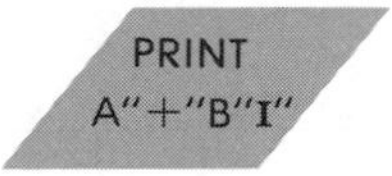

19. Trace the flowchart below. DATA 10, 90, 43, 11

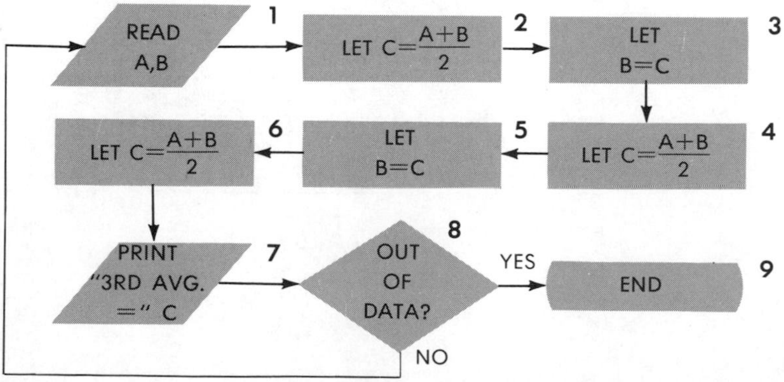

C Use the flowchart below for Exercises 20 through 22.

20. Trace the flowchart. No data are needed.

21. Would the flowchart produce the same output if boxes 7 and 8 were reversed so that box 8 comes before box 7?

22. The flowchart automatically starts I at 0 and J at 1. The algorithm could be made more flexible by allowing the two starting values to be input from data. Explain how the flowchart below can be modified to allow this flexibility.

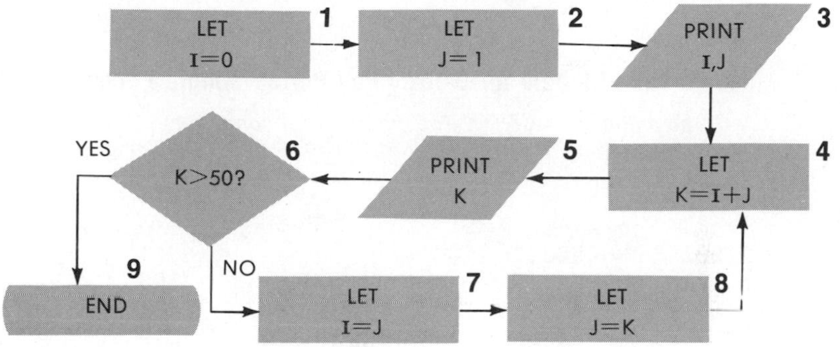

Computers in Business

By far the most widespread use of computers is in business. A common business application is calculating the payroll of a company. Perhaps the chief complication in determining an employee's take-home pay is deciding how much income tax to withhold from the salary.

PROBLEM: Suppose a company pays its employees each week. Then the withholding tax might be computed according to the following tables.

Income Tax Withheld for Weekly Pay Period: Single Person

If the amount of wages is:		*The amount of income tax to be withheld shall be:*	
Not over $27		0	
Over—	*But not over—*		*of excess over—*
$27	—$63	15%	—$27
$63	—$131	$5.40 plus 18%	—$63
$131	—$196	$17.64 plus 21%	—$131
$196	—$273	$31.29 plus 26%	—$196
$273	—$331	$51.31 plus 30%	—$273
$331	—$433	$68.71 plus 34%	—$331
$433		$103.39 plus 39%	—$433

Income Tax Withhold for Weekly Pay Period: Married Person

If the amount of wages is:		*The amount of income tax to be withheld shall be:*	
Not over $46		0	
Over—	*But not over—*		*of excess over—*
$46	—$127	15%	—$46
$127	—$210	$12.15 plus 18%	—$127
$210	—$288	$27.09 plus 21%	—$210
$288	—$369	$43.47 plus 24%	—$288
$369	—$454	$62.91 plus 28%	—$369
$454	—$556	$86.71 plus 32%	—$454
$556		$119.35 plus 37%	—$556

A flowchart is to be made to compute an employee's net pay and the amount of tax withheld. The input will be the employee's gross pay (P) for the week and a code number (M) indicating the employee's marital status (0 = single, 1 = married).

The program must first decide whether the employee is single or married. In either case a sequence of decisions must be used to determine which tax rate applies to this employee. The decisions can start either at the low end or the high end of the tables above. For example, one approach is the following, where T represents the tax to be withheld.

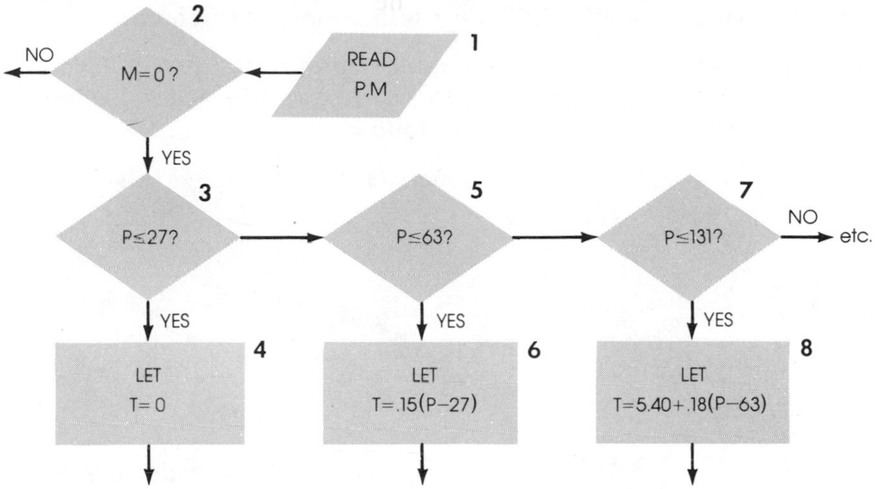

For the NO branch of box 2, a similar sequence of decisions is needed: P ≤ 46? P ≤ 127? P ≤ 210? and so forth. Regardless of which branch is taken, T is computed. Then the net pay (N) is calculated by subtracting the tax (T) from the gross pay (P). Finally, P, T, and N are printed. The program then returns to the top to read the data for the next employee.

Projects

1. Draw up the complete flowchart for the payroll problem above.
2. Expand the payroll flowchart in Project 1 as follows: Calculate the total gross pay of all employees, the total tax withheld, and the total net pay. Total gross pay (G) can be calculated by LET G = G + P . The other two totals can be computed by similar steps. In order to do this, put a code number, say 9999, along with another extra number, say 0, at the end of the DATA list. After reading P and M (box 1), insert a decision: P = 9999? . If the answer is YES, jump to a box which prints the total gross pay, tax, and net pay that have been accumulated. No ØUT ØF DATA? decision is used.

CHAPTER SUMMARY

Every computer system, large or small, can perform the functions of *input, storage, processing,* and *output.* Programs and data are entered into the system by means of a keyboard. The keyboard is usually part of a *terminal,* which may also include a television-like screen or a printer.

Before writing a program, a programmer often constructs a *flowchart,* which is a diagram of the steps to be followed in accomplishing a given task. The symbols used are as follows.

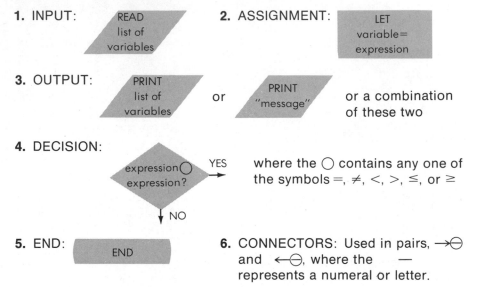

1. INPUT:

2. ASSIGNMENT:

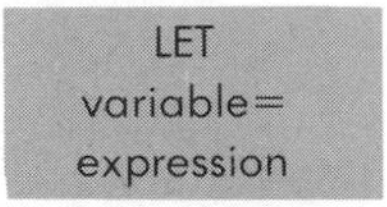

3. OUTPUT:

or

or a combination of these two

4. DECISION:

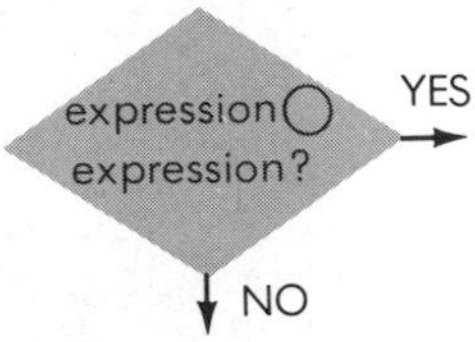

where the ○ contains any one of the symbols =, ≠, <, >, ≤, or ≥

5. END:

6. CONNECTORS: Used in pairs, →⊖ and ←⊖, where the — represents a numeral or letter.

A *trace* is used to check whether an algorithm gives correct results. For a trace, sample data are used and the programmer executes the steps of the flowchart, keeping track of the values of the variables.

Most flowcharts are constructed to handle numerous sets of data and therefore include an OUT OF DATA? decision.

CHAPTER OBJECTIVES AND REVIEW

Objective: To decide whether a given flowchart box is valid and, if it is not, to explain why it is not valid. *(Sections 1-2 and 1-4)*

State whether each box is a valid flowchart box. If not, explain why.

1.

2.

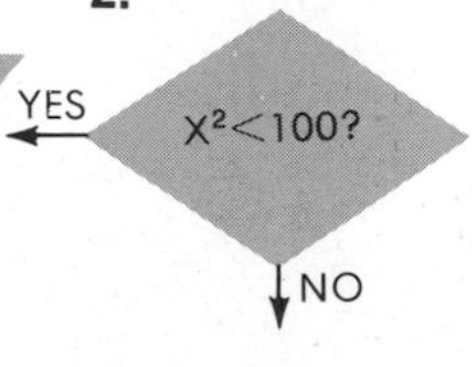

3.

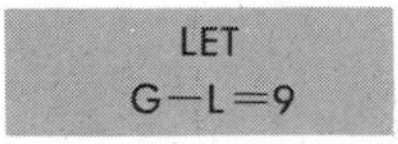

4.

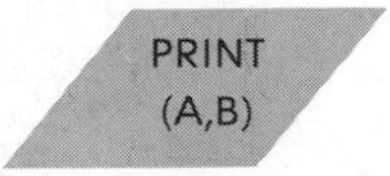

5.

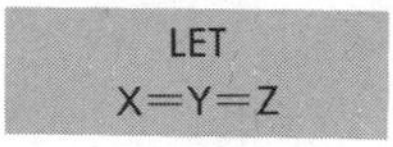

6.

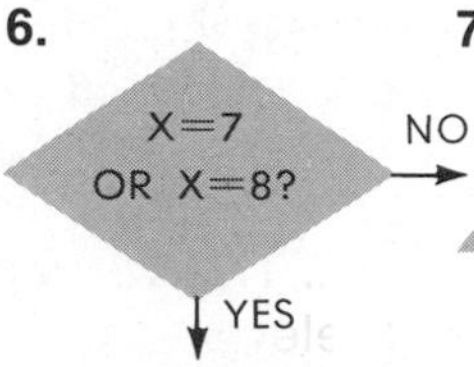

7.

8.

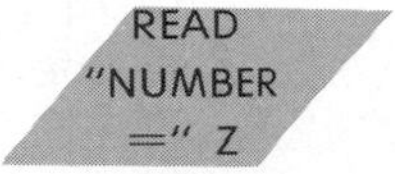

Objective: To draw a flowchart box or sequence of boxes to execute a given task. *(Section 1-3)*

Draw a flowchart box to execute each task.

9. Input values for the variables R, Y, and Z.
10. Test whether X is greater than 7.
11. Halt the program.
12. Assign to Y the sum of twice X and 7.
13. Output the message HELP!
14. Take the square of the number in location M and copy this square into location T.
15. Print the value in memory location P.
16. Accept a value for the variable K.

Construct a section of a flowchart that does what is stated each time.

17. If M = N, then print "ZERO"; otherwise, print "NOT ZERO".
18. Read X and Y. If X > Y, let Z = X; if X ≤ Y, assign Y to Z.
19. If $X^2 + 4X = 7$ is true, print X "IS A ROOT"; if it is false, END.
20. Print Y. If I > 10, go to the OUT OF DATA? decision box; otherwise read Y.

Objective: To complete a given partial flowchart. *(Sections 1-2 and 1-5)*

21. Hero's (or Heron's) Formula is used to compute the area of a triangle given the lengths of the sides. The formula is $\text{Area} = \sqrt{s(s-a)(s-b)(s-c)}$ where *a*, *b*, and *c* are the lengths of the sides and *s* is the "semiperimeter" (half the perimeter) of the triangle. Complete the partial flowchart below which, given the lengths of the sides, computes and prints the area.

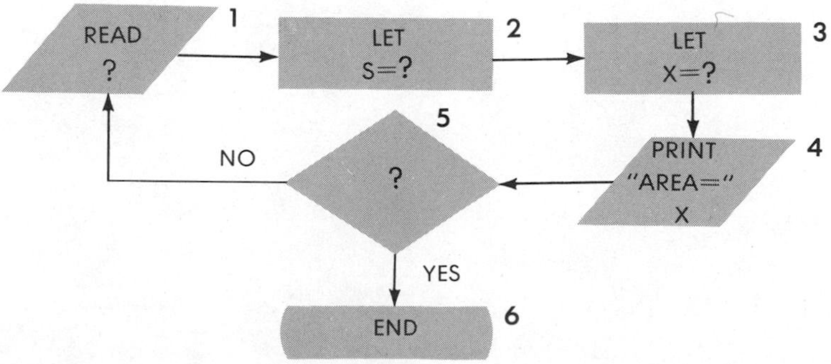

Objective: To trace a given flowchart either using given data values or making up data values that test all possible branches of the flowchart. *(Sections 1-3, 1-4, and 1-5)*

22. Trace the flowchart that you completed in Exercise 21. Use the following data list: 5, 4, 3, 4, 4, 6.

Objective: To determine whether a variable has its value in memory changed by a given flowchart box. *(Section 1-4)*

Write *Yes* or *No* to show whether each flowchart box below would change the value in Q.

23.

24.

25

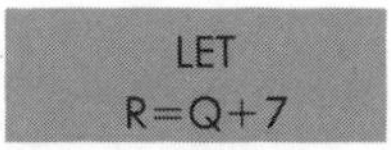

26.

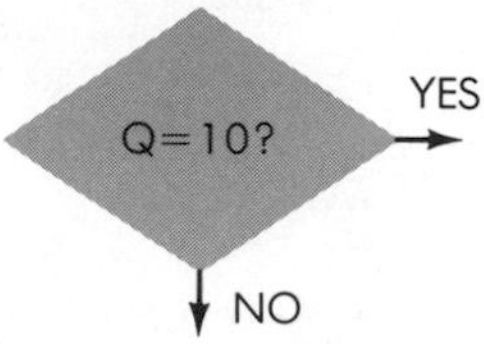

27.

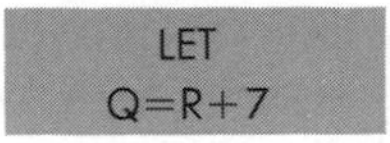

28.

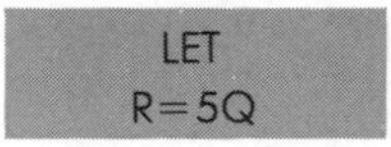

Objective: To draw a complete flowchart to solve a given problem, the flowchart to process many sets of data. *(Sections 1-4 and 1-5)*

29. Given the principal (P), the rate of interest (R), and the time of the investment in years (T), compute the amount of interest using the formula I = PRT.

Objective: To correct all errors in a given flowchart. *(Section 1-5)*

30. Correct all errors in the flowchart below.

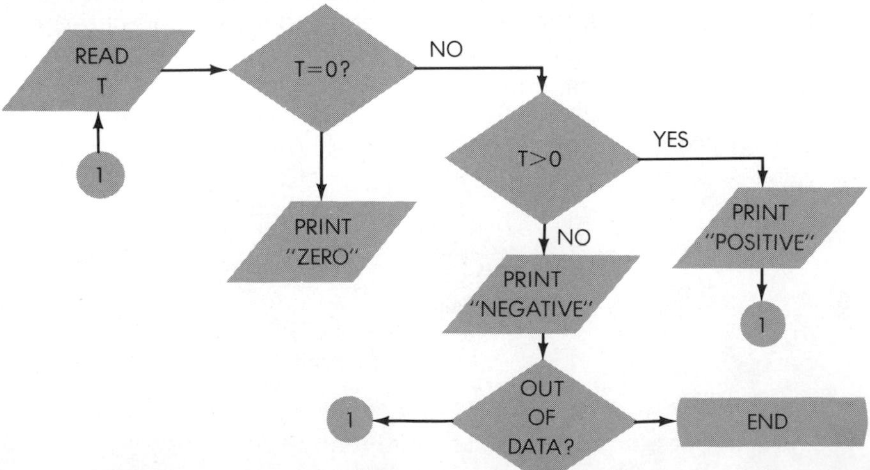

ROUND ONE: *FLOWCHARTS FOR STUDENT ASSIGNMENT*

GENERAL INSTRUCTIONS:

1. In each exercise on pages 31 through 39, draw a flowchart to handle as many sets of data as needed.
2. Include steps in the flowchart to handle all possibilities.
3. If your teacher requires it, trace the flowchart for a variety of data values. The data should be chosen so that each box of the flowchart is executed at least once. Regardless of the number of paths through the flowchart, the trace should process at least three sets of data.
4. Research may be necessary to learn the meaning of a word or to find the formula needed for a calculation.

ALGEBRA ONE

1. Read a real number. Print the number and its absolute value. (Assume that there is no "built-in" way for the computer to take the absolute value of a number.)
2. Find the slope of the line through two given points in the coordinate plane. Include the possibility that the slope may be undefined.
3. Input two real numbers. Without actually multiplying the numbers, determine whether their product is positive, negative, or zero.
4. Accept the coordinates of two points on the real number line. Subdivide the line segment determined by these two points into four equal subsegments. Print the coordinates of the endpoints of each segment.

   Example: Suppose the given points are 0 and 1. The endpoints of the subdivisions are 0, .25, .5, .75, and 1.
5. Read the coordinates of a point in the *xy*-plane. Decide the number of the quadrant in which the point lies or, if it lies on an axis, decide whether it lies on the *x*-axis, on the *y*-axis, or on both.
6. A die is tossed several times. Enter the number of ones, the number of twos, the number of threes, and so on, that turn up. Print the percent of tosses that are ones, the percent that are twos, and so on.
7. Given five real numbers, print only the smallest. Do not assume that the numbers are listed in the data in any special order.

In Exercises 8 through 11 read rational numbers A, B, and C, which are the coefficients of a linear equation of the form $Ax + By = C$. (Assume that A and B are not both zero.)

8. Compute and print the slope of the graph of the equation. Remember that the slope may be undefined.

9. Print the x-intercept of the graph as an ordered pair.

10. Print the y-intercept of the graph as an ordered pair.

11. Input real numbers R and S. Decide whether the point (R, S) lies on the graph of $Ax + By = C$.

12. Input a real number X. Print X, its additive inverse, and (if it has one) its multiplicative inverse.

13. Read real numbers A and B. Without computing A + B, decide whether the sum of A and B is positive, negative, or zero.

14. Given the number of a baseball team's wins and losses, compute its winning percentage. Assume that there are no ties.

15. Input the number of a team's wins, losses, and ties, and print its winning percentage. Assume that a tie game counts as a full game played and a half-game won.

16. Students in a certain course take two examinations. If a score is less than 40 on either exam, then the student fails the course. If the average on the two exams is below 60, the student also fails the course. An average of 60 to 90, inclusive, is passing (without honors). An average above 90 is passing with honors. Given a student's scores on the two exams, print whether he or she fails, passes (without honors), or passes with honors.

17. Arrange a set of three numbers in descending order. For example, for the data values 8, 11, −3, print 11 8 −3 . Two or three of the numbers may be equal.

18. Given a linear equation $Ax + B = C$ (A, B, C real numbers), solve for x. For example, if the equation is $7x + 5 = 19$, print X = 2.

19. Given an inequality $Ax + B > C$ (A, B, C real numbers), solve for x. For example, if the inequality is $7x + 5 > 19$, print $x > 2$.

GEOMETRY

20. Given the length of a side of a square, compute the perimeter.

21. Given the length of a side of a square, compute the area.

22. Given an angle measure greater than 0 and less than 180, classify the angle as ACUTE, RIGHT, or OBTUSE.

23. Given the lengths of any two sides of a right triangle, the Pythagorean Theorem enables you to compute the third side. Design a flowchart which finds the length of the missing side whether it is a leg or the hypotenuse. One way to accomplish this is to READ A, B, C but enter 0 for the unknown side. Then test whether A = 0, B = 0, or C = 0 and branch to one of three assignment steps to compute the missing length and print it.

24. Input the radius of a sphere and compute its volume.

25. Input the radius of a sphere and compute its surface area.

26. Accept L, the length of one side of an equilateral triangle, and compute the perimeter.

27. Accept L as defined in Exercise 26 and compute the area.

28. Read the measure of the vertex angle of an isosceles triangle. Print the measure of a base angle of the triangle.

29. Read three positive numbers A, B, and C. Determine whether these could be the lengths of the sides of a right triangle. (Note: You must first check that A, B, and C can be sides of *any* triangle.)

30. Input N, a positive integer denoting the number of sides of a polygon. Compute the sum of the measures of the interior angles of the polygon.

31. Input N as defined in Exercise 30. Assume that the N-gon is regular and print the measure of each interior angle.

In Exercises 32 and 33 triangle ABC is isosceles with AB = AC. Input the lengths of $\overline{BC}$ and $\overline{AB}$.

32. Compute the perimeter of the triangle.

33. Compute the area of the triangle.

34. Find the slant height of a regular square pyramid, given the length of a side of the base and the length of a lateral edge.

35. Given the coordinates of three points in the *xy*-plane, determine whether the points are collinear.

36. In Exercise 35, if the points are not collinear, decide whether the triangle formed by joining the three points is ISOSCELES, EQUILATERAL, or SCALENE.

37. In Exercise 35, if the points are not collinear, print the perimeter of the triangle formed by joining the three points.

38. Given the measures of two angles of a triangle, print the measure of the third angle.

In Exercises 39 and 40 triangles ABC and DEF are given. Read the lengths of the three sides of triangle ABC and the lengths of the three corresponding sides of triangle DEF.

39. Determine whether the triangles are congruent.

40. Determine whether the triangles are similar.

41. Read the lengths of the four sides of a quadrilateral. Determine whether the quadrilateral is equilateral.

42. Read the lengths of the five sides of a pentagon. Determine whether the pentagon is equilateral.

43. Given the coordinates of four points in the xy-plane, determine whether the quadrilateral formed by joining the points in order is a parallelogram.

44. Knowing the ratio of the measures of the angles of a triangle, determine the measure of each angle. For example, if the ratio of the angle measures is 2:3:4, input 2, 3, 4 as data.

In Exercises 45-48 right triangle ABC is given with altitude CD drawn to the hypotenuse AB. Let *a, b, c, h, x,* and *y* represent lengths as shown in the figure at the right below. Find each indicated length.

45. *a,* given *c* and *x* **46.** *h,* given *c* and *x*

47. *b,* given *a* and *h* **48.** *b,* given *h* and *x*

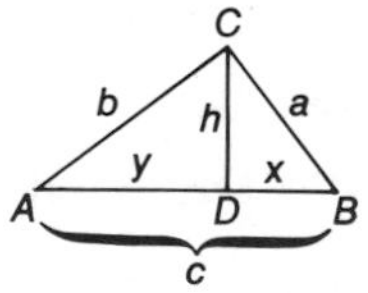

In Exercises 49 and 50 the coordinates of two points A and B in the coordinate plane are given.

49. Compute the length of segment AB.

50. Determine the coordinates of the midpoint of $\overline{AB}$.

51. Compute the perimeter of a triangle, given the lengths of its sides.

52. Compute the perimeter of a right triangle, given the lengths of the two legs.

53. Compute the perimeter of a right triangle, given the length of the hypotenuse and the length of one leg.

ALGEBRA TWO

54. A cubic polynomial function is defined by $y = Ax^3 + Bx^2 + Cx + D$ (A, B, C, D rational). Read A, B, C, D, and N. Compute *y* for $x = N$ and print N and *y*.

55. Given the coordinates of two points in the xy-plane, print the equation of the line through the two points.

In Exercises 56-59 A, B, and C are the real coefficients of quadratic equation $\text{A}x^2 + \text{B}x + \text{C} = 0$. Read A, B, and C.

56. Determine whether the equation has real roots. Print either REAL ROOTS or NO REAL ROOTS. Do not actually compute the roots.

57. Determine whether the equation has zero, one, or two real roots. Do not actually compute the roots.

58. Determine the sum and product of the roots without actually computing the roots. (This applies whether the roots are real or not.)

59. If the equation has one or more real roots, compute and print the root(s).

In Exercises 60-65, a system of linear equations is given as follows.

$$\begin{cases} \text{A}x + \text{B}y = \text{C} \\ \text{D}x + \text{E}y = \text{F} \end{cases}$$

Input the coefficients A, B, C, D, E, and F.

60. Determine whether the graphs of the equations are parallel. (Here "parallel to" means "having the same slope" so that parallel lines might coincide.)

61. Determine whether the graphs of the equations are perpendicular.

62. Determine whether the graphs intersect. If they do, do they intersect in one point or in infinitely many points?

63. Determine whether the solution set of the system is the null (empty) set, a one-element set, or an infinite set.

64. If the solution set has one element, print it as an ordered pair.

65. Determine whether the equations are consistent or inconsistent, and dependent or independent.

In Exercises 66-70, a parabola is defined by $y = \text{A}x^2 + \text{B}x + \text{C}$, $\text{A} \neq 0$. Read rational numbers A, B, and C. Then print the indicated item.

66. the coordinates of the vertex of the parabola

67. whether the vertex is a maximum or minimum point

68. the equation of the axis of symmetry

69. the coordinates of the focus

70. the equation of the directrix

71. Input a real number X such that $1 < \text{X} < 10^9$. Print X and the characteristic of its common logarithm. For example, if X = 73, print 73 1 .

72. The equation of an ellipse with its center at the origin is $\frac{x^2}{A^2}+\frac{y^2}{B^2}=1$. Read A and B (neither is zero) and print the coordinates of the foci of the ellipse. Remember that the foci sometimes are on the *x*-axis and sometimes are on the *y*-axis.

73. Solve absolute value equations of the form $|x - A| = B$ (A and B real).

74. Read a real number X. Print the cube root of X. Then, if X is nonnegative, print the principal fourth root of X. If X is negative, print NO REAL FOURTH ROOT.

75. Given a quadratic equation $ax^2 + bx + c = 0$ and a proposed real root R. Determine by substitution whether R is a root.

In Exercises 76-78 $f(X) = 3X + 4$ and $g(X) = X^2 - 14$.

76. Find $f(g(X))$ for X-values that you select.

77. Find $g(f(X))$ for X-values that you select.

78. Determine in each case whether $f(g(X)) = g(f(X))$.

79. Accept two ordered pairs that represent coordinates of two points and print the equation of the perpendicular bisector of the line segment determined by these points.

80. Compute and print the square roots of any real number including imaginary roots.

81. To input a complex number $A + Bi$, read A and B, the "real" and "imaginary" parts respectively. ("*i*" has no special significance to a computer; it is regarded as if it were just another real variable.) Compute and print the absolute value of $A + Bi$.

82. Given pure imaginary numbers Ai and Bi, read A and B and print the product of Ai and Bi.

ADVANCED MATHEMATICS

83. Test the addition of two-dimensional vectors to determine whether it is commutative.

84. Test the addition of two-dimensional vectors to determine whether it is associative.

85. Test the addition of three-dimensional vectors to determine whether it is commutative.

86. Test the addition of three-dimensional vectors to determine whether it is associative.

87. Input the lengths of the legs of a right triangle. Compute and print the values of the six trigonometric functions of either acute angle of the triangle.

88. An angle of rotation in standard position in the coordinate plane may have any measure, positive, negative, or zero. Read a measure M ($-360 \leq$ M ≤ 360); determine in which quadrant the terminal side of an angle with measure M lies or, if the terminal side lies on an axis, which part of which axis.

89. Given sin x and the quadrant in which x lies, compute and print (**a**) cos x, (**b**) tan x, (**c**) cot x, (**d**) sec x, and (**e**) csc x. Remember that tan, cot, sec, or csc may be undefined. Since SIN X may not be used as a variable in a flowchart, let S = sin x and READ S. Similarly use single letters for the other five trigonometric functions.

90. Compute and print the determinant of a 2×2 matrix $\begin{bmatrix} A & B \\ C & D \end{bmatrix}$.

In Exercises 91 and 92 an arithmetic sequence is given. Read A, the first term, D, the common difference, and N, a positive integer.

91. Print the Nth term of the sequence.

92. Print the sum of the first N terms of the sequence.

93. Input real numbers X and Y (X $\neq$ Y). Print three arithmetic means between X and Y.

In Exercises 94 and 95, a geometric sequence is given. Input A, the first term, R, the common ratio (R $\neq 1$), and N, a positive integer.

94. Print the Nth term of the sequence.

95. Print the sum of the first N terms of the sequence.

96. Given three consecutive terms of a sequence of real numbers, decide whether the sequence is arithmetic, geometric, or neither.

In Exercises 97 and 98, two two-dimensional vectors are given. Input the components of the two vectors.

97. Decide whether the vectors are perpendicular.

98. Decide whether the vectors are parallel.

99. Find the distance from a point to a line in the xy-plane, given the coordinates of the point and A, B, and C from the equation of the line, Ax + By + C = 0. Use the formula $d = \frac{|\text{A}x + \text{B}y + \text{C}|}{\sqrt{\text{A}^2 + \text{B}^2}}$. If $d = 0$, print that the point is on the line.

100. In the *xy*-plane, find the distance from a point to a line, given the coordinates of the point and the coordinates of two points on the line. (See Ex. 99, p. 37.)

101. Compute the distance between two points in a three-dimensional coordinate system.

In Exercises 102 and 103, S and T are the components of a given vector, $\vec{V} = (S, T)$. Read S and T.

102. Compute and print the norm of $\vec{V}$.

103. Input a scalar K and print the product $K\vec{V}$.

BUSINESS

104. Assume that the cost, not including tax, for sending a telegram from Chicago to Los Angeles is $4.50 for the first fifteen words or less, plus $0.15 for each additional word beyond fifteen. Design a flowchart that, given the number of words in a telegram (Chicago-Los Angeles), computes the cost of the telegram.

105. Assume that a baby-sitter works for a rate of $1.20 per hour until 11 P.M. and $1.80 per hour thereafter. Given the time that he or she begins and the time that he or she ends, compute the fee for an evening's work. (Hint: Input the times in terms of the twenty-four hour clock; e.g., for 7 P.M. input 1900.)

106. Input the sales and expenses of the Acme Trucking Company for the past year. Calculate the profit as sales minus expenses. Then compute the tax by the following rule.
If 0 < profit ≤ $20,000, the tax is 30% of the profit;
if profit > $20,000, the tax is 30% of the $20,000 plus 50% of the profit above $20,000;
if profit ≤ 0, the tax is zero.
Print the profit, the net tax, and the ratio of the tax to the profit.

107. Liberty Bank imposes a service charge based on the amount in an account at the end of the month.

Balance at end of month	Service change
$ 0-99	$ .75
100-199	.50
200-299	.25
300 or more	none

Given the ending balance in an account and the account number, print the service charge and the net amount in that account.

108. In a certain city taxis charge according to the following schedule: 95¢ for the first $\frac{1}{6}$ of a mile plus 30¢ for each additional $\frac{1}{6}$ of a mile. Read the distance traveled and print the total fare for the trip.

109. The monthly rates charged by Tiger Electric Company are as follows.

Base charge	$0.95
First 100 kwhrs of use	0.0985 per kwhr
Next 225 kwhrs	0.0885 per kwhr
Over 325 kwhrs	0.0785 per kwhr

Given the number of kilowatt hours (kwhrs), print the total monthly charge for electricity.

110. Employees of the Tiger Electric Company are given raises as follows: salespeople: 12%; production workers: 8%; managerial staff: 15%. Given an employee's payroll number, current weekly salary, and a code number (1, 2, or 3) indicating the job category of the worker, print the employee's new weekly salary.

PHYSICAL SCIENCES

111. Given the mass and velocity of an object, print its momentum and its kinetic energy.

112. Given the mass of an object moving in a circular path, its velocity, and the radius of the circle, compute the centripetal force.

113. Given the population of a city, state, or country at the beginning of a year and the population at the end of the year, print the percent of change in population. If there is a gain, print the message XX% INCREASE. If there is a loss, print XX% DECREASE.

114. Given the distance of an object from the center of a thin lens and given the focal length of the lens, calculate the distance of the object's image from the center of the lens and state whether the image is on the same side of the lens as the object or on the side of the lens that is away from the object.

115. Determine the number of calories needed to raise a given amount of H_2O (as ice, liquid water, or water vapor) from a given starting temperature (degrees Celsius) to a given final temperature. Assume normal atmospheric pressure.

116. Water (H_2O) can exist in any of three phases: solid, liquid, or gas. Two of the phases are mixed at standard atmospheric pressure and the mixture is allowed to reach equilibrium. Given the temperature (degrees Celsius) of each phase and the amount of H_2O in each phase, determine the final temperature of the mixture.

2

ELEMENTARY PROGRAMS

Beginning with this chapter and continuing throughout the rest of the book, you will learn how to write programs in the BASIC language. The flowcharts of Chapter 1 were prepared with BASIC in mind, so you should find it easy to move from flowcharting to programming.

2-1 AN EXAMPLE

We begin by studying the BASIC program shown at the right.

Let's take a closer look at this same program, making comments along the way.

Program 2-1

```
10 READ L,W
20 LET P=2*L+2*W
30 PRINT "PERIMETER = " P
40 DATA 6.5,2.3
50 END
```

This is a statement number (a positive integer).

Note this comma.

```
10 READ L,W
```

There is no punctuation at the end of a line.

These blank spaces are not necessary but make the reading easier.

On most systems the word "Let" may be omitted.

```
20 LET P=2*L+2*W
```

These are multiplication symbols, which must always be explicitly shown.

These are optional blanks.

"Print" means "print on the terminal."

```
30 PRINT "PERIMETER = " P
```

P *has a value from line 20 and that value is printed at this point.*

Some systems require a ";" here.

The computer will print everything between two quotation marks.

The first number will be read by the computer as the value of the first variable "L" in the READ *step.*

`40 DATA 6.5,2.3` ← *This second number will be read as the value for the second variable "W" in the* READ *step.*

This line supplies the data needed in the READ *step.*

`50 END` ← *This line tells the computer that there are no more lines in the program.*

Here is the BASIC program alongside the corresponding flowchart.

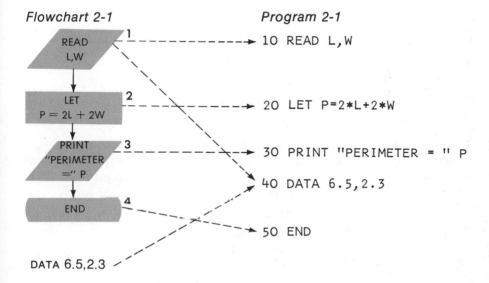

Flowchart 2-1

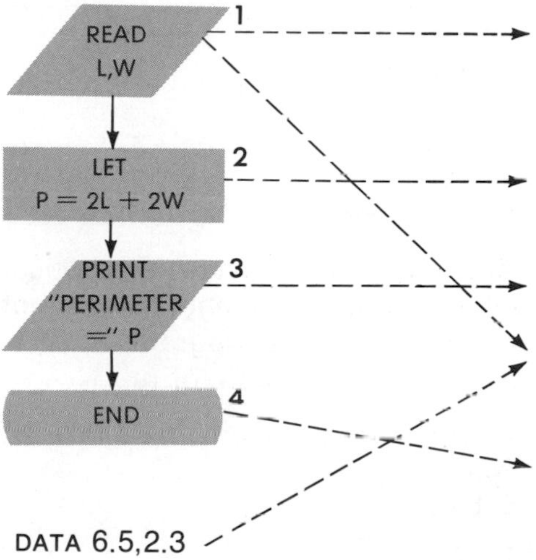

Program 2-1

```
10 READ L,W

20 LET P=2*L+2*W

30 PRINT "PERIMETER = " P
40 DATA 6.5,2.3

50 END
```

The dashed arrows show the relationship between the flowchart and the program steps. The READ box requires that there be both a READ statement and a DATA statement in the program.

There are many other correct ways of writing the above program. Here are some. Study each and notice how it differs from Program 2-1.

```
10 DATA 6.5, 2.3
20 READ L,W
30 LET P=2*L+2*W
40 PRINT "PERIMETER = " P
50 END
```

```
10 READ L, W
20 DATA 6.5, 2.3
30 LET P=2*L+2*W
40 PRINT "PERIMETER="P
50 END
```

```
10 READ L,W
20 LET P = 2*L + 2*W
30 DATA 6.5,2.3
40 PRINT "PERIMETER = " P
50 END
```

These alternate ways of writing the program emphasize these points.

1. The DATA step may appear anywhere in the program as long as it comes before the END statement.
2. After the statement number has been typed, blank spaces are ignored (with one exception mentioned below). The calculation step of Program 2-1 on page 40 could have been typed in many ways.

```
20LETP=2*L+2*W
20 LET P=2*L+2*W
20 LET P=2*L + 2*W
20 LET P = 2*L + 2*W
20 LET P = 2 * L + 2 * W
20 L E T P = 2 * L + 2 * W
```

On some systems the two versions shown below are *not* acceptable.

Do not indent a line.

```
 20 LET P=2*L+2*W
2 0 LET P = 2*L + 2*W
```

The computer may assume a zero here and hence read this as line "200."

There is one other area in a program where blank spaces are critical: in a message dictated between quotation marks in a PRINT statement. The following versions of the PRINT statement of the program would all print differently spaced messages (with the same value for P).

```
30 PRINT "PERIMETER=" P
30 PRINT "PERIMETER =" P
30 PRINT " PERIMETER = " P
30 PRINT "P E R I M E T E R = " P
```

EXERCISES 2-1

A Each of these programs contains at least one error. Identify each error and correct it. (If necessary, rewrite the entire statement or, if a statement has been omitted, write it with the proper number.)

1.
```
10 READ X;Y
20 LET P = X*Y
30 PRINT "RESULT IS" P
40 DATA 6,8
50 END
```

2.
```
10 LET R = 6
20 READ S
30 LET X = R+2*S.
40 PRINT X
50 END
```

3.
```
10 READ S
20 LET T=S*S;
30 PRINT SQUARE IS T
40DATA 6.8
50 END
```

4.
```
10 READ X,Y,Z,
20 LET A=(X+Y+Z)
30 PRINT "SUM = A"
40 DATA 821.3 287.6
50 END
```

5.
```
READ M,N
20 LET Q=MN+3
30 PRINT Q
40 DATA 78,61
50 END
```

6.
```
10 R E A D R
20 LET R*4=S
30 PRINT S
40 DATA 71
50 END
```

B Construct a flowchart that corresponds to each program.

7.
```
10 READ X
20 PRINT "NUMBER IS " X
30 LET Y = X*X
40 PRINT "SQUARE IS " Y
50 DATA -4
60 END
```

8.
```
10 LET P = 3.14159
20 READ D
30 LET C = P * D
40 PRINT C
50 DATA 10
60 END
```

In Exercises 9 and 10, write a program for the flowchart shown.

9.

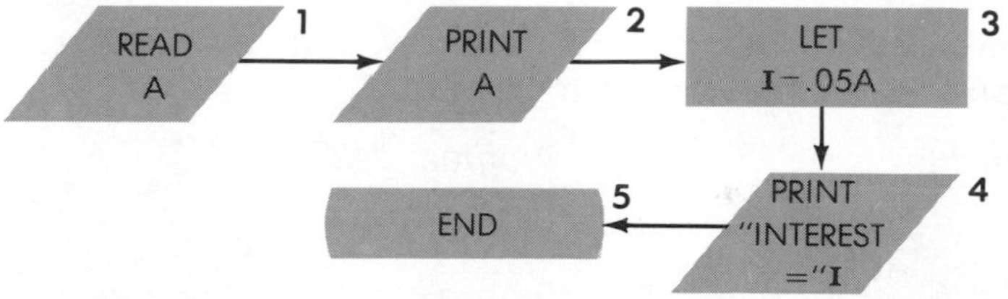

10.

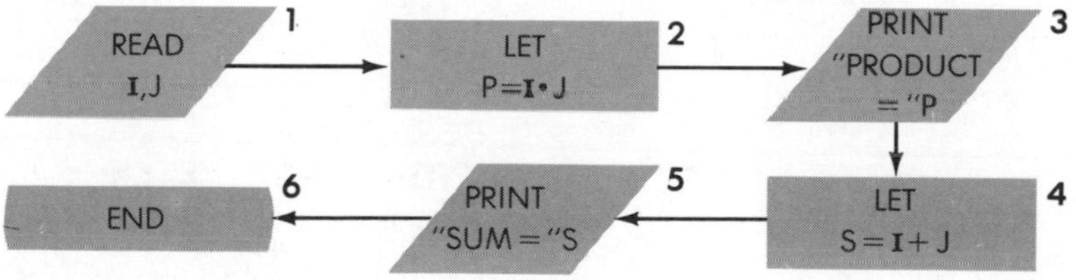

2-2 PROCESSING MORE THAN ONE SET OF DATA

Program 2-1 on page 40 processes just one set of data, that is, it computes the perimeter of only one rectangle. Suppose we want perimeters of several rectangles. Adding one step to the program allows us to process as many sets of length-width values as we wish.

Program 2-2

```
10 READ L,W
20 LET P=2*L+2*W
30 PRINT "PERIMETER = " P
40 GØ TØ 10
50 DATA 6.5,2.3,7.86,6.03,21,17
60 END
```

On many microcomputers, line 40 is written as GØTØ 10.

Comment:

In programming it is necessary to distinguish between the letter "O" and the digit "0" because these are two different keys on a card punch or on a terminal and are coded differently in the computer. Hence it is customary to put a slash through one of them to distinguish it from the other. In this book "Ø" will represent the letter and "0" the digit. On some terminals however, the reverse is true: "Ø" represents the digit and "0" the letter. On others, neither symbol is slashed.

The output from Program 2-2 will be as follows.

```
PERIMETER = 17.6
PERIMETER = 27.78
PERIMETER = 76

ØUT ØF DATA LINE # 10
```

This message will vary from system to system.

The flowchart for Program 2-2 is below, with the correspondence of boxes and statements shown by arrows.

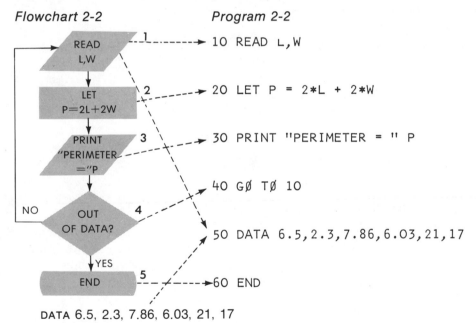

Flowchart 2-2 *Program 2-2*

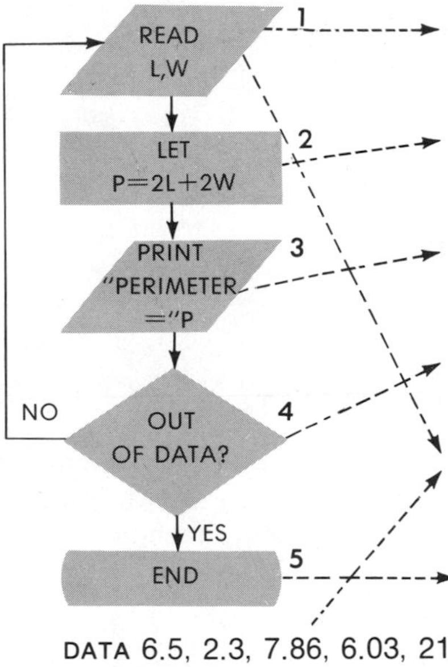


```
10 READ L,W
20 LET P = 2*L + 2*W
30 PRINT "PERIMETER = " P
40 GØ TØ 10
50 DATA 6.5,2.3,7.86,6.03,21,17
60 END
```

Each time the computer reaches the GØ TØ 10 step, it returns to the READ statement and inputs the next two items from the data list. Since there are six numbers in line 50, the computer calculates and prints three perimeters. The fourth time it returns to the READ step, it finds that there are no more numbers in the data list. The computer branches to the END statement and prints ØUT ØF DATA LINE # 10 or a similar message and stops.

There are five errors to be avoided in DATA statements.

1. Putting semicolons in place of commas. This would make the DATA statement of Program 2-2 on page 44 look like this.

```
50 DATA 6.5,2.3; 7.86,6.03; 21,17 <---- Wrong!
```

The temptation is to use the semicolon to group the pairs of length-width values. This may help the programmer organize his DATA but it will cause rejection of the program by the computer. 10 READ L,W will have the effect of grouping the data since the computer is thus instructed to read *two* data items at a time, calling the first L and the second W.

2. Grouping data with extra spacing. It would be erroneous to omit the commas in an attempt to group DATA.

```
50 DATA 6.5,2.3  7.86,6.03  21,17 <---- Wrong!
```

3. Putting operation signs in DATA lists. On many systems the statement

```
50 DATA 6.5,2.3,3/4,6.03,21,17
```

should be written as follows.

```
50 DATA 6.5,2.3,.75,6.03,21,17
```

4. Putting variables in DATA lists.
5. Including in DATA lists special characters such as $ or %. However, decimal points and negative signs are allowed.

If the data list is so long that it cannot fit on one line, it may be broken into several lines, but each line must be numbered and the word DATA repeated each time. For example, if the data values are 6.5, 2.3, 7.86, 6.03, 21, 17, 0.01, 2.34, 81.7, 6.43, 9.13, 10.2, 1.87, 61, 90, .23, 11.4, 67.54, 89.07, 34.2, and 45.06, then they should be entered in the program like this.

```
50 DATA 6.5,2.3,7.86,6.03,21,17,0.01,2.34,81.7,6.43,9.13
51 DATA 10.2,1.87,61,90,.23,11.4,67.54,89.07,34.2,45.06
```

On many systems a comma at the end of line 50 would not cause any error.

"Amazing! It would take four thousand mathematicians four thousand years to make a mistake like that!"

Drawing by Alan Dunn, © 1968. The New Yorker Magazine, Inc.

EXERCISES 2-2

A Correct any errors in these DATA statements.

1. `60 6.5,2.3,7.86,6.03,21,17`
2. `100 DATA 76,-81,2 .5,173`
3. `41 DATA $8.01,7.63,9.12;$8.42,61.01,10.30`
4. `80 DATA 12%,81%,14%, 18%,104%,61%,.5%`
5. `90 DATA 4,16,25,40,3,55,10,60,40,6,8,-7,9,12,11, 2,-5,1.1,5,1000,.03,20,10000,-5,1.1,5,1000,.03, 20,10000,.05,40,1,.50,50,2.25,35,1.5`
6. `20 DATA A,B,C`
7. 1,834,614 is one of the items in a DATA list. It is entered like this: 60 DATA 1,834,614 . How will the computer interpret this line?

Write a program for each of these flowcharts.

8. DATA 6, 4, −3, 7, 8, 8, 5, −2

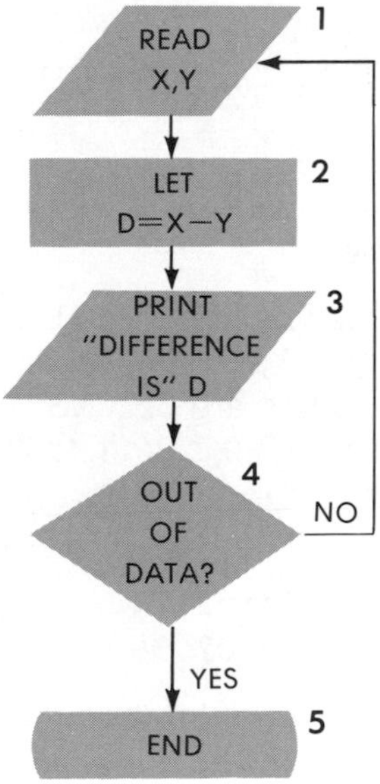

9. DATA 2, −3, 5, 0

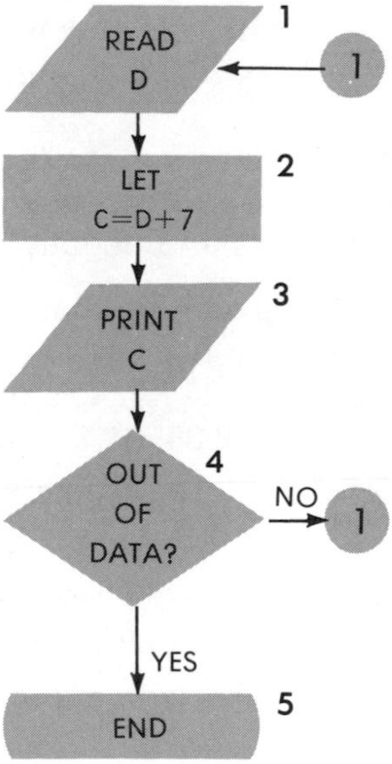

Flowchart each of these programs.

10.
```
10 READ S
20 LET T = S*S-S+7
30 PRINT T
40 GØ TØ 10
50 DATA 1,3,5
60 END
```

11.
```
5 DATA 6,8,-4,4,10,20
10 READ M,N
20 LET A = (M+N)/2
30 PRINT "AVERAGE = " A
40 GØ TØ 10
50 END
```

2-3 TRACING A PROGRAM

Just as a flowchart can be traced, so can a program be traced. The following trace illustrates the format to be used and the steps involved in tracing a program. The data listed in line 50 will be used.

Program 2-2

```
10 READ L,W
20 LET P=2*L+2*W
30 PRINT "PERIMETER = " P
40 GØ TØ 10
50 DATA 6.5,2.3,7.86,6.03,21,17
60 END
```

Table 2-1 Trace of Program 2-2

Step Number	Statement Number	Values of Variables L	W	P	Test	Yes or No?	Output
1	10	6.5	2.3				
2	20			17.6			
3	30						PERIMETER = 17.6
4	40				Out of Data?	No	
5	10	7.86	6.03				
6	20			27.78			
7	30						PERIMETER = 27.78
8	40				Out of Data?	No	
9	10	21	17				
10	20			76			
11	30						PERIMETER = 76
12	40				Out of Data?	Yes	
13	END						

The steps generally follow the procedure used for flowcharts, but a word of explanation is necessary for steps 4, 8, and 12 in the trace shown above. They correspond to line 40 of the program, GØ TØ 10. This is the only convenient point in the trace to show the ØUT ØF DATA? test which is performed inside the computer as it attempts to execute 10 READ L,W. A DATA statement never appears directly in the trace.

As in flowchart traces, when a value is entered in a column for a variable, it remains the value until a new numeral is entered in the column.

Now study a new program and its trace.

Program 2-3

```
10 LET P = 3.14159
20 READ R
30 DATA 5,7
40 LET C = 2*P*R
50 PRINT "CIRCUMFERENCE = " C
60 GØ TØ 20
70 END
```

Table 2-2 Trace of Program 2-3

Step Number	Statement Number	Values of Variables P	R	C	Test	Yes or No?	Output
1	10	3.14159					
2	20		5				
3	40			31.4159			
4	50						CIRCUMFERENCE = 31.4159
5	60				Out of Data?	No	
6	20		7				
7	40			43.98226			
8	50						CIRCUMFERENCE = 43.98226
9	60				Out of Data?	Yes	
10	END						

Given the radius, the program computes the circumference of a circle using the formula $c = 2\pi r$. The symbol "π" does not appear on the keyboard of standard card punches and terminals. Hence a constant approximating pi must be entered into the program. 3.14159 is suggested here since most BASIC systems use six significant digits. (Some versions of BASIC allow the word "PI" for 3.14159 in a program.) Since 3.14159 is a constant, we can eliminate line 10 and revise line 40 as follows: 40 LET C = 2 * 3.14159 * R.

EXERCISES 2-3

A

1. In Program 2-2 on the previous page, replace line 50 with 50 DATA 4, 5, 10, 7.5, 11, 3 . Now prepare a table like the one on the previous page and trace the program.
2. Draw a flowchart for Program 2-3 above.
3. In Program 2-3 replace line 30 with 30 DATA 2, 10 . Prepare a table like the one above and trace the program.

Prepare tables like the ones on pages 47 and 48 and trace each program.

4.
```
10 READ X,Y
20 LET A = X + Y
30 PRINT "SUM="A
40 GØ TØ 10
50 DATA 10,12,6,5,-4,8
60 END
```

5.
```
10 DATA 100,200,50
20 LET R = .05
30 READ P
40 LET I = P*R
50 PRINT "INTEREST = " I
60 GØ TØ 30
70 END
```

B

6. Prepare a flowchart for the program in Exercise 4.

7. Prepare a flowchart for the program in Exercise 5.

8. Trace the programs in Exercises 8 through 11 on page 46.

2-4 NUMBERING STATEMENTS

Program 2-2, shown again at the right, illustrates one reason for numbering the statements of a program: statements such as GØ TØ 10 refer to another line of the program and line 10 must be identified for the computer.

Program 2-2

```
10 READ L,W
20 LET P=2*L+2*W
30 PRINT "PERIMETER = " P
40 GØ TØ 10
50 DATA 6.5,2.3,7.86,6.03,21,17
60 END
```

The second reason for numbering statements results from a convenient editing capability of BASIC. The following example illustrates the possibilities. Suppose a student types Program 2-2 as follows.

```
10 READ L,W
20 LET P=2*L+2*W
30 PRINT "PERIMETER = " P
50 DATA 6.5,2.3,7.86,6.03,21,17
60 END
```

He has forgotten line 40. However, this is no problem; just type it now, numbering it "40." Externally, the program will look like this.

```
10 READ L,W
20 LET P=2*L+2*W
30 PRINT "PERIMETER = " P
50 DATA 6.5,2.3,7.86,6.03,21,17
60 END
40 GØ TØ 10
```

Inside the computer, the above lines are sorted into numerical order. Thus, line 40 is moved to its correct position in the program.

Before proceeding with this explanation, we stop to explain what a compiler is, because it is the compiler that allows us to add a statement at the end of the program as we have just done. Once entered into the computer system, a BASIC program is stored in memory where the BASIC compiler, part of the software of the system, "decodes" it. A *compiler* (or *interpreter*) is a program that translates a program from a source language such as BASIC to machine language, which is the only language the central processor can actually "understand" and execute. The compiler finds any errors of form or syntax, and also sorts the statements into numerical order before translating into machine language for execution. This ability of the compiler makes possible the editing procedures being explained in this lesson.

Why, in the programs shown thus far, are the statements numbered with multiples of 10? Why not type the program in the following ways?

Program 2-2A

```
1 READ L,W
2 LET P=2*L+2*W
3 PRINT "PERIMETER = " P
4 GØ TØ 1
5 DATA 6.5,2.3,7.86,6.03,21,17
6 END
```

Program 2-2B

```
18 READ L,W
71 LET P=2*L+2*W
213 PRINT "PERIMETER = " P
476 GØ TØ 18
812 DATA 6.5,2.3,7.86,6.03,21,17
999 END
```

To the compiler there is nothing wrong with these numberings. To understand why multiples of 10 are preferred, consider Program 2-2A. Suppose a student types the program in the manner shown below.

```
1 READ L,W
2 LET P=2*L+2*W
3 GØ TØ 1
4 DATA 6.5,2.3,7.86,6.03,21,17
5 END
```

He realizes that he has forgotten the PRINT statement. To add the omitted line, he must now type the correct version of line 3 and then retype the original lines 3, 4, and 5. His completed program, as it would look on the printer or screen, is shown on the next page.

```
1 READ L,W
2 LET P=2*L+2*W
3 GØ TØ 1
4 DATA 6.5,2.3,7.86,6.03,21,17
5 END
3 PRINT "PERIMETER = " P
4 GØ TØ 1
5 DATA 6.5,2.3,7.86,6.03,21,17
6 END
```

There are now two steps numbered "3," two numbered "4," and two numbered "5." When a statement is retyped, the compiler automatically replaces the earlier version of that line in memory with the later version. Hence a statement can be retyped as many times as necessary until it is correct.

If the lines of program 2-2A on page 50 had been numbered with multiples of 10, adding the omitted PRINT statement would have been easy.

```
10 READ L,W
20 LET P=2*L+2*W
30 GØ TØ 10
40 DATA 6.5,2.3,7.86,6.03,21,17
50 END
25 PRINT "PERIMETER = " P
```

By proceeding in this way the student does not have to retype lines 30, 40, or 50.

There is another rather important editing capability in BASIC programming: deleting a step. Suppose that a student types the program shown at the left below. She realizes that since she has only one data value to process, she does not need line 40. She can delete this line simply by typing "40" and leaving the remainder of the line blank. The completed program would then look like the one at the right below.

```
10 READ X
20 LET Y=8.6201*X*X
30 PRINT Y
40 GØ TØ 10
50 DATA 76.1
60 END
```

```
10 READ X
20 LET Y=8.6201*X*X
30 PRINT Y
40 GØ TØ 10
50 DATA 76.1
60 END
40
```

REMEMBER: In memory the lines of a program are stored in statement number order. The sequence in which the lines are typed is not significant.

EXERCISES 2-4

A State whether or not each of the programs below is equivalent to the program at the right. ("Is equivalent to" means "produces the same output as.")

```
10 READ X
20 LET S=X*X
30 PRINT S
40 DATA 7.26,8.91,6.081
50 GØ TØ 10
60 END
```

1.
```
10 READ X
30 PRINT S
40 DATA 7.26,8.91,6.081
50 GØ TØ TEN
60 END
20 LET S=X*X
```

2.
```
1 READ X
2 LET S=X*X
3 PRINT S
4 DAA
4 DATA 7.26,8.91,6.081
5 GØ TØ 1
6 END
```

3.
```
5 READ X
30 END
10 LETS=X*X
20 PRINT S
15 GØ TØ 5
25 DATA 7.26,8.91,6.081
```

4.
```
10READ X
20 LET S=X*X
30 PRINT S
40 DATA 7.26,8.91,6.081
50 END
```

What would be the output from each program below?

5.
```
10 READ J,K
20 LET S=J+K
30 GØ TØ 10
40 PRINT S
50 DATA 2,3,8,10,-6,14
60 END
```

6.
```
10 READ X,Y
20 LET Z=X+Y
30 PRINT "ANSWER IS " Z
40 DATA 8,-3,0,16,-2.7
45 DATA -6,8
50 END
```

Suppose a student has written the program at the right. He types this program on the keyboard but makes mistakes. He attempts to correct his errors. Which version(s) below, if any, is (are) equivalent to the program he wishes to run?

```
10 READ R
20 LET X=.5*R*R
30 PRINT X
40 DATA 86.1
50 END
```

7.
```
10 RA
10 READ R
20 LET X=.5*R
30 PRINT X
40DATA 86.1
50 END
20 LET X=.5*R*R
```

8.
```
1Ø READ R
10 READ R
20 LET X=.5*R*R
30 DATA 86.1
40 PRINT X
50 END
```

9.
```
10 READ R
20 PRINT X
30 LET X=.5*R*R
20
40 PRINT X
50 DATA 86.1
60 END
```

2-5 LEGAL VARIABLE NAMES AND SIGNS OF OPERATION

In all flowcharts and programs thus far, only single letters have been used for numerical variables. Actually, there are also two other types.

> A numerical variable may be denoted by:
>
> **1.** a single letter such as A, B, C, D, . . . , X, Y, Z,
> **2.** a letter followed by a single digit, for example, A0, A1, A2, . . . , Z8, Z9, or
> **3.** a subscripted variable such as X(I) or Y(J, K). (See Chapter 5.)

(Many microcomputer systems also allow double-letter variables, such as AA, AB, . . . , AZ.) Each variable used in a program corresponds to a distinct memory location chosen by the compiler.

Several signs of operation have already been introduced. Here is a complete list. Note that there are *three* symbols for exponentiation. However, each system uses just one of the three symbols.

Sign	**Operation**
+	addition
−	subtraction
*	multiplication
/	division
↑	exponentiation (raising to a power)
∧ or **	exponentiation (alternate symbols)

Every formula used in a program must lie in a single line, with no superscripts, subscripts, or built-up fractions.

Examples:

Algebra	**BASIC**
$t = \frac{d}{r}$	`10 LET T = D/R`
$y = x^2 + 3x - 7$	`10 LET Y = X↑2 + 3*X - 7`
$M = \frac{y_2 - y_1}{x_2 - x_1}$	`10 LET M = (Y2-Y1)/(X2-X1)`

The last example shows the need for parentheses in a LET statement.

What would be the algebraic equivalent of this BASIC statement?

```
10 LET M = Y2 - Y1/X2 - X1
```

To answer this question we need an understanding of the *hierarchy of operations* followed by the computer. This "hierarchy" is the order of precedence given to the symbols of a formula.

1. Operations within parentheses are worked out, from the innermost parentheses outward, from left to right. Within a set of parentheses follow the order given in steps 2, 3, and 4 below.
2. Exponentiations are performed, left to right.
3. Multiplications and divisions are performed in order from left to right.

   Multiplication and division are of equal standing. This rule does not mean that multiplications are worked out first, then divisions. It means that, after any exponentiations have been completed, the compiler scans the formula from left to right, working out multiplications or divisions as it hits either one. Addition and subtraction (step 4) are also of equal rank and are handled in a similar fashion.
4. Additions and subtractions are performed in order from left to right.

Example:

Identify the order of operations in the statement below.

```
20 LET S = (X - Y)/Z↑3 + X*Y - Z
```

Here is the formula again with numerals indicating the order in which the computer will perform the operations.

```
20 LET S = (X - Y)/Z↑3 + X*Y - Z
               1    3 2  5  4  6
```

Adding another pair of parentheses, like this:
20 LET S=((X−Y)/Z) ↑ 3 + X∗Y − Z changes the order to the following.

```
20 LET S = ((X - Y)/Z)↑3 + X*Y - 2
                1    2  3  5  4  6
```

(In BASIC neither brackets nor braces are used because they do not universally appear on terminal keyboards.)

Three "rules of thumb" will help you to write correct expressions.

1. Every expression must contain an *even* number of parentheses. The number of left parentheses must equal the number of right parentheses.
2. There is no way that two operation signs can appear next to each other. For example, A ∗ −B is not a valid expression but A ∗ (−B) is.
3. Multiplication signs are never understood.

ab	must be written	A∗B.
2(*x*+*y*)	must be written	2∗(X+Y).
(7+*a*)(*b*−6)	must be written	(7+A)∗(B−6).

EXERCISES 2-5

A Write *Yes* or *No* to tell whether each of the following is a legal BASIC variable name.

1. A	**2.** B	**3.** AB	**4.** SUM	**5.** (R)	**6.** AZ
7. Z23	**8.** X1	**9.** L.	**10.** 1X2	**11.** K9	**12.** Z0
13. TØ	**14.** 42G	**15.** 7B	**16.** E2	**17.** .Y	**18.** R+S

Shown below are a number of mathematical expressions and corresponding BASIC expressions. Each BASIC expression contains at least one error. Correct each error, rewriting the expression if necessary.

19. $\frac{x+2}{y+4}$; X + 2/Y + 4 **20.** $\frac{ab}{c+2}$; AB/(C + 2)

21. $\left(\frac{x+a}{2z}\right)^2$; (X + A)/(2*Z) ↑ 2 **22.** $\left(\frac{x}{y}\right)^{n-1}$; (X/Y) ↑ N−1

What is the order of evaluation in each of the following BASIC expressions? As in the example on page 54, place a numeral under each sign to show the correct order.

23. B ↑ 2 − 4*A*C **24.** A/B/C*D **25.** −B/2*A
26. A/C*B/D **27.** A ↑ B/3 **28.** A+(C−D*(X/3+Y/2) ↑ 2)+6

For each of the following expressions, write a single BASIC statement that will compute each quantity. Start each statement with 10 LET Z = . . .

29. $3b - 2c$ **30.** $\frac{c-d}{3}$ **31.** $\frac{n-7}{6.5+m}$ **32.** $x + y^3$

33. $x^{\frac{1}{2}}$ **34.** $-a + \frac{b}{c+d}$ **35.** $\frac{7}{-ab}$

36. $\left(\frac{a+b}{c+d}\right)^2 + x^2$ **37.** $\frac{xy}{3}$ **38.** $(c-d)(m+n)$

If A = 3, B = 5, and C = 2, what value is assigned to X by each of these LET statements?

39. 20 LET X = A + B * C **40.** 30 LET X = A * B + C
41. 25 LET X = A + B/C **42.** 60 LET X = (A + B)/C
43. 50 LET X = A + C↑2
44. 15 LET X = (A + C)↑2
45. 70 LET X = A/B + C
46. 80 LET X = A/B*C
47. 85 LET X = A/(B*C)
48. 90 LET X = A + B / C + 7
49. 60 LET X = A + B / C ↑ 2
50. 40 LET X = (A + B)↑2/(B - C)↑2

B 51. Two resistors, with resistances R_1 and R_2, are connected in parallel. The equivalent resistance between the input point and the output point is given by the formula $R = \dfrac{R_1 R_2}{R_1 + R_2}$. Write a LET statement containing this formula.

2-6 TAKING ROOTS

In programming there is no radical sign ($\sqrt{\ }$) because this symbol usually does not appear on computer keyboards. The corresponding fractional power must be used to compute a root, as the following examples show.

$y = \sqrt{x}$ becomes
```
10 LET Y = X↑(1/2) or
10 LET Y = X↑.5
```

$y = \sqrt[3]{x}$ becomes
```
10 LET Y = X↑(1/3)
```

$y = \sqrt[4]{a + 7}$ becomes
```
10 LET Y = (A + 7)↑(1/4) or
10 LET Y = (A + 7)↑.25
```

In algebra, great care is taken to define when a radical expression may be legitimately used, that is, when it names a real number. For example, $\sqrt{x}$ names a real number if $x = 4$ but not if $x = -4$. Since computers deal only with real numbers, fractional powers may be computed only when the expression names a real number.

For example, if x = −4, the following expressions would *not* name real numbers and would cause some type of error message during execution of a program.

x ↑ .5   x ↑ .25   x ↑ (1/6)   x ↑ (3/4)   x ↑ (5/2)   etc.

Thus, no fractional powers may be computed if the numerator is odd, the denominator even, and the base negative.

For x = −4, the following expressions *would* yield real numbers and are acceptable.

x ↑ (1/3)   x ↑ (1/5)   x ↑ (3/7)   etc.

Thus, odd roots of negative numbers are real numbers and can be computed.

CAUTION: Computing powers is an area of BASIC where systems differ from one another. Consult the manual for your system and experiment with a variety of power expressions and values to see which ones are accepted and what results are printed each time. (See Ex. 24, p. 57.)

EXERCISES 2-6

A Write each of these formulas in a LET statement.

1. $z = \sqrt[5]{x}$ **2.** $z = \sqrt{x^2 - y^2}$

3. $z = \sqrt{y + 2x}$ **4.** $z = \sqrt{2xy - 6}$

5. $z = \dfrac{\sqrt[3]{7}}{x}$ **6.** $z = \dfrac{4.5}{\sqrt{8.6}}$

7. $z = \dfrac{1}{1 + \sqrt{x}}$ **8.** $z = \sqrt[4]{\dfrac{x}{3}}$

9. $z = \dfrac{1 - 2\sqrt{x}}{3\sqrt{x} + 2}$ **10.** $z = \sqrt{\dfrac{x + 5}{4 - x}}$

11. A student writes $y = \sqrt{x}$ in a BASIC statement like this.

```
10 LET Y = X↑1/2
```

Will this statement actually assign to Y the principal square root of X? If not, what is computed by the right side of the assignment statement?

B If X = −8, which of these LET statements would produce an error message because the right side would not yield a real number?

12. `20 LET Z = X↑.5` **13.** `30 LET Z = X↑(1/3)`
14. `50 LET Z = (X↑2)↑.5` **15.** `60 LET Z = -X↑.5`
16. `45 LET Z = (-X)↑.5` **17.** `90 LET Z = X↑(1/X)`

State whether each BASIC expression below is defined for all values of X. If an expression is not always defined, state the value(s) of X for which it is not defined.

Example: X ↑ .5 **Answer:** Undefined for X < 0

18. X ↑ (1/9) **19.** X ↑ (2/3)
20. 0 ↑ (−X) **21.** X ↑ (3/2)
22. X ↑ 0 **23.** (−X) ↑ .5

C **24.** Run the program below on your system and note what value or error message is printed for each set of data. Also notice whether an error terminates the run or whether the system processes the remaining data anyway. Also note if any mathematically incorrect answers are printed for Y.

```
10 READ N,X
20 LET Y = X ↑ (1/N)
30 PRINT N,X,Y
40 GØ TØ 10
50 DATA 2,4,2,-4,2,0,3,8,3,-8,3,0,0,6,6,0,-4,0
60 END
```

2-7 ERRORS IN LET STATEMENTS

This program contains an error associated with line 20.

```
10 READ X,Y
20 LET Q = X + Y - 2*Z
30 PRINT Q
40 DATA 61,-83
50 END
```

The variable Z has not received a value. In some languages this would cause rejection of the program. In BASIC, however, most compilers automatically assign a value of zero to a variable that is otherwise undefined. What then would be the output of the above program?

Another common error is illustrated by the following program involving the Pythagorean Theorem.

```
10 READ A,B
20 LET C↑2 = A↑2 + B↑2
30 PRINT C↑2
40 DATA 6.3,8.9
50 END
```

The error lies in line 20: the expression to the left of = in a LET statement may not contain an operation sign. A LET statement is called an *assignment* statement. Recall the explanation of the assignment box in chapter one. In the statement 20 LET X = Y + 2 * Z, the value of Y + 2 * Z is being assigned to the variable X. The left expression in an assignment statement must be simply a variable name.

The program above should be written as follows.

```
10 READ A,B
20 LET C = (A↑2 + B↑2)↑.5
30 PRINT C
40 DATA 6.3,8.9
50 END
```

EXERCISES 2-7

A State whether each of the following is a valid LET statement.

1. 20 LET Z1 = 7
2. 40 LET 9 = C
3. 80 LET Z = A + B
4. 90 LET A + B = Z
5. 100 LET X = Y = 0
6. 120 LET C/2 = A/2

Correct all errors in the following programs.

7.
```
10 READ S, T, U
20 LET R + S = T + U
30 PRINT R
40 DATA 76.891,-3.074
50 END
```

8.
```
5 READ A, B, C
10 LET P = A/B + C/D
20 PRINT P
30 DATA 7, 1, 3, 2, 8
999 END
```

Write a program for each of the following.

9. Given the lengths of the legs of a right triangle, compute the length of the hypotenuse.

10. Given the lengths of the hypotenuse and one leg of a right triangle, compute the length of the other leg.

C State whether each of the following is a valid LET statement.

11. 95 LET C = C + 1

12. 80 LET A = 2*A

13. 100 LET X = Y↑2 + X

14. 20 LET N = N - 1

If, when line 50 is reached in the program, I = 10, what value is assigned to I by each of these statements?

15. 50 LET I = I + 1

16. 50 LET I = I - 1

17. 50 LET I = I - 2

18. 50 LET I = I + 2

19. 50 LET I = 2*I

20. 50 LET I = I↑2

2-8 CALCULATIONS IN A PRINT STATEMENT

A feature of BASIC that we shall now discuss allows the alert programmer to save a step by putting a formula into a PRINT statement. This principle is applied to Program 2-1 (perimeter of a rectangle).

Program 2-1 (page 40)

Old Version
```
10 READ L,W
20 LET P = 2*L + 2*W
30 PRINT "PERIMETER = " P
40 DATA 6.5,2.3
50 END
```

New Version
```
10 READ L,W
20 PRINT "PERIMETER = " 2*L + 2*W
30 DATA 6.5,2.3
40 END
```

The variable P is not needed in the new version. In fact it would be *incorrect* to write a PRINT statement such as the following one: 20 PRINT P = 2 * L + 2 * W . However, the following statement *would* be acceptable: 20 PRINT "P = " 2 * L + 2 * W . The quotation marks make P = a message to the computer and not a part of the formula.

This new technique is not recommended if the perimeter is needed in a later step of the program. In this case use the original method and store the perimeter in location P for further use. For example, suppose the perimeters of two rectangles must be computed and added. Then the following program could be used.

Program 2-4A

```
10 READ L1,W1
20 LET P1 = 2*L1 + 2*W1
30 PRINT "1ST PERIMETER = " P1
40 READ L2,W2
50 LET P2 = 2*L2 + 2*W2
60 PRINT "2ND PERIMETER = " P2
70 PRINT "SUM ØF PERIMETERS = " P1 + P2
80 DATA 6,4,10,9
90 END
```

The values for P1 and P2 are needed in line 70. Hence it is wise to use LET statements 20 and 50 to compute *and store* the two perimeters.

Compare version A of the program with version B.

Program 2-4B

```
10 READ L1,W1
30 PRINT "1ST PERIMETER = " 2*L1 + 2*W1
40 READ L2,W2
60 PRINT "2ND PERIMETER = " 2*L2 + 2*W2
70 PRINT "SUM ØF PERIMETERS = " 2*L1+2*W1 + 2*L2+2*W2
80 DATA 6,4,10,9
90 END
```

Notice in version B how a programmer must type the expressions in line 70

$$2 * L1 + 2 * W1 \text{ and } 2 * L2 + 2 * W2$$

twice each. For expressions that are longer than these it becomes even more advisable to use a LET statement to compute and store a value in a location, such as P1 or P2. The programmer can then simply refer to the stored variable or variables from that point on in the program.

You may also print a constant, as illustrated below.

```
50 PRINT 1
60 PRINT "X = " 7
30 PRINT 0 " IS THE SØLUTIØN"
```

EXERCISES 2-8

A State whether each of the following is a valid PRINT statement.

1. `35 PRINT -4` **2.** `10 PRINT A↑2 + B↑2`

3. `20 PRINT X = R + S` **4.** `97 PRINT "RØØT IS " O`

5. `98 PRINT "RØØT IS O"` **6.** `99 PRINT "RØØT IS" ZERØ`

In Exercises 7-14, C = 8, D = 7, and E = 5. Show what will be printed by each of the PRINT statements.

Example: `90 PRINT "RESULT = " C + D - E`
Answer: `RESULT = 10`

7. `110 PRINT C - 6`
8. `15 PRINT C * D + E`
9. `20 PRINT "X = " D/E`
10. `90 PRINT D/E " = D/E"`
11. `30 PRINT D "/" E " = " D/E`
12. `40 PRINT 2 * C + E↑2`
13. `25 PRINT C " + " D`
14. `50 PRINT C + D " = " C " + " D`

15. Rewrite the program for Exercise 9 on page 59 so that it does not contain a LET statement.
16. Rewrite the program for Exercise 10 on page 59 so that it does not contain a LET statement.

B **17.** Let us now agree to allow in flowcharts the same shortcut as in BASIC: calculations in a PRINT statement (box). Hence for Program 2-4A on page 60, line 70 would correspond to the box at the right. With this agreement in mind, make a flowchart for Program 2-4A.

7

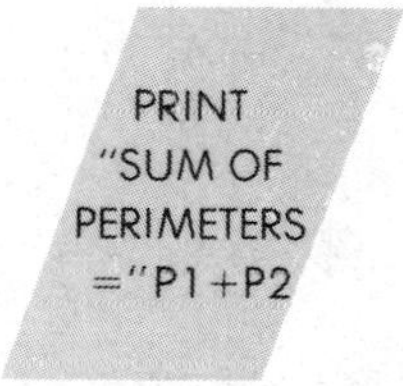

18. Trace Program 2-4A.

For each problem below write a two-step program that uses no variables.
19. Compute the number of seconds in a week.
20. Compute the number of minutes in a 30-day month.
21. Compute the number of seconds in a 30-day month.
22. Calculate the number of seconds in one 365-day year.

2-9 "INPUT" STATEMENTS

The READ statement causes data to be read from a DATA list that has already been placed in the program itself. The INPUT statement allows a user to enter data while the program is being run.

Examples:

```
10 INPUT X          20 INPUT A, B, C
50 INPUT R1,R2
```

When the computer reaches an INPUT statement in a program, it shows a "?" on the terminal and waits for the user to type the required values. Once this is done, program execution continues.

Often the INPUT statement is preceded in the program by one or more PRINT statements that explain to the user what he is to do.

Example:

Program 2-5

```
10 PRINT "PRØGRAM CØMPUTES PERIMETER ØF A RECTANGLE."
20 PRINT "GIVE THE LENGTH AND WIDTH ØF THE RECTANGLE."
30 INPUT L,W
40 PRINT "THE PERIMETER IS " 2*L + 2*W
50 END
```

Lines 10 and 20 inform the user that he is to type two values and what these values signify. The program's output is shown below.

```
PRØGRAM CØMPUTES PERIMETER ØF A RECTANGLE.
GIVE THE LENGTH AND WIDTH ØF THE RECTANGLE.
?
```

At this point the user types two numerals separated by commas. (Some systems allow numerals to be separated by blank spaces when an INPUT command is being executed.) Then he hits the RETURN or the ENTER key. The remainder of the program is then executed. A complete printout from Program 2-5 might look like this.

```
PRØGRAM CØMPUTES PERIMETER ØF A RECTANGLE.
GIVE THE LENGTH AND WIDTH ØF THE RECTANGLE.
? 7,6
THE PERIMETER IS 26
```

If "45 GØ TØ 30" were put into Program 2-5, the computer would type another "?" and wait for new values for L and W. The program would contain an infinite loop. On most systems the run could be ended by pressing the ESC (escape) key or the BRK (break) key.

In many programs an INPUT statement is preceded by one or more PRINT statements that prompt a desired response. For that reason, many BASIC systems allow a message in the INPUT command itself.

Examples:

```
10 INPUT "GIVE THE LENGTH AND WIDTH.";L,W
5 INPUT "WHAT IS YØUR AGE";A
```

In the second example no "?" is included in the message between quotation marks because the INPUT statement will automatically print a "?" to tell the user to enter one or more data values.

For the time being a user must enter only numerals to an INPUT command. (Handling alphabetical data will be explained in Chapter 7.) For example, if a program asks the question WHAT IS YØUR AGE? the response should be just 18 and not I AM 18 or 18 YEARS ØLD . Most systems would respond to either of these last two inputs with ILLEGAL CHARACTER or some such error message. Some versions of BASIC would then stop the program while others would repeat the INPUT command and give the user another chance to give a valid response.

EXERCISES 2-9

A Write *Yes* or *No* to show whether each of the following is a valid BASIC statement for your system.

1. `10 INPUT X`
2. `5 INPUT X,`
3. `5 INPUT D,E`
4. `20 INPUT C?`
5. `12 INPUT A;B;C`
6. `10 INPUT "GIVE THE LENGTH ØF A SIDE";S`
7. `20 INPUT "WHAT IS THE NUMBER?"`
8. `30 INPUT "ENTER THE LENGTH AND WIDTH.";L,W`

Below are computer-user dialogs with each "?" signaling the execution of the command INPUT N. What is wrong with each response?

9. `HØW MANY CHILDREN DØ YØU HAVE? I HAVE 4.`
10. `WHAT IS YØUR ANNUAL INCØME? $9000`
11. `WHAT IS YØUR ANNUAL INCØME? 8,500`

12. As shown on the right, an INPUT command can be placed in a flowchart just like a READ command. Make a flowchart for Program 2-5.

13. Trace the program below. Choose any appropriate value for S.

```
10 PRINT "INPUT LENGTH ØF A SIDE ØF THE SQUARE."
20 INPUT S
30 LET A = S*S
40 LET P = 4*S
50 PRINT "AREA = " A
60 PRINT "PERIMETER = " P
70 END
```

2-10 FUNCTIONS

Many calculations involve standard mathematical functions such as sine, cosine, log, etc. BASIC handles a number of functions, provided they are abbreviated correctly. Each function is designated by a three-letter code.

Function	*Explanation*
ABS(X)	absolute value of *x*
SQR(X)	square root of *x* ($x \geq 0$)
SIN(X)	sine *x*, *x* measured in radians
CØS(X)	cosine *x*, *x* measured in radians
TAN(X)	tangent *x*, *x* measured in radians
ATN(X)	arctangent *x*, answer in radians
CLG(X)	common logarithm (base ten) of *x*

(Note: The system you are working with may use different abbreviations for some of these functions and undoubtedly has others not listed here. Consult the manual that explains your system.)

In the list above, X is used as the "argument" of each function. Actually the argument may be any valid BASIC expression and may even itself contain a function. (On most systems, principal values are given for the arctangent function. These values are between $-\frac{\pi}{2}$ and $\frac{\pi}{2}$.)

Correct statements:

```
10 LET Y = SIN(2*A)
25 PRINT CØS(P+Q)
50 LET Z = SQR(TAN(X))
15 PRINT ABS(X) + CLG(Y↑2 - 6.1)
```

There is no way one of these functions could correctly appear to the left of the equal sign in a LET statement. Nor could a function occur in a READ statement.

Incorrect statements:

```
20 LET SIN(X) = SQR(1 - CØS(X) * CØS(X))
35 LET ABS(X) = (A - B)/2
15 LET CLG(Y*Z) = CLG(Y) + CLG(Z)
25 READ ABS(X)
```

In each of these incorrect statements, a legitimate variable, such as *R* or *S*, should be substituted for SIN(X), ABS(X), or CLG(Y*Z). A message in a PRINT statement can be used to label R or S correctly as "SINE" or "ABSØLUTE VALUE" or "LØG".

EXERCISES 2-10

A State whether each of the following is a valid BASIC statement.

1. `20 LET ABS(X) = -X`
2. `30 LET Y = SQR Z`
3. `15 PRINT ABS VALUE (R - 1)`
4. `50 PRINT SQRT(M*N)`
5. `25 LET M = SQR(ABS(N+7)`
6. `60 PRINT "SQUARE RØØT = " SQR(Z)`
7. `5 READ X, SQR(X)`
8. `70 LET X2 = ABS(SQR(X) - 6*X)`
9. `35 LET SQ. ØF DISC = SQR(B↑2 + 4*A*C)`
10. `255 PRINT "ABSØLUTE VALUE ØF" A " = "ABS(A)`

Write a LET statement for each of these formulas.

11. $y = |x|$
12. $z = \sqrt{-x}$
13. $t = |2r - 3|$
14. $x = \sqrt{7 + 6v}$
15. $z = \sqrt{|e + g|}$
16. $c = \sqrt{a^2 + b^2}$
17. $m = |x| - 7$
18. $v = |6x| - |x + 9|$

B Correct any errors in these BASIC expressions.

19. `SINE(X) + CØS(3*Z↑2)`
20. `TAN*SIN(Y) - 8.312*ATN(-1)`
21. `SIN↑2(X) + CØS↑2(X)`
22. `SQR(TAN(P+Q) - CLG(16*Z)`

Write a LET statement for each of these formulas.

23. $q = \dfrac{1 - \sin x}{1 + \sin x}$
24. $c = 2r \sin \frac{1}{2}\theta$
25. $s = a \sin kw - b \cos kw$
26. $y = \dfrac{1}{1 + |\tan x|}$
27. $f = \cos^2 x + 1$
28. $c = \log_{10}(x + \sqrt{x^2 + 1})$

Check the accuracy of several of the BASIC functions on your system by writing and running the following programs.

29. Calculate and print $\sin^2 x + \cos^2 x$ for x values between 0 and 1, inclusive.
30. Calculate and print $(\sqrt{x})^2$ for positive x values. Do not choose just integers for x.

C 31. Design a BASIC program directing the computer to solve the equation

$$\tan^2 x - 3 \tan x + 2 = 0 \text{ for } -\frac{\pi}{2} < x < \frac{\pi}{2}.$$

Computers in the Physical Sciences

Most "glamorous" applications of computers are in the physical sciences. Space shots to the moon, Mars, Jupiter, and Saturn rely on computers to plot the course and control the photographic, telescopic, and other recording equipment on board.

The simplest scientific applications involve the use of standard formulas from physics or chemistry. Often the challenge of programming the solution of a problem lies in finding the right formula and solving it for the unknown variable.

PROBLEM: The period T (in seconds) of a simple pendulum of length L (in meters) is given by $T = 2\pi\sqrt{\frac{L}{g}}$, where g is the gravity constant (in meters/second^2). Given L and g, compute T.

Program

```
10  READ L, G
20  LET T = 2 * 3.14159 * SQR(L/G)
30  PRINT "FØR A SIMPLE PENDULUM ØF LENGTH " L " METERS,"
40  PRINT "THE PERIØD IS " T " SECØNDS."
50  GØ TØ 10
60  DATA 10, 9.8, 24.8, 9.79, 12, 9.6
70  END
```

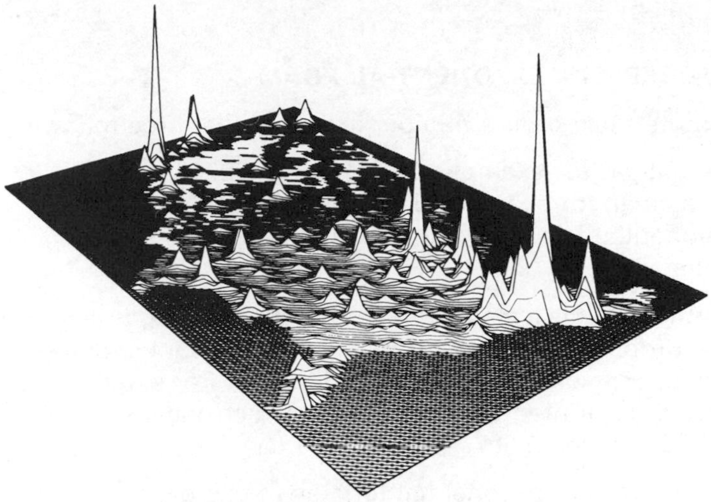

This three-dimensional graphic of population density was drawn by a computer.

The program was straightforward because the formula (line 20) was already solved for T. But suppose the problem is changed so that T and g are given, and L must be found. Now the formula must be solved for L, as follows.

$$T = 2\pi\sqrt{\frac{L}{g}}$$

$$\frac{T}{2\pi} = \sqrt{\frac{L}{g}} \longleftarrow \text{Divide both sides by } 2\pi.$$

$$\frac{T^2}{4\pi^2} = \frac{L}{g} \longleftarrow \text{Square both sides.}$$

$$\frac{T^2 g}{4\pi^2} = L \longleftarrow \text{Multiply both sides by } g.$$

Now a program can be written to find L, given T and g.

Projects

1. Given the period T (in seconds) of a simple pendulum and the gravity constant g, write a program that finds and prints the length L (in meters) of the pendulum.
2. Given the length L (in meters) and the period T (in seconds) of a simple pendulum, write a program that computes and prints the gravity constant g.
3. The distance d (in feet) an object falls and the time t (in seconds) it takes to fall are related by the formula $d = 16t^2$. (See Exercises 14 and 15 on page 11.) Given d, write a program that computes and prints t.

2-11 NUMBERS IN EXPONENTIAL FORM

The computer may print a number in one of the three following forms:

1. As an integer, for example, 8, −71, 8341, 927683.
2. As a decimal, for example, 6.2, −.192308, .067.
3. In exponential form, for example, 1.36424E2, −6.92308E3, 1.92308E−3.

BASIC normally prints a maximum of *six* significant digits. Nonsignificant zeros are dropped. When the number of significant positions exceeds six, the answer is printed in exponential form. For example, an answer of .00192308 is printed as 1.92308E−3, which means 1.92308×10^{-3}. 93,000,000 is printed 9.3E7.

Data can be READ in exponential form as in this program.

```
10 READ L,W
20 LET P = 2*L + 2*W
30 PRINT P
40 DATA 2.67E4, .81920E-2
50 END
```

Numbers in E-form may also appear in LET and PRINT statements.

EXERCISES 2-11

A Write the number represented by each exponential form.

Example: $9.861\text{E}2 = 9.861 \times 10^2 = 986.1$

1. 6.07E2 **2.** 1.92308E3 **3.** 1.15385E−2
4. 1E6 **5.** 8.4615E−2 **6.** 3.63798E−12
7. 1.86E3 **8.** 6.6430E9

B **9.** The amount of energy E (ergs) of a nuclear particle of mass M (grams) traveling at a speed v (centimeters per second) is given by the formula $E = \frac{1}{2}Mv^2$. For an alpha particle, $M = 6.6430 \times 10^{-24}$ g (grams). Write a BASIC program to compute the energy of an alpha particle traveling 2.2×10^9 cm/sec (centimeters per second). Write constants in exponential form in the program.

10. According to the theory of relativity, if the length of a spacecraft at rest on the launching pad is L_0, then its length when it moves at a speed v will be $L = L_0\sqrt{1 - \frac{v^2}{c^2}}$, in which $c = 3 \times 10^8$ m/sec (meters per second) or 186,000 mi/sec (miles per second). Write a BASIC program to compute and print L for input values of L_0 and v.

11. The speed of light is 2.99776×10^8 m/sec. Write a BASIC program to compute the number of meters in one light year.

2-12 REM STATEMENTS

Consider the program below.

Program 2-6

```
1 REM FIND THE AREA ØF A CIRCLE, GIVEN ITS RADIUS.
10 READ R
20 LET A = 3.14159 * R * R
30 REM A SIX-DIGIT APPRØXIMATIØN IS USED FØR PI.
40 PRINT "AREA IS " A
50 DATA 10,20
60 GØ TØ 10
70 END
```

"REM" is short for "REMARK." A REM statement is ignored by the compiler and does not affect execution. It provides the programmer a means of explaining the procedures to other readers. It is also useful to the programmer who is reviewing his or her own programs.

A REM statement may appear anywhere in a program before END but must have a line number. If the remark takes more than one line, all lines of the remark must be numbered and start with the REM abbreviation (just as all DATA lines must have a statement number and the word DATA). DATA and REM statements are both called "nonexecutable" statements because neither gives a command to the computer. Similarly, neither statement appears in a flowchart of a program.

In Program 2-6 above, notice that line 60 says GØ TØ 10 and not GØ TØ 1. On most systems GØ TØ 1 would cause no error, but since a REM statement is a nonexecutable statement, it is logically better to return to the READ.

SUGGESTION: Use one or more REM statements at the beginning of each program you write to give your name, the round and number (or page and number) of the problem, and perhaps a brief description of the program.

Example:

```
10 REM   TED CHANG
15 REM   RØUND TWØ  NØ. 170
20 REM   CØMPUTES THE PERIMETER ØF A RECTANGLE GIVEN
30 REM   THE LENGTH AND WIDTH.
40 READ L,W
50 PRINT "P = " 2*L + 2*W
60 GØ TØ 40
70 DATA 21,17,83,46
80 END
```

On some computers a remark is enclosed between single quotes (').

Example: `50 LET X = (A + B)/2 'X IS AVERAGE OF A AND B.'`

Here are the steps that you should follow when assigned a program.

1. Write the program on paper (flowcharting the logic first, if necessary, or if required by your teacher).
2. Enter your program into the computer. Depending on your system, this can be done directly from a keyboard or by means of punched cards, paper tape, cassette tape, or disk. Follow the specific directions of your teacher and system manual.
3. RUN the program using, if necessary, the editing features explained in this chapter.
4. If necessary, correct all errors and run the program again until the right output is obtained.
5. When the program is compiled and executed correctly, submit it to your teacher if he or she directs you to do so.

EXERCISES 2-12

A Correct any errors in these programs.

1.
```
1  SUE BAGERT   NØ. 84
10 READ X
20 PRINT "AREA = " X*X
30 GØ TØ 10
40 END
```

2.
```
100 REM  THIS PRØGRAM CALCULATES THE CIRCUMFERENCE
101      ØF A CIRCLE GIVEN THE RADIUS R.
110 READ R
120 PRINT C = 3.14159 * 2R
130 DATA 10,20
140 GØ TØ 100
9999 END
```

3.
```
10 DATA 71.6,82.05
20 READ L,W
30 REM   L IS THE LENGTH ØF THE RECTANGLE.
         W IS THE WIDTH.
40 LET P = 2*(L + W)
50 PRINT "PERIMETER = P"
60 END
```

B **4.** Flowchart Program 2-6 on page 69. **5.** Trace Program 2-6.

CHAPTER SUMMARY

In BASIC, simple programs can be written using statements of the kind illustrated below.

Purpose of the BASIC Statement	Sample of a BASIC Statement
Input	10 READ L, W or 10 INPUT L, W
Computation	20 LET P = 2*L + 2*W
Output	30 PRINT "PERIMETER =" P
Jump	40 GØ TØ 10
End	50 END

A *trace* of a program can show whether it gives correct results.

When entered into a computer, a program is analyzed by the BASIC *compiler,* which finds errors such as misspellings, extra commas, and so on. Each statement in the program must have a line number. The compiler sorts the statements by line numbers, and the programmer can use this feature to add, delete, or change statements in a program.

So far two types of variables have been used: a single capital letter (such as A or X) and a capital letter followed by a digit (such as X1 or Y2).

The *order of operations* in an arithmetic expression is as follows.

Order of Operations

1. Operations in parentheses are performed first, from the innermost parentheses outward.
2. Exponentiations (↑) are done from left to right.
3. Multiplications (*) and divisions(/) are done from left to right.
4. Finally, addition (+) and subtraction (−) are done from left to right.

BASIC provides a set of functions for use in programs, including ABS (absolute value), SQR (square root), SIN, CØS, TAN, ATN (arctangent), and CLG (common log).

The REM statement can be used to insert comments anywhere in a program.

CHAPTER OBJECTIVES AND REVIEW

Objective: To decide whether a given BASIC statement is legal and, if it is not, to correct it. *(Sections 2-1, 2-2, 2-7, and 2-12)*

Correct all errors, if any, in each of the following BASIC statements.

1. `1.5 READ (X, Y)`
2. `30 INPUT Ø, A/B`
3. `45 LET X + Y = R`
4. `70 LET M = 2K - 7`
5. `100 LET N = SQR X`
6. `80 PRINT O`
7. `1DATA 6,7;8,3`
8. `80 LET Y = SQR((ABS(Y))`
9. `90 PRINT 9.3E7/2.8E-2`
10. `86 PRINT "TIME IS" T (HØURS)`
11. `80 LET S = X*2      REM   S IS THE STRESS.`

Objective: To construct a flowchart for a given program and vice-versa. *(Sections 2-2 and 2-3)*

12. Construct a flowchart for the program shown at the right.

```
10 READ A,B,C
20 DATA 2,4,6,1,3,2
30 LET D = B * C / A
40 PRINT "4TH TERM =" D
50 GØ TØ 10
60 END
```

13. Write a BASIC program for the flowchart below.

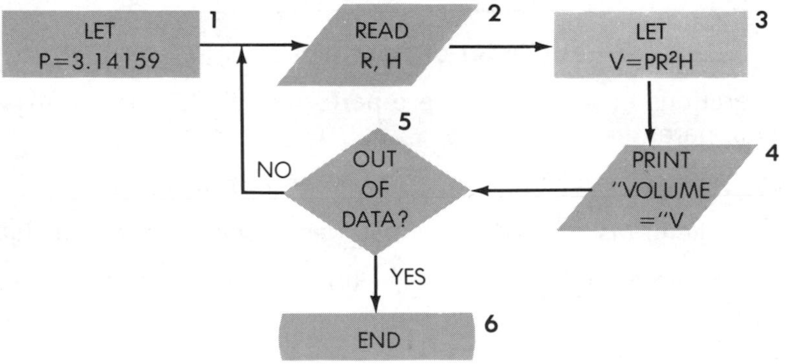

Objective: To trace a given program. *(Sections 2-3 and 2-9)*

14. Trace the program of Exercise 12 for the DATA listed in line 20.

Objective: To edit a BASIC program, keying on the line numbers. *(Section 2-4)*

15. A student entered her program into a computer. In checking, she noticed three errors. List the three lines she must type in order to correct the errors.

```
10 READ X,
20 LET Y = X↑3
30 PRINT X, X↑3
40 DATA 2, -1, 3
50 END
```

Objective: To decide whether a given expression is a legal BASIC variable. *(Section 2-5)*

Which of the following are not BASIC variables?

16. x9 **17.** 2z **18.** 7 **19.** (Y1)
20. NET **21.** E−2 **22.** P − Q **23.** GØ

Objective: To use the rules for order of operations in BASIC to compute the value assigned to a variable by a given LET statement for given values of variables on the right side of the LET statement. *(Section 2-5)*

If W = 2, X = 4, and Y = −2, what value is assigned to Z by each of the LET statements of Exercises 24-29?

24. `10 LET Z = -W ↑ 3`
25. `20 LET Z = 2 * X ↑ .5`
26. `30 LET Z = X - 3 * W + Y`
27. `40 LET Z = (X + Y) / W + ABS(Y)`
28. `50 LET Z = W * X / Y * 5`
29. `60 LET Z = SQR(X) * Y / W`

Objective: To write a given algebraic expression in BASIC. *(Sections 2-5, 2-6, and 2-10)*

Write each of these expressions in a LET statement. Start each statement with 20 LET M = . . .

30. $6s - t^2$ **31.** $(6 + 2s)^4$

32. $\sqrt[4]{\dfrac{r}{2t}}$ **33.** $\dfrac{a+b}{2c+d^2}$

34. $\sqrt{uv - 7z}$ **35.** $|16 - t^{\frac{1}{3}}|$

36. $-7(c - 2f)$ **37.** $(k + 9)(k - 1)$

38. $\left(\dfrac{x^2}{6}\right)^{n+1}$ **39.** $\dfrac{xy}{z^3}$

Objective: To write a BASIC program that processes many sets of DATA to solve a given problem, using the READ (or INPUT), LET, PRINT, GØ TØ, DATA, END, or REM statements. *(Sections 2-7 and 2-8)*

40. Write a BASIC program for the following: given the measures of two angles of a triangle, print the measure of the third angle. (See Ex. 38, p. 33.)

ROUND TWO: ***PROGRAMS FOR STUDENT ASSIGNMENT***

GENERAL INSTRUCTIONS:

1. In each exercise on pages 74 through 85, write and run a program that will do what is specified in the exercise.
2. Research may be necessary to learn the meaning of a word or to find the formula needed for a calculation.
3. Print results with an appropriate message, for example, "AREA =" or "SØLUTIØN IS", etc.
4. The program should be written to handle numerous DATA sets.
5. Include at least three sets of DATA. As a check, calculate the first answer yourself and have it ready to compare with the computer output.
6. If your teacher requires it, submit a flowchart.

ALGEBRA ONE

1. Find the arithmetic mean of two real numbers.
2. The "slugging percentage" of a baseball hitter is the ratio of his total bases to his at-bats. Given his number of singles, doubles, triples, home runs, and at-bats, print a player's slugging percentage. Note: Like batting average, slugging percentage is expressed as a three-place decimal. A slugging percentage over .500 is considered outstanding.
3. A coin is flipped repeatedly. Input the number of heads and the number of tails that occur. Compute the percent of the total flips that are heads and the percent that are tails.
4. Given a linear equation $AX + B = C$ ($A \neq 0$), input A, B, and C and solve for x. For example, if the equation is $7x + 5 = 19$, print $X = 2$.
5. Read a positive integer N and print the product P of the four consecutive integers N, N + 1, N + 2, and N + 3. If the program runs correctly, P + 1 will be a perfect square each time.
6. A baseball pitcher's "earned-run average" is computed using the formula $ERA = \frac{R \cdot 9}{I}$ where R = number of earned runs allowed and I = innings pitched. Given R and I, compute and print a pitcher's ERA. Assume that a whole number of innings is pitched.
7. A die is tossed several times. Enter the number of ones, the number of twos, the number of threes, and so on, that turn up. Print the percent of tosses that are ones, the percent that are twos, and so on. (See Ex. 6, p. 31.)

8. Accept the coordinates of two points on the real number line. Subdivide the line segment determined by these two points into four equal subsegments. Print the coordinates of the endpoints of each segment. (See Ex. 4, p. 31.)

9. Given the number of a baseball team's wins and losses, compute its winning percentage. Assume there are no ties. (See Ex. 14, p. 32.)

10. Input the number of a team's wins, losses, and ties, and print its winning percentage. Assume that a tie game counts as a full game played and a half-game won. (See Ex. 15, p. 32.)

11. Compute a baseball player's "fielding percentage," given his put-outs, assists, and errors.

$$\text{fielding percentage} = \frac{\text{chances handled successfully}}{\text{total chances}} = \frac{P + A}{P + A + E}$$

In Exercises 12-16 you are given two positive numbers, X and Y.

12. Determine what percent X is of Y.

13. Determine what percent Y is of X.

14. Compute D, the absolute value of the difference between X and Y.

15. Print the percent D is of X. (See Exercise 14.)

16. Print the percent D is of Y. (See Exercise 14.)

17. Given values for A, B, and C, test the Distributive Property by printing the values A(B + C) and AB + AC for each set of input data.

18. A person has P pennies, N nickels, D dimes, Q quarters, and H half-dollars. How much money does he or she have?

GEOMETRY

19. Find the sum of the measures of the interior angles of a polygon, given its number of sides. (See Ex. 30, p. 33.)

20. Find the measure of each angle of a regular polygon, given the number of sides. (See Ex. 31, p. 33.)

21. Find the number sides of a polygon, given the sum of the measures of the interior angles.

22. Find the number of sides of a regular polygon, given the measure of each interior angle.

23. Find the geometric mean (mean proportional) of two positive real numbers.

24. Find the measure of an exterior angle of a triangle, given the measures of the two remote interior angles.

25. Input the radius of a sphere and compute its volume. (See Ex. 24, p. 33.)

26. Input the radius of a sphere and compute its surface area. (See Ex. 25, p. 33.)

In Exercises 27-29 the length, width, and height of a rectangular prism are given.

27. Compute the length of a diagonal of the prism.

28. Compute the total surface area of the prism.

29. Compute the volume of the prism.

In Exercises 30 and 31 triangle ABC is isosceles with AB = AC. Input the lengths of $\overline{BC}$ and $\overline{AB}$. (See Ex. 32-33, p. 33.)

30. Compute the perimeter of the triangle.

31. Compute the area of the triangle.

32. Given the measure of angle A of isosceles triangle ABC with AB = AC, find the measure of angle B.

In Exercises 33-35 suppose that two triangles ABC and XYZ are similar (have the same shape).

33. Given AB, XY, and BC, find YZ.

34. Given AB, XY, and the perimeter of ΔABC, find the perimeter of ΔXYZ.

35. Given AB and XY, print the ratio of the areas of the two triangles.

36. Find the area of a triangle, given the lengths of the three sides. (See Ex. 21, p. 29.)

37. Convert an angle from degrees, minutes, and seconds to degrees with a decimal fraction.

In Exercises 38-41, a regular square pyramid is given. Also given are the length of a side of the base of the pyramid and the length of a lateral edge.

38. Find the slant height of the pyramid. (See Ex. 34, p. 33.)

39. Find the lateral area of the pyramid.

40. Find the total surface area of the pyramid.

41. Find the volume of the pyramid.

42. Given the lengths of three segments formed by two intersecting chords in a circle, find the length of the fourth segment.

In Exercises 43-48 compute the area of the figures described.

43. a triangle, given the base and height

44. an equilateral triangle, given the length of a side (See Ex. 27, p. 33.)

45. a parallelogram, given the length and height

46. a rhombus, given the lengths of the diagonals

47. a trapezoid, given the height and the lengths of the bases

48. a regular polygon, given the number of sides and the measures of the apothem and one side.

In Exercises 49-51, a right circular cylinder is given. Also given are the length of the altitude and the radius of the base.

49. Find the lateral area of the cylinder.

50. Find the total surface area of the cylinder.

51. Find the volume of the cylinder.

52. Given that a segment of length L is divided into two segments whose ratio is L_1 to L_2, find the length of each segment.

53. Knowing the ratio of the measures of the angles of a triangle, determine the measure of each angle. For example, if the ratio of the angle measures is 2:3:4, input 2, 3, 4 as data. (See Ex. 44, p. 34.)

In Exercises 54-57, a right triangle ABC is given with altitude CD drawn to the hypotenuse AB. Let *a, b, c, h, x,* and *y* represent lengths as indicated in the figure. (See Ex. 45-8, p. 34.)

54. Given *c* and *x*, find *a*.

55. Given *c* and *x*, find *h*.

56. Given *h* and *a*, find *b*.

57. Given *h* and *x*, find *b*.

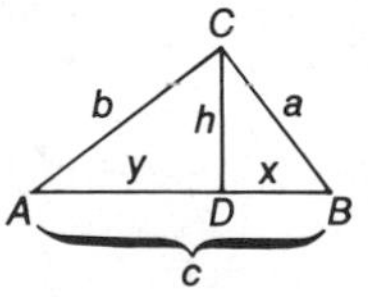

In Exercises 58 and 59 the coordinates of two points A and B in the coordinate plane are given. (See Ex. 49 and 50, p. 34.)

58. Compute the length of $\overline{AB}$.

59. Determine the coordinates of the midpoint of $\overline{AB}$.

60. Compute the perimeter of a right triangle, given the lengths of the two legs. (See Ex. 52, p. 34.)

61. Compute the perimeter of a right triangle, given the length of the hypotenuse and the length of one leg. (See Ex. 53, p. 34.)

In Exercises 62-64 an isosceles right triangle is given.

62. Find the length of the hypotenuse, given the length of a leg.

63. Find the length of a leg, given the length of the hypotenuse.

64. Find the perimeter, given the length of a leg.

In Exercises 65 and 66 input the number of degrees in an acute angle.

65. Print the measure of its complement.

66. Print the measure of its supplement.

In Exercises 67-69 the altitude and the radius of the base of a right circular cone are given.

67. Find the lateral area.

68. Find the total surface area.

69. Find the volume.

70. In parallelogram *ABCD* at the right, $m\angle A = 45°$. Given x and b, find the area of *ABCD*.

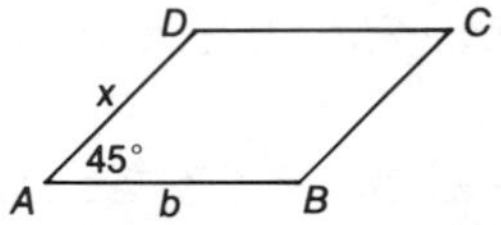

71. In parallelogram *WXYZ* at the right, $m\angle W = 30°$. Given l and w, find the area of *WXYZ*.

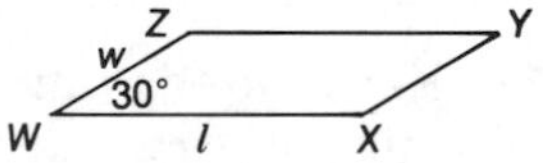

ALGEBRA TWO

72. A cubic polynomial function is defined by $y = Ax^3 + Bx^2 + Cx + D$ (A, B, C, D are rational). Read A, B, C, D, and N. Compute Y for $x = N$ and print N and y. (See Ex. 54, p. 34.)

73. Repeat Exercise 72 for the fourth-degree polynomial function $y = Ax^4 + Bx^3 + Cx^2 + Dx + E$ (A, B, C, D, E rational).

In Exercises 74-76, quadratic equation $Ax^2 + Bx + C = 0$ is given. Input A, B, and C (A, B, and C rational, $A \neq 0$).

74. Read a value for x and print x and the value of $Ax^2 + Bx + C$.

75. Evaluate the discriminant.

76. Determine the sum and product of the roots without actually computing the roots. This applies whether the roots are real or not. (See Ex. 58, p. 35.)

77. For the complex number A + Bi (A and B real), input A and B and print the absolute value of the complex number. (See Ex. 81, p. 36.)

78. Given pure imaginary numbers Ai and Bi, read A and B and print the product of Ai and Bi. (See Ex. 82, p. 36.)

79. Input the slope of an oblique line l in the xy-plane. (An "oblique" line is neither horizontal nor vertical.) Print the slope of any line perpendicular to l.

In Exercises 80-83, a parabola is defined by $y = \mathrm{A}x^2 + \mathrm{B}x + \mathrm{C}$, $\mathrm{A} \neq 0$. Read rational numbers A, B, and C.

80. Print the coordinates of the vertex of the parabola. (See Ex. 66, p. 35.)

81. Print the equation of the axis of symmetry. (See Ex. 68, p. 35.)

82. Print the coordinates of the focus. (See Ex. 69, p. 35.)

83. Print the equation of the directrix. (See Ex. 70, p. 35.)

84. Given a positive real number X and a rational number Y, print XY. (Note: one or more of the computer's answers may not agree with the answer you would get with pencil and paper.)

85. A function f is defined by $\mathrm{Y} = 2\mathrm{X} - 7$. The domain of f is $\{-5, -2, -1, 0, 3, 11\}$. For each member of the domain, print X and the corresponding Y.

86. For a repeating decimal of the form .ABABAB. . . , input A and B and print the rational number for that decimal. Use a statement such as PRINT X "/" Y.

87. Repeat Exercise 86 for a repeating decimal of the form .ABBBBB. . . .

88. Find $f(g(\mathrm{X}))$ where $f(\mathrm{X}) - 3\mathrm{X} + 4$ and $g(\mathrm{X}) = \mathrm{X}^2 - 14$ for X-values that you select. (See Ex. 76, p. 36.)

89. For the same functions f and g as defined in Exercise 88, find $g(f(\mathrm{X}))$ for X-values that you select. (See Ex. 77, p. 36.)

Given a point $P(x, y)$, print the ordered pair of the point that is symmetric to P with respect to each of the following.

90. the x-axis.

91. the y-axis

92. the origin

93. the line defined by $y = x$

ADVANCED MATHEMATICS

94. Given the radian measure of an angle, compute the degree measure.

95. Given the degree measure of an angle, compute the radian measure.

96. Given A and B (in radians), find cosine (A + B) without using "CØS(A + B)".

97. Given the lengths of the hypotenuse and one leg of a right triangle, find the sine, cosine, and tangent of either one of the acute angles of the triangle.

In Exercises 98-101, the length of the hypotenuse and the measure of one acute angle of a right triangle are given.

98. Compute the measure of the other acute angle.

99. Compute the length of each leg.

100. Compute the perimeter of the triangle.

101. Compute the area of the triangle.

102. Compute the area of a triangle by taking one-half the product of the lengths of two sides times the sine of the included angle.

103. Given the lengths, a and b, of two adjacent sides of a parallelogram and the measure, A, of the included angle, find the length, l, of a diagonal of the parallelogram using the formula
$l = \sqrt{a^2 + b^2 + 2ab \cos A}$.

In Exercises 104-106, use the diagram at the right, where a, b, and c represent the lengths of the sides of the triangle and A, B, and C represent the measures of the angles.

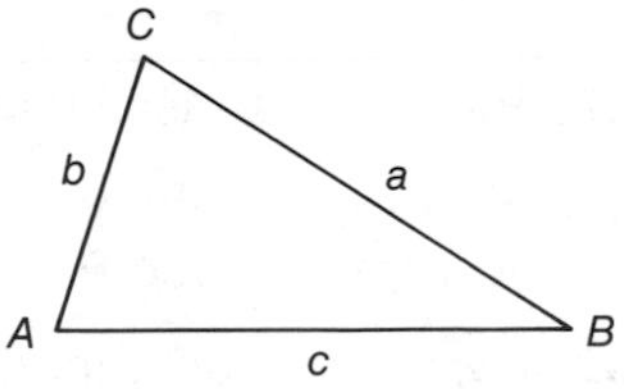

104. Given a, b, and c, use the formula

$$\tan \frac{A}{2} = \sqrt{\frac{(a+b-c)(a-b+c)}{(b+c+a)(b+c-a)}}$$ to find A.

105. Given b, c, and A, find the area of the triangle where

$$\text{area of } \triangle ABC = bc \sin \frac{A}{2} \cos \frac{A}{2}.$$

106. Given A, C, and b, find the area of the triangle using the formula

$$\text{area of } \triangle ABC = \frac{b^2 \sin A \sin C}{2 \sin B}.$$

107. Compute and print the determinant of a 2 × 2 matrix $\begin{bmatrix} A & B \\ C & D \end{bmatrix}$. (See Ex. 90, p. 37.)

In Exercises 108 and 109 an arithmetic sequence is given. Input A, the first term, D, the common difference, and N, a positive integer. Print each of the following. (See Ex. 91 and 92, p. 37.)

108. the Nth term

109. the sum of the first N terms

110. Input real numbers X and Y (X ≠ Y). Print three arithmetic means between X and Y. (See Ex. 93, p. 37.)

In Exercises 111 and 112, a geometric sequence is given. Input A, the first term, R, the common ratio (R ≠ 1), and N, a positive integer. Print each of the following. (See Ex. 94 and 95, p. 37.)

111. the Nth term

112. the sum of the first N terms

113. A ball is dropped straight down from a tower 102 feet high and rebounds each time to 36% of its previous height. What is the total vertical distance traveled by the ball before it comes to rest? (Since this problem has built-in data, you may ignore General Instructions 4 and 5.)

114. Compute the distance between two points in a three-dimensional coordinate system. (See Ex. 101, p. 38.)

In Exercises 115 and 116, S and T are the components of a vector, $\vec{v}$ = (S, T). Read S and T. (See Ex. 102 and 103, p. 38.)

115. Compute and print the norm of $\vec{v}$.

116. Input a scalar K and print the product K$\vec{v}$.

In Exercises 117 and 118, S and T are the components of $\vec{v}$ = (S, T). X and Y are the components of a vector $\vec{w}$. Read S, T, X, and Y.

117. Print the sum of $\vec{v}$ and $\vec{w}$.

118. Print the inner product (dot product) of $\vec{v}$ and $\vec{w}$.

119. Accept the components of two three-dimensional vectors, $\vec{y}$ and $\vec{z}$. Print the cross-product of $\vec{y}$ and $\vec{z}$.

BUSINESS

120. Given the list price of an item and the rate of discount, print the amount of the discount and the net price.

121. Given the list and net prices of an item, find the amount of discount and the percent (rate) of discount.

122. Often a "chain discount" is applied to an item. First one and then another discount is applied. Given the original price and the two discount rates, compute the final net price of the item.

123. Given the cost price and the percent of margin (markup) of an item, calculate the selling price and the gross profit.

124. Input the total amount of a sales and the sales tax rate. Find the amount of tax and the net sale after taxes.

125. The withholding tax on a weekly salary (let us assume) is computed as follows: 14% of the difference between a person's gross pay and $13 times the number of dependents he or she claims. Read the values for the gross pay and the number of dependents; print the withholding tax.

126. Calculate a person's gross weekly pay, given the rate per hour, overtime rate per hour, number of regular hours worked that week, and number of overtime hours that week.

In Exercises 127 and 128 the mileage records of four automobiles are as given at the right.

Car	Miles	Gallons Used
1	420	25.1
2	305	21.5
3	227	14.9
4	195	15.2

127. Compute each car's average number of miles per gallon.

128. Compute the average number of miles per gallon of all four cars.

In Exercises 129 and 130, a finance charge is imposed on merchandise purchased on an installment plan.

129. Input the cash selling price of an item, the down payment, the monthly payment, and the number of monthly payments to be made. Find the finance charge.

130. Given the unpaid cash balance of an item, the finance charge, and the number of months of payments, calculate the monthly payment.

131. An investor makes regular purchases of the stock of an automobile manufacturer. Read the number of shares that the investor owns and the dividend rate on each share. Print the total dividend.

132. Calculate the effective annual interest rate for a known initial investment that amounts to a known future value in a specified number of years. This rate expresses the actual rate of interest earned annually on the investment. The formula is

$$\text{effective annual interest rate} = \left(\frac{\text{future value}}{\text{initial investment}}\right)^{\frac{1}{\text{years}}} - 1.$$

133. Calculate the amount required as a regular deposit to provide a stated future value in a specified number of years. Input the future value (T), the nominal annual interest rate (i), the number of deposits per year (N), and the number of years (Y).

The formula is $$R = T\left[\frac{\frac{i}{N}}{\left(1+\frac{i}{N}\right)^{NY} - 1}\right].$$

134. Compute the annual depreciation rate of an investment. Given is the original value of the investment, its current value, and its age in years. Use the formula

$$\text{depreciation rate} = 1 - \left(\frac{\text{current value}}{\text{original value}}\right)^{\frac{1}{\text{age}}}$$

135. Compute the number of years needed to repay a loan. Given are the amount of the loan (P), the amount of the payments (R), the number of payments to be made per year (N), and the annual interest rate on the loan (i).

The formula is $$Y = -\frac{\log\left(1-\frac{iP}{NR}\right)}{\log\left(1+\frac{i}{N}\right)} \cdot \frac{1}{N}.$$

PHYSICAL SCIENCES

In Exercises 136-138, an electric circuit carries direct current. In the circuit, I (the amount of current in amps), E (the voltage in volts), and R (the resistance in ohms) are related by the formula $E = IR$. (This is known as Ohm's Law.)

136. Given the voltage and the resistance, find the amount of current.

137. Given the amount of current and the voltage, find the resistance.

138. Given the amount of current and the resistance, find the voltage.

In Exercises 139-141, an electric circuit carries alternating current. The voltage is given by $E = E_{max} \sin \theta$, where E = the instantaneous voltage, E_{max} = the maximum voltage attained in one cycle, and θ = the displacement angle.

139. Given E_{max} and θ, find E.

140. Given E and θ, find E_{max}.

141. Given E and E_{max}, find θ. (Note: most versions of BASIC do not have an arcsin function. Thus, you will need to find out a way to use the ATN function to find θ.)

142. The length, L, of a belt around two wheels can be computed by L = 3.26(R1 + R2) + 2D, where R1 and R2 are the radii of the wheels and D is the distance between the centers of the wheels. Given R1, R2, and D, find L.

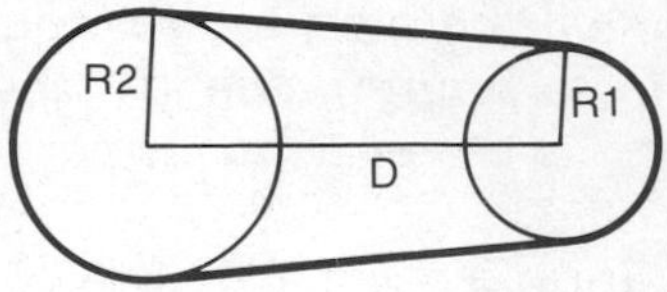

143. The French mathematician Marin Mersenne (1588-1648) discovered the formula $f = \frac{1}{2L}\sqrt{\frac{P}{m}}$, where f = frequency of a musical note in cycles per second (hertz), L = length in centimeters of the vibrating string or wire, P = stretching force (or tension) in dynes, and m = mass in grams of one centimeter of the string or wire. Given *L, P,* and *m,* find *f.*

In Exercises 144-147, an object moves at a uniform (constant) acceleration, *a*. It can be shown that the object's final velocity, v_f, is given by the formula $v_f = \sqrt{v_1^2 + 2a\Delta s}$, where v_1 = the object's initial velocity (often 0) and Δs = its displacement (change of position).

144. Given v_1, a, and Δs, find v_f.

145. Given v_f, a, and Δs, find v_1.

146. Given v_f, v_1, and Δs, find a.

147. Given v_f, v_1, and a, find Δs.

148. In the summer the weather bureau puts out the "temperature humidity index" (THI). The formula is THI = .4(W + D) + 15, where W = the wet bulb thermometer reading and D = the dry bulb thermometer reading. Given W and D, find the THI.

149. Assume that one ounce of hamburger contains 80 calories, that a bun has 200 calories, and that one French fry has 14 calories. Given the number of ounces of hamburger, whether a person has a bun (1 = Yes, 0 = No), and the number of French fries, calculate the number of calories in a person's meal.

In Exercises 150 and 151, the mass and velocity of an object are given.

150. Compute its momentum.

151. Compute its kinetic energy.

152. The intensity, B, in decibels, of a sound is given by the formula $B = 10 \log \frac{I}{I_0}$, where I is in watts/cm^2 and I_0 is the intensity of the threshold of hearing (usually about 10^{-16}watts/cm^2). Given I, compute B.

In Exercises 153 and 154 a planet is revolving around the Sun. According to Kepler's law of planetary motion, if P is the number of Earth years for one revolution of the planet around the Sun, and D is the planet's average distance (in kilometers) from the Sun, then $\frac{P^2}{D^3} = 2.985 \times 10^{-25}$. (For DATA, use actual values for the planets in our solar system.)

153. Given P, compute D.

154. Given D, compute P.

155. Given the mass of an object moving in a circle, its velocity, and the radius of the circle, compute the centripetal force on the object. (See Ex. 112, p. 39.)

156. Calculate the volume of a given number of moles of a gas at a given temperature and pressure using the ideal gas equation $pV = nRT$.

157. One form of Van Der Waal's equation of state for a gas is

$$p = \frac{nRT}{V - nb} - \frac{an^2}{V^2},$$

where p = the pressure in atmospheres, V = the volume in liters, T = the absolute temperature in degrees Kelvin, n = the number of moles, R = the gas constant, and a and b are empirical constants for the specific gas. Given n, R, T, V, a, and b, compute p.

158. Given the mass (in grams) and volume (in cubic centimeters) of a body, compute its mass density.

In Exercises 159-164, make the indicated conversion of temperatures.

159. Celsius to Fahrenheit.

160. Celsius to Kelvin.

161. Fahrenheit to Celsius

162. Fahrenheit to Kelvin.

163. Kelvin to Celsius

164. Kelvin to Fahrenheit.

165. Given the height from which an object falls, determine the time it will take to fall. (See Ex. 14 and 15, p. 11.)

166. The period T (in seconds) of a simple pendulum of length L (in meters) is given by $T = 2\pi\sqrt{\frac{L}{g}}$, where g is the gravity constant. Given L and g, compute T.

167. Convert pH values to the corresponding hydrogen ion concentrations.

168. Given the candle power of a light source and its distance from an object, compute the illumination on the object.

3

CONTROLLING OUTPUT; IF...THEN STATEMENTS

The output rules explained in the first six lessons of this chapter are intended to cover the majority of BASIC compilers. However, the explanations given here may sometimes differ from those that apply to the system that you are using. Consult the manual and experiment with your system to determine if the rules given here are followed exactly.

3-1 COMMAS

In many programs we want to print several numbers as output. Here is an example.

Example: Given a nonzero real number, print the number along with its additive inverse and its multiplicative inverse.

Program 3-1

```
10 READ X
20 PRINT X, -X, 1/X
30 GØ TØ 10
40 DATA 5,-100,4
50 END
```

In line 20 notice the commas separating the quantities to be printed. In addition to serving as separators, they tell the compiler how to space the numerals to be printed. Each execution of a PRINT statement normally produces one line of output.

The output from Program 3-1 on the previous page is shown below.

```
   5              -5              .2
-100             100            -.01
   4              -4             .25
```

If we want the number, its additive inverse, and its multiplicative inverse on separate lines, we would write the program as shown below.

Program 3-2

```
10 READ X
20 PRINT X
30 PRINT -X
40 PRINT 1/X
50 GØ TØ 10
60 DATA 5,-100,4
70 END
```

Here is the output of Program 3-2.

```
 5
-5
 .2
-100
 100
-.01
 4
-4
 .25
```

The method of Program 3-1 on page 86 is better since it saves space and keeps associated values together on the same line.

We have still not explained exactly how commas govern the spacing of numerals printed. Most terminals can print a maximum of 75 characters across the page or screen. These "print positions" are numbered 1 to 75 left-to-right. Let us look again at the output from Program 3-1, but this time with the print positions indicated.

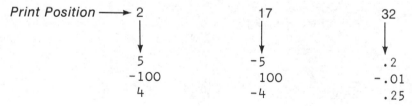

```
Print Position ──→ 2              17              32
                   │               │               │
                   ↓               ↓               ↓
                   5              -5              .2
                -100             100            -.01
                   4              -4             .25
```

RULE:
When the output expressions are separated by commas in a PRINT statement, the compiler automatically assigns each quantity to a print zone. (The width of the zone varies from system to system.)

When commas separate expressions in a PRINT statement, the output line is usually divided into five "zones": columns 1 through 15, 16 through 30, 31 through 45, 46 through 60, and 61 through 75. For numerical output the first position in each zone is reserved for a negative sign. For example, in the output of Program 3-1, the first 5 falls in column two rather than in column one. The first significant digit of each numeral is actually printed in column 2, 17, 32, 47, or 62.

What happens when we try to print six expressions separated by commas, as in this program?

Program 3-3

```
10 READ A,B
20 PRINT A+B,A-B,A*B,A/B,A↑B,B↑A
30 GØ TØ 10
40 DATA 5, 2, 2, 3
50 END
```

Since only the first five expressions of line 20 can fit on one line, the sixth (B ↑ A) is printed on the next line, like this.

Print
Position⟶

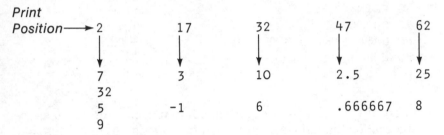

```
2              17             32             47             62
↓              ↓              ↓              ↓              ↓
7              3              10             2.5            25
32
5              -1             6              .666667        8
9
```

EXERCISES 3-1

A As in the examples of this lesson, show the output from each of these programs, with the leftmost print position of each quantity numbered.

1.
```
10 READ R
20 PRINT R,R↑2,R↑3
40 DATA 2, 6
50 GØ TØ 10
60 END
```

2.
```
5 READ S, T
10 PRINT S,T,S*T,S/T,T/S
15 GØ TØ 5
20 DATA 12, 6, 3, 4
25 END
```

3.
```
20 READ X,Y,Z
21 PRINT X*Y,X*Z,Y*Z
22 PRINT X-Y,X-Z,Y-Z
23 DATA 4, 2, 3
24 END
```

4.
```
10 READ C, D
20 PRINT C,D,-C,-D,1/C,1/D
30 DATA 2,4,8,10
40 GØ TØ 10
50 END
```

5. Show the output from Program 3-2 on page 87 if it is revised as shown at the right (with line 45 added).

```
10 READ X
20 PRINT X
30 PRINT -X
40 PRINT 1/X
45 PRINT "END ØF DATA SET"
50 GØ TØ 10
60 DATA 5,-100,4
70 END
```

3-2 SEMICOLONS

The use of semicolons in a **PRINT** statement permits an alternate output format that packs together the numerals more closely than commas do. Let us rewrite Program 3-1 on page 86 to illustrate this fact.

Program 3-1A

```
10 READ X
20 PRINT X;-X;1/X
30 GØ TØ 10
40 DATA 5,-100,4
50 END
```

Putting semicolons in line 20 causes the output to look like the following.

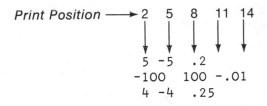

```
Print Position ——→ 2  5  8  11 14
                   ↓  ↓  ↓  ↓  ↓
                   5 -5  .2
                -100  100 -.01
                   4 -4  .25
```

The semicolon in a **PRINT** statement causes most compilers to organize the output in a format according to the following rules.

1. It prints the first quantity, beginning in print position one if the quantity is negative, in print position two if it is positive or zero.
2. If the next quantity is negative, it skips one space, prints the negative sign and then the significant digits of the numeral.
3. If the next quantity is positive or zero, it skips two spaces and prints the next numeral.

There is nothing wrong with mixing semicolons and commas in **PRINT** statements, as the following examples show.

```
30 PRINT A;B,C
40 PRINT X+Y, X-Y; X↑Y; Y↑X, X/Y
```

In a **PRINT** statement such as

```
50 PRINT "PERIMETER = " P
```

most systems assume that there is an understood semicolon between the second quotation mark and the variable P. On some systems the semicolon must be explicitly shown, like this.

```
50 PRINT "PERIMETER = "; P
```

CAUTION: The rules just stated for semicolon output apply only to numerical output. For alphamerical output (*alpha*betical characters in combination with nu*merical*), such as messages, no spaces are skipped *before* an open quotation mark. Hence if P = 25, the statement

```
50 PRINT P "= PERIMETER"
```

would produce the line

```
25= PERIMETER
```

with no space skipped between the numeral (25) and the message (= PERIMETER). To space the message better, use

```
50 PRINT P " = PERIMETER"
```

since the spaces inside the quotation marks will be honored by the compiler.

By understanding this rule, a programmer can avoid producing the awkward output of a statement such as this.

```
50 PRINT "L = " L "W = " W "P = " 2*L+2*W
```

If L = 5 and W = 3, then line 50 would print the following.

```
L =    5W =    3P =    16
```

Notice that no space is skipped at either of these points.

Revise line 50 to the following.

```
50 PRINT "L = " L " W = " W "  P = " 2*L+2*W
```

Notice the spaces included at these points inside *quotation marks.*

The output would now look like this.

```
L =    5  W =    3  P =    16
```

EXERCISES 3-2

A Show each output, indicating the print positions as in earlier examples.

1.
```
10 READ S
20 LET Y = S↑2 - 7
30 PRINT S;Y
40 GØ TØ 10
50 DATA 2, -3
60 END
```

2.
```
10 READ N
20 PRINT N↑3, N↑4; -N
30 GØ TØ 10
40 DATA 1, -2, 3
50 END
```

If P = 30, show the line produced by each of these PRINT statements. Use an underline to indicate a blank space.

Example: 50 PRINT "PERIM =" P
Answer: PERIM_=__30

3. 50 PRINT "P ="P   **4.** 50 PRINT "P = "P

5. 50 PRINT P "= P"   **6.** 50 PRINT P " = PERIMETER"

B If L = 4 and W = 3, show the output from each of these PRINT statements. Use an underline to indicate a blank space.

7. 60 PRINT "L =" L " W =" W " P =" 2*L+2*W

8. 60 PRINT L "= L" W "= W" 2*L+2*W "= P"

9. 60 PRINT "LENGTH" L " WIDTH" W " PERIMETER" 2*L+2*W

3-3 SKIPPING LINES

Returning to Program 3-1 on page 86, let us assume that the programmer would like the output double-spaced, like this.

```
 5              -5              .2

-100             100            -.01

 4              -4              .25
```

This can be accomplished by using a "dummy" PRINT statement (line 30 below).

Program 3-1B

```
10 READ X
20 PRINT X, -X, 1/X
30 PRINT
40 GØ TØ 10
50 DATA 5,-100,4
60 END
```

The "dummy" PRINT is equivalent to a line like this.

```
30 PRINT "              "
```

where the "message" being printed is just a line of blanks.

EXERCISES 3-3

A **1.** What would be the output if Program 3-1B on the previous page were written in the following manner?

```
5 PRINT
10 READ X
20 PRINT X, -X, 1/X
30 GØ TØ 5
40 DATA 5, -100, 4
50 END
```

Show the output of each of these programs.

2.
```
10 READ R
20 PRINT R↑2, R↑3
30 PRINT
40 DATA 2, 6
50 GØ TØ 10
60 END
```

3.
```
10 PRINT
20 READ S
30 LET T = 4*S↑2
40 PRINT S; T
50 PRINT
60 GØ TØ 10
70 DATA 2, 3, 4
80 END
```

3-4 COLUMNS AND COLUMN HEADINGS

Programmers often print output in tabular form with columns of figures, each column identified with a heading. As a simple example, suppose we want the output from Program 3-1 on page 86 to look like this.

```
 X              -X              1/X
 5              -5               .2
-100             100            -.01
 4              -4               .25
```

The program would have to be tailored as follows.

Program 3-1C

```
5 PRINT " X"," -X"," 1/X"
10 READ X
20 PRINT X, -X, 1/X
30 GØ TØ 10
40 DATA 5, -100, 4
50 END
```

Comment:

In statement 5, note the space at the beginning of each message. This space shifts the heading so that it begins over the first significant digit (or decimal point) of each numeral since the first column of each print zone is reserved for a negative sign.

Before any READ or calculation is performed, the headings are printed. Note that line 5 is executed only once, at the beginning of the program. Line 30 returns control to line 10 for the second set of data so that the headings will not be repeated.

An extension of this technique is to skip a line before and after printing the headings so that the output looks like this.

```
      X                  -X                 1/X

      5                  -5                 .2
   -100                 100                -.01
      4                  -4                 .25
```

This effect can be accomplished by adding the lines 4 PRINT and 6 PRINT to Program 3-1C.

EXERCISES 3-4

A Show the output of each of these programs.

1.
```
10 PRINT "REAL NØ.","SQRT"
20 READ A
30 PRINT A, SQR(A)
40 GØ TØ 20
50 DATA 4, 16, 25
60 END
```

2.
```
5 PRINT
6 PRINT "DISTANCE","RATE","TIME"
7 PRINT
10 READ R,T
20 PRINT R*T,R,T
30 GØ TØ 10
40 DATA 40,3,55,10,60,40
50 END
```

3.
```
5 PRINT "X";"X*X"
10 READ X
20 PRINT X;X*X
30 GØ TØ 10
40 DATA 2,-5,1.1
50 END
```

Identify and correct any error(s) in each program.

4.
```
10 PRINT "YEARS,""PRINCIPAL,""RATE,""INTEREST"
20 READ Y,P,R
30 LET I=P*R*Y
40 PRINT Y,P,R,I
50 GØ TØ 10
60 DATA 5,1000,.03,20,10000,.05
70 END
```

5.
```
5 PRINT "HØURS, RATE, PAY"
10 READ H,R
20LET P=H*R
30 PRINT H,R,P
40 DATA 40,1.50,50,2.25,35,1 1/2
50 GØ TØ 10
60 END
```

3-5 SUPPRESSING LINE FEED

In all programs written thus far each answer has been printed on a separate line. This procedure wastes space and, unless there are special requirements, can be avoided by putting either a comma or a semicolon at the end of the PRINT statement, as in the examples below.

The comma at the end of the PRINT line causes the compiler to allot each value fifteen spaces, as explained earlier. The semicolon makes the computer print the values closer together. In either case, the "," or ";" at the end of the PRINT statement stops the printer from advancing to the next line.

```
50 PRINT S,
50 PRINT S;
50 PRINT X+Y;
50 PRINT 2*A-4*B,
50 PRINT X,Y,
50 PRINT "NØS. ARE:";
```

EXERCISES 3-5

A State whether each of the following is a valid PRINT statement.

1. `20 PRINT`

2. `20 PRINT "    "`

3. `20 PRINT "    ";`

4. `20 PRINT "THE LIST IS",`

5. `20 PRINT P = "PERIMETER"`

6. `20 PRINT X1,X2;" AND " Y`

Show the output from each of these programs.

7.
```
10 READ L,W
20 PRINT 2*L+2*W;
30 GØ TØ 10
40 DATA 2,3,5,6
50 END
```

8.
```
10 READ L,W
20 PRINT 2*L+2*W,
30 GØ TØ 10
40 DATA 2,3,5,6
50 END
```

B **9.** Let's indulge in some computer "art." A program is shown at the left below for printing a geometric pattern.

```
10 PRINT "*      *"
20 PRINT "**    **"
30 PRINT "***  ***"
40 PRINT "********"
50 PRINT "********"
60 PRINT "***  ***"
70 PRINT "**    **"
80 PRINT "*      *"
90 END
```

```
NN     N
N N    N
N  N   N
N   N  N
N    N N
N     NN
```

Write programs to create your own patterns. For example, print your name or your initials. One interesting technique is to use the letter whose shape is being printed to form the shape as shown at the right above.

3-6 "TAB" FUNCTION

On a typewriter, "tab" stops can be set so that when the tabulator key is pressed, the carriage jumps to the next tabbed position to the right. BASIC has a TAB function that gives a similar result.

Example: `60 PRINT TAB(10);X;TAB(22);Y`

Line 60 gives the following output format: the first nine print positions are skipped; X is printed beginning in position 10 (recall that the first position in a numeric zone is reserved for a possible negative sign); Y is printed beginning in position 22. Thus, if X = 1.2 and Y = −13, the output from line 60 would look like this.

```
Print Position ——→ 10          22
                   |           |
                   ↓           ↓
                   1.2         -13
```

The TAB function allows you to create your own print zones when neither the comma nor the semicolon formats, explained in earlier lessons, are applicable. For example, if you want to print six numbers on the same line, you must use the TAB function.

The argument of TAB may be a variable. For example, 50 PRINT X;TAB(N);Y means that X is printed, then the machine moves to the print position corresponding to the current value of N (an integer) and prints Y. The argument of TAB may even be an expression. An example of this is 50 PRINT X;TAB (2*N-1);Y. As in the examples just shown, semicolons are used to separate TAB expressions from adjacent items. If more than one TAB expression is used in a PRINT statement, the numerical values of the arguments must get progressively larger with enough space between TAB's for what is being printed. If insufficient space is allowed, the next TAB position will be overrun, as on a typewriter.

Program 3-4 below uses the TAB function in lines 10 and 40 to print the headings over the columns of output (see next page).

Program 3-4

```
 5 PRINT
10 PRINT "LENGTH";TAB(20);"WIDTH";TAB(40);"PERIMETER"
20 PRINT
30 READ L,W
40 PRINT L;TAB(20);W;TAB(40);2*L+2*W
50 GØ TØ 30
60 DATA 6,8,3,7,10,5,2,11
70 END
```

The output for Program 3-4 is shown below.

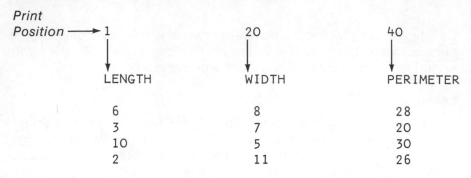

```
Print
Position ——→ 1                  20                  40
             |                  |                   |
             ↓                  ↓                   ↓
             LENGTH             WIDTH               PERIMETER

              6                  8                   28
              3                  7                   20
              10                 5                   30
              2                  11                  26

             ØUT ØF DATA LINE #10
```

EXERCISES 3-6

A State whether each statement is valid for your system.

1. `50 PRINT X;TAB(20);Y`
2. `85 PRINT TAB(15);A`
3. `30 PRINT "RATE";TAB(25);"TIME";TAB(50);"DISTANCE"`
4. `100 PRINT X;TAB(I);Y;`
5. `130 PRINT A - B;TAB(2*K);A + B`
6. `145 PRINT L,W;TAB(50);"PERIMETER ="2*(L+W)`
7. `45 PRINT X;TAB(20);Y,Z`

In Exercises 8-10, assume that A = 10 and B = 5. For each PRINT statement, show the output with the key columns labeled.

8. `5 PRINT TAB(5);"A";TAB(15);"B";TAB(25);"A/B"`
9. `20 PRINT A;TAB(10);B`
10. `5 PRINT "A="A;TAB(20);"B="B;TAB(35);"A/B="A/B`

B Write a program using TAB's to print each pattern on the terminal.

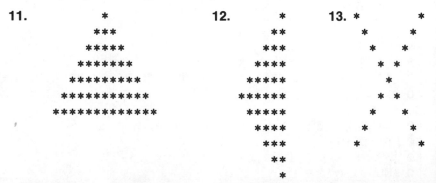

11.

```
      *
     ***
    *****
   *******
  *********
 ***********
*************
```

12.

```
     *
    **
   ***
  ****
 *****
******
 *****
  ****
   ***
    **
     *
```

13.

```
*       *
 *     *
  *   *
   * *
    *
   * *
  *   *
 *     *
*       *
```

3-7 DECISIONS: IF . . . THEN STATEMENTS

We now return to the problem of Flowchart 1-3 on page 7.

Example:

Read a real number x. If x is nonnegative, give the square root. If x is negative, print NØ REAL SQUARE RØØT.

We now write the program and trace the program.

Program 3-5

```
10 READ X
20 IF X >= 0 THEN 50
30 PRINT "NØ REAL SQUARE RØØT"
40 GØ TØ 10
50 PRINT X↑.5
60 GØ TØ 10
70 DATA 81,-2,0
80 END
```

Comment:

Unlike Flowchart 1-3, Program 3-5 has been written to process several values of x.

Table 3-1 Trace of Program 3-5

Step Number	Statement Number	Value of Variable x	Test	Yes or No?	Output
1	10	81			
2	20		81 >= 0?	Yes	
3	50				9
4	60		OUT OF DATA?	No	
5	10	−2			
6	20		−2 >= 0?	No	
7	30				NØ REAL SQUARE RØØT
8	40		OUT OF DATA?	No	
9	10	0			
10	20		0 >= 0?	Yes	
11	50				0
12	60		OUT OF DATA?	Yes	
13	END				

The decision of the program is made in line 20, an IF . . . THEN statement. Such statements must be written in the following form.

IF (equation or inequality) THEN (statement number)

Note that, while it might be grammatically correct to use a comma before the word THEN, none is inserted. The statement number may be the number of a statement earlier in the program or of one that comes later. That is, the IF . . . THEN statement may branch the computer forward or backward.

Here are examples of valid IF . . . THEN statements.

```
15 IF Y = Z THEN 40
20 IF A + B < B - 16 THEN 100
40 IF R >= 71 THEN 10
60 IF X/Y < Z↑3 THEN 40
50 IF A <> B THEN 80
```

Refer to Table 3-2 below to interpret the inequality symbols used in the examples. Many systems allow alternate forms: >< as well as <>, =< instead of <= and => for >=. Some systems use # for ≠.

Table 3-2 Relation symbols

Algebra	BASIC
=	=
<	<
>	>
≠	< >
≤	< =
≥	> =

Unlike LET statements, IF . . . THEN statements may have operation signs on either or both sides of the equation or inequality in the IF clause.

IF . . . THEN statements are handled by the computer as follows.

The machine tests the condition stated in the IF clause.

1. If this condition holds true, the computer branches to the statement whose number appears after the word THEN.
2. If the condition is false, the computer ignores the THEN clause and continues to the next line of the program in regular sequence.

Many versions of BASIC allow more complicated IF . . . THEN statements. Some of these are explained in Section 7-8.

Example:

Read a real number; print whether it is positive, negative, or zero.

Program 3-6

```
10 READ X
20 IF X > 0 THEN 60
30 IF X < 0 THEN 80
40 PRINT "ZERØ"
50 GØ TØ 10
60 PRINT "PØSITIVE"
70 GØ TØ 10
80 PRINT "NEGATIVE"
90 GØ TØ 10
100 DATA 8,-16,0,73,-124
110 END
```

Notice that both Program 3-5 on page 97 and Program 3-6 above have several GØ TØ 10 statements. In Program 3-5, both GØ TØ statements are needed. If you are puzzled by this, study Program 3-5 without the first GØ TØ 10 statement.

```
10 READ X
20 IF X >= 0 THEN 50
30 PRINT "NØ REAL SQUARE RØØT"
50 PRINT X↑.5
60 GØ TØ 10
70 DATA 81,-2,0
80 END
```

Trace the program until you find the error that develops. It will occur when $X = -2$.

A common mistake is to write an IF . . . THEN statement which is no decision at all, as in this program segment.

```
        . . .
30 IF X = Y THEN 40
40 LET Z = X + 7
        . . .
```

If $X = Y$, the THEN clause directs the computer to go to line 40. If $X \neq Y$, the machine goes to the next statement, which is 40. In either case it goes to 40; there is no decision, no breaking into two branches.

RULE:

In an IF . . . THEN statement, the statement number after THEN should not be the number of the statement immediately following the IF . . . THEN statement.

Another common mistake is to follow an IF . . . THEN statement with a GØ TØ statement. Compare these two versions of the same program.

Version A (poor)

```
10 READ X
20 IF X < 0 THEN 40
30 GØ TØ 60
40 PRINT "NEGATIVE"
50 GØ TØ 10
60 PRINT "NØNNEGATIVE"
70 GØ TØ 10
80 DATA 6, -5, 0
90 END
```

Version B (good)

```
10 READ X
20 IF X >= 0 THEN 60
40 PRINT "NEGATIVE"
50 GØ TØ 10
60 PRINT "NØNNEGATIVE"
70 GØ TØ 10
80 DATA 6, -5, 0
90 END
```

Notice how line 30 in version A is eliminated in version B because in line 20 the inequality sign in the IF clause has been reversed and the computer sent directly to line 60.

RULE: In a good program an IF . . . THEN statement is almost never followed by a GØ TØ statement.

An IF . . . THEN statement is often used with an INPUT statement to give a user a choice during the running of a program. For example, consider this program.

Program 3-7

```
10 INPUT "ENTER LENGTH AND WIDTH ØF A RECTANGLE";L,W
20 PRINT "PERIMETER =" 2*L + 2*W
30 INPUT "DØ YØU WISH TØ CØNTINUE (1 = YES, 0 = NØ)";X
40 IF X = 1 THEN 10
50 END
```

Line 30 gives the user a code for indicating whether he wishes to enter more data. His response (1 or 0) is stored as "X". Then in line 40, if $x = 1$ (YES response), the computer returns to line 10 and asks for more data. But if $x \neq 1$, the run ends.

An extension of this thinking allows the programmer to give the user a "menu" of choices. Then, depending on which selection is made, the computer is sent to various sections of the program. As an example, consider these lines from a program.

```
10 PRINT "ENTER NUMBER ØF PLAN YØU WISH TØ ANALYZE."
20 PRINT
30 PRINT TAB(10);"1. SIMPLE INTEREST"
40 PRINT TAB(10);"2. INTEREST CØMPØUNDED YEARLY"
```

```
50 PRINT TAB(10);"3. INTEREST CØMPØUNDED SEMI-ANNUALLY"
60 PRINT TAB(10);"4. INTEREST CØMPØUNDED QUARTERLY"
70 PRINT TAB(10);"5. INTEREST CØMPØUNDED MØNTHLY"
80 PRINT
90 INPUT Z
100 IF Z = 1 THEN 210
110 IF Z = 2 THEN 330
120 IF Z = 3 THEN 470
130 IF Z = 4 THEN 595
140 IF Z = 5 THEN 710
150 PRINT "INCØRRECT RESPØNSE. PLEASE TRY AGAIN."
160 GØ TØ 90
170 . . .
```

Lines 150 and 160 are included to cover the possibility that the user accidentally enters a number other than 1, 2, 3, 4, or 5.

In conjunction with the program section just shown, an ØN statement can be used to replace lines 100-140 with a single line:

```
100 ØN Z GØ TØ 210,330,470,595,710
```

For a fuller explanation of the ØN statement, see Section 7-6.

EXERCISES 3-7

A State whether each of the following is a valid IF . . . THEN statement for your system.

1. `20 IF A + B > 6 THEN -30`
2. `20 IF M - N <> 0 THEN 75`
3. `30 IF X↑2 + Y↑2 = R↑2 THEN 210`
4. `20 IF A = B = C THEN 63`
5. `20 IF (K+1)*(K+1) > M THEN GØ TØ 90`
6. `20 IF D = 0, THEN 80`
7. `20 IF X*Y = Y*Z THEN 20`
8. Is this program equivalent to Program 3-5 on page 97? Trace until you can decide whether the output will be the same.

```
10 READ X
20 IF X < 0 THEN 50
30 PRINT X↑.5
40 GØ TØ 10
50 PRINT "NØ REAL SQUARE RØØT"
60 GØ TØ 10
70 DATA 81,-2,0
80 END
```

Write BASIC statements that implement the flowchart decision section shown.

Example:

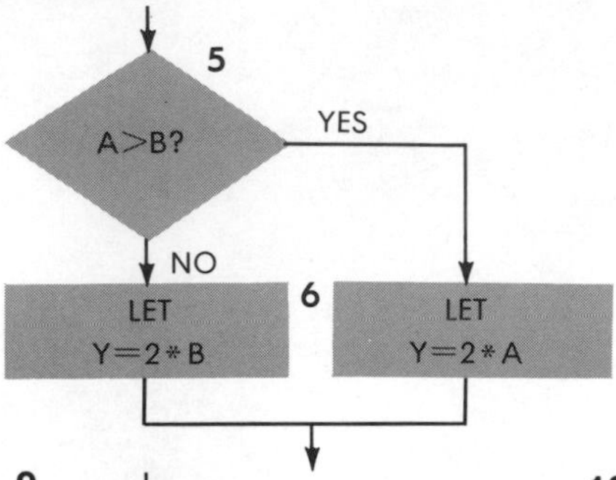

Answer:

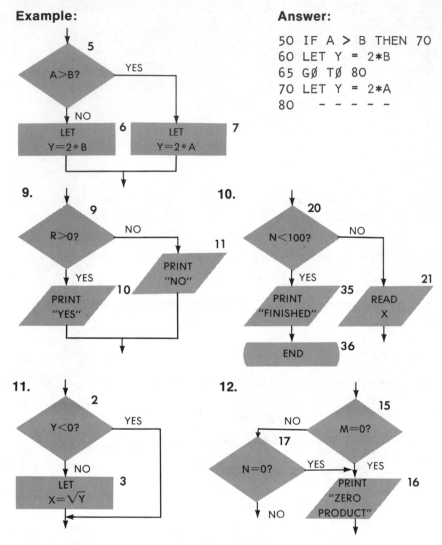

```
50 IF A > B THEN 70
60 LET Y = 2*B
65 GØ TØ 80
70 LET Y = 2*A
80   - - - - -
```

9.

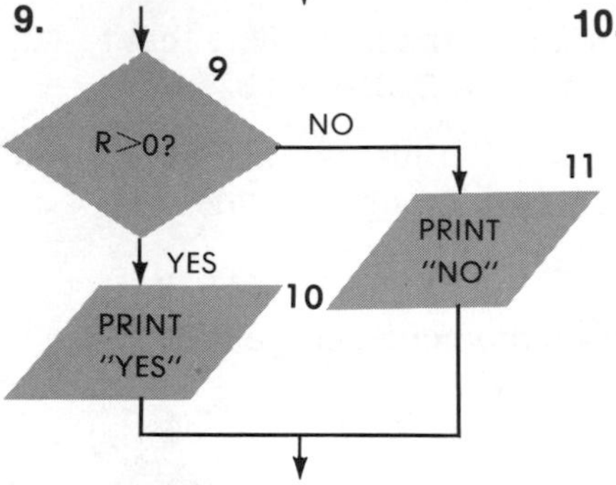

10.

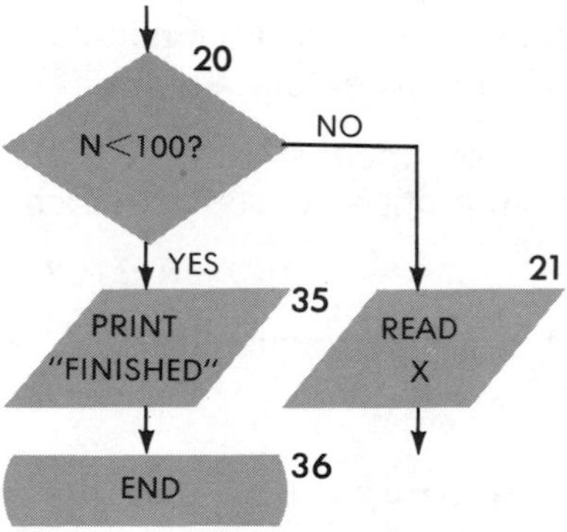

11.

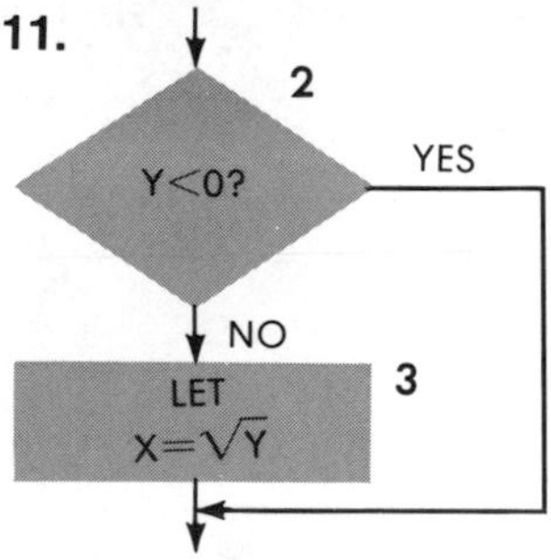

12.

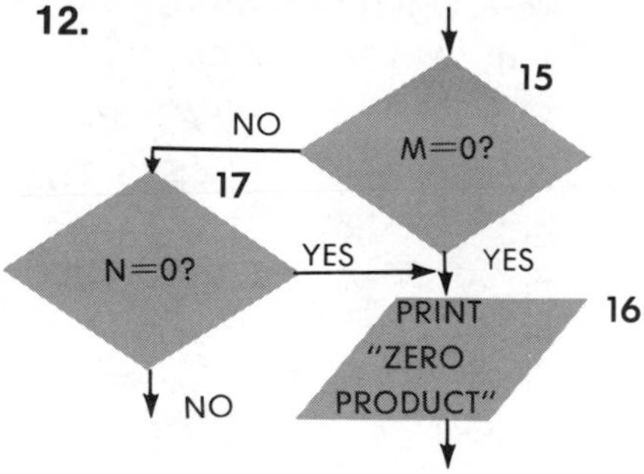

Use the program at the right to do Exercises 13 and 14.

13. Flowchart the program.

14. Trace the program.

```
10 READ H
20 IF H > 40 THEN 50
30 LET P = H*2.00
40 GØ TØ 60
50 LET P = 80 + (H-40)*3.00
60 PRINT "PAY = " P
70 GØ TØ 10
80 DATA 30,50,40
90 END
```

15. Write a program for the flowchart below. DATA 0, 2, −3

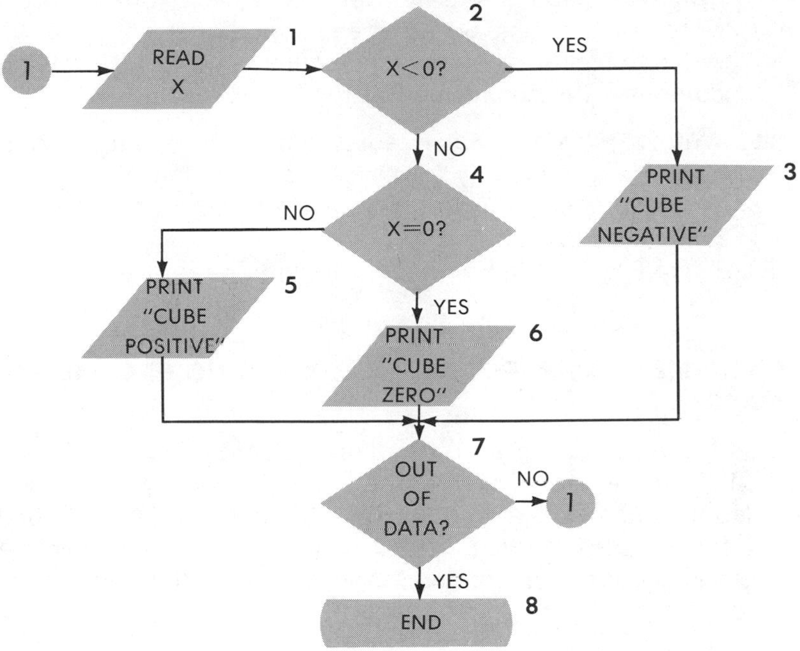

16. Trace the program that you wrote for Exercise 15.

17. Revise the program below to eliminate line 30.

```
10 INPUT A, B
20 IF A > B THEN 40
30 GØ TØ 60
40 PRINT A " LARGER"
50 GØ TØ 10
60 PRINT B " LARGER"
70 GØ TØ 10
80 END
```

Write BASIC programs for each of Exercises 18-21.

18. Read two unequal real numbers X and Y. Print either "$X > Y$" or "$Y > X$." (See Ex. 16, p. 11.)

19. Given a quadratic equation of the form $AX^2 + BX + C = 0$, determine whether the equation has real roots without actually computing the roots. (See Ex. 56, p. 35.)

20. Given a real number, print the number and its absolute value without using the ABS function of BASIC. (See Ex. 1, p. 31.)

21. Assume that the cost, not including tax, for sending a telegram from Minneapolis to San Francisco is \$4.20 for the first fifteen words or less, plus \$0.11 for each additional word over fifteen. Write a program that, given the number of words in a telegram, computes the cost. (See Ex. 104, p. 38.)

B **22.** Write a program that is equivalent to Program 3-6 but with a different inequality for at least one IF clause of a decision.

23. Trace your program for Exercise 22 using the DATA listed in Program 3-6.

24. Trace Program 3-6 with lines 50 and 70 removed.

3-8 MATHEMATICAL APPLICATIONS REQUIRING SPECIAL PRINT FORMATS

Suppose the output from a program is a set of points in the *xy*-plane. We usually list the coordinates of the points between parentheses and separated by commas, like this: (2, 7); (−3, 8); (0, −9); (−1.5, −6). If, as usual, X and Y represent the first and second coordinates, then a PRINT statement to produce the desired output would be the following.

```
40 PRINT "(" X "," Y ")"
```

Printing complex numbers is another application requiring a special format. A complex number is of the form A + B*i*, where "*i*" is the imaginary unit such that $i^2 = -1$. However, I is just another real variable in programming and has no special significance. When a complex number is to be printed, the "real part" (A) and the "imaginary part" (B) must be computed separately. "I" must be dictated between quotes in the PRINT statement; the "+" must also be inserted by means of quotes, as in the following example.

```
60 PRINT A " + " B " I"
```

This type of PRINT statement, however, produces a difficulty if B is negative. For example, if B = −4 the output would look like this, 6 + −4I, which is awkward. In order to avoid such situations, any program that prints complex numbers must include two PRINT statements with a decision based on the value of B. This is shown below.

```
...
60 IF B < 0 THEN 90
70 PRINT A " + " B " I"
80 GØ TØ 10
90 PRINT A; B " I"
100 GØ TØ 10
...
```

If B is negative, no "+" sign is dictated (line 90).

A similar approach is needed when the programmer must print a polynomial. Suppose the output will be a quadratic polynomial of the form $ax^2 + bx + c$. Decisions must be included to handle negative values for either *b* or *c* or both. The following sequence of steps would be one way of handling the problem.

```
...
60 IF B < 0 THEN 100
70 IF C < 0 THEN 130
80 PRINT A "X↑2 + " B " X + " C
90 GØ TØ 10
100 IF C < 0 THEN 150
110 PRINT A "X↑2 " B " X + " C
120 GØ TØ 10
130 PRINT A "X↑2 + " B " X " C
140 GØ TØ 10
150 PRINT A "X↑2 " B " X " C
160 GØ TØ 10
...
```

In this example it was assumed that the output would always be quadratic polynomials. Handling polynomials of varying degrees involves subscripted variables and will be explained in Chapter 5.

The program could be made more complicated and handle zero coefficients and one coefficients so that a polynomial such as $x^2 - 7$ would be printed simply as x↑2−7 and not as 1x↑2+0x−7 .

EXERCISES 3-8

A Show the output of each of these programs.

1.
```
10 READ X,Y
20 PRINT "("X","Y")"
30 GØ TØ 10
40 DATA 2,3,-4,17,0,-2
50 END
```

2.
```
10 READ X,Y
20 PRINT "("X","Y")";
30 GØ TØ 10
40 DATA 2,3,-4,17,0,-2
50 END
```

3.
```
10 DATA 7,4,8,-6,-2,0
20 READ A,B
30 PRINT A " + " B " I"
40 GØ TØ 20
50 END
```

4.
```
10 READ A,B
20 DATA 7,4,8,-6,-2,0
30 IF B < 0 THEN 60
40 PRINT A " + " B " I"
50 GØ TØ 10
60 PRINT A; B " I"
70 GØ TØ 10
80 END
```

5.
```
20 READ A,B,C
40 PRINT A "X↑2 + " B " X + " C
60 GØ TØ 20
80 DATA 7,4,3,8,-2,10,-1,4,-8,6,-7,0
100 END
```

6.
```
10 READ A,B,C
20 IF B < 0 THEN 60
30 IF C < 0 THEN 90
40 PRINT A "X↑2 + " B " X + " C
50 GØ TØ 10
60 IF C < 0 THEN 110
70 PRINT A "X↑2 " B " X + " C
80 GØ TØ 10
90 PRINT A "X↑2 + " B " X " C
100 GØ TØ 10
110 PRINT A "X↑2" B " X " C
120 GØ TØ 10
130 DATA 7,4,3,8,-2,10,-1,4,-8,6,-7,0
140 END
```

Correct any error(s) in each of these programs.

7.
```
10 READ A,B
20 LET Z = A + B*I
30 PRINT "THE COMPLEX NØ. IS" Z
40 GØ TØ 10
50 DATA 7,4,3,-2,-1,10
60 END
```

8.
```
10 READ A,B,C
20 LET P = A*X↑2 + B*X + C
30 PRINT "THE QUADRATIC IS " P
40 DATA 7,-10,8,4,2,-7
50 END
```

9.
```
10 READ X,Y
20 PRINT (X, Y) "IS THE VERTEX"
 30 GØ TØ 10
40 DATA 7,-2,4,0,-8,10
END
50 END
```

10.
```
1 READ X,Y
2 PRINT "("X,Y")"
3 GØ TØ 1
4 DATA 7,-2,4,0,-8,10
5 END
```

Correct any error(s) in each of the following programs.

11.
```
10 READ X,Y
20 PRINT "("X","Y")
30 GØ TØ 10
40 DATA 7,-2,4,0,-8,10
50 END
```

12.
```
10 READ A,B
20 IF B < 0 THEN 40
30 PRINT A " + " B " I"
40 PRINT A; B " I"
50 GØ TØ 10
60 DATA 7,4,-2,-8,0,-7
70 END
```

B **13.** Write a program that, given A and B, prints the linear polynomial AX + B.

C **14.** Rewrite the program segment that was given on page 105 for printing polynomials so that it also eliminates the printing of coefficients that are either zero or one.

3-9 DIFFICULTY OF DETERMINING EXACT EQUALITY

Consider the following statement: 40 IF SQR(D) = X/Y THEN 100. Its meaning is clear; if the square root of D equals the quotient of X divided by Y, branch to statement 100. Otherwise continue to the next statement in numerical sequence.

This seems straightforward, but there is a problem and it lies with the meaning of "=". The computer will branch to line 100 only if SQR(D) *exactly equals* X/Y. When a programmer traces his program using pencil and paper, he does the calculations himself. For example, if D = 4, X = 8, and Y = 4, then SQR(4) = 8/4 and the programmer expects the computer to branch to line 100. However, he should not be surprised if it does not, for reasons we will now explain.

Computers do not perform calculations the same way humans do. For one thing the computer represents numbers in the binary system. For integers this causes no inaccuracy but for fractions a finite decimal in base ten often converts to an infinite decimal in base two. Here is an example.

$$.3_{ten} = .010011001\ldots_{two}$$

No computer can store this entire infinite repeating decimal. It must be "chopped off" after a certain number of digits.

Secondly, computers can only add. All other operations must be reduced to an addition process or a process of finding a tabular value. Thus the square root of 4, when calculated in base two by a complicated process and reconverted to base ten, may not turn out to be *exactly* two. Then the test in the IF clause of line 40 will yield "NO", the computer will not branch to line 100, and the program will go on to produce erroneous results.

What can be done to avoid this error?

The square root of 4 may not be calculated as precisely 2 but it will be close, say, 1.99999999. It will lie within a certain *tolerance* or margin of error of the true result. Instead of demanding exact equality, the programmer should test to see if the two quantities, SQR(D) and X/Y in the example above, lie within a specified tolerance of each other. Line 40 can be rewritten as the following.

```
40 IF ABS(SQR(D) - X/Y) < .00001 THEN 100
```

The tolerance is .00001. The test now is whether SQR(D) and X/Y are within .00001 of each other. The assumption is that if they are that close, the difference is probably due to roundoff or conversion to and from the binary system.

In algebraic notation the test is written as follows.

$$|\sqrt{D} - X/Y| < .00001 \text{ ?}$$

The absolute value sign is needed because it is not known whether $\sqrt{D}$ will be slightly larger or slightly smaller than X/Y. If it is slightly larger, $\sqrt{D} - X/Y$ is positive; if it is smaller, $\sqrt{D} - X/Y$ is negative. But in either case as long as $\sqrt{D}$ lies within .00001 of X/Y, we want to assume equality and branch to 100.

Not all decisions of equality need be complicated by considerations of tolerance. For example, if a program begins like this,

```
10 READ X
20 IF X = 0 THEN 100
        ...
```

there is no need to revise line 20. X is being read from DATA and is not the result of a computation. Testing X for exact equality to 0 should cause no problem and the program should work as planned.

Similarly, if all values are integers and only the four operations of addition, subtraction, multiplication, and division are used, the program should proceed as in a pencil-and-paper trace. For example, if A and B are integers, a decision such as 20 IF A − B = B THEN 100 should cause no problem, and no tolerance is needed. But 20 IF A ↑ (1/3) = B THEN 100 probably requires a tolerance.

The size of the tolerance is determined by several factors and no general rule can be given. The tolerance depends on the number of digits and method of computation used by the computer in question. If a program is not executing as planned because expected equality is not occurring, you should experiment with different tolerances until desired results are obtained.

EXERCISES 3-9

A Rewrite each statement to introduce the tolerance specified.

Example 1: `50 IF X = Y/3 THEN 80 ; .0005`
Answer: `50 IF ABS(X - Y/3) < .0005 THEN 80`

Example 2: `20 IF M <> SQR(K + 1) THEN 50 ; .001`
Answer: `20 IF ABS(M - SQR(K + 1)) >= .001 THEN 50`

1. `12 IF C/D = .5 THEN 90 ; .0001`
2. `35 IF (2*N)↑(1/5) = P THEN 10 ; .00001`
3. `25 IF R - S <> L/2 THEN 75 ; .005`
4. `67 IF A↑2 + B↑2 = C↑2 THEN 110 ; .00005`

Write an IF . . . THEN statement that corresponds to each algebraic decision.

5. If $|x - a| < .1$, then 100.
6. If $|2r - s^2| > .01$, go to 80.
7. If $|z| < .0005$, then go to 75.
8. If $|x^2 - 2x + 1| < .005$, then go to 79.
9. If $|m - \sqrt{p}| \leq .00001$, then 47.

Write BASIC statements that implement the flowchart portions shown below.

10.

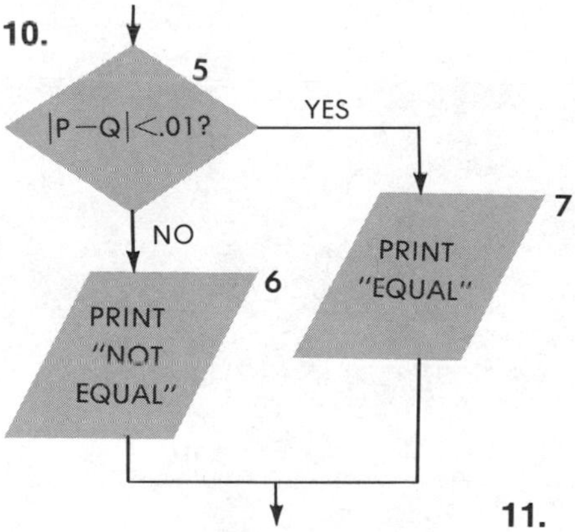

11.

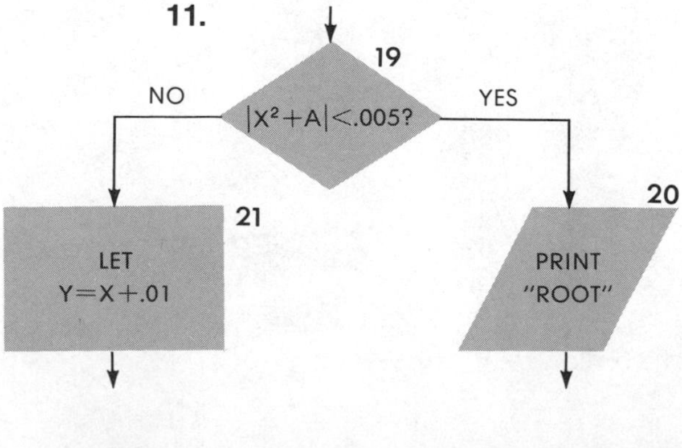

Computers in Education

Computers have long been used in the administrative aspects of education. Perhaps your schedule of classes this year was created or printed by a computer. Another educational application is shown by the following problem.

PROBLEM: The input consists of a student's code number, total quality points (grades) for the latest marking period (A = 4, B = 3, C = 2, D = 1, F = 0), and number of courses. Write a program to compute the student's grade-point-average (G.P.A.) and decide whether the student is on the "alpha" honor roll (3.5 G.P.A. or better) or the "beta" honor roll (minimum of 3.0 G.P.A.). Print the results in the following form.

STUDENT NØ.	G.P.A.	ALPHA H.R.	BETA H.R.
0603	3.64	X	
0641	3.05		X
0725	2.67		
0742	3.43		X
0756	1.89		
	. . .		

A printout of a class schedule being examined by a teacher

Probably the trickiest part of the task is printing the last two columns of output. Here is an outline of the program showing some of the key statements.

Program Outline

1. Print the headings with the following lines.

```
PRINT
PRINT "STUDENT NØ.","G.P.A.","ALPHA H.R.","BETA H.R."
PRINT
```

2. Read N (student code number), Q (total quality points), and C (number of courses).

3. Compute the G.P.A.

```
LET G = Q/C
```

4. Print the student number and G.P.A. but stay on the same output line until alpha and beta honor roll possibilities are checked.

```
PRINT N, G,
```

5. Decide whether $G \geq 3.5$. If so, print an X in the third output zone, get off that output line, and return to the READ statement for new DATA.

6. If $G < 3.5$, test whether $G \geq 3.0$. If it is, skip to the fourth zone, print an X, and get off that output line, like this.

```
PRINT , "X"
```

   Then return to the READ statement.

7. If $G < 3.0$, use a dummy PRINT to get off that output line before returning for more DATA.

Projects

1. Write the complete program for the honor roll example above.
2. Revise the program in Project 1 so that the complete titles "ALPHA HØNØR RØLL" and "BETA HØNØR RØLL" are printed. (Note that "ALPHA HØNØR RØLL" requires *16* print spaces.)
3. Write the program for the flowchart of Project 1 on page 27 (withholding taxes for payroll).
4. Write the program for the flowchart of Project 2 on page 27 (extension of withholding tax program).

CHAPTER SUMMARY

In order to display a program's output in an attractive manner, a programmer may use the PRINT statement together with a suitable choice of commas or semicolons. For even greater flexibility in spacing the output, the programmer may also use the TAB function.

Sample Statement	Effect of the Statement
50 PRINT X, Y	The numerical value of X is printed in the first print zone (up to 16 positions wide). The value of Y is printed in the second zone.
70 PRINT X; Y	The value of X is printed, one space is skipped, and the value of Y is printed.
90 PRINT	The printer advances to the next line.
95 PRINT TAB(10);X;TAB(20);Y	The value of X is printed, starting at position 10. The value of Y begins at position 20.

Decisions are made using the IF . . . THEN statement. The general form is

IF (equation or inequality) THEN (statement number).

Examples: 50 IF X = Y THEN 100   80 IF A > B THEN 10

Printing ordered pairs, complex numbers, and polynomials requires special use of quotation marks in PRINT statements.

Examples: 50 PRINT "(" X "," Y ")"   70 PRINT A "X↑2"

CHAPTER OBJECTIVES AND REVIEW

Objective: To show the output from a program involving PRINT statements that contain commas, semicolons, TAB functions or quotation marks. *(Sections 3-1 through 3-6 and Section 3-8)*

Show the output from each program. Number the key print positions.

1.
```
10 READ X
20 IF X < 0 THEN 10
30 PRINT X,-X
40 GØ TØ 10
50 DATA 5,-2,0,.5
60 END
```

2.
```
10 PRINT "PERIMETERS = ";
20 READ L,W
30 PRINT 2*L+2*W;
40 GØ TØ 20
50 DATA 4,3,10,5
60 END
```

3.
```
10 READ R, S
20 PRINT TAB(7); R*S; TAB(14); R/S
30 GØ TØ 10
40 DATA 3, 2, -8, 4, 0, 6
50 END
```

Objective: To correct all errors in a given program that involves one or more PRINT or IF . . . THEN statements. *(Sections 3-4 and 3-8)*

Correct all errors in the following programs.

4.
```
10 INPUT A,B
20 IF A > B THEN 50
30 IF A = B THEN 60
40 IF A < B THEN 70
50 PRINT A "GREATER"
60 PRINT "EQUAL"
70 PRINT B "GREATER"
80 GØ TØ 10
90 DATA 6,4,5,5,2,11
100 END
```

5.
```
5 PRINT "ØRDERED PAIR IS":
10 READ (X,Y)
20 IF ABS(X) > ABS(Y) THEN 50
30 PRINT "CLØSER TØ Y-AXIS"
40 GØ TØ 60
50 PRINT "CLØSER TØ X-AXIS"
60 GØ TØ 10
70 DATA 11,3,-4,-1,0,9
80 END
```

Objective: To decide whether a given PRINT or IF . . . THEN statement is valid for your system. *(Sections 3-5, 3-6, and 3-7)*

Which of the following are valid IF . . . THEN statements?

6. `10 IF X = Y ØR X = Z THEN 50`

7. `20 IF X = 9 THEN LET Q = 4`

8. `50 IF A/B >= C - 2 THEN 10`

9. `15 IF R*7 < S THEN GØ TØ 60`

Which of the following are valid PRINT statements?

10. `11 PRINT`

11. `30 PRINT X,Y;Z`

12. `83 PRINT "AREA"= A`

13. `101 PRINT S "= SUM"`

14. `15 PRINT "("X",Y")"`

15. `20 PRINT R + 2`

16. `100 PRINT "SIDE ="S"PERIM ="4*S`

17. `48 PRINT "X ="X,`

Objective: To write a program for a given flowchart that involves at least one decision besides ØUT ØF DATA? *(Sections 3-7 and 3-9)*

18. Write a program for the flowchart below. Input DATA −16,81,0.

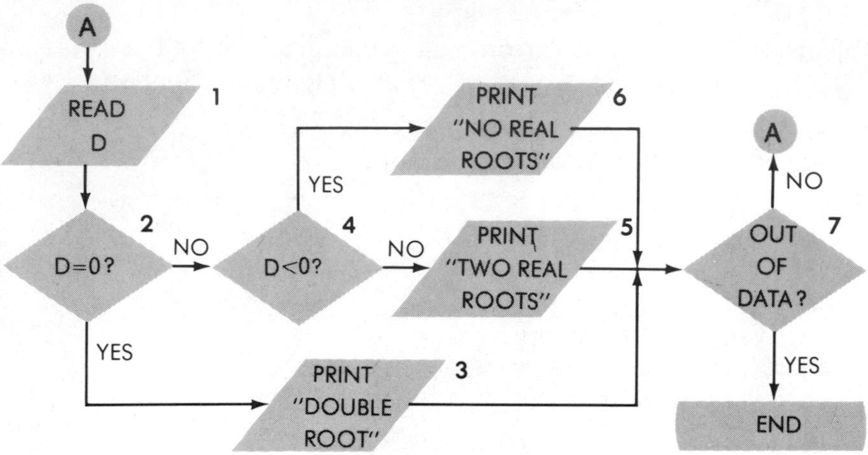

Objective: To flowchart a given program that involves at least one IF . . . THEN statement. *(Section 3-7)*

19. Flowchart the program shown at the right.

```
10 READ M
20 IF M↑2 > 50 THEN 50
30 PRINT "SQUARE <= 50"
40 GØ TØ 10
50 PRINT "SQUARE > 50"
60 GØ TØ 10
70 DATA 5,10,7
80 END
```

Objective: To trace a program involving at least one IF . . . THEN statement. *(Section 3-7)*

20. Trace the program of Exercise 19.

Objective: To use at least one IF . . . THEN statement in writing a BASIC program to solve a given problem. *(Section 3-7)*

21. Write a BASIC program to read real numbers A and B. If B $\neq$ 0, print A/B. If B = 0, print "QUØTIENT UNDEFINED."

Objective: To write an IF . . . THEN statement that tests whether two expressions are within a given tolerance of each other. *(Section 3-9)*

22. Write an IF . . . THEN statement such that if A = B within a tolerance of .0005, then the computer jumps to statement 100.

ROUND THREE: *PROGRAMS FOR STUDENT ASSIGNMENT*

GENERAL INSTRUCTIONS:

1. In each exercise on pages 115 through 125, write and run a program that will do what is specified in the exercise.
2. If the program has several possible outcomes, the DATA must produce each outcome at least once.
3. Regardless of the possible outcomes, the program must process at least three sets of DATA.
4. Label output with appropriate messages or headings.
5. If your teacher requires it, submit a flowchart.

ALGEBRA ONE

1. Read nonzero real numbers A, B, C, and D. Are these numbers proportional in the order given? That is, does $\frac{A}{B} = \frac{C}{D}$?
2. Find the slope of the line through two given points in the coordinate plane. Include the possibility that the slope may be undefined. (See Ex. 2, p. 31.)
3. Input two real numbers. Without actually multiplying the numbers, determine whether their product is positive, negative, or zero. (See Ex. 3, p. 31.)
4. Given a positive real number, compute its square root by using the SQR function, the .5 power, and the 1/2 power. Print the output in four labeled columns.

```
NUMBER        SQR        .5 PØWER        1/2 PØWER
```

5. Read the coordinates of a point in the *xy*-plane. Decide the number of the quadrant in which the point lies or, if it lies on an axis, decide whether it lies on the *x*-axis, on the *y*-axis, or on both. (See Ex. 5, p. 31.)

Use a variety of values for A and B to test the truth of the following.

6. $|A + B| = |A| + |B|$ **7.** $|A \cdot B| = |A| \cdot |B|$ **8.** $|A - B| = |B - A|$

In Exercises 9 through 12 read rational numbers A, B, and C, which are the coefficients of a linear equation of the form $Ax + By = C$. Assume that A and B are not both zero. (See Ex. 8 through 11, p. 32.)

9. Compute and print the slope of the graph of the equation. Remember that the slope may be undefined.

10. Print the x-intercept of the graph as an ordered pair.

11. Print the y-intercept of the graph as an ordered pair.

12. Input real numbers R and S. Decide whether the point (R, S) lies on the graph of $\text{A}x + \text{B}y = \text{C}$.

13. Input a real number X. Print X, its additive inverse, and (if it has one) its multiplicative inverse. (See Ex. 12, p. 32.)

14. Read real numbers A and B. Without computing A + B, decide whether the sum of A and B is positive, negative, or zero. (See Ex. 13, p. 32.)

15. Four dice are rolled. Accept the four numbers which appear on the top faces of the dice and decide whether 0, 2, 3, or 4 of the dice show the same value, or whether two show one value and the other pair show another value.

16. Given five real numbers, print only the smallest. Do not assume the numbers are listed in the DATA in any specific order. (See Ex. 7, p. 31.)

17. Students in a certain course take two examinations. If a score is less than 40 on either exam, then the student fails the course. If the average on the two exams is below 60, the student also fails the course. An average of 60 to 90, inclusive, is passing (without honors). An average above 90 is passing with honors. Given a student's scores on the two exams, print whether he or she fails, passes (without honors), or passes with honors. (See Ex. 16, p. 32.)

18. Arrange a set of three numbers in descending order. For example, for the data values 8, 11, −3, print 11   8   −3. Two or three of the numbers may be equal. (See Ex. 17, p. 32.)

19. Given a linear equation $\text{A}x + \text{B} = \text{C}$, solve for x. For example, if the equation is $7x + 5 = 19$, print $x = 2$. A, B, and C are real numbers. Do *not* assume that $\text{A} \neq 0$. (See Ex. 18, p. 32.)

20. Given an inequality $\text{A}x + \text{B} > \text{C}$ (A, B, C real numbers), solve for x. For example, if the inequality is $7x + 5 > 19$, print $x > 2$
(See Ex. 19, p. 32.)

21. Given the coordinates of a point in the xy-plane, decide whether the point lies in the graph of the solution set of the following system of inequalities.

$$\begin{aligned} 2x - y &< 3 \\ x &\leq 3 - 3y \\ x &> 0 \\ y &> 0 \end{aligned}$$

GEOMETRY

22. Read three positive numbers. Determine whether these could represent the lengths of the sides of a triangle. (See Ex. 19, p. 11.)

23. Given an angle measure greater than 0 and less than 180, classify the angle as ACUTE, RIGHT, or ØBTUSE. (See Ex. 22, p. 32.)

24. Given the lengths of any two sides of a right triangle, the Pythagorean Theorem enables you to compute the third side. Design a program that finds the length of the missing side whether it is a leg or the hypotenuse. One way to accomplish this is to READ A, B, C but enter 0 for the unknown side. Then test whether A = 0, B = 0, or C = 0 and branch to one of three assignment steps to compute the missing length and print it. (See Ex. 23, p. 33.)

25. Given the radius of a circle, compute the area by using $3\frac{1}{7}$ for pi and 3.1416 for pi. Find the difference each time. Print the output in three labeled columns.

26. Determine the number of points of intersection of a circle with center at (X_1, Y_1) and radius R_1 with the circle with center (X_2, Y_2) and radius R_2. Assume that neither circle lies in the interior of the other.

27. Given the coordinates of four points in the *xy*-plane, determine whether the quadrilateral formed by joining the points in order is equilateral.

28. Read three positive numbers A, B, and C. Determine whether these could be the lengths of the sides of a right triangle. Note: You must first check that A, B, and C can be sides of *any* triangle. (See Ex. 29, p. 33.)

29. Given the lengths of the sides of a triangle, determine whether the triangle is EQUILATERAL, ISØSCELES, or SCALENE. (See Ex. 20, p. 11.)

30. Given the coordinates of four points in the *xy*-plane, determine whether the quadrilateral formed by joining the points in order is a parallelogram. (See Ex. 43, p. 34.)

In Exercises 31 and 32 read the lengths of three sides of a triangle and the lengths of the three corresponding sides of a second triangle. (See Ex. 39 and 40, p. 34.)

31. Are the triangles congruent? **32.** Are the triangles similar?

33. Read the lengths of the four sides of a quadrilateral. Decide whether the quadrilateral is equilateral. (See Ex. 41, p. 34.)

34. Read the lengths of the five sides of a pentagon. Decide whether the pentagon is equilateral. (See Ex. 42, p. 34.)

35. Given the coordinates of three points in the *xy*-plane, determine whether the points are collinear. (See Ex. 35, p. 33.)

36. In Exercise 35, if the points are not collinear, decide whether the triangle formed by joining them is ISØSCELES, EQUILATERAL, or SCALENE. (See Ex. 36, p. 33.)

37. In Exercise 35, if the points are not collinear, print the perimeter of the triangle formed by joining them. (See Ex. 37, p. 33.)

38. In Exercise 35, if the points are not collinear, compute the area of the triangle formed by joining them. (See Ex. 21, p. 29.)

39. In Exercise 35, if the points are not collinear, decide whether the triangle is a right triangle by computing the slopes of the three sides to see whether the product is −1 for any pair. A vertical side must be handled as a special case.

40. Determine whether a given point (X_1, Y_1) lies within, on, or outside a circle with center (X_2, Y_2) and radius R. (If you have not done so already, read Lesson 3-9: "Difficulty of Determining Exact Equality" on pages 107-109.)

41. Given two positive real numbers X and Y, print X, Y, their arithmetic mean, their geometric mean, and which of the two means is larger. Run the program for at least ten X-Y pairs.

42. Given the coordinates of the vertices of quadrilateral *ABCD* in the *xy*-plane, what kind of quadrilateral is formed when the midpoints of the sides of *ABCD* are joined?

ALGEBRA TWO

43. Given the coordinates of the center and the length of its radius, print the equation of a circle.

44. Given the coordinates of two points in the *xy*-plane, print the equation of the line through the two points. (See Ex. 55, p. 35.)

45. Given the coordinates of two points in the XY-plane, print the equation of the perpendicular bisector of the segment determined by the two points. (See Ex. 79, p. 36.)

In Exercises 46 and 47 read real numbers A, B, and C, which are the coefficients of a quadratic equation $AX^2 + BX + C = 0$.

46. Decide whether the equation has zero, one, or two real roots. Do not actually compute the roots. (See Ex. 57, p. 35.)

47. If the equation has one or more real roots, compute and print the root(s). (See Ex. 59, p. 35.)

48. Input the coefficients of a quadratic equation $Ax^2 + Bx + C = 0$ (A, B, and C rational with $A \neq 0$) and a proposed root $D + Ei$. Check by substitution whether $D + Ei$ is a root.

49. Given two integers that are the roots of a quadratic equation, print the equation in the form $Ax^2 + Bx + C = 0$.

In Exercises 50-56, a system of linear equations is given as shown at the right. Input the coefficients. (See Ex. 60-65, p. 35.)

$$\begin{cases} Ax + By = C \\ Dx + Ey = F \end{cases}$$

50. Determine whether the graphs of the equations are parallel. Assume that a straight line may be parallel to itself.

51. Determine whether the graphs of the equations are perpendicular.

52. Determine whether the graphs intersect. If they do, do they intersect in one point or in infinitely many points?

53. Determine whether the solution set of the system is the null (empty) set, a one-element set, or an infinite set.

54. If the solution set has one element, print it as an ordered pair.

55. Determine whether the equations are consistent or inconsistent.

56. Determine whether the equations are dependent or independent.

57. Find the intersection, if it exists, of two lines whose equations are given in slope-intercept form.

58. Find the intersection, if it exists, of two lines in the *xy*-plane, given the coordinates of two points on each line.

59. A quadratic polynomial can be written as $Ax^2 + Bx + C$ or as $A(x - K)^2 + H$. Given the first form, derive the second.

60. For the parabola defined by $y = Ax^2 + Bx + C$, read rational numbers A, B, and C and then print the coordinates of the vertex and whether the vertex is a MAXIMUM or MINIMUM point. (See Ex. 67, p. 35.)

61. The equation of an ellipse with its center at the origin is $\frac{x^2}{A^2} + \frac{y^2}{B^2} = 1$.

Read A and B (neither is zero) and print the coordinates of the foci of the ellipse. Remember that the foci sometimes are on the *x*-axis and sometimes are on the *y*-axis. (See Ex. 72, p. 36.)

62. Solve absolute value equations of the form $|x - A| = B$ (A and B real). (See Ex. 73, p. 36.)

63. Read a real number X. Print the cube root of X. Then, if X is non-negative, print the principal fourth root of X. If X is negative, print NØ REAL FØURTH RØØT. (See Ex. 74, p. 36.)

64. Let a function f be defined by $f(x) = 3x + 4$ and let g be defined by $g(x) = x^2 - 14$. Use a variety of values for x and decide in each case whether $f(g(x)) = g(f(x))$. (See Ex. 78, p. 36.)

In Exercises 65-69 you are given the ordered pairs of three noncollinear points in the *xy*-plane and the triangle formed by joining these points.

65. Print the equations of the lines that contain the three medians.

66. Print the equations of the lines that contain the altitudes.

67. Print the equations of the lines that contain the perpendicular bisectors of the sides.

68. Compute the coordinates of the center of the circumscribed circle.

69. Compute the length of the radius of the circumscribed circle.

In Exercises 70 and 71 consider a complex number A + B*i* and input A and B.

70. Print the conjugate of A + B*i*.

71. Print the reciprocal of A + B*i*.

In Exercises 72-74 you are given complex numbers A + B*i* and C + D*i*. Print the following in standard form.

72. Their sum

73. Their product

74. The quotient (if it exists) of A + B*i* divided by C + D*i*

75. Given a real number (positive, negative, or zero), print its square roots. Include imaginary roots. (See Ex. 80, p. 36.)

ADVANCED MATHEMATICS

76. Given the coordinates of a point in the *xy*-plane, compute the trigonometric functions of the angle in standard position having that point on its terminal side. Assume that the point is not the origin but allow the possibility that the point may lie on an axis.

77. Given sin *x* and the quadrant in which *x* lies, compute and print: (**a**) cos *x*; (**b**) tan *x*; (**c**) cot *x*; (**d**) sec *x*; (**e**) csc *x*. Remember that tan, cot, sec, or csc may be undefined. Do not use any of the BASIC trigonometric functions available on your system. (See Ex. 89, p. 37.)

In Exercises 78 and 79 you are given the quadrant in which an angle x lies. (Note: Most versions of BASIC do not have any built-in arcsin or arccos function, just ATN.)

78. Given sin *x*, find *x* in degrees.

79. Given cos *x*, find *x* in degrees.

For Exercises 80 and 81, you are given $\cos x$ and the quadrant in which $x/2$ lies.

80. Find $\sin\frac{x}{2}$ using the formula $|\sin\frac{x}{2}| = \sqrt{\frac{1-\cos x}{2}}$.

81. Find $\cos\frac{x}{2}$ using the formula $|\cos\frac{x}{2}| = \sqrt{\frac{1+\cos x}{2}}$.

In Exercises 82-85 you are given the following combinations of data for a right triangle. Solve for the remaining parts.

82. HL (hypotenuse-leg)
83. HA (hypotenuse-acute angle)
84. LA (leg-acute angle)
85. LL (leg-leg)

For a nonright triangle, given the right combination of three of the parts of the triangle, it is possible to "solve" the triangle, that is, to find the remaining three parts (side and angles). In Exercises 86-90 solve nonright triangles, given the following combinations of data.

86. ASA
87. SAA
88. SSS
89. SAS

90. SSA (This is the so-called "ambiguous case.")

91. Given the coordinates of a point in the Cartesian plane, convert to polar coordinates.

92. Given the polar coordinates of a point, convert to Cartesian coordinates.

93. Given a linear equation $Ax + By = C$ (A, B, and C rational), convert it to polar form.

94. Given the Cartesian coordinates of a point in three-dimensional space, print the spherical coordinates of the point.

In Exercises 95 and 96, consider a complex number $A + Bi$ and input A and B. Print each of the following.

95. The square roots of $A + Bi$
96. The polar form of $A + Bi$

97. Given a complex number in polar form, convert it to standard form.

98. Find the roots of any quadratic equation with rational coefficients. Solve over C, the field of complex numbers.

99. Solve cubic equations using the formula discovered by Tartaglia and later published by Cardan.

100. Given the equation $Ax^2 + Bxy + Cy^2 + Dx + Ey + F = 0$ (all coefficients rational), determine whether the graph of the equation is a circle, parabola, ellipse, hyperbola, two lines, one line, a point, or the empty set.

101. Given a 2×2 matrix, print its multiplicative inverse (if it has one).

102. Given three consecutive terms of a sequence of real numbers, decide whether the sequence is arithmetic, geometric, or neither. (See Ex. 96, p. 37.)

In Exercises 103-105, the components of the two-dimensional vectors, $\vec{u}$ and $\vec{v}$, are given.

103. Determine whether $\vec{u}$ and $\vec{v}$ are perpendicular. (See Ex. 97, p. 37.)

104. Determine whether they are parallel. (See Ex. 98, p. 37.)

105. Decide whether they satisfy the Triangle Inequality $|\vec{u}+\vec{v}| \leq |\vec{u}|+|\vec{v}|$, where $|\vec{u}|$ represents the norm of $\vec{u}$.

In Exercises 106-109, you are given two three-dimensional vectors, $\vec{v}$ and $\vec{w}$. Input the components of the vectors.

106. Decide whether the vectors are perpendicular.

107. Decide whether the vectors are parallel.

108. Compute the cosine of the angle between the vectors, neither of which is the zero vector. Use this formula: $\cos A = \dfrac{\vec{v} \cdot \vec{w}}{|\vec{v}| \cdot |\vec{w}|}$, where $0 \leq A \leq \pi$, $|\vec{v}|$ represents the norm of $\vec{v}$, and $\vec{v} \cdot \vec{w}$ represents the inner product ("dot" product) of $\vec{v}$ and $\vec{w}$.

109. Compute the direction cosines of $\vec{v}$ and of $\vec{w}$.

In Exercises 110-112, you are given a scalar R and the components of two two-dimensional vectors, $\vec{v}$ and $\vec{t}$. Decide for each set of data whether the following properties of scalar multiplication hold.

110. Commutative Property: $R\vec{v} = \vec{v}R$

111. Distributive Properties: $R(\vec{v} + \vec{t}) = R\vec{v} + R\vec{t}$ and $(\vec{v} + \vec{t})R = \vec{v}R + \vec{t}R$

112. Norm property: $|R\vec{v}| = |R| \cdot |\vec{v}|$

113. Find the distance from a point to a line in the *xy*-plane, given the coordinates of the point and the equation of the line, $Ax + By + C = 0$. Use the formula $d = \dfrac{|Ax + By + C|}{\sqrt{A^2 + B^2}}$. (See Ex. 99, p. 37.)

114. In the *xy*-plane, find the distance from a point to a line, given the coordinates of the point and the coordinates of two points on the line. (See Ex. 100, p. 38.)

115. Given the degree measure of an angle and its sine and the degree measure of another angle and its sine, interpolate to find the sine of a desired angle between the first two.

116. Compute square roots of positive integers using Newton's Method, which consists of alternately dividing and averaging. Stop when the square of the estimate is within .001 of the given number.

117. Use the Euclidean Algorithm to find the greatest common divisor of two positive integers.

BUSINESS

118. Calculate the selling price of an item, given a particular cost and a desired markup. The markup can be based on either cost (enter a code number of 1) or selling price (code number 2).

119. Do flowchart Exercise 105, p. 38, as a programming exercise.

120. Do flowchart Exercise 106, p. 38, as a programming exercise.

121. Do flowchart Exercise 107, p. 38, as a programming exercise.

122. Enter an employee's Social Security number (without hyphens), year-to-date earnings, and year-to-date Social Security tax withheld. Also input this week's earnings for the employee. Calculate the proper Social Security tax based on this rule: The tax rate is 6.70% but no more tax is to be withheld when the year-to-date earnings reach $31,800. Print the employee's Social Security number, new year-to-date earnings, Social Security tax withheld this week, and new year-to-date Social Security tax withheld.

123. In an attempt to encourage consumers to use lower horsepower cars and conserve energy, a state adopted a set of annual license fees based upon the power rating of each car.

Horsepower	License Fee
Up to 50 hp	$ 0
More than 50 but 100 hp or less	30
More than 100 but 200 hp or less	70
More than 200 but 300 hp or less	150
More than 300 hp	500

Given the auto's horsepower, print the license fee.

124. Do flowchart Exercise 108, p. 39, as a programming exercise.

125. Do flowchart Exercise 109, p. 39, as a programming exercise.

126. Do flowchart Exercise 110, p. 39. (raises granted to employees of the Tiger Electric Company) as a programming exercise.

127. In Exercise 126, suppose that in addition to the 12%, 8%, or 15% raises, any worker who has been with the company five years or more receives an extra 2% raise. Thus, in addition to the input of Exercise 126, also enter the number of years the employee has worked for Tiger Electric. Print the new weekly salary.

128. In a certain city if you get a speeding ticket, your fine is based on the amount by which you exceeded the speed limit.

Amount over Limit (miles per hour)	Fine
1-10 mph	$ 5
11-20 mph	10
21-30 mph	20
31-40 mph	40
above 41 mph	80

Given the speed limit and the speed arrested at, print the fine.

129. Suppose that discounts for direct-dial long-distance calls are figured as follows (where the times are at the calling points).

Time	Day	Discount
7 A.M.–5 P.M.	Weekdays	None
5–11 P.M.	Any day	20%
11 P.M.–7 A.M.	Any day	40%
7 A.M.–11 P.M.	Saturday	20%
7 A.M.–5 P.M.	Sunday	40%

For each call enter the day of the week (1 = Sunday, 2 = Monday, . . . , 7 = Saturday) and the time the call originated (in terms of a twenty-four hour clock; e.g., for 7 P.M., use 1900). Print the discount rate for the call.

PHYSICAL SCIENCES

130. Do flowchart Exercise 113, p. 39, as a programming exercise.

131. Do flowchart Exercise 115, p. 39, as a programming exercise.

132. Do flowchart Exercise 116, p. 39, as a programming exercise.

133. A quantity of carbon dioxide (CO_2) is held at standard temperature (273° K) and standard pressure (1 atmosphere). Given one of the following—the number of molecules, the number of moles, or the weight of the gas—find the volume of the CO_2 at a second temperature and pressure. The user will input a code number (1, 2, or 3) indicating whether the next number entered will represent number of molecules, number of moles, or weight. Also entered will be the second temperature and pressure.

134. The volume, pressure, and temperature (degrees Kelvin) of an ideal gas are related by the formula $v_2 = \frac{p_1 T_2 v_1}{p_2 T_1}$. The subscripts refer to the state of the gas at two different times. Given the values of any five variables, find the sixth. Read all six variables but enter zero for the missing one.

135. Density (d) is mass (m) per unit volume (v). Given values for any two of the variables, find the third. Read values for all three variables but with zero for the unknown one. Then use the appropriate formula to compute the missing quantity.

136. As in Exercises 136-138 on page 83, consider the relationship in an electric circuit among the voltage, E, the current, I, and the resistance, R. Given values of any two of the variables, find the third. The program is to read all three variables but in each set of DATA, the unknown one is entered as zero. The computer is to use the appropriate formula to calculate this missing quantity.

137. Coulomb's law of electrostatics states that $F = k\,\frac{Q_1 Q_2}{s^2}$, where F = the force between two point charges (in newtons), Q_1 and Q_2 are the magnitudes of the charges (in coulombs), and s is the distance (in meters) between the sources. In a vacuum, $k = 8.987 \times 10^9 \frac{\text{newton-meter}^2}{\text{coulomb}^2}$; in air $k = 8.93 \times 10^9 \frac{\text{N-m}^2}{\text{coul}^2}$.

Enter a code number that tells whether the charges are in a vacuum or in air. Then, given Q_1, Q_2, and s, determine F.

138. The change in pitch produced by the relative motion between a source of sound and a listener is known as the *Doppler effect.* Assume that the listener is stationary. Enter a code number that tells whether the sound source is moving toward or away from the listener. In either case, given the frequency of the emitted sound, the velocity of the sound in the medium, and the speed of the moving source, determine the frequency of the sound reaching the stationary listener.

139. Repeat Exercise 138 but now assume that the sound source is stationary and the listener is moving. Again distinguish between two cases: listener moving away from the source and listener moving toward the source. In either case, given the frequency of the emitted sound, the velocity of the sound in the the medium, and the speed of the moving listener, compute the frequency of the sound reaching the listener.

140. Do flowchart Exercise 114, p. 39, as a programming exercise.

4

LOOPS

4-1 COUNTING

How can we program a computer to count? Accomplishing this task will open the door to numerous programs in widespread use. To start with a simple example, suppose we want the computer to count from one to ten, that is, to print 1, 2, 3, 4, 5, 6, 7, 8, 9, 10.

In an earlier chapter we used the word *algorithm.* An **algorithm** is a set of steps for performing a task, usually a repetitive task. You have learned many algorithms. Every time you perform long division you use an algorithm. You have developed your own algorithm for traveling to school each morning. BASIC, like FORTRAN, is called an "algorithmic" programming language because it was created with problem-solving in mind.

When confronted with a problem, the programmer's first job is to create an algorithm to accomplish the task. To guide his thinking he may want to state the steps in words. For example, our count-to-ten problem could be handled by this algorithm.

1. Start I at zero.
2. Add one to I.
3. Print I.
4. Is I < 10? If it is, go back to step 2.
   If it is not, go to step 5.
5. End.

The following flowchart illustrates these five steps.

Flowchart 4-1

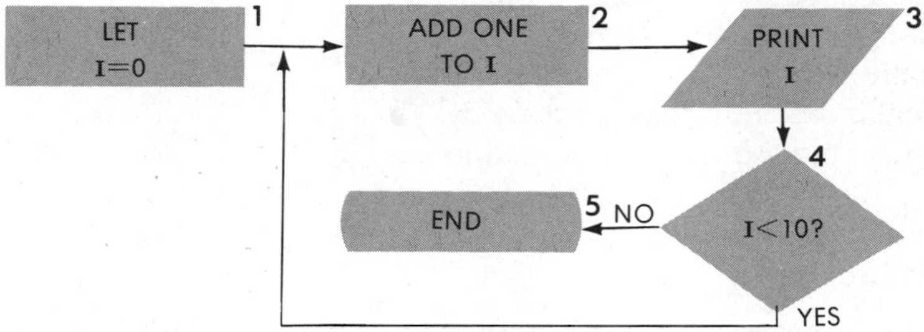

The flowchart shows that this algorithm contains a three-step **loop,** that is, a set of steps that is performed many times (ten in this case).

The only step of the program that involves a new idea is step 2: "Add one to I." We will need a LET statement to accomplish this. We add one to I by writing this statement.

```
20 LET I = I + 1
```

This is not an algebraic equation. If it were, it would have no solution. It is a LET statement in a BASIC program and it must be interpreted the way the computer will interpret it.

In handling a LET statement

1. The machine starts with the expression to the *right* of the equal sign.
2. Using the current values of any variables in this expression, it evaluates the formula according to the rules discussed in Lesson 2-5 on page 54. The right side is thus reduced to a single value.
3. The computer now examines the left side of the equality to find what name (that is, what memory location) the programmer wishes to assign to the value computed from the right-hand formula.

Let us apply this procedure to our key line 20 LET I = I + 1 .

1. The computer starts with "I + 1."
2. It adds the current value of I (which has been set to zero by step 1) to 1, getting 1 as the answer.
3. It stores this 1 as the *new* value of I.

Thus the effect of line 20 was to change location I from 0 to 1. The next time the statement is executed, I changes from 1 to 2, then from 2 to 3, and so on. The program is working because the location "I" in memory is serving as a *counter.* Because of the statement "I = I + 1," the computer is counting. The program itself can now be written.

In Program 4-1 at the right, line 10 is not needed. Most BASIC compilers start all variables at zero automatically. Also, the semicolon is optional in line 30. It saves space by printing 1 to 10 on a single line rather than one numeral per line.

Program 4-1

```
10 LET I = 0
20 LET I = I + 1
30 PRINT I;
40 IF I < 10 THEN 20
50 END
```

EXERCISES 4-1

A Write *Yes* or *No* to show whether each of the following is a valid LET statement.

1. `20 LET S = 2*S`
2. `10 LET I + 2 = I`
3. `50 LET S = S + K`
4. `90 LET K = K + 4*(T-2)`

If, entering line 20, I = 5, what value is assigned to I by each LET statement?

5. `20 LET I = I + 5`
6. `20 LET I = 3*I`
7. `20 LET I = I - 1`
8. `20 LET I = I * I`

Write programs for Exercises 9 through 12. In each exercise have your program resemble Program 4-1 except in one line.

9. Count by 2's from 2 to 10. **10.** Count from 1 to 20.
11. Count from 1 to 10, printing each numeral on a separate line.
12. Count from 4 to 10.

13. Write a BASIC program to count backwards from 10 to 1.
14. A costly error has been made in the following program. What will be the output (if any)?

```
20 LET I = 0
30 LET I = I + 1
40 PRINT I;
50 IF I < 10 THEN 20
60 END
```

(In connection with this exercise, it is appropriate to point out that on many systems, striking the 'ESC' (escape) key, the 'BRK' (break) key, or some other special key pulls the computer out of a program that is giving erroneous results.)

B For each program: (**a**) trace; (**b**) flowchart.

15.
```
10 LET N = 6
20 PRINT N;
30 LET N = N - 1
40 IF N >= 1 THEN 20
50 END
```

16.
```
10 LET N = 6
20 IF N < 1 THEN 99
30 PRINT N;
40 LET N = N - 1
50 GØ TØ 20
99 END
```

For each flowchart: (**a**) trace; (**b**) write a program.

17. DATA: none needed

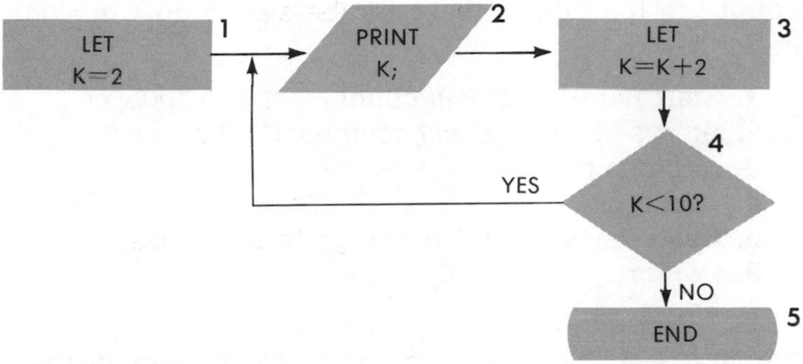

18. DATA 3, 10, 8, 5

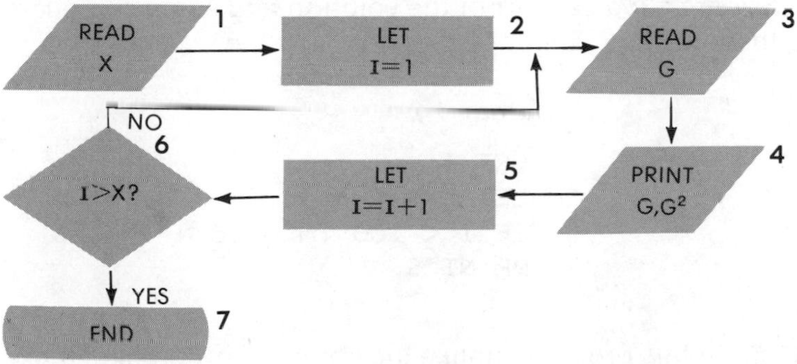

C **19.** DATA: none needed

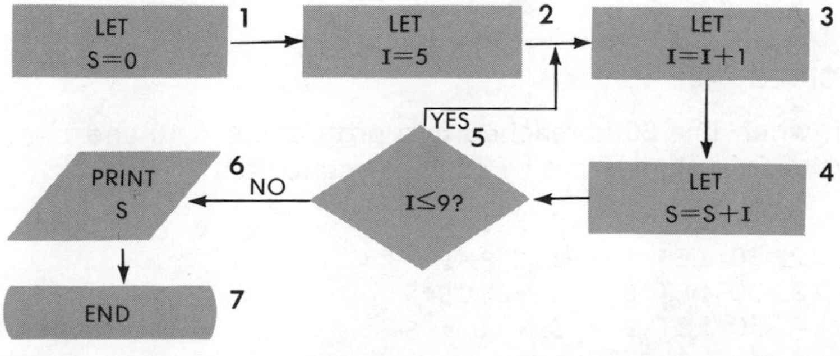

4-2 SUMMATIONS

Example:

A triangular brick wall is to be built with one brick on the top row, two bricks on the second row, three on the third, etc., for 100 rows. How many bricks are needed?

A mathematical model for this problem is: Add the whole numbers from 1 to 100. The algorithm builds on the work of the last lesson. We must count 1 to 100, adding these numbers as we go. Our algorithm can be stated this way.

1. Start I at 0. *(I will count from 1 to 100.)*
2. Start S at 0. *(S will accumulate the sum.)*
3. Add one to I.
4. Add I to S.
5. Has I reached 100? If not, go to 3. If it has, go to 6.
6. Print S.
7. End.

Recalling that BASIC handles steps 1 and 2 for us, we write the following program. (We will continue to state steps 1 and 2 in the algorithm because they are a logical part of the solution and some compilers do not handle these steps.)

Program 4-2

```
10 LET I = I + 1
20 LET S = S + I
30 IF I < 100 THEN 10
40 PRINT S
50 END
```

Notice that in this program, unlike the counting program of the previous lesson, the PRINT statement is outside the loop. We do not print S until the total sum has accumulated, that is, until I has reached 100.

EXERCISES 4-2

A If, when line 30 is reached in a program, $S = 10$ and $I = 4$, what value is assigned to S by each LET statement?

1. `30 LET S = S - I`
2. `30 LET S = I↑2 + S`
3. `30 LET S = S + .05*S`
4. `30 LET S = S + I * S`

Write programs for Exercises 5 through 8.

5. Add the even whole numbers 2 to 100.

6. Add the whole numbers from 1 to 200.

7. Add the whole numbers from 4 to 10.

8. Add the whole numbers from 1 to 100, printing each sum (1, 3, 6, 10, 15, etc.).

B Discuss the output of each program below.

9.
```
10 LET I = I + 1
20 LET S = S + I
30 IF I < 100 THEN 20
40 PRINT S
50 END
```

10.
```
10 LET I = I + 1
20 LET S = S + 1
30 IF I < 100 THEN 10
40 PRINT S
50 END
```

11.
```
10 LET I = 1
20 LET S = S + I
30 LET I = I + 1
40 IF I <= 100 THEN 20
50 PRINT S
60 END
```

12.
```
10 LET I = 1
20 LET S = S + I
30 LET I = I + 1
40 IF I <= 100 THEN 10
50 PRINT S
60 END
```

13. Prepare a flowchart for Program 4-2 on page 130.

14. Trace and flowchart the program at the right.

```
10 LET I = 0
20 READ L,W
30 LET A = L * W
40 PRINT A
50 LET I = I + 1
60 IF I < 4 THEN 20
70 DATA 1,2,8,10,6,4,5,5
80 END
```

Discuss the result of replacing line 30 in Program 4-2 with each of these steps.

15. `30 IF I <= 100 THEN 10`

16. `30 IF I <= 99 THEN 10`

17. `30 IF I < 101 THEN 10`

18. `30 IF I < 99 THEN 10`

For the flowchart: (**a**) trace; (**b**) write a program.

19. DATA: none needed

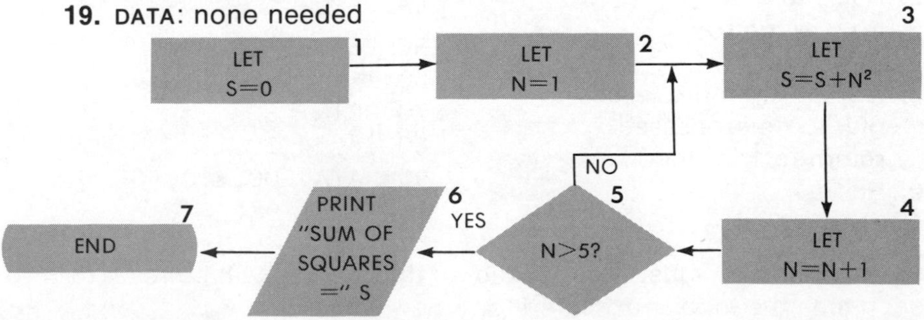

For the flowchart: (**a**) trace; (**b**) write a program.

20. DATA 5

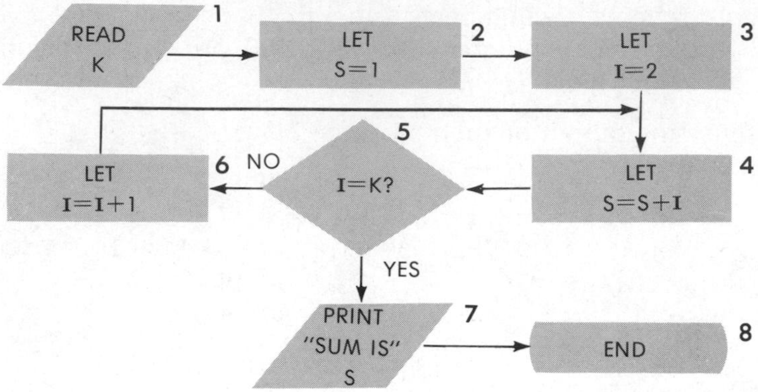

4-3 VARIABLE LOOPS

Thus far in the lessons and exercises we have written one program to add from 1 to 100, another to add from 1 to 200, another to add 4 to 10, and so on. Is it possible to write one flexible program that will handle all such problems? Yes, it is, and in this lesson we develop such a program in stages. At the left below is an algorithm for adding from 1 to N, where N is read from a DATA statement each time we execute the program. The program appears at the right below.

1. Start I at 0.
2. Start S at 0.
3. Read N.
4. Add 1 to I.
5. Add I to S.
6. If I < N, go to 4.
7. Print S.
8. If there are more values of N to be processed, return to 1.
9. End.

Program 4-3

```
10 LET I = 0
20 LET S = 0
30 READ N
40 LET I = I + 1
50 LET S = S + I
60 IF I < N THEN 40
70 PRINT S
80 GØ TØ 10
90 DATA 100,200,50
100 END
```

Lines 10 and 20 must be included so that I and S will be reset to zero each time the loop is executed for a new value of N.

The next logical extension of the algorithm is to vary the initial value of the summation, that is, to add the whole numbers from J to N, where J and N are made explicit in a DATA statement. See Program 4-4 at the right.

The final stage of generalizing the program is to vary the step between values. For example, add the *even* whole numbers 2 to 100. See Exercise 4 below.

Program 4-4

```
10 READ J,N
20 LET I = J
30 LET S = J
40 LET I = I + 1
50 LET S = S + I
60 IF I < N THEN 40
70 PRINT S
80 GØ TØ 10
90 DATA 1,100,1,200,50,150
100 END
```

EXERCISES 4-3

A Discuss the output of the following programs. Change each program so that correct output can be obtained.

1.

```
10 READ N
20 LET I = I + 1
30 LET S = S + I
40 IF I < N THEN 20
50 PRINT S
60 GØ TØ 10
70 DATA 100,50
80 END
```

2.

```
10 READ J,N
20 LET I = J
30 LET S = 0
40 LET I = I + 1
50 LET S = S + I
60 IF I < N THEN 30
70 PRINT S
80 GØ TØ 10
90 DATA 1, 100, 50, 150
100 END
```

3. Is the program at the right equivalent to Program 4-4? Trace until you can decide whether the output is the same.

```
10 READ J,N
20 LET I = J
30 LET S = 0
40 LET S = S + I
50 LET I = I + 1
60 IF I <= N THEN 40
70 PRINT S
80 GØ TØ 10
90 DATA 1,100,1,200,50,150
100 END
```

B **4.** Write a program to add the whole numbers from a variable initial value to a variable final value, with a variable step between numbers.

5. Prepare a flowchart for Program 4-3.

6. Write the algorithm and prepare a flowchart for Program 4-4.

4-4 ANATOMY OF A LOOP

Loops are the heart of programming and deserve careful study. The diagram at the right illustrates the essential components of any loop.

While these components may occur in a different order from the one shown, they must all be present in a loop. Initialization is always first but the other phases can occur in any order.

Figure 4-1: Components of a Loop

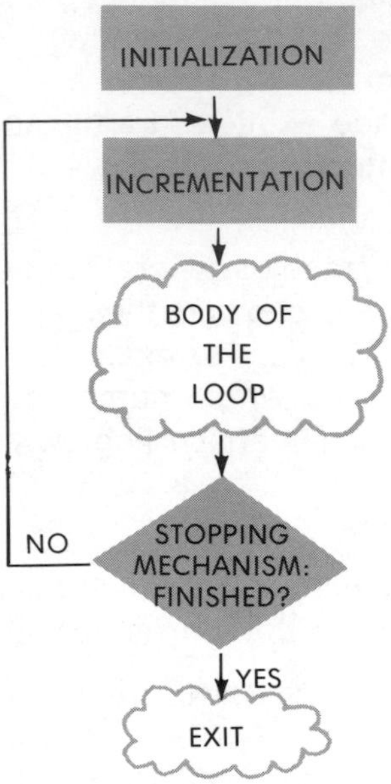

Here is an explanation of each component.

INITIALIZATION: One or more statements that assign to one or more variables their starting values entering the loop. Initialization can be accomplished by **READ** or **LET** statements.

Examples:

```
10 READ A,B     5 LET I = 0     20 LET J = K
   50 LET L = K + 1     35 LET D = SQR(N)
```

INCREMENTATION: One or more **LET** statements that increase or decrease the values of one or more variables involved in the loop.

Examples:

```
20 LET I = I + 1     40 LET J = J - 5     80 LET K = 2*K
```

BODY OF THE LOOP: The statement or set of statements that accomplishes the objective(s) of the loop; for example finding the average of a set of numbers, finding the largest value, or computing the weekly pay of each employee of a company. A typical loop may include **READ**, **LET**, and **PRINT** statements.

STOPPING MECHANISM: A decision step that determines whether the loop is finished or should continue at least one more time.

Examples:

```
50 IF J = 10 THEN 60        40 IF I < 100 THEN 10
50 IF K > L THEN 20         35 IF M <> 50 THEN 100
```

EXIT: EXIT does not necessarily mean END. When a loop is completed, the computer exits to the first executable step after the loop. This may or may not be the END statement. Often a large segment of the program follows a loop.

To make sense out of the diagram on page 134 and the explanation, let us identify these components as they occur in Programs 4-1 and 4-3.

Program 4-1

```
10 LET I = 0 ←———————————————— INITIALIZATION
20 LET I = I + 1 ←———————————— INCREMENTATION
30 PRINT I; ←————————————————— BODY OF THE LOOP
40 IF I < 10 THEN 20 ←———————— STOPPING MECHANISM
50 END ←—————————————————————— EXIT
```

Program 4-3

```
10 LET I = 0 ┐
20 LET S = 0 ├ ←—————————————— INITIALIZATION
30 READ N    ┘
40 LET I = I + 1 ←———————————— INCREMENTATION
50 LET S = S + I ←———————————— BODY OF THE LOOP
60 IF I < N THEN 40 ←————————— STOPPING MECHANISM
70 PRINT S ←—————————————————— EXIT
80 GØ TØ 10 ←————————————————— This statement creates a simple "outer
90 DATA 100,200,50             loop" that restarts the program for a new
100 END                        value of N; the stopping mechanism for
                               this outer loop is BASIC's built-in ØUT ØF
                               DATA? test.
```

In both these programs the components occur in the order shown in Figure 4-1 on page 134, and the body of the loop consists of just one statement. To illustrate a different configuration of the stages and a larger body of the loop, consider the following program.

Program 4-5 (See Ex. 14, p. 131.)

```
10 LET I = 0<------------------------------INITIALIZATION

20 READ L,W    }
30 LET A = L * W} <------------------------BODY OF THE LOOP
40 PRINT A     }

50 LET I = I + 1<--------------------------INCREMENTATION

60 IF I < 4 THEN 20<-----------------------STOPPING MECHANISM

70 DATA 1,2,8,10,6,4,5,5

80 END<------------------------------------EXIT
```

The body of the loop, three statements, comes before incrementation. The loop of the program serves merely to process a predetermined number of DATA sets, four in this case.

Strange as it may seem the stopping mechanism could even come before the body of the loop. Consider this revised version of Program 4-1.

Program 4-1A

```
10 LET I = 0<------------------------------INITIALIZATION

20 LET I = I + 1<--------------------------INCREMENTATION

30 IF I > 10 THEN 60<----------------------STOPPING MECHANISM

40 PRINT I; }
50 GØ TØ 20 }<-----------------------------BODY OF THE LOOP

60 END<------------------------------------EXIT
```

Trace Program 4-1A until you are convinced that it executes in the same manner as Program 4-1 on page 128. It has an additional statement but the point is that a loop in a particular configuration can be recast into a different one.

Loops occur so frequently in algorithm design that it is convenient to introduce a new flowchart symbol, the *iteration box.* ("Iteration" means "repetition.")

Example: Count from 5 to 8. *Flowchart 4-2*

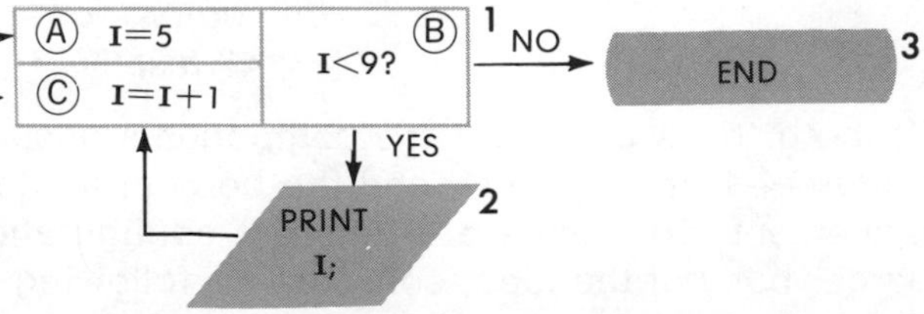

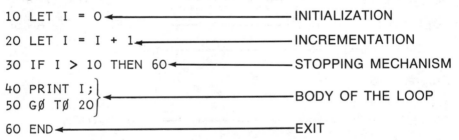

*Note: to save space "*LET*" is omitted from compartments* Ⓐ *and* Ⓒ.

The iteration box is understood to have its own inner flow from compartment to compartment.

Figure 4-2: Flow within the iteration box

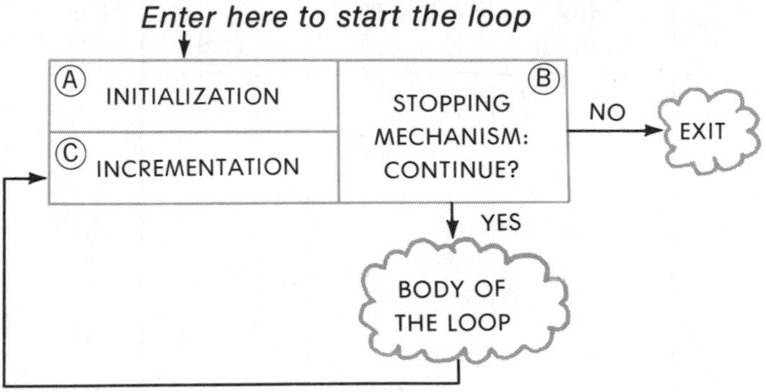

Begin the loop by entering compartment Ⓐ and initializing the variable (I in Flowchart 4-2 on page 136) which is called the *index* of the loop. Compartment Ⓐ will be entered only once during execution of the loop. Now jump to compartment Ⓑ and apply the test. At this point the YES outlet will undoubtedly be followed and the body of the loop executed. Return to compartment Ⓒ and increment the index. Then move to Ⓑ and apply the stopping mechanism. Continue this procedure until the test yields a NO result and the loop is satisfied.

A diagram of the sequence looks like this.

Figure 4-3: Order of steps in execution of the Iteration Box

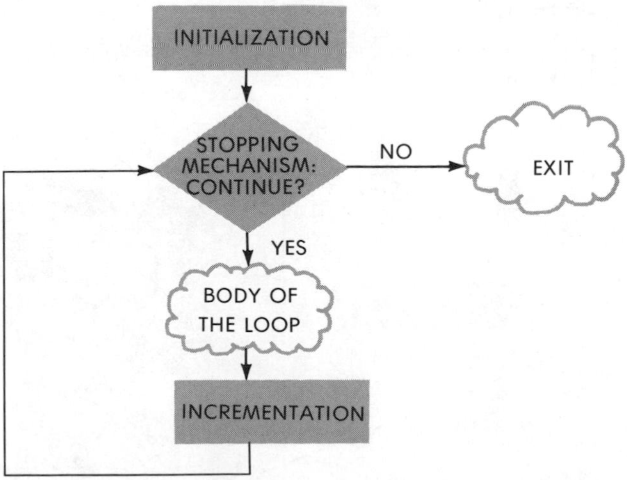

A trace of flowchart 4-2 on page 136 is now shown.

Table 4-1 Trace of Flowchart 4-2

Step Number	Box Number	Value of Variable I	Test	Yes or No?	Output
1	1A	5			
2	1B		5 < 9?	Yes	
3	2				5
4	1C	6			
5	1B		6 < 9?	Yes	
6	2				6
7	1C	7			
8	1B		7 < 9?	Yes	
9	2				7
10	1C	8			
11	1B		8 < 9?	Yes	
12	2				8
13	1C	9			
14	1B		9 < 9?	No	
15	END				

In the second column of the trace, A, B, and C are used to distinguish which compartment of box 1 is entered at each step.

The iteration box is equivalent to two assignment boxes and one decision box. The following diagram of Flowchart 4-2 both with and without an iteration box illustrates this fact.

Flowchart 4-2 *Flowchart 4-2 without Iteration Box*

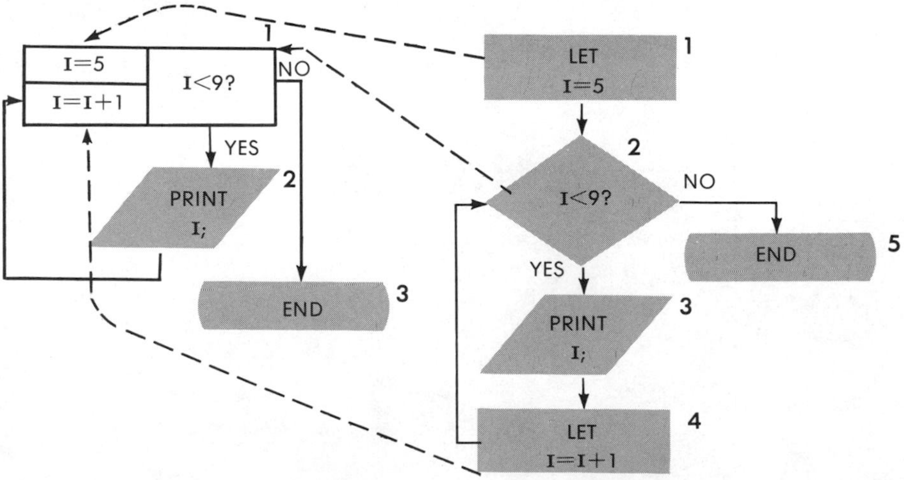

EXERCISES 4-4

A 1. In all possible configurations of a loop, what phase always comes first?

For each program of Exercises 2 through 5, (**a**) identify the components of each loop and name the index, (**b**) trace the program, (**c**) prepare a flowchart without using the iteration box, (**d**) prepare a flowchart using the iteration box, and (**e**) explain what the program does.

2.
```
10 LET I = 10
20 LET I = I + 10
30 PRINT I;
40 IF I < 50 THEN 20
50 END
```

3.
```
10 LET K = 10
20 IF K < 0 THEN 60
30 PRINT K;
40 LET K = K - 2
50 GØ TØ 20
60 END
```

4.
```
10 READ N
20 LET L = 1
30 PRINT L;
40 LET L = L + 1
50 IF L <= N THEN 30
60 GØ TØ 10
70 DATA 3,5
80 END
```

5.
```
5 LET S = 0
10 LET I = 1
20 READ L,W
30 LET P = 2*(L + W)
40 LET S = S + P
50 LET I = I + 1
60 IF I < 5 THEN 20
70 PRINT "SUM ØF P =" S
80 DATA 2,3,5,5,10,4,8,2
90 END
```

B For each flowchart, (**a**) trace, and (**b**) write a BASIC program.

6. DATA: none needed

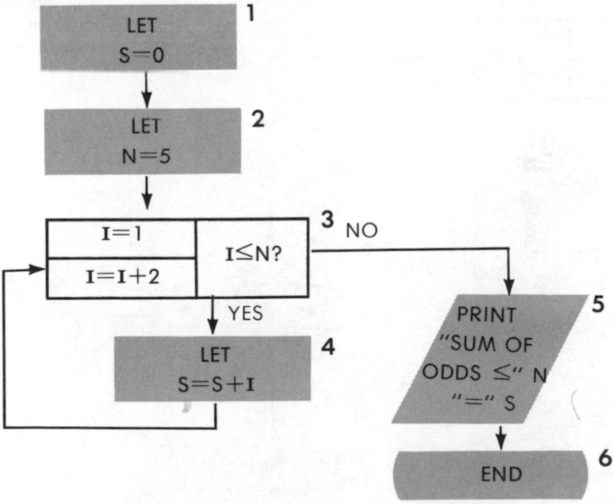

For each flowchart, (**a**) trace, and (**b**) write a BASIC program.

7. DATA: none needed

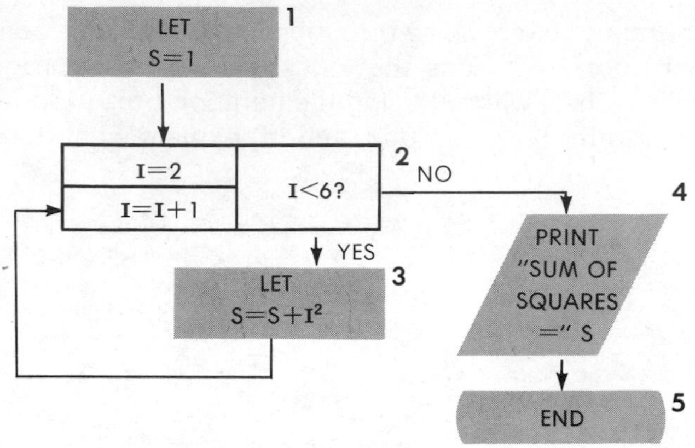

8. DATA 0, 4, 11, 21

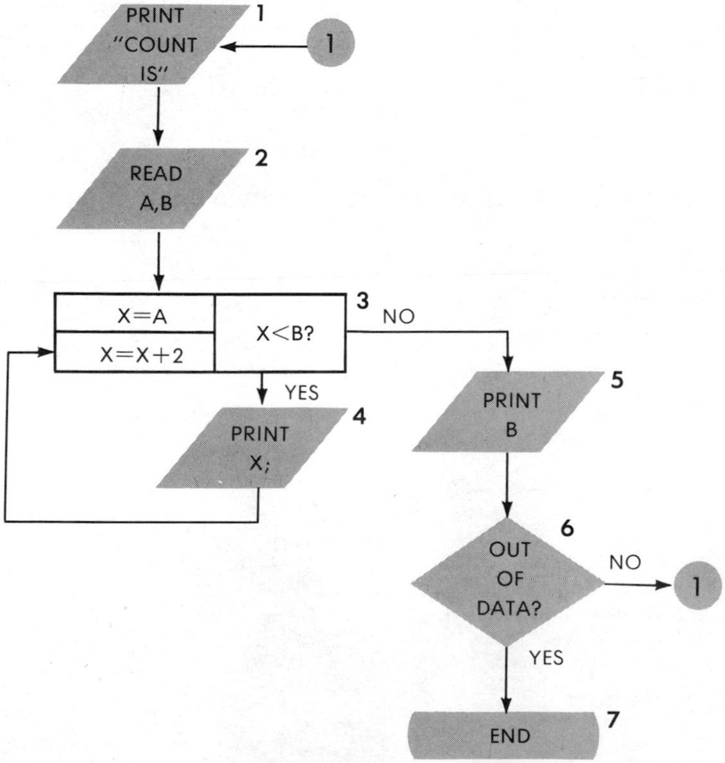

9. DATA 4, 18, 15, 63, 12

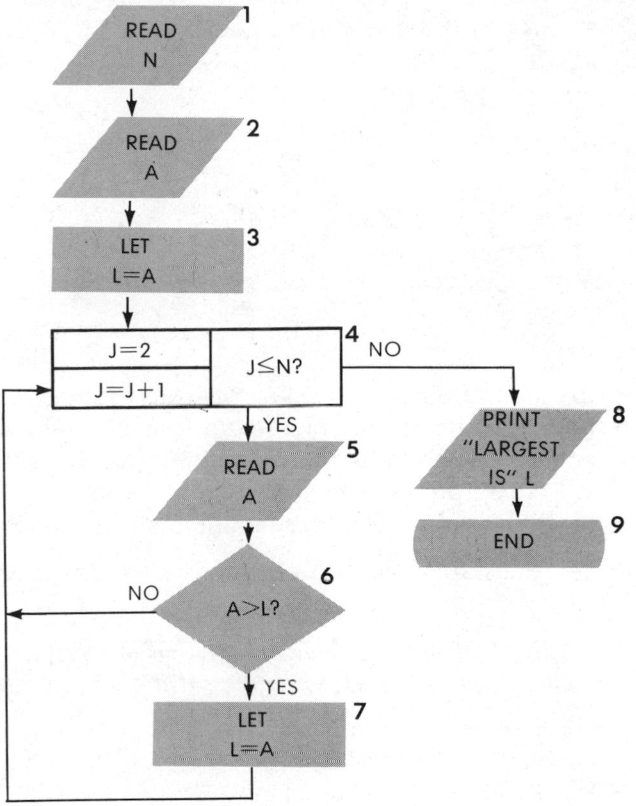

C **10.** DATA: none needed

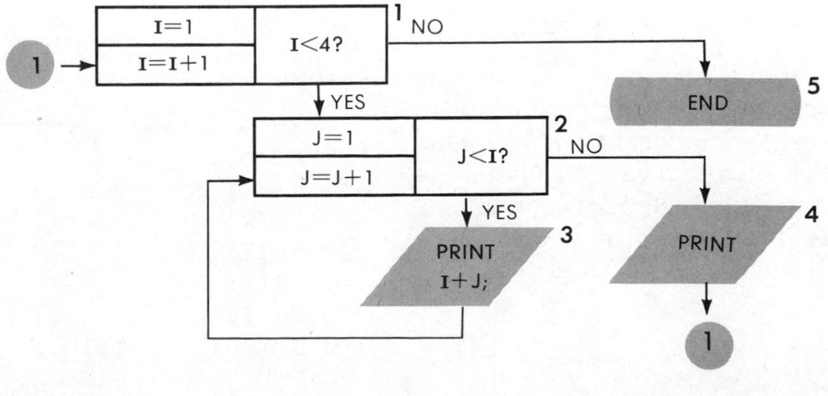

4-5 FØR-NEXT LOOPS

BASIC (like all algorithmic languages) provides an easy method for constructing loops: the FØR and NEXT statements. The two programs below are equivalent. (They each add the whole numbers from 4 to 200.)

Program 4-6

Version A

```
10 LET I = 4
20 LET S = S + I
30 LET I = I + 1
40 IF I <= 200 THEN 20
50 PRINT S
60 END
```

Version B

```
10 FØR I = 4 TØ 200
20 LET S = S + I
30 NEXT I
40 PRINT S
50 END
```

In version B, lines 10, 20, and 30 constitute a "FØR-NEXT loop." Such a loop may contain more than three statements but it must begin with a FØR statement and end with a NEXT statement. Furthermore the variable after the word FØR (I in Program 4-6) must match the variable after the word NEXT. The general form of the FØR statement is shown below.

FØR (variable) = (expression) TØ (expression) STEP (expression)

- (variable) ↗ *INDEX*
- (expression) ↗ *INITIAL VALUE of the index*
- (expression) ↗ *FINAL VALUE of the index*
- (expression) ↗ *INCREMENT (optional if the step is one)*

Examples:

1. `25 FØR I = 0 TØ 100 STEP 2`
2. `80 FØR X = I+1 TØ J`
3. `90 FØR K1 = X/Y TØ Z↑2 STEP L+1`
4. `60 FØR J = 100 TØ 1 STEP -1`

Example 1 would cause I to take on the successive values 0, 2, 4, 6, . . . , 96, 98, 100. If no STEP is listed, as in Example 2, the compiler assumes a STEP of one. Hence the following statements are equivalent.

```
80 FØR X = I+1 TØ J          80 FØR X = I+1 TØ J STEP 1
```

In previous lessons a program was developed in which you added the whole numbers from a variable initial value to a variable final value with a variable step between values. This program can now be written in the manner shown at the right.

Program 4-7

```
10 READ J,N,D
20 LET S = 0
30 FØR I = J TØ N STEP D
40 LET S = S + I
50 NEXT I
60 PRINT S
70 GØ TØ 10
80 DATA 1,5,1,1,10,2
90 END
```

The FØR-NEXT combination brackets the body of the loop and provides the initialization, incrementation, and stopping mechanism. In Program 4-6B, repeated at the left below, the index I is initialized at 4. Since $4 \leq 200$, the loop is executed. When NEXT I is encountered, I is incremented by the understood step of one. Since $5 \leq 200$, the loop is executed again. This sequence is repeated until $I = 201$. Since $201 > 200$, this last value of I is discarded and the computer branches to the first statement after NEXT I that can be executed, that is, to 40 PRINT S.

Program 4-6B

```
10 FØR I = 4 TØ 200
20 LET S = S + I
30 NEXT I
40 PRINT S
50 END
```

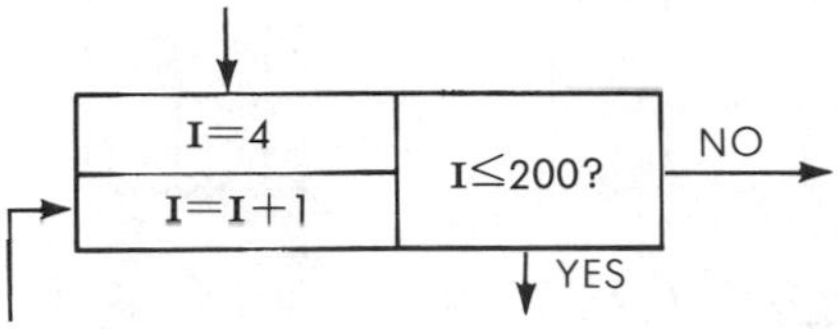

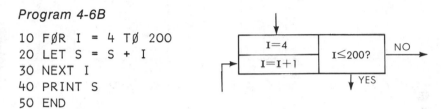

This sequence follows the order of events built into the iteration box shown at the right above. This is no fluke since the iteration box was designed in anticipation of FØR-NEXT loops of BASIC. However, there is no flowchart box corresponding to the FØR statement nor a box for NEXT. Instead the iteration box is used, as in this flowchart for Program 4-7 on page 142.

Flowchart 4-3

Program 4-7

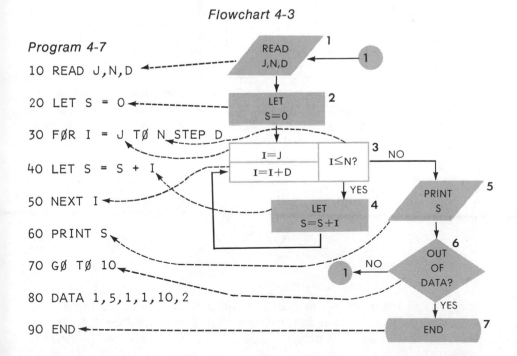

```
10 READ J,N,D
20 LET S = 0
30 FØR I = J TØ N STEP D
40 LET S = S + I
50 NEXT I
60 PRINT S
70 GØ TØ 10
80 DATA 1,5,1,1,10,2
90 END
```

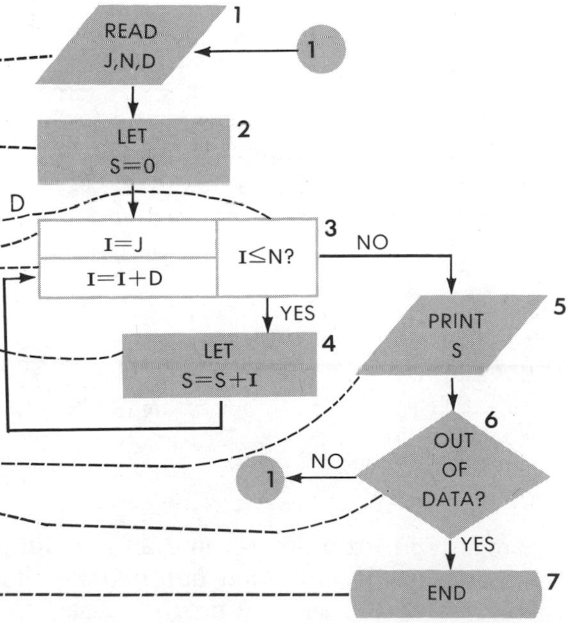

FØR-NEXT statements affect traces as is shown below.

Table 4-2 Portion of the trace of Program 4-7 for the first set of DATA (1,5,1)

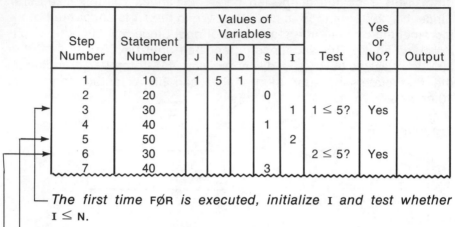

Step Number	Statement Number	Values of Variables J	N	D	S	I	Test	Yes or No?	Output
1	10	1	5	1					
2	20				0				
3	30					1	$1 \leq 5$?	Yes	
4	40				1				
5	50					2			
6	30						$2 \leq 5$?	Yes	
7	40				3				
16	40				15				
17	50					6			
18	30						$6 \leq 5$?	No	
19	60					5			15
20	70						OUT OF DATA?	No	

The first time FØR *is executed, initialize* I *and test whether* $I \leq N$. (step 3)

When NEXT I *is reached, increment* I. (step 5)

Then on each succeeding FØR, *test whether* $I \leq N$. (step 6)

When the loop is satisfied, most compilers restore the index (I) *to the last value that was actually used in the loop (5 here).* (step 19)

A common mistake occurs when the programmer does not realize all that the FØR-NEXT combination does for him and writes his own incrementation or decision steps in the FØR-NEXT loop. For example, in Program 4-8 line 30 is not needed and in fact interferes with the operation of the loop. 40 NEXT I causes the I to be incremented.

Program 4-8

```
10 FØR I = 1 TØ 10
20 LET S = S + I
30 LET I = I + 1
40 NEXT I
50 PRINT "SUM = " S
60 END
```

NOT NEEDED!

Program 4-9

```
10 FØR I = 1 TØ 10
20 LET S = S + I
30 IF I > 10 THEN 50
40 NEXT I
50 PRINT "SUM = " S
60 END
```

Similarly in Program 4-9 line 30 is redundant. When executing a FØR-NEXT loop, the computer *automatically* tests the index each time it is incremented to see if it has gone past the final value listed in the FØR statement.

At the right is shown a revised version of Program 4-5 on page 136 using a FØR-NEXT loop. This program shows that the index need not even enter the calculations within the loop. I serves merely as a counter, clicking off the four times the programmer wants the loop executed.

Program 4-5A

```
10 FØR I = 1 TØ 4
20 READ L,W
30 LET A = L*W
40 PRINT A
50 NEXT I
60 DATA 1,2,8,10,6,4,5,5
70 END
```

Here are some miscellaneous points concerning FØR-NEXT loops.

1. If the STEP is negative, then the stopping mechanism is slightly different from the one discussed earlier. For example, the statement

```
10 FØR I = 10 TØ 0 STEP -2
```

is equivalent to the iteration box shown at the right. The decision is $I \geq 0$. Compare this to loops with positive STEPS in which cases the decision is of the form $I \leq N$ (N the final value).

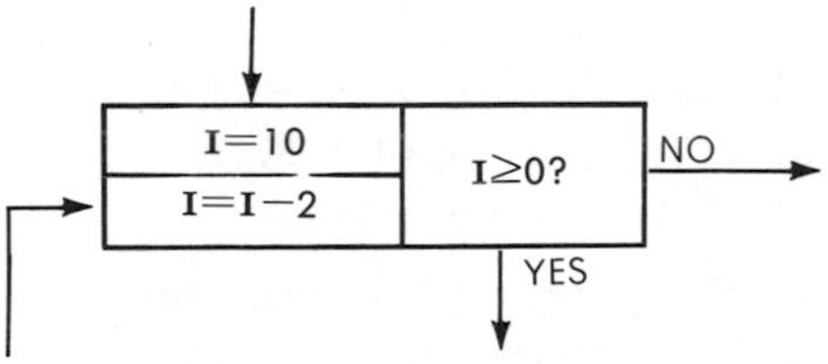

2. A good compiler tests the initial value of the index immediately to see if it is already outside the range of values intended for the loop. Some loops might be over before they start. For example, if $N = 3$, a loop beginning 20 FØR I = 2 TØ SQR(N) should not be executed even once since $2 > \sqrt{3}$.

To test whether your compiler follows this rule, run this program.

Test Program 1

```
10 READ N
20 FØR I = 2 TØ SQR(N)
30 PRINT I
40 NEXT I
50 PRINT "LØØP FINISHED FØR N = " N
60 GØ TØ 10
70 DATA 1,2,3,4
80 END
```

If the compiler operates as expected, the loop should not be executed at all for $N = 1$, 2, or 3 and should be executed once when $N = 4$.

If the compiler does not automatically test the initial value but rather blindly executes the loop once before applying the stopping mechanism, you may have to write steps to get around this defect.

3. As indicated in Table 4-2 on page 144 (step 19), good compilers return the index to the last value for which the loop was actually executed when control transfers out of the loop to the first executable statement after NEXT. For example, if a loop begins 50 FØR J = 0 TØ 10 STEP 2 then the last time the loop is executed, J = 10. When J is incremented to 12, the loop is satisfied, since 12 > 10. Before continuing the program, most compilers restore the value 10 to J. To test how your compiler operates, run this program.

Test Program 2

```
10 FØR I = 1 TØ 5
20 PRINT I;
30 NEXT I
40 PRINT
50 PRINT "ØUT ØF LØØP NØW; I = " I
60 END
```

The question is whether line 50 will print I = 5 or I = 6. For example, most microcomputer systems will yield I = 6. In either case you have learned for later programs a useful fact about your compiler.

4. The index of the loop may not be changed in the body of the loop. If, for example, a loop begins 50 FØR I = 1 TO 10 , then each of the following statements is illegal in the body of the loop.

```
60 READ I              55 LET I = J + 1
70 READ A, B, I        95 LET I = I - 1
```

Each of these statements assigns a new value to I, thus contradicting the use of I as the index of the loop. I may be used on the right-side of "=" in an assignment statement or in a PRINT or IF . . . THEN statement because none of these uses changes its value. The index can legitimately be changed only when NEXT I is reached.

5. Do not use the index to the right of "=" in the FØR statement. Avoid statements such as the following.

```
15 FØR I = I TØ 10              30 FØR J = 0 TØ J
25 FØR D = 10 TØ 30 STEP D      50 FØR K = K/2 TØ 7
10 FØR M = 1 TØ 5*M             93 FØR A = 2 TØ 40 STEP A+1
```

Different compilers would react differently to these statements. Some would reject them immediately. Others would run the program but bog down during execution. For example, the problem with the statement 10 FØR M = 1 TO 5*M is that the index, M, is constantly changing in value. Yet the stopping mechanism hinges on M. This loop would never end because as M increases (1,2,3,4, . . .), 5*M increases also (5,10,15, 20, . . .) and the test M ≤ 5*M? never yields a NO answer.

EXERCISES 4-5

A Give the NEXT statement that must appear in a program with each of these FØR statements. Choose any appropriate number for the NEXT statement.

1. `50 FØR D = X TØ Z`
2. `20 FØR I = 15 TØ 50 STEP 5`
3. `110 FØR K = 1E6 TØ 1E7 STEP 1E2`
4. `35 FØR M1 = L1 TØ R*S STEP D`

Correct any errors in the following programs.

5.
```
10 IF I = 1 TØ 10
20 LET Y = I↑2 + 3*I - 7
30 PRINT Y
40 NEXT Y
50 END
```

6.
```
10 READ M,N
20 FØR J = M,N STEP 5
30 LET S = S + J
40 NEXT J
50 PRINT S
60 GØ TØ 10
70 END
```

7.
```
10 FØR I = 1 TØ 10
20 LET Y = 4*I + 6
30 PRINT Y;
40 LET I = I + 1
50 NEXT I
60 END
```

8.
```
10 READ N
15 LET S = 0
20 FØR I = 1 TØ N
30 LET S = S + I
40 IF I < N THEN 20
50 NEXT I
60 PRINT "SUM IS " S
70 DATA 10,100,75
80 END
```

Rewrite the program at the right below using a FØR-NEXT loop so that the output is as follows.

9. Vertical.
3
6
9
.
.
.

10. Horizontal.
3 6 9 12 . . .

```
10 LET N = 1
20 IF N > 20 THEN 60
30 PRINT 3*N
40 LET N = N + 1
50 GØ TØ 20
60 END
```

Use a FØR-NEXT loop in rewriting each of these programs.

11.
```
10 LET I = 0
20 LET I = I + 1
30 IF I > 5 THEN 60
40 LET S = S + I
50 GØ TØ 20
60 PRINT "SUM IS " S
70 END
```

12.
```
10 LET J = 1
20 PRINT J, J↑2, J↑3
30 LET J = J + 1
40 IF J <= 5 THEN 20
50 END
```

B 13. For each revised program in Exercises 11 and 12, using a FØR-NEXT loop, flowchart the program and trace it.

For each iteration box, write a FØR statement and its NEXT companion.

Example:

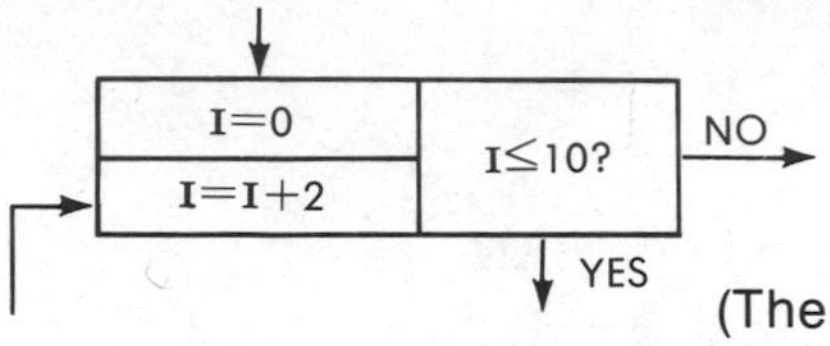

Answer:

```
10 FØR I = 0 TØ 10 STEP 2
   .
   .
   .
50 NEXT I
```

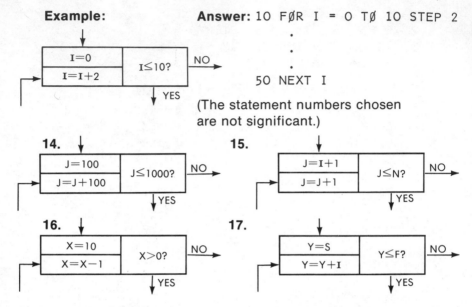

(The statement numbers chosen are not significant.)

14.

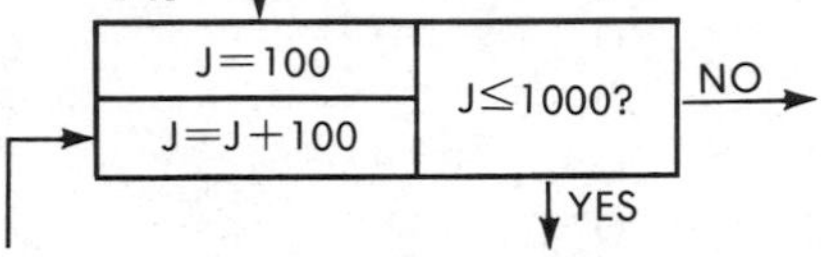

15.

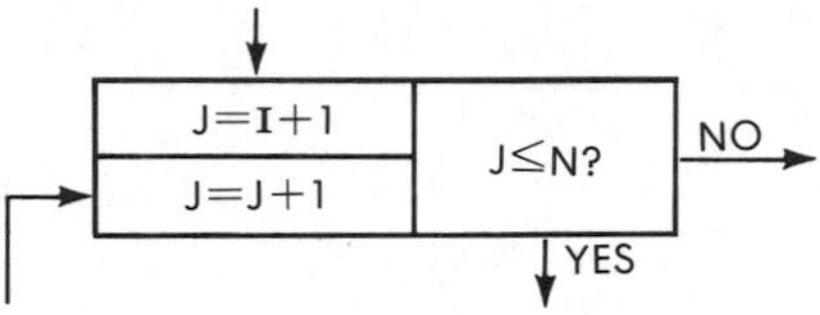

16.

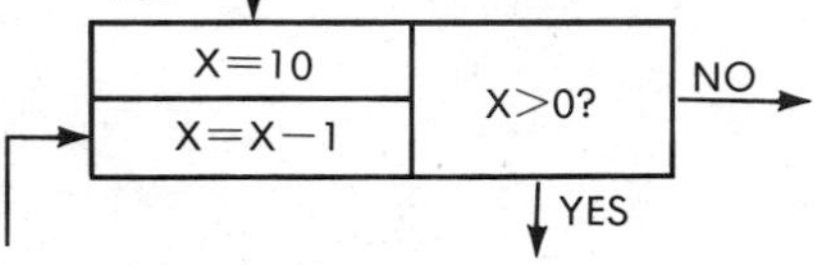

17.

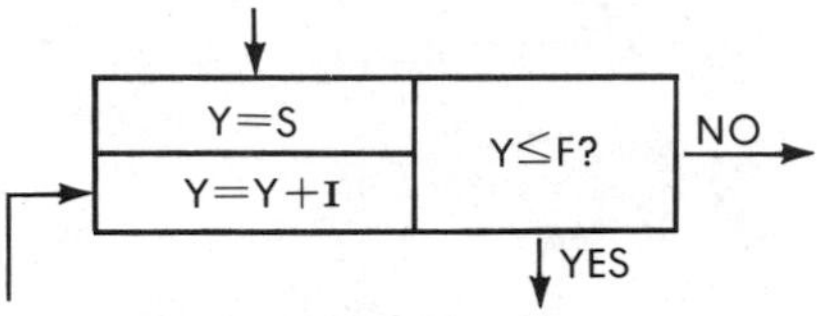

Draw an iteration box corresponding to each FØR-NEXT combination.

18.

```
100 FØR L = 1 TØ 50
    . . .

200 NEXT L
```

19.

```
50 FØR R = K TØ 1 STEP -2
   . . .

80 NEXT R
```

20.

```
30 FØR D = 3 TØ SQR(P) STEP 2
   . . .

100 NEXT D
```

21.

```
20 FØR J = X/Y TØ Z↑2 STEP D+2
   . . .

80 NEXT J
```

Use a FØR-NEXT loop in writing these programs.

22. Add the odd whole numbers from 1 to 99.

23. Print the whole numbers from 1 to 1000.

24. Compute Y as a function of X according to the formula $Y = 16.7x + 9.2x^2 - 1.02x^3$ for x values from 1.0 to 2.0 in increments of .1. Print the output in two labeled columns.

Use an iteration box in flowcharting each of these programs.

25.
```
5 PRINT "EVEN NUMBERS ARE:";
10 FØR J = 2 TØ 50 STEP 2
20 PRINT J;
30 NEXT J
40 END
```

26.
```
5 LET S = 1000
10 READ N
20 FØR M = 1 TØ N
30 LET S = S + .05*S
40 NEXT M
50 PRINT "TØTAL AMØUNT AFTER"M" MØNTHS=" S
60 GØ TØ 5
70 DATA 12,24,36
80 END
```

Use a FØR-NEXT loop in programming each flowchart.

27.

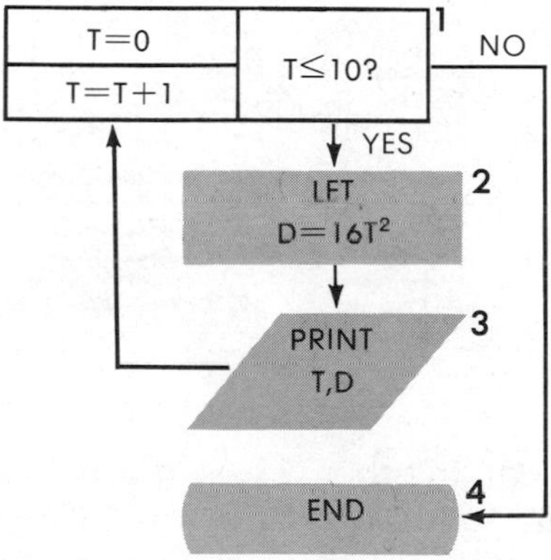

28.

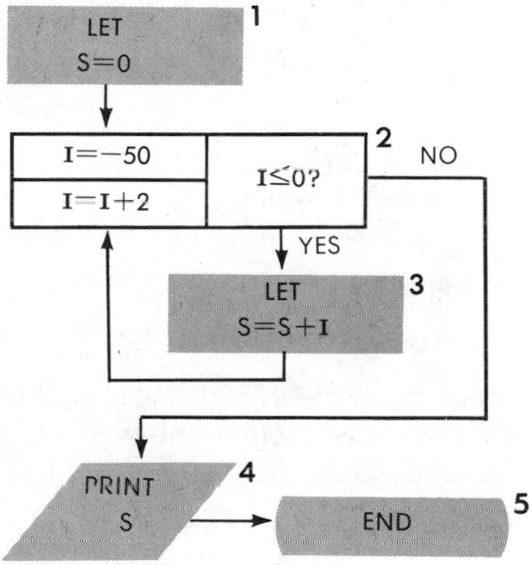

4-6 LOOPS CONTAINING DECISIONS

Example: Add all integers from 1 to 50 that are multiples of 3.

From previous lessons we realize that this program involves a loop. However, within the loop there must be a decision: Is the integer a multiple of 3? The algorithm can be written as at the right.

1. Start I at 0.
2. Start S at 0.
3. Add one to I.
4. Is I a multiple of 3?
   If it is not, go to step 6.
5. Add I to S.
6. I < 50? If so, go to step 3.
7. Print S.
8. End.

The flowchart of the algorithm on page 149 is shown at the right.

Flowchart 4-4

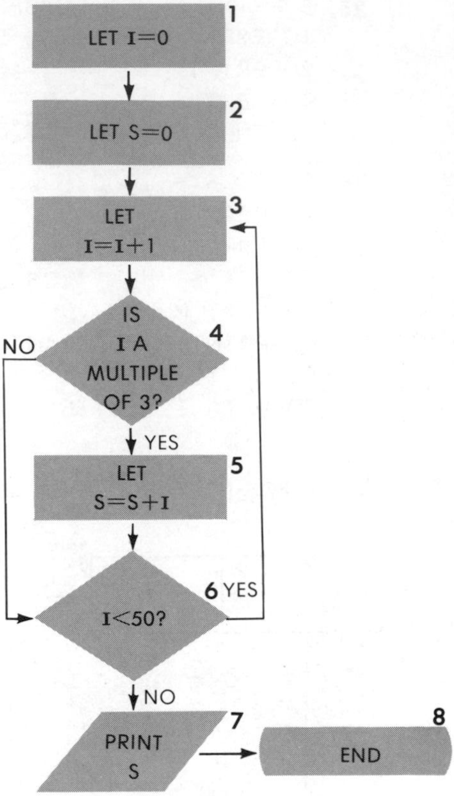

Steps 1 and 2 will be handled by the BASIC compiler. Steps 3 through 6 will form a loop.

```
10 FØR I = 1 TØ 50
   :
40 NEXT I
```

Adding I to S will be accomplished by the statement 30 LET S = S + I . "PRINT S" and "END" pose no problems. So the program looks like this now.

```
10 FØR I = 1 TØ 50
20
30 LET S = S + I
40 NEXT I
50 PRINT S
60 END
```

Only the decision "Is I a multiple of 3?" (line 20) cannot be written from what we know already. We will need a statement of this form:

20 IF (I not a multiple of 3) THEN 40.

I is a multiple of 3 if it is *divisible* by 3 or, in other words, if 3 is a *factor* of I. To understand how the computer can be programmed to check this, we must stop and study the INT (integer) function of BASIC.

INT(X) means "the greatest integer less than or equal to X." In mathematics books this expression is usually written $[x]$. Here are examples.

INT(1.2) = 1	INT(0) = 0	INT(3.14159) = 3
INT(71) = 71	INT(−3.4) = −4	INT(−83) = −83

Applying this concept to the program at hand, we note that if I is a multiple of 3, then I/3 is an integer and hence INT(I/3) = I/3. Test this last statement for particular values of I.

12 is a multiple of 3.
INT(12/3) = 4 and 12/3 = 4.
Hence INT(I/3) = I/3.

31 is not a multiple of 3.
INT(31/3) = 10 but 31/3 = 10.33 . . .
Hence INT(I/3) ≠ I/3.

So asking if I is a multiple of 3 is the same as asking if INT(I/3) = I/3.

Our program can now be completed as follows.

Program 4-10

```
10 FØR I = 1 TØ 50
20 IF INT(I/3) <> I/3 THEN 40
30 LET S = S + I
40 NEXT I
50 PRINT S
60 END
```

Line 20 had to end "THEN 40" and not "THEN 10". Branching back to line 10 would start the loop over with I = 1; I would never reach 50 and the program would never end.

The following example illustrates an error to be avoided in programs involving loops.

```
10 FØR I = 1 TØ 10
20 READ X
30 IF X > 100 THEN 70
40 PRINT "LESS THAN ØNE HUNDRED"
50 NEXT I
60 GØ TØ 100
70 PRINT "GREATER THAN ØNE HUNDRED"
80 GØ TØ 50
90 DATA 84,113,97,101,105,33,12,99,134,82
100 END
```

The mistake lies in branching out of the loop when X is greater than 100 (line 30) and then attempting to reenter the loop by returning to "NEXT I" (line 80). Changing line 80 to "GØ TØ 10" would also be erroneous because returning to line 10 directly without passing through 50 NEXT I causes the loop to be restarted with I = 1 again.

Here is the correct version of the program.

Program 4-11

```
10 FØR I = 1 TØ 10
20 READ X
30 IF X > 100 THEN 60
40 PRINT "LESS THAN ØNE HUNDRED"
50 GØ TØ 70
60 PRINT "GREATER THAN ØNE HUNDRED"
70 NEXT I
80 DATA 84,113,97,101,105,33,12,99,134,82
90 END
```

The correct and incorrect "jumps" or branches in and out of loops are illustrated by the diagrams below. A bracket [is used to represent a loop. The top of the bracket is anchored on the FØR statement and the bottom on the NEXT statement.

Legal Jumps

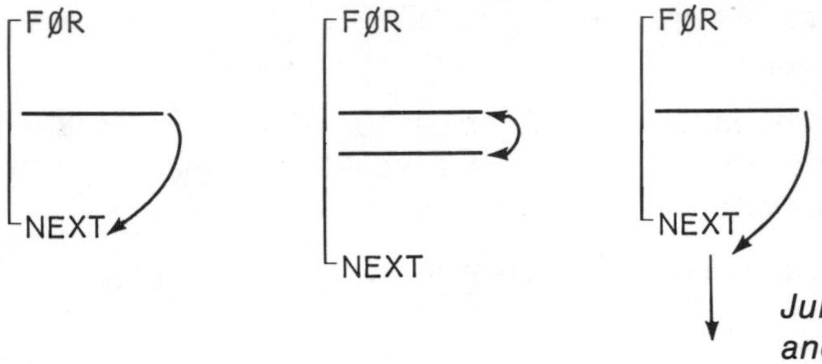

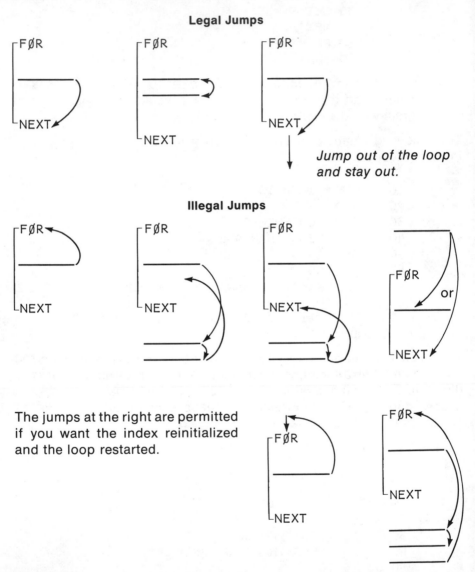

Jump out of the loop and stay out.

Illegal Jumps

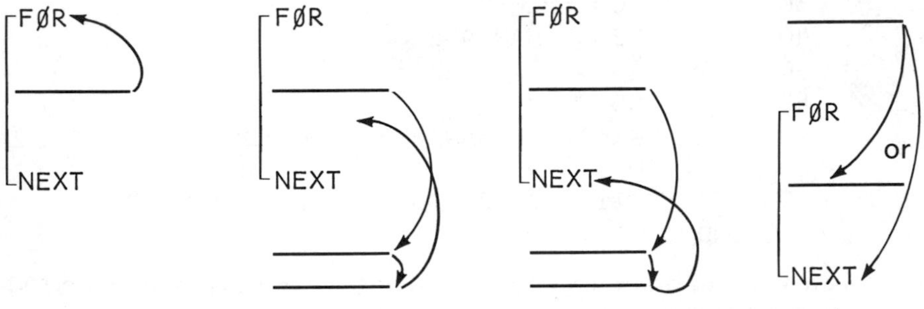

The jumps at the right are permitted if you want the index reinitialized and the loop restarted.

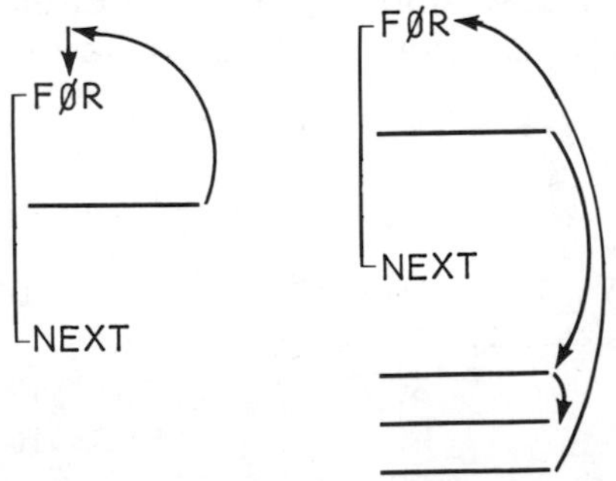

SUMMARY: A program may not branch out of the body of a loop and then return to the body of the loop again. Once the program branches out of the loop, the loop may be reentered only through the FØR statement and the index will be reset to its starting value.

EXERCISES 4-6

A Fill the following blanks.

1. INT(6.7) = __?__ **2.** INT(3/5) = __?__
3. INT(−4.5) = __?__ **4.** INT(43) = __?__
5. INT(−67) = __?__ **6.** INT(SQR(15)) = __?__

Write IF . . . THEN statements for each of these decisions.

7. If X is a multiple of 4, then go to line 30.
8. If I is even, then go to 45.
9. If Y is not a multiple of 7, then 60.
10. If Z is not divisible by 5, then 81.

11. Write a program to read integers X and Y and determine whether X is a factor of Y.

Correct any errors in the following programs.

12.
```
10 FØR J = 1 TØ 100
20 LET S1 = S1 + J
30 IF J/6 = INT(J/6) THEN 10
40 LET S2 = S2 + J
50 NEXT J
60 PRINT "SUM ØF INTEGERS 1 TØ 100 IS S1"
70 PRINT "SUM ØF MULTIPLES ØF SIX FRØM 1 TØ 100
   IS S2"
80 END
```

13.
```
10 READ N
20 FØR I = 1 TØ N
30 READ X,Y
40 IF X*Y < 0 THEN 90
50 PRINT "PRØDUCT NØN-NEGATIVE"
60 LET S = S + X*Y
70 NEXT I
80 PRINT "SUM ØF PRØDUCTS = " S
85 GØ TØ 120
90 PRINT "PRØDUCT NEGATIVE"
100 GØ TØ 60
110 DATA 4,8,5,-2,4,0,6,6,3
120 END
```

B Use the INT function to write an assignment statement that will *round* the variable Z to each nearest digit indicated below.

14. integer **15.** tenth **16.** hundredth **17.** ten

18. Write a program to find all positive integers *n* less than 20 such that $2^n + 1$ is divisible by 3.

4-7 NESTED LOOPS

An investor plans to invest a sum of money at $5\frac{1}{2}\%$ interest. He must decide the amount to invest and the number of years. A computer can guide his decision by calculating the interest he would receive for various amounts and various time periods. The formula is I = P * T * .055 where I = interest, P = principal or amount, and T = time, in years.

Let us suppose that the investor is considering investing $1000, $2000, $3000, or $4000 for 1, 2, 3, 4, or 5 years. Then the calculations can be accomplished by the program below.

Program 4-12

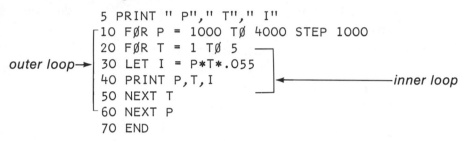

```
             5 PRINT " P"," T"," I"
            ┌10 FØR P = 1000 TØ 4000 STEP 1000
            │20 FØR T = 1 TØ 5   ──┐
outer loop→ │30 LET I = P*T*.055   │
            │40 PRINT P,T,I        │←────── inner loop
            │50 NEXT T           ──┘
            └60 NEXT P
             70 END
```

This program contains a "loop-within-a-loop" or a "nested loop." The output will look like this.

```
P         T         I
1000      1         55
1000      2         110
1000      3         165
1000      4         220
1000      5         275
2000      1         110
2000      2         220
...       ...       ...
4000      4         880
4000      5         1100
```

T (the inner loop index) varies more rapidly than P (the outer loop index). P is fixed at its first value (1000) and T is run through its cycle of values from 1 to 5. Then P is stepped to 2000 and T starts its cycle again. This procedure continues until P has reached 4000 and T completes 1 to 5 a last time.

For a nested loop the index in the *first* FØR statement must match the index in the *last* NEXT statement. Similarly the indices must match in the *second* FØR and the *second-to-last* NEXT.

Two, three, four, or more loops may be nested. Here is an example.

Program 4-13

```
10 READ X,Y,Z
20 FØR I = 1 TØ X
30 FØR J = 1 TØ Y
40 FØR K = 1 TØ Z
50 LET S = I↑3 + J↑2 - K
60 PRINT I,J,K,S
70 NEXT K
75 PRINT "K-LØØP FINISHED"
80 NEXT J
85 PRINT "J-LØØP FINISHED"
90 NEXT I
95 PRINT "I-LØØP FINISHED"
100 DATA 3,2,2
110 END
```

As illustrated at the right, the index of an inner loop may key onto the value of an outer loop.

```
30 FØR I = 1 TØ N-1
40 FØR J = I+1 TØ N
```

The following diagrams show legal and illegal ways of nesting loops.

Legal nesting

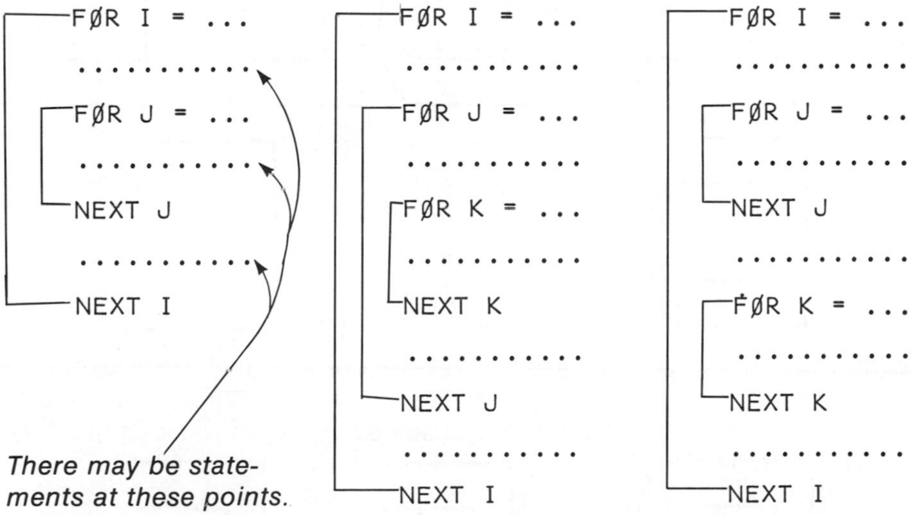

The above diagrams show the nesting of two loops and three loops. Similar nestings exist for four or more loops but will not be shown (see Exercise 14 on page 157).

Illegal nesting

```
FØR I = ...
...........
FØR J = ...
...........
NEXT I
...........
NEXT J
```

```
FØR I = ...
...........
FØR I = ...
...........
NEXT I
```

```
FØR I = ...
...........
NEXT I
...........
NEXT I
```

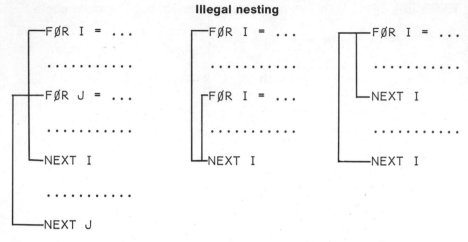

Each of these configurations would produce an error message such as the one shown below.

```
NEXT NØT MATCHED WITH FØR LINE #---
```

The following diagrams illustrate some legal and illegal ways of jumping within nested loops.

Legal Jumps

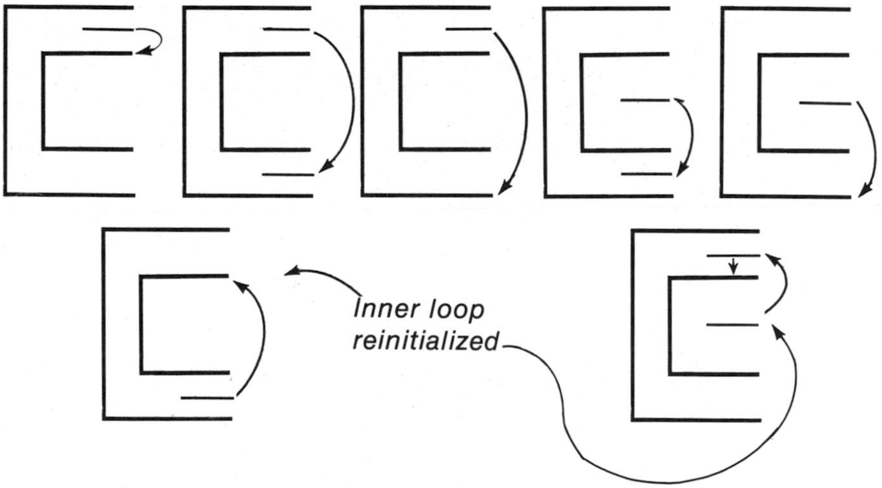

Illegal Jumps

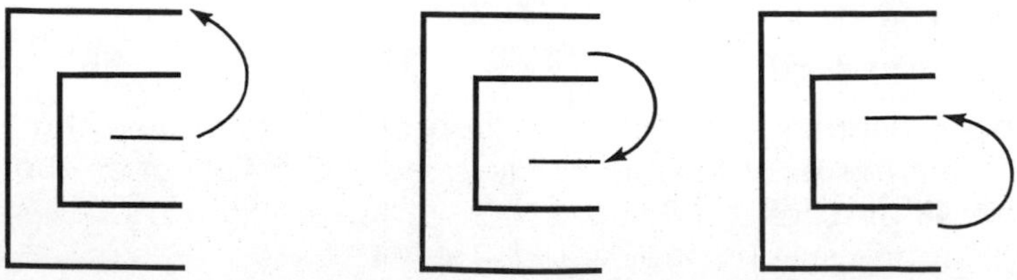

EXERCISES 4-7

A In Program 4-12 how many times is each of these lines executed?

1. 5 **2.** 30 **3.** 40

Correct any errors in each of the following programs.

4.
```
10 READ X
20 FØR J = 1 TØ X
30 READ M
40 IF M < 0 THEN 70
50 LET P = P + 1
60 NEXT J
70 LET N = N + 1
80 NEXT J
90 PRINT "SUM ØF PØSITIVES =" P
100 PRINT "SUM ØF NEGATIVES = " N
110 DATA 6,2,-3,5,-4,17
120 END
```

5.
```
10 READ R,S
20 FØR I = 1 TØ R
30 FØR J = 1 TØ S
40 IF I < J THEN 30
50 PRINT I, J, I+J
60 NEXT I
70 NEXT J
80 END
```

Consider the program at the right.

6. Show the first five lines of output.

7. Show the last five lines of output.

```
10 PRINT "LENGTH","WIDTH","AREA"
20 FØR L = 1 TØ 2 STEP .1
30 FØR W = 1 TØ 2 STEP .1
40 PRINT L,W,L*W
50 NEXT W
60 NEXT L
70 END
```

Consider the revised version of Program 4-12 that is shown at the right.

8. Show the first ten lines of output.

9. Show the last ten lines of output.

```
1 PRINT
5 PRINT " P"," T"," I"
6 PRINT
10 FØR P = 1000 TØ 4000 STEP 1000
20 FØR T = 1 TØ 5
30 LET I = P*T*.055
40 PRINT P,T,I
50 NEXT T
55 PRINT
60 NEXT P
70 END
```

10. Write a program to number twelve lines on the paper in three sets of four (1234 1234 1234).

11. Write a program to print the sum $x + y$ for all integer pairs (x, y) such that $-5 \leq x \leq 5$ and $0 \leq y \leq 10$.

B **12.** Prepare a flowchart for Program 4-13 on page 155.

13. Prepare a flowchart for the program of Exercises 6 and 7.

C **14.** Draw bracket-diagrams to illustrate all the ways in which three loops may be nested inside a fourth loop.

Computers in Insurance

In setting its premium rates for life insurance, an insurance company uses a **mortality table.** Part of one is shown below.

Age	Number Living (Jan. 1)	Deaths Each Year	Death Rate per 1000	Age	Number Living (Jan. 1)	Deaths Each Year	Death Rate per 1000
0	10,000,000	70,800	7.08	10	9,805,870	11,865	1.21
1	9,929,200	17,475	1.76	11	9,794,005	12,047	1.23
2	9,911,725	15,066	1.52	12	9,781,958	12,325	1.26
3	9,896,659	14,449	1.46	13	9,769,633	12,896	1.32
4	9,882,210	13,835	1.40	14	9,756,737	13,562	1.39
5	9,868,375	13,322	1.35	15	9,743,175	14,225	1.46
6	9,855,053	12,812	1.30	16	9,728,950	14,983	1.54
7	9,842,241	12,401	1.26	17	9,713,967	15,737	1.62
8	9,829,840	12,091	1.23	18	9,698,230	16,390	1.69
9	9,817,749	11,879	1.21	19	9,681,840	16,846	1.74

In the table, "Age 0" means "Under 6 months of age." To structure a mortality table, a large amount of data has to be gathered and many computations have to be made. To compute the annual death rate per 1000, an **actuary** (a statistician for an insurance company) uses the following proportion.

$$\frac{x}{1000} = \frac{\text{Number dying during the year}}{\text{Number living at start of the year}}$$

For the table above, the death rate per 1000 for four-year olds was calculated as follows:

$$\frac{x}{1000} = \frac{13{,}835}{9{,}882{,}210}$$

$$x = \frac{13{,}835{,}000}{9{,}882{,}210}, \text{ or } 1.40$$

Thus, out of every set of 1000 four-year-olds insured by the company, it is expected that on the average 1.4 will die before reaching age five.

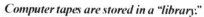

Computer tapes are stored in a "library."

The mortality table can also be used to answer more long-range questions. For example, what is the number of four-year-olds that can be expected to be alive at age 20, at age 30, and so forth? From such considerations actuaries can decide the amount of money (the **premium**) each policy holder should pay each year.

A specific program that arises from this situation is the following.

PROBLEM: Given the death rate per 1000 for each age group from 0 through 19, and a starting population, determine the number expected to be alive at age A $(0 < A \leq 20)$.

Program

```
100     INPUT "WHAT IS THE STARTING PØPULATIØN"; P
110     INPUT "AT WHAT AGE (<= 20) DØES PRØJECTIØN END" ; A
120
130     FØR I = 0 TØ A-1
140       READ D
150
160 REM   D = DEATHS PER 1000 FØR AGE-GRØUP I.
170
180       LET P = INT(P - P*D/1000 + .5)
190     NEXT I
200
210     PRINT
220     PRINT "NØ. EXPECTED ALIVE AT AGE ";A;" IS ";P
230     PRINT
240
250     DATA 7.08, 1.76, 1.52, ...
          .
          .
          .
300     END
```

Projects

1. For the program above insert statements to test for bad input data. Print statements such as "The starting population P must be greater than 0" and "A cannot be greater than 20."

2. Given the death rate per 1000 and the starting population, write a program to compute the number of persons from age 0 through 19 who are expected to die each year and print the mortality table.

3. Given the starting population and the number who die each year, write a program to compute the death rate per 1000 for persons from age 0 through 19 and print the mortality table.

4-8 A SUGGESTED FORMAT FOR PROGRAMS

To emphasize logical groupings, programs will sometimes be shown with indented lines, blank lines, or both. The following revision of Program 4-12 illustrates these and other features of a more open format.

```
100   REM     PRØGRAM 4-12 IN THE NEW FØRMAT
110
120   REM     THE PRØGRAM CALCULATES INTEREST ØN $1000,
130   REM     $2000, $3000, ØR $4000 FØR 1 TØ 5 YEARS.
140
150   REM      VARIABLES:  P = PRINCIPAL
160   REM                  T = TIME
170   REM                  I = INTEREST
180
190          PRINT " P", " T", " I"
200
210          FØR P = 1000 TØ 4000 STEP 1000
220
230            FØR T = 1 TØ 5
240              LET I = P * T * .055
250              PRINT P, T, I
260            NEXT T
270
280          NEXT P
290
300          END
```

Comments about the new format:

1. REMarks are used freely to explain what the program is doing and what each variable represents.
2. In order to make blocks of the program easier to see, blank lines are inserted above and below the explanatory comments and above and below each FØR-NEXT loop. Note: On some systems, blank lines are automatically removed by the compiler. In that case, you can type "REM" right after the line number in each line that is to be blank. This will achieve almost the same effect.
3. Lines are indented to show where they fit into the structure of the program. For example, lines 230-260 (the body of the P-loop), are all indented further than the FØR and NEXT statements of that loop (lines 210 and 280). Then lines 240 and 250 (the body of the nested T-loop) are indented further. Notice that each NEXT is indented the same amount as the corresponding FØR.
4. To insure uniform indents, line numbers of equal width are used.
5. Within each line, blank spaces are used to improve readability.

The next program shows a key programming technique needed in some of the Round Four exercises. That technique involves taking a whole number and splitting off its digits.

```
100    REM     PRØGRAM 4-14:  DIGIT REVERSAL
110
120    REM     PRØGRAM FØRMS THE REVERSAL ØF A 3-DIGIT
130    REM     NUMBER. EXAMPLE: 187; PRINT 781. DIGITS ØF
140    REM     NUMBER ARE NØT ENTERED SEPARATELY NØR ARE
150    REM     DIGITS ØF REVERSAL PRINTED SEPARATELY.
160
170    REM     VARIABLES:  X = ØRIGINAL NUMBER
180    REM                 H = HUNDREDS DIGIT ØF X
190    REM                 T = TENS DIGIT ØF X
200    REM                 U = UNITS DIGIT ØF X
210    REM                 R = THE REVERSAL ØF X
220    REM                 Z = A VARIABLE (0 ØR 1) USED TØ
230    REM                     DECIDE WHETHER TØ STØP
240
250           INPUT "ENTER A THREE-DIGIT WHØLE NUMBER."; X
260
270    REM     LINES 290-310 CHECK FØR BAD INPUT.
280
290           IF X <> INT(X) THEN 320
300             IF X < 100 THEN 320
310               IF X < 1000 THEN 370
320                 PRINT "A 3-DIGIT WHØLE NUMBER, PLEASE"
330                 GØ TØ 250
340
350    REM     LINES 370-420 FØRM AND PRINT REVERSAL ØF X.
360
370           H = INT(X/100)
380           T = INT((X - 100*H)/10)
390           U = X - (100*H + 10*T)
400           R = 100*U + 10*T + H
410           PRINT "THE REVERSAL IS " R
420           PRINT
430
440    REM     LINES 470-480 DECIDE WHETHER THE USER WANTS
450    REM     TØ CØNTINUE.
460
470           INPUT "WANT TØ STØP (1 = YES, 0 = NØ)"; Z
480           IF Z = 0 THEN 250
490
500           END
```

EXERCISES 4-8

A Rewrite each of these programs in the new format.

1. Program 4-7 **2.** Program 4-11 **3.** Program 4-13

4. Give at least two reasons why it is important to write programs that are as easy as possible to read and follow.

5. Give a reason why you might not be able to use completely the new format for a very large program.

B Write a program to do each of the following.

6. Given a two-digit whole number, print its reversal.
7. Given a four-digit whole number, print its reversal.
8. Given a five-digit whole number, print its reversal.

CHAPTER SUMMARY

A computer that is programmed to use an algorithm, such as the steps for long division, must be able both to count and to accumulate a sum of integers. The computer's *counter* is a variable, such as I, with the key step being LET I = I + K. Here, K is the *increment* and often has the value 1. To accumulate a sum in location S, use LET S = S + I.

The components of a *loop* are initialization, incrementation, body, and stopping mechanism. In BASIC, initialization, incrementation, and stopping mechanism are included in the FØR and NEXT statements. The general form of the FØR statement is as follows.

FØR (variable) = (expression) TØ (expression) STEP (expression)

(variable)	(expression)	(expression)	(expression)
INDEX	*INITIAL VALUE of the index*	*FINAL VALUE of the index*	*INCREMENT (optional if the step is one)*

The general form of the NEXT statement is NEXT (variable). The same index, such as I, follows both FØR and NEXT.

Example:

```
50 FØR I = 1 TØ X STEP N

        . . .

90 NEXT I
```

A program may not branch out of the body of a loop and then return directly to the body of the loop again. Once the program leaves a loop, the loop may be reentered only through the FØR statement and the index is reset to its initial value. One or more loops may be nested inside another loop.

The INT function is used to test whether one integer is divisible by another. For example, to test whether an integer X is divisible by 3, check to see whether INT (X/3) = X/3.

A suggested format for programs includes the following features: the free use of REMarks, the use of blank lines above and below blocks of copy, the use of deep indents to emphasize loop structure, the choice of line numbers of equal width (usually three characters), and the insertion of extra space within lines to improve readability.

CHAPTER OBJECTIVES AND REVIEW

Objective: To decide whether a given LET, IF . . . THEN, FØR, or NEXT statement is valid. *(Sections 4-1, 4-5, and 4-6)*

Write *Yes* or *No* to show whether each of the following is a valid BASIC statement.

1. `35 LET I - 1 = I`
2. `60 FØR J = 1,10`
3. `50 LET K2 = K2 + 2`
4. `100 NEXT I + 1`
5. `85 FØR M = X + 7 TØ W*Z STEP K`
6. `70 IF INT(X/Y = X/Y) THEN 91`
7. `150 FØR L = L TØ L + 10 STEP L`

Objective: To write a program to add integers from a given starting value to a given last value with a given increment between values. *(Sections 4-2 and 4-3)*

8. Write a program to find the sum of the odd integers from −21 to 99 inclusive. Do not use a FØR–NEXT loop.

Objective: To identify the four components of a loop in a given program. *(Section 4-4)*

9. Identify the four components (initialization, incrementation, body, and stopping mechanism) of the loop in the program below.

```
10 LET S = 0
20 READ X
30 LET I = 1
40 IF I = X THEN 80
50 LET S = S + I
60 LET I = I + 1
70 GØ TØ 40
80 PRINT "SUM = " S
90 DATA 11
100 END
```

Objective: To trace a given program that contains a loop. *(Section 4-4)*

10. Trace the program at the right.

```
10 LET K = 2
20 LET K = K + 1
30 PRINT K;
40 IF K < 8 THEN 20
50 END
```

Objective: To use an iteration box in drawing a flowchart for a given program that contains a loop. *(Section 4-4)*

11. Flowchart the program of Exercise 10. Use an iteration box.

Objective: To use the FØR and NEXT statements in revising a given program that contains a loop and is not in FØR-NEXT form. *(Section 4-5)*

12. Rewrite the program of Exercise 10 using a FØR-NEXT loop.

Objective: To correct all errors in a given program involving FØR and NEXT statements. *(Sections 4-5, 4-6, and 4-7)*

13. Correct all errors in the program at the right.

```
13 FØR M = 0 TØ 6 STEP 1
17 READ K
22 IF K < 0 THEN 39
24 LET P = P + K
28 LET M = M + 1
31 NEXT M
34 GØ TØ 47
39 LET N = N + K
41 GØ TØ 28
47 PRINT P,N
86 DATA 83,-11,-17,42,91,13
99 END
```

Objective: To use the INT function in decisions about divisibility. *(Section 4-6)*

Write an IF . . . THEN statement for each decision.

14. If X is an integer, then 20.
15. If Y is a multiple of 5, branch to 100.
16. If M + N is not divisible by 6, then go to 90.

Objective: To use at least one FØR-NEXT loop in writing a program to solve a given problem. *(Section 4-8)*

17. Write a program that reads ten DATA values, adds the positive numbers in S1, adds the negative numbers in S2, and prints S1, S2, and the sum of all ten values.

ROUND FOUR: *PROGRAMS FOR STUDENT ASSIGNMENT*

GENERAL INSTRUCTIONS:

1. In each exercise on pages 165 through 183 write and run a program that will do what is specified in the exercise.
2. If the program has several possible outcomes, the DATA must produce each outcome at least once.
3. Regardless of the possible outcomes, every program must process at least three sets of DATA.
4. Most programs should include at least one FØR-NEXT loop.

ALGEBRA ONE

1. Given an integer A and a positive integer N, compute A^N without using exponentiation (raising to a power; see p. 53).
2. Extend Exercise 1 to handle any integer N. (Caution: Zero raised to a nonpositive power is undefined.)
3. Read ten values of X and ten values of Y (the X and Y-values alternate in the DATA). Compute the sum of the X-values, the sum of the Y-values, and sum of the products XY.
4. There are only two whole numbers less than 10,000 that are multiples of their reversals (where the reversal does not equal the original number). Both these integers are greater than 8700. Find both numbers. (See Program 4-14, p. 161.)
5. There are two more integers less than 100,000 (see Ex. 4) that are multiples of their reversals (excluding the trivial case where the reversal equals the original number). These two integers lie between 87,900 and 99,000. Find them. (See Program 4-14, p. 161.)

Given fractions $\frac{a}{b}$ and $\frac{c}{d}$ (a, b, c, and d integers, b and d not zero), print the following in the lowest terms.

6. their sum
7. their product
8. the quotient of $\frac{a}{b}$ divided by $\frac{c}{d}$ (Test first whether $c = 0$.)
9. Find the abscissa values of the points that result when the segment from (1, 0) to (2, 0) on the x-axis is divided into eight equal parts.
10. Input a set of twenty numbers. Print the number of positive values and the number of negative values in the set.

11. The number 153 has an interesting property. It equals the sum of the cubes of its digits, that is, $153 = 1^3 + 5^3 + 3^3$. There are no two-digit or four-digit whole numbers with this property and only four three-digit numbers (including 153). Find these four whole numbers. A check on the program is that the first integer found should be 153. Do not list the digits separately in the DATA statement. (See Program 4-14, p. 161.)

12. Find every two-digit whole number that equals the sum of the squares of its digits. (See Ex. 6, p. 162.)

13. Find every four-digit whole number that equals the sum of the fourth powers of its digits. To save computer time, start the search with 1600. (See Ex. 7, p. 162.)

14. Decide whether a positive integer N ($N \leq 100$) is a perfect square.

15. Given a trinomial $Ax^2 + Bx + C$ (A, B, and C integers with $A \leq 100$ and $C \leq 100$), input A, B, and C and determine whether the trinomial is a perfect square over the integers.

16. Extend the program for Exercise 15 so that for a trinomial that is a perfect square, the program prints the square root. For example, for $4x^2 - 12x + 9$, print (2x−3) .

17. Given a three-digit whole number, compute the product of the digits. For example, for 423, print 24 (that is, $4 \times 2 \times 3$). Do not list the digits separately in the DATA statement. For example, do not use DATA 4, 2, 3 but rather DATA 423.

18. Find all three-digit whole numbers that are divisible by the product of their digits. There are twenty such numbers. Note: Any number with a zero digit must be excluded to avoid a zero divisor. This problem can be modified to find all the two-digit numbers divisible by the product of their digits. (See Program 4-14, p. 161.)

19. Find the forty four-digit whole numbers that are divisible by the product of their digits. Exclude any number with a zero digit to avoid division by zero. (See Ex. 7, p. 162.)

20. Convert a given improper fraction to a mixed number. For example, change $\frac{11}{8}$ to $1\frac{3}{8}$. Input the $\frac{11}{8}$ with DATA 11, 8 . Be sure that the fraction part of the mixed number is in lowest terms. For example, for $\frac{12}{8}$ output $1\frac{1}{2}$ and not $1\frac{4}{8}$.

21. Convert a mixed number to an improper fraction in lowest terms. Use three items of DATA to input the mixed number. For example, for $1\frac{3}{8}$ put DATA 1, 3, 8

22. There are times when illegal cancellation produces correct results. For example, $\frac{16}{64} = \frac{1\not{6}}{\not{6}4} = \frac{1}{4}$. Cases like this have been humorously called "mathematical misteaks." There are three other proper fractions with two-digit numerator and two-digit denominator where this illegal cancellation gives a correct result. Find the four fractions (including $\frac{16}{64}$).

23. Input a four-digit integer and determine whether all its digits are even. Do not feed the digits of the integer separately. For example, for 8675 use DATA 8675 .

24. Given a four-digit number that represents a year, decide whether it is a leap year. (Note: The algorithm for determining whether a year is a leap year is more complicated than simply dividing by four.)

25. Read two four-digit numbers A and B, which stand for years. Print all leap years that occur between A and B. Include in the DATA statement the pair A = 1898, B = 2001.

26. Given a year, determine the next year in which January 1 will fall on the same day of the week.

27. A high school teacher uses the following grading scale on her tests.

94-100 = A, 85-93 = B, 77-84 = C, 70-76 = D, below 70 = F

First read N, which represents the number of students in a class. Then read the exam grade of each student and count the number of A's, B's, C's, D's, and F's in the class.

28. Find the sum of the squares of the first ten consecutive positive integers.

GEOMETRY

29. Find the number of distinct triangles with sides of integral length no greater than ten. If the lengths of the sides are A, B, and C, the program can be made more efficient by assuming A ≤ B ≤ C. Then the following statements can be used to generate the integer combinations to be tested.

```
50 FØR A = 1 TØ 10
60 FØR B = A TØ 10
70 FØR C = B TØ 10
```

30. Using the conditions of Exercise 29, count and print the combinations for which A, B, and C are relatively prime (that is, the conditions under which 1 is their only common factor).

31. A man has contracted for 36 meters (36 m) of fencing for a rectangular yard. Many rectangles have 36 meter perimeters, for example 10×8, 12×6, $17.5 \times .5$, and 9×9. Which of the possible rectangles has the largest area? Answer by printing the length, width, and area of the rectangles with lengths from 9 m to 17.5 m in increments of 0.5 m.

32. Reverse Exercise 31. Fix the area of the rectangle at 36 square meters (36 m^2). Decide which rectangle has the largest perimeter by letting the length range from 6 m to 36 m in increments of 1 m.

33. Approximate π by finding the perimeters of regular N-gons inscribed in a circle of diameter one for $N = 4, 8, 16, 32, 64, 128, 256$.

34. In 1650 the English mathematician John Wallis discovered the following formula.

$$\frac{\pi}{2} = \frac{2}{1} \cdot \frac{2}{3} \cdot \frac{4}{3} \cdot \frac{4}{5} \cdot \frac{6}{5} \cdot \frac{6}{7} \cdot \frac{8}{7} \cdot \cdots$$

Use this formula to approximate π. Continue multiplying factors until the difference between successive products is less than .00005. Then multiply the last approximation by two to obtain the final result.

35. In 1674 Leibniz found the following formula.

$$\frac{\pi}{4} = 1 - \frac{1}{3} + \frac{1}{5} - \frac{1}{7} + \frac{1}{9} - \cdots + \frac{(-1)^{n-1}}{2n-1} + \cdots$$

Use the formula to approximate π. Continue adding terms until two successive approximations differ by less than .00005.

In Exercises 36-38, approximate π by using each of the following formulas. Use the stopping mechanism explained in Exercise 35.

36. $$\frac{\pi^2}{8} = 1 + \frac{1}{9} + \frac{1}{25} + \cdots + \frac{1}{(2n-1)^2} + \cdots$$

37. $$\frac{\pi^2}{6} = 1 + \frac{1}{4} + \frac{1}{9} + \frac{1}{16} + \cdots + \frac{1}{n^2} + \cdots$$

38. $$\frac{\pi^4}{90} = 1 + \frac{1}{16} + \frac{1}{81} + \frac{1}{256} + \cdots + \frac{1}{n^4} + \cdots$$

In Exercises 39-43, you need to know that a **Pythagorean Triple** is a set of three positive integers A, B, and C such that $A^2 + B^2 = C^2$.

39. Find all Pythagorean Triples whose components are all less than or equal to fifty. Computer time can be saved by assuming that $A < B < C$. (Note that if $A = B$, C cannot be an integer.) Then the integers to be tested can be generated by the following statements.

```
10 FØR A = 1 TØ 48
20 FØR B = A + 1 TØ 49
30 FØR C = B + 1 TØ 50
```

40. Eliminate the C-loop of Exercise 39 by generating A and B and testing whether $\sqrt{A^2 + B^2}$ is an integer less than or equal to fifty.

41. Print only the *primitive* Pythagorean Triples whose components are all less than or equal to fifty. That is, print only those triples for which A, B, and C are relatively prime. (See Ex. 30.)

42. Verify that the product of a Pythagorean Triple is always divisible by sixty.

43. Find and test a relationship between the areas of primitive Pythagorean triangles (see Exercise 41) and the number six.

In addition to the equation $a^2 + b^2 = c^2$, other formulas have been discovered for generating Pythagorean Triples (see Exercises 39-43). In Exercises 44-46 use the given formulas to print Triples. (In all cases, m and n are positive integers and $m > 1$.)

44. $(m, \frac{m^2 - 1}{2}, \frac{m^2 + 1}{2})$ and m is odd. This formula is attributed to Pythagoras himself (540 B.C.).

45. $(2m, m^2 - 1, m^2 + 1)$ This is Plato's formula (400 B.C.).

46. $(m^2 - n^2, 2mn, m^2 + n^2)$ and $m > n$ Euclid's formula (320 B.C.)

By the Pythagorean Theorem, if squares are constructed on the sides of a right triangle, then the area of the square on the hypotenuse (III) equals the sum of the areas of the squares on the two legs (I and II).

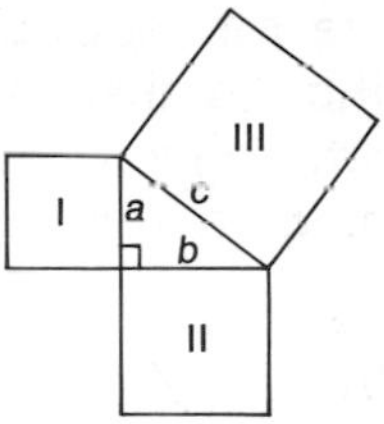

47. Suppose that instead of constructing squares on the sides of the triangle, we construct semicircles. Does the sum of the areas of semicircles I and II equal the area of semicircle III? Generate Pythagorean Triples and test the conjecture.

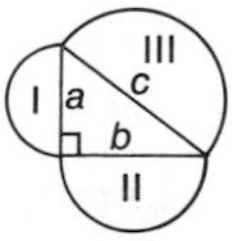

48. Construct equilateral triangles on the sides of right triangles and test whether, for each right triangle, the sum of the areas of the two equilateral triangles on the legs equals the area of the equilateral triangle on the hypotenuse.

ALGEBRA TWO

49. Print a $\frac{3}{2}$ power table for $x = 1, 2, 3, \ldots, 10$, i.e., $1^{\frac{3}{2}}, 2^{\frac{3}{2}}, \ldots, 10^{\frac{3}{2}}$.

50. Calculate logarithms to the base eight for $n = 1, 2, 3, \ldots, 20$. Print the output in two columns: n and $\log_8 n$.

51. Input a real number X such that $.0001 < X < 10^9$. Print X and the characteristic of its common logarithm. Do not use the INT or CLG functions (or the equivalent on your system).

52. Solve $x^x = 2$ for a value of x correct to the nearest hundredth. Use a trial-and-error method with a tolerance. (See Lesson 3-9.)

53. Given positive integers A and B, use the INT function to print the whole number part of the quotient and the remainder when A is divided by B. Do not assume that A > B.

54. Do Exercise 53 without using the INT function.

55. Print a table of cube and fourth roots of x, $x = 1, 2, 3, \ldots, 10$.

56. Determine whether the equation $x^n + y^n = z^n$ has a solution for positive integers $x, y, z < 10$ and $3 \leq n < 10$. (For $n = 2$, the equation is the Pythagorean formula.)

57. Given a positive integer $x > 1$, evaluate $\sqrt{x + \sqrt{x + \sqrt{x + \sqrt{x + \sqrt{x}}}}}$.

58. Extend the pattern of the expression in Exercise 57 to include ten x's. Then evaluate the expression.

59. Evaluate the expression in Exercise 57 with all the radicals changed to cube roots.

60. The rational numbers can be lined up in an order and counted (though the counting does not end). Print the rational numbers between zero and one that are of the form A/B, where A and B are integers from 1 to 10, inclusive. The list will look like this.

1/2	1/3	1/4	1/5	1/6	1/7	1/8	1/9	1/10
2/3	2/4	2/5	2/6	2/7	2/8	2/9	2/10	
. . .			. . .			. . .		
8/9	8/10							
9/10								

61. In the list of Exercise 60 the same number occurs several times. For example, 1/2 = 2/4 = 3/6 = 4/8 = 5/10. Avoid this repetition by printing only the fractions A/B that are in lowest terms.

62. Find i^n for any natural number n (where i is the imaginary unit such that $i = \sqrt{-1}$).

63. Extend Exercise 62 to all integers n.

ADVANCED MATHEMATICS

64. Compute N! for N = 1 to 10. Print the output in two labeled columns, N and N-FACTØRIAL.

65. Print a table of the six trigonometric functions in a ten-degree range in intervals of 15 minutes. Let the user specify which ten-degree range is desired.

66. In trigonometry any angle whose degree measure is greater than 90 or less than zero has a "reference angle" between 0 and 90, inclusive. Given the degree measure of an angle between −720 and 720, inclusive, print the measure of its reference angle.

67. Given polar coordinates (r, θ) and (s, α) such that $-720° < \theta < 720°$ and $-720° < \alpha < 720°$. Decide whether the two sets of polar coordinates designate the same point.

68. The function $\sin x$ is increasing at $x = 0$. Find experimentally the smallest positive value of x (to the nearest hundredth) at which the function starts decreasing. Trigonometry specifies this value as $\frac{\pi}{2}$.

69. Given two real numbers X and Y and a positive integer N, compute N arithmetic means between X and Y.

70. Given two real numbers X and Y and a positive integer N, compute (if possible) N geometric means between X and Y. Sometimes there may be more than one set of means. For example, if X = 1, Y = 16, and N = 3, one set of means is 2, 4, 8 and another is −2, 4, −8.

In Exercises 71 and 72 you are given the complex roots of a quadratic equation. Print the equation.

71. Assume that the quadratic polynomial has real coefficients. (This implies something about the roots.)

72. Do not assume that the equation has real coefficients.

Descartes' Rule of Signs establishes a connection between the number of sign changes between consecutive terms of a polynomial P and the number of possible real roots of the equation $P = 0$. Read the integral coefficients of a cubic polynomial $Ax^3 + Bx^2 + Cx + D = 0$ and do Exercises 73 and 74.

73. Count the number of sign changes and print the maximum number of positive real roots the equation may have.

74. Decide the maximum possible number of negative real roots.

75. Evaluate $\sin x$ by this series and compare with the SIN(X) of BASIC.

$$\sin x = x - \frac{x^3}{3!} + \frac{x^5}{5!} - \frac{x^7}{7!} + \ldots \text{ (}x\text{ in radians)}$$

76. Evaluate arcsin x using the following series.

$$\arcsin x = x + \frac{x^3}{2 \cdot 3} + \frac{1 \cdot 3x^5}{2 \cdot 4 \cdot 5} + \frac{1 \cdot 3 \cdot 5x^7}{2 \cdot 4 \cdot 6 \cdot 7} + \cdots \qquad (x^2 < 1)$$

77. Compute the sum of the series $1 + \frac{1}{2} + \frac{1}{3} + \frac{1}{4} + \ldots + \frac{1}{100}$.

78. Find n such that $1 + \frac{1}{2} + \frac{1}{3} + \frac{1}{4} + \ldots + \frac{1}{n}$ exceeds five.

Use the computer to verify each of the following.

79. $1 + 2 + 3 + \ldots + n = \dfrac{n(n+1)}{2}$

80. $1 + 4 + 9 + \ldots + n^2 = \dfrac{n(n+1)(2n+1)}{6}$

Use the computer to compare the convergence of each of the following pairs of sequences.

81. $\left(-\frac{100}{101}\right)$ and $\left(\frac{1}{10}\right)^n$

82. $1 + \left(\frac{2}{3}\right)^n$ and $\left(1 + \frac{2}{3}\right)^n$

Use the computer to examine the convergence of each of the following sequences.

83. $\dfrac{n^2 + 3n - 1}{n}$

84. $\dfrac{n-1}{(n+1)(n-2)}$

85. $\dfrac{1}{n!}$

86. $1 + \dfrac{1}{n^n}$

87. Determine the limit of $\dfrac{\sin x}{x}$ as x approaches zero by printing x and $\dfrac{\sin x}{x}$ for $x = 1, .5, .25, .125, \ldots$ until the difference between successive values of the ratio is less than .00005.

88. Repeat Exercise 87 for $\dfrac{\log x}{x}$ as x increases without bound ($x = 2, 3, 4, \ldots$).

89. In the complex number system any number has two square roots, three cube roots, four fourth roots, . . . , n nth roots. Use De Moivre's Theorem to calculate the n nth roots (in standard form) of a complex number.

NUMBER THEORY

90. Given a positive integer, print its positive integral factors.

91. Given an integer N and an integer M > 1, find the congruence class (modulo M) to which N belongs.

92. Accept integers J and N and decide whether they are congruent modulo M (M is an integer and is greater than 1).

93. Print a multiplication table modulo M for the integers 0, 1, 2, . . . , M − 1.

94. Find the LCM (least common multiple) of two integers.

95. Find the LCM of three integers.

96. Find the GCF (greatest common factor) of two integers.

97. Find the GCF of three integers.

98. Decide whether two given integers are relatively prime.

99. Decide whether three given integers are relatively prime.

100. A positive integer N is *prime* if and only if N ≠ 1 and N has no positive factors except itself and one. A positive integer greater than one is *composite* if and only if it is not prime. Every even integer is composite except two. One is the only positive integer that is neither prime nor composite. We develop the following algorithm for determining whether a given positive integer is prime, composite, or neither.

(a) Read N (a positive integer).
(b) If N = 1, print NEITHER and go to **g**.
(c) If N = 2, print PRIME and go to **g**.
(d) Test whether N is divisible by 2. If it is, print CØMPØSITE and go to **g**.
(e) Decide whether N is divisible by any *odd* integer from 3 to $\sqrt{N}$. If it is, print CØMPØSITE and go to **g**.
(f) If steps **d** and **e** result in no divisor, print PRIME.
(g) Out of data? If no, go to **a**. If yes, END.

Read a positive integer. Is it prime, composite, or neither?

101. Given a positive integer, print its prime factors. For example, for 315 output the list   3   5   7   .

102. For a positive integer print its prime factorization, showing by exponents the number of times each prime is used as a factor. For example, for 315 output   3 ↑ 2 * 5 * 7   .

103. "Twin primes" are two consecutive primes that differ by two. For example, 5 and 7, 11 and 13, 41 and 43 are twin primes. Find the number of twin primes in each of the intervals 3–100, 101–200, 201–300, . . . , 901–1000. Print the results in tabular form. (Will the number of twins in each interval decrease as you reach larger and larger integers?)

104. A "palindromic prime" is a prime that is also a prime when its digits are reversed. 11, 13, and 17 are such primes. Find ten others.

105. Let $f(n) = n^2 - n + 41$. Test that $f(n)$ is prime for $n = 1, 2, 3, \ldots, 40$ but not prime for $n = 41$. Print the output in columns: n, $f(n)$, prime or composite.

106. Many formulas have been tried to see whether they always produce primes. (None has thus far been found. See Exercise 105.) Test each of the formulas below and verify that they produce primes for the values indicated but do not produce a prime for the next value in succession:

$n^2 + n + 17$	for $n = 0, 1, 2, \ldots, 15$
$n^3 - 31n^2 + 320n - 1117$	for $n = 0, 1, 2, \ldots, 24$
$2n^2 + 29$	for $n = 0, 1, 2, \ldots, 28$
$3n^2 - 3n + 23$	for $n = 0, 1, 2, \ldots, 22$

107. Three sailors, shipwrecked with a monkey on a desert island, have gathered a pile of coconuts that are to be divided early the next day. During the night one sailor arises, divides the pile into three equal parts, and finds one coconut left over, which he gives to the monkey. He then hides his share. Later during the night, each of the other two sailors arises separately and repeats the performance of the first sailor. In the morning all three sailors arise, divide the pile into three equal shares, and find one left over, which they give to the monkey. By trial-and-error compute the smallest integer that could represent the number of coconuts in the original pile.

108. All primes congruent to one (modulo 4) can be expressed as a unique sum of two integral squares (Fermat's "Two Square" Theorem). For example, $5 = 1^2 + 2^2$, $29 = 2^2 + 5^2$, and so forth. For the ten smallest primes that satisfy the conditions of Fermat's Theorem, print the number as the sum of two squares.

109. Find twelve consecutive composite integers. Do not use a trial-and-error method. (Hint: Find an algorithm that involves a factorial.)

110. Multiply pairs of positive base-ten integers by repeated addition. Execution time will be saved if the larger integer is used as the multiplicand and the smaller as the multiplier. For example, it is quicker to multiply 82×13 by adding 82 thirteen times than to add 13 eighty-two times.

111. Extend Exercise 110 to allow the multiplicand to have a decimal part. For example, 82.43×13.

112. Print the largest proper factor (any factor less than the number itself) for each odd integer from 1001 to 1019, inclusive.

113. A "perfect number" is a whole number that equals the sum of its proper factors. (See Ex. 112.) Find and print all perfect numbers that are less than 100.

114. A whole number *n* is "abundant" if the sum of its proper factors exceeds *n*, and "deficient" if the sum is less than *n*. Given a positive integer, classify it as perfect, abundant, or deficient.

115. Convert the binary representation of a whole number to its decimal form. Arrange the DATA in the following way: the number of digits in the binary numeral, followed by the digits separately. For example, for 1101_{two}, use DATA 4,1,1,0,1. (Note that the digits are listed left-to-right and not right-to-left.) For 1101, the program should print 13.

116. The British mathematician G. H. Hardy once casually mentioned to the brilliant young Indian mathematician Ramanujan that he. Hardy, had just ridden in a taxi with an "uninteresting" identification number. Upon being told the number, Ramanujan promptly replied that the number was quite interesting because it was the smallest integer that could be written as the sum of two cubes in two different ways. Find the number of Hardy's taxi. Warning: This program takes a large amount of computer time!

117. The integers 12 and 13 have the following characteristic: $12 \times 12 = 144$, $21 \times 21 = 441$; and $13 \times 13 = 169$; $31 \times 31 = 961$. Find a three-digit integer (if one exists) for which this same kind of relationship holds.

118. Goldbach's Conjecture, which has never been proved or disproved, claims that every even number greater than four is the sum of two odd primes. For example, $44 = 13 + 31$. (This pair is not unique: $44 = 41 + 3$, $44 = 37 + 7$.) Test the Conjecture for the even integers up to fifty. Print the result for each integer as an equation such as $44 = 3 + 41$. (Any one pair of odd primes is sufficient for each integer.) If the program gives faulty results, read Lesson 3-9 on pages 107 and 108.

119. Find all two-digit whole numbers that have the property that if the final digit of the numeral is deleted, the original number is divisible by the new number. For example, 2<u>4</u> is divisible by 2 but 2<u>5</u> is not divisible by 2.

120. 220 and 284 are called "friendly" or "amicable" numbers because the sum of the proper factors of each equals the other. Find another pair of amicable whole numbers.
Warning: This program can take a large amount of computer time!

121. In his *Laws,* Book 5, Plato recommends that a city be divided into plots of land so that the number of plots has as many proper divisors as possible (thus insuring the maximum flexibility for further subdivisions). He suggested 5040 because it has 59 proper divisors, a very large number. However, computer research reveals that the largest number of proper divisors that a number less than 10,000 can have is 63, which tops Plato's number by four divisors. There are just two such 63-divisor numbers. One is 9240. Find the other.

122. A novel method of multiplying two integers is the "Russian peasant method." For example, to find the product of 19 and 23, write these numbers at the top of two columns. Each number on the left is divided by two, ignoring any remainder (truncating). Each time division takes place, the corresponding number on the right is multiplied by two. This process continues until the number on the left is reduced to 1. The procedure is shown in Table 1.

19 ×	23
9	46
4	92
2	184
1	368

Table 1

19 ×	23
9	46
4	~~92~~
2	~~184~~
1	368

Table 2

Now each time an even number appears on the left, its corresponding number on the right is crossed out. The columns would now appear as shown in Table 2. The sum of the remaining numbers in the right column is 19 × 23. Program the computer to use this method of multiplying positive integers.

123. A man born in the 18th century was x years old in the year x^2. How old was he in 1776? Is there a corresponding puzzle for the 19th century? If so, find the man's age in 1876. Show that there is no corresponding puzzle for the 20th century.

124. Find the number of positive integers that leave a remainder of 24 when divided into 4049.

125. Find all positive integers less than 200 that leave a remainder of 1 when divided by 5 and a remainder of 2 when divided by 7.

126. Repeat Exercise 125 but change the first remainder to 2 and the second remainder to 1.

127. "Euler's phi-function" is defined as follows: For any positive integer n, $\phi(n)$ equals the number of positive integers less than n that are relatively prime to n. Find $\phi(n)$ for $n = 1, 2, 3, \ldots, 50$.

128. The mathematician Stanislav Ulam of the University of Colorado hypothesized that any positive integer would always converge to 1 if treated as follows. If it is odd, multiply it by three and add one; if it is even, divide it by two. This procedure is then applied to the result of each calculation. For example, starting with eleven produces the following sequence.

11 34 17 52 26 13 40 20 10 5 16 8 4 2 1

Test whether the procedure just described works for every integer from 1 to 100 inclusive.

129. A conjecture known as the "Four Square Theorem" states that every positive integer is either a square or the sum of two, three, or four squares (i.e., the equation $n = x^2 + y^2 + z^2 + w^2$, where x, y, z, and w are nonnegative integers, has a solution for every positive integer n). Use the computer to verify or disprove the conjecture for all integers n from 1 to 100.

In Exercises 130-134, use the computer to verify each of the given divisibility tests.

130. Divisibility by 13: Multiply the units digit of the number by four and add the product to the number represented by the remaining digits. This sum is divisible by 13 if and only if the original number is divisible by 13.

131. Divisibility by 17: Multiply the units digit of the number by five and subtract the product from the number represented by the remaining digits. This difference is divisible by 17 if and only if the original number is divisible by 17.

132. Divisibility by 19: Multiply the units digit of the number by two and add the product to the number represented by the remaining digits. This sum is divisible by 19 if and only if the original number is divisible by 19.

133. Divisibility by 31: Triple the units digit of the number and subtract the triple from the number represented by the remaining digits. This difference is divisible by 31 if and only if the original number is divisible by 31.

134. Divisibility by 11: Form a new number from the number being tested by **(a)** deleting the units digit and **(b)** subtracting the deleted digit from the shortened number. Repeat this two-step process until only two digits remain. The remaining two-digit number is divisible by 11 if and only if the original number is divisible by 11. This test for divisibility by 11 was given in 1897 by Charles L. Dodgson (Lewis Carroll).

BUSINESS

(Note: In many of the programs of this section, you can use the formula worked out in Exercise 16 on page 153 to print monetary output to two decimal places only.)

Many of the programs below involve *compound interest,* which is not the same as *simple interest.* An example will show the contrast.

Suppose a principal of $100 is invested at 6% simple interest. After one year the investment earns .06 × $100 of $6.00 interest. The $6 interest is not added to the principal. Thus the second year again yields $6 interest and the principal remains $100.

If the $100 is invested at 6% compound interest, the $6 interest after the first year is added to the $100 and for the second year the principal is $106. Hence the second year's interest is .06 × $106 or $6.36. The principal for the third year is then $112.36.

In all exercises the interest rates are *annual* rates unless explicitly stated otherwise.

135. Manhattan Island was purchased in 1626 for $24. If those early buyers had invested the same amount at 6% interest, compounded annually, how much would their investment be worth today?

136. A woman plans to borrow $100 and wants to compare various loan plans. Suppose that Company A will lend her the money at compound interest at 1% monthly, and Company B will lend her the money at simple interest at $1\frac{1}{8}$% per month. Compare how much she would have to pay under each plan after 12, 24, or 36 months.

137. An employee of the Colonel Motors Company receives life insurance in an amount equal to three times his or her yearly salary to the next highest $100. For example, if an employee earns $7950 per year, he receives 3 × $8000 or $24,000 worth of insurance. Determine the amount of policy for an employee whose *weekly* salary is given. (An employee at Colonel Motors is paid for fifty-two weeks of the year, including vacation.)

138. $100 is invested at 5% compounded quarterly. Print the value of the account each year for ten years. Note: "Compounded quarterly" means that the interest is compounded four times a year (every three months). Remember, though, that the 5% is an annual interest rate. Use the quarterly rate ($1\frac{1}{4}$%).

139. Job A lasts thirty days and pays $25 per day; job B lasts thirty days and pays as follows: $1 first day, $2 second day, $3 third day, and so forth. Which job pays more?

140. Many cash registers in use today automatically return the correct change. Write a program to simulate this procedure. Assume that the cost of the purchase is less than one dollar. The program will accept as input the cost of the purchase (in cents) and will output the coins that will be returned if a dollar bill were given to the cashier. The number of coins returned should be kept to a minimum. Thus you do not want to return only pennies. For example, if the purchase price were 29 cents, the coin returned would be two quarters, two dimes, and one penny. Assume that half-dollars are not used.

141. An individual has an account with a principal of $10,000. He withdraws $100 at the beginning of each month. Assuming that the bank adds interest at $5\frac{1}{4}$% on the minimum balance during the previous month, print the monthly balance for one year.

142. Suppose that you purchase the Newtown Spears, a minor league baseball team, for $72,000. The league tells you that the profit (in $1,000 units) of the franchise can be projected for the next eight years by using the formula

$$P = T^3 - 5T^2 + 10T - C$$

where P = profit, T = time in years, C = cost in thousands (72). Calculate and print your profit or loss for each of the next eight years. Also calculate and print your net profit (or loss) at the end of eight years.

143. Show the transactions during one month for a person's bank account. (In effect you are writing a checkbook-balancing program.) Enter the balance at the beginning of the month. Then input the transactions in chronological order, entering first the day number of the transaction, a code to indicate whether it was a debit or credit, and the amount. Use a code number to signal the last transaction of the month. Have the computer print a record of the month in four columns as follows.

DAY	DEBIT	CREDIT	CURRENT BALANCE

At the bottom print the balance at the end of the month.

144. Expand Exercise 143 to include a bank service charge. The charge is $.25 per month but if at any time during the month the balance falls below $300, an additional $.25 is debited. (Thus the maximum monthly service charge is $.50.)

145. Given the net profit and the number of partners of a company, enter the percent of ownership of each partner. Print the profit of each partner.

146. Calculate and print a loan repayment schedule. The schedule is to provide the following outputs: (**a**) payment number, (**b**) amount of each payment paid as interest, (**c**) amount of the loan amortized with each payment, (**d**) balance remaining on the principal at the time of each payment, and (**e**) the amount of the last payment. The input is the amount of the regular payment, the term of payment, the number of payments per year, the amount of the principal, and the annual interest rate.

147. Each week the Tiger Electric Company pays its employees in cash. Thus, the treasurer needs to know exactly how much money to get from the bank. The input for each employee is his net pay amount for the week. Prepare the output in the following form.

$20 bills	xxx	Quarters	xxx
$10 bills	xxx	Dimes	xxx
$ 5 bills	xxx	Nickels	xxx
$ 1 bills	xxx	Pennies	xxx

Total net pay: $xxxx.xx

148. Print a compound interest table for an investment of $1000 at interest rates of $5\frac{1}{2}$%, 6%, . . . , 9%. The interest is compounded monthly for one year. Prepare the output in the form illustrated in the table below.

Month	5.5%	6%	6.5%	7%
1	4.58333	5.00000	5.41666	5.83333
.	.	.	.	.
12	.	.	.	.

Month	7.5%	8%	8.5%	9%
1	.	.	.	.
.	.	.	.	.
12	.	.	.	.

149. Suppose that the charge for a direct-dial call between New York and Los Angeles is $.94 per minute. (61 seconds count as a two-minute call.) Use the discount rates listed in Exercise 129 on page 124. Given the day of the week and the time at which the call originated and the number of seconds the call lasted, print the charge.

150. Given a date (month, day, year) for a loan payment, find what day of the year it is. January 1 = day 1, February 1 = day 32, . . . , December 31 = day 365 (day 366 if leap year).

151. Depreciation is that part of the original cost of an asset that a business charges to its expenses of operation over the estimated life of the asset. The two most common methods of depreciation are *straight-line* and *sum-of-the-year's digits.* The straight-line method charges the same amount per year, the amount being determined by dividing the depreciation base (original cost minus estimated scrap value) by the estimated life. The sum-of-the-year's digits is an accelerated method that allows the business owner to charge proportionately more than the straight-line amount in the early years of the asset and less in later years. With this method, it is necessary to determine a fraction that will be multiplied times the depreciation base. The denominator of that fraction is found by adding the whole numbers from one through the number of years of the asset's estimated life. For instance, the denominator would be six for an asset whose estimated life is three years (1 + 2 + 3). The denominator remains the same for all the annual calculations for that asset. The numerator of the fraction in the first year is the number that represents the estimated life. The numerator declines by one for each subsequent year until it is just one in the last year. Thus for an asset with a three-year life, one-half ($\frac{3}{6}$) is written off the first year, one-third ($\frac{2}{6}$) in the second, and one-sixth ($\frac{1}{6}$) in the third year. The program is to calculate the depreciation of an asset for any cost, scrap value, and life, and display, side-by-side, the results obtained by the two methods. Show not only the annual depreciation but also the depreciation as it accumulates and the resulting book value (original cost minus accumulated depreciation).

PHYSICAL SCIENCES

152. Produce a table listing the Fahrenheit temperature for each Celsius temperature from 0° C to 100° C in increments of 5° C.

153. A projectile is propelled vertically. Given its initial velocity, print the height of the projectile each second until it returns to its starting point.

154. In an electric circuit, if resistances R_1, R_2, R_3, . . . are in series, then the total resistance R is given by the formula,

$$R = R_1 + R_2 + R_3 + \cdots .$$

Given the number of resistances in series in a circuit, input the amount of each resistance. Then print the total resistance.

155. If resistances are in parallel, then the equivalent resistance R of a circuit is given by the formula

$$\frac{1}{R}=\frac{1}{R_1}+\frac{1}{R_2}+\frac{1}{R_3}+\cdots.$$

Given the number of resistances in parallel in a circuit, input the amount of each resistance. Then print the equivalent resistance of the circuit.

156. Assume that in 1960 the population figures for the United States and Mexico were 180,000,000 and 85,000,000 respectively and that the annual rate of growth of the U.S. is 1.23% and of Mexico, 2.23%. If these growth rates remain constant, in what year will the population of Mexico equal or exceed that of the United States?

157. Suppose that the world population is 4.5 billion. Each year it increases by 1.9%. Calculate the number of years from now in which world population will be double its current level and the number of years from now in which it will be triple its current level (assuming that the current growth rate remains constant).

158. The current population of a certain city is 40,000. Studies show that people move into the city at an annual rate of .6% and move out at an annual rate of .4%. The annual birthrate is 1.7%. The annual death rate is .9%. Print a table showing the city's population each year for the next 10 years. After 10 years summarize by printing the net increase or decrease and percent of change for the decade.

159. Calculate the percent of water in a hydrate from data that have been collected in a laboratory by heating weighted samples of hydrate to drive off the water and then determining the mass of the residue. Handle up to 20 samples. A line of output looks like the following.

```
SAMPLE NØ. XX     XXX PERCENT WATER
```

160. The diagram below shows the forces (n and p) acting on a body on an inclined plane of angle θ. If w represents the weight of the object, than $p=w \sin\theta$ and $n=w\cos\theta$. For a given w, print the two components n and p for values of θ from 10° to 80° in increments of 5°.

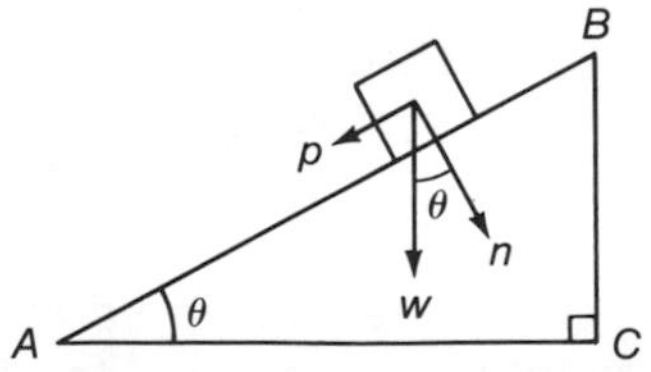

161. In the Bohr model of the atom, $E = -\frac{me^4}{8k^2h^2n^2}$, where E = the energy of an electron, m = its mass, e = its electronic charge, $k = 8.854 \times 10^{-12} \frac{\text{coulomb}^2}{\text{newton-meter}^2}$, h = Planck's constant, and n = the principal quantum number. Calculate E for an electron in each of the four energy levels (n = 1, 2, 3, 4).

162. Given the number of grams of a radioactive substance and its half-life, print the amount of the substance remaining after each of one-tenth half-life increments up to one half-life.

163. If a colony of bacteria grows at the rate of 9% per hour, then in eight hours the colony will double its size. Thus, the *doubling time* is eight hours. The so-called "rule of 72" can be used to compute doubling times. If a quantity grows by R percent in a single period of time, then the number of periods required for the quantity to double is approximately 72/R. Given the growth rate and the original quantity, print the hourly size of the bacteria colony until it doubles. Have the computer compare the doubling time found by this approach with the answer from the "rule of 72."

164. The index of refraction for a substance is to be computed as follows. Data from an experiment list five angles of incidence and the corresponding five angles of refraction for light entering the substance. Compute the average index of refraction for the five sets of data. (Assume that the angle of incidence is measured in a vacuum.)

165. An object is dropped from a height of 1000 m. Given the mass of the object (in kg), print the kinetic and potential energy of the object at heights of 1000 m, 900 m, 800 m, · · · , 100 m, 0 m. (Ignore air resistance.)

5

SUBSCRIPTED VARIABLES

5-1 COMPUTING THE AVERAGE OF A SET OF NUMBERS

Example:

Read a list of ten numbers and compute the average of the set.

A natural approach to programming this problem might be to start with either of the following statements.

```
        10 READ A,B,C,D,E,F,G,H,I,J
    or  10 READ A0,A1,A2,A3,A4,A5,A6,A7,A8,A9
```

Then the average could be computed with either of these statements.

```
      20 LET X = (A+B+C+D+E+F+G+H+I+J)/10
  or  20 LET X = (A0+A1+A2+A3+A4+A5+A6+A7+A8+A9)/10
```

These statements would work; they would compute the average of ten numbers. But suppose you must average one hundred numbers. Your READ and LET statements would grow so long as to become unwieldy.

The program does not require ten variable names (that is, ten storage locations) for the input numbers. Only one is needed since the numbers can be read and summed one at a time, as in this program.

Program 5-1

```
110 REM      CALCULATE THE AVERAGE ØF TEN NUMBERS.
120 REM      I SERVES AS A CØUNTER.
130
140           FØR I = 1 TØ 10
150             READ A
160             LET S = S + A
170           NEXT I
180           PRINT "AVERAGE = " S/10
```

```
190
200          DATA 71,67,73,84,52,58,64,80,68,71
210          END
```

Program 5-1 can be taken a step further.

Example:

Read a list of ten numbers and compute the average of the set; print the list of numbers followed by their average.

Program 5-1 used one memory location (A) over and over in order to hold the input numbers one at a time. The variable A will also suffice for the restated problem because each number can be printed as soon as it is read. Just insert the following lines in Program 5-1.

```
155            PRINT A;
175            PRINT
```

Program 5-1 processes ten DATA values—no more and no less. To allow more flexibility, the first number in the DATA could be the *number* of values in the set. This value would be read into location N and used to control the FØR-NEXT loop that reads, prints, and adds the remaining DATA values, as in the following program.

Program 5-2

```
110    REM     CALCULATE THE AVERAGE ØF N NUMBERS; N IS
120    REM     THE FIRST NUMBER IN DATA LIST (LINE 240).
130
140            READ N
150            FØR I = 1 TØ N
160              READ A
170              PRINT A;
180              LET S = S + A
190            NEXT I
200            PRINT
210            PRINT "AVERAGE = " S/N
220
230
240            DATA 10,71,67,73,84,52,58,64,80,68,71
250
260            END
```

This is not an element of the set to be averaged but a preliminary numeral signifying the number of elements in the list that follows. (arrow points to the 10 in line 240)

Even the approach on the previous page becomes inconvenient in case a large number of values must be processed. It would be tedious to count 50, 100, or more values for the program's input. To avoid this difficulty, you may use a code number, or sentinel, to indicate the end of the DATA list. Use any number that you know will not appear in the DATA list. Thus, if all of the DATA are positive, you can use zero or a negative number as an end-of-data sentinel.

This idea is implemented in Program 5-3 below. Note that there is no need for a preliminary number at the head of the DATA list. Instead a decision step (line 22) is included to test whether the sentinel (9999) has been reached. As soon as it is reached, the program branches out of the read-print-and-add loop and prints the average of the DATA values.

Program 5-3

```
10 FØR I = 1 TØ 1000
20   READ A
22   IF A = 9999 THEN 45
25     PRINT A;
30     LET S = S + A
40 NEXT I
45 PRINT
50 PRINT "AVERAGE = " S/(I-1)
60 DATA 71,67,73,84,52,58,64,80,68,71,9999
70 END
```

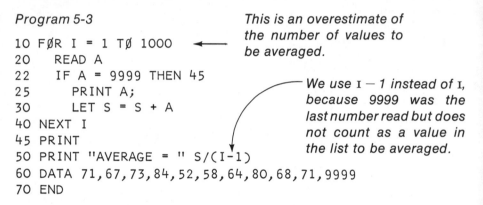

This is an overestimate of the number of values to be averaged. (line 10)

We use I − 1 *instead of* I, *because 9999 was the last number read but does not count as a value in the list to be averaged.* (line 50)

EXERCISES 5-1

A **1.** A student believes that she can write Program 5-3 without using a FØR-NEXT loop. Her program is listed below. Will it do the job? If not, what changes can be made (without introducing a FØR-NEXT loop) so that it will give the desired output?

```
10 READ A
20 LET N = N + 1
30 PRINT A;
40 LET S = S + A
50 GØ TØ 10
60 PRINT
70 PRINT "AVERAGE = " S/N
80 DATA 71,67,73,84,52,58,64,80,68,71
90 END
```

2. Input a number X and then a list of twenty numbers. Determine the number of times X occurs in the list.

3. Write a program that accepts a list of numbers and prints the average of the positives and the average of the negatives.

B 4. Given a list of whole numbers, find the sum of those that are multiples of both three and five.

5. Given a list of whole numbers, find the sum of those that are multiples of either three or five.

6. Given a list of whole numbers, find the sum of those that are even multiples of seven.

7. Trace this program.

```
10 READ X
20 IF X < 0 THEN 60
30 LET S = S + X
40 LET C = C + 1
50 GØ TØ 10
60 PRINT "AVERAGE IS " S/C
70 DATA 30,20,6,4,-1
80 END
```

Draw a flowchart for each of the following programs.

8. 5-1 9. 5-2 10. 5-3

5-2 SUBSCRIPTED VARIABLES

Lesson 5-1 developed a program to calculate the average of a set of numbers. We now move a step further.

Example:

Read a list of numbers; compute the average of the set; then determine how far from the average (above or below) each element in the list lies.

In Programs 5-1 to 5-3 on pages 184 through 186, it was possible to use one memory location, A, to hold, one at a time, each input value so that it could be printed and added to the sum S. Since the element was no longer needed, the next number in the list could be read into the same location.

For the problem above, however, this scheme will not work because after the average is computed, we must go back to each element and subtract the average from it. The algorithm might be stated as follows.

1. Read and store a list of numbers.
2. Find the sum of the list.
3. Compute the average of the set.
4. Subtract the average from each number in the list.
5. Print each number and its distance from the average.
6. Stop.

Steps 1 and 2 might be combined into one loop, as in Programs 5-1 through 5-3. Similarly steps 4 and 5 could be combined into another loop, after the average has been computed.

One thought might be to return to using a list of variables. If there are ten DATA items, the following program would work.

Program 5-4

```
10 READ A,B,C,D,E,F,G,H,I,J
20 LET X = (A+B+C+D+E+F+G+H+I+J)/10
30 PRINT A, A-X
40 PRINT B, B-X
50 PRINT C, C-X
60 PRINT D, D-X
70 PRINT E, E-X
80 PRINT F, F-X
90 PRINT G, G-X
100 PRINT H, H-X
110 PRINT I, I-X
120 PRINT J, J-X
130 DATA 71,67,73,84,52,58,64,80,68,71
140 END
```

For a list of ten numbers fourteen statements were required in Program 5-4. No loop was used. For longer lists of values the program quickly gets out of hand. There must be a better way.

The solution lies in using a *subscripted variable.* In mathematics a list of numbers is often designated using subscripts.

$$a_1, a_2, a_3, \ldots, \text{ or in general } a_i$$

These variables are read "*a* sub one," "*a* sub two," and so on, or in general "*a* sub *i*." In BASIC, since a terminal cannot print actual subscripts below the line, this list is written

A(1), A(2), A(3), . . . , A(I).

The "subscript" actually appears in parentheses right after the variable. The advantage of this notation is that the subscript is itself a variable and can therefore have values as large as needed. For the averaging problem ten numbers could be named A(1), A(2), A(3), . . . , A(10); that is, A(I) with I running from 1 to 10. Ninety-eight numbers could be stored as A(1), A(2), A(3), . . . , A(98); that is, A(I) with I running from 1 to 98. In both cases only two letters are needed: A and I.

A set of values named by one letter with a changing subscript is called a *list, vector,* or **array**. The number of values in the list is called the **dimension** (length) of the array. The variable representing the subscript (I above) is called the **index**. A one-dimensional array has one index; a two-dimensional array needs two indices (plural of "index"); three indices are used for a three-dimensional array, and so forth. For this chapter we limit ourselves to one-dimensional arrays.

Mathematically there is no limit to the number of subscripts a variable may have. In computer programming, however, the size of the machine being used and the rules of the programming language set an upper limit. Most versions of BASIC allow at most *two* subscripts.

In BASIC any one-letter variable may be subscripted. (Some systems may allow a variable such as A1 to be subscripted also.) Any one-letter variable (for example A) or one-letter-one-digit variable (such as A5) may be used as an index. Here are examples of subscripted variables in mathematical and BASIC notations.

Mathematical Notation	BASIC Notation
x_1	X(1)
a_0	A(0)
$R1_5$	Usually not permitted
z_v	Z(V)
p_{n+1}	P(N+1)
r_{2j-1}	R(2*J−1)

In many versions of BASIC a subscript must be a positive integer. Some compilers, however, allow zero subscripts. The subscript may be a constant, a variable, or a legitimate arithmetic expression. For some BASIC compilers the subscript, if it involves operations, must work out to an integer; otherwise an error message is printed and execution stops. For other versions of BASIC, if the computed subscript is positive but not an integer, the INT function is applied and execution continues. For example, if K = 3 and M = 2, then A(K/M) would become A(1).

For each computer there is a maximal value a subscript may attain. The limit is undoubtedly large enough for the programs you will write but if in doubt, consult the manual for your system.

When we wish to display the elements of an array, we do so between brackets. See the example below.

$$X = [31 \quad -6 \quad 1.5 \quad 83 \quad -17]$$

If the array is called X, then mathematically X_1 refers to an individual element. If indexing begins at one, then the elements of array X are $X_1 = 31$, $X_2 = -6$, $X_3 = 1.5$, $X_4 = 83$, and $X_5 = -17$. If the index is started at 0, then $X_0 = 31$, $X_1 = -6$, $X_2 = 1.5$, $X_3 = 83$, and $X_4 = -17$.

X, I, and X(I) are three different variables whose values are stored in three separate locations in memory. Some compilers may not permit the use of X both subscripted and not subscripted in a program. But if both X and X(I) are permitted, then one memory location is reserved for X and separate locations for X(1), X(2), X(3), . . . , to the last element of the array. If I is used as the index, then I itself requires a storage location.

To input the array X on the previous page, use the loop at the right.

```
10 FØR I = 1 TØ 5
20   READ X(I)
30 NEXT I
40 DATA 31,-6,1.5,83,-17
      :
```

Before execution of this loop, the compiler establishes a memory location for I and for X(1), X(2), X(3), X(4), and X(5).

Subscripted variables may be used in algebraic expressions just like other variables and inserted into READ, LET, PRINT, or IF . . . THEN statements. However, a subscripted variable may not be used as the index for a FØR statement or in NEXT statements.

Mathematical Notation	**BASIC Notation**
$a_1 + a_2 + a_3 + a_4$	A(1) + A(2) + A(3) + A(4)
$x_1^2 + x_2^2$	X(1) ↑ 2 + X(2) ↑ 2
$(a - r_1)(z - r_2)$	(A − R(1))*(Z − R(2))
$1.5(z_{i+1} - z_i)$	1.5 * (Z(I + 1) − Z(I))

Here are sample BASIC statements involving subscripted variables.

```
10 INPUT A(I)
20 READ X(1),X(2),X(3)
20 LET Z = X(I)*2
20 LET F(I+1) = F(I) + F(I-1)
25 LET R = SQR(A(J))
30 PRINT X(I);
40 PRINT Z(D+1)/Z(D)
50 PRINT X(1),X(2),X(3)
50 IF X(I) = Z(J) THEN 100
50 IF A(I+1)/A(I) = SQR(A(I)) THEN 80
50 IF INT(R(D)) = INT(B(J))THEN 100
60 FØR X = 0 TØ M(J)
60 FØR S = Y(1) TØ Y(N) STEP .5
60 FØR T = 1 TØ 10 STEP X(I)
```

Subscripted variables may be used in the flowchart boxes corresponding to these statements.

These may not be allowed on your system. (referring to the three FØR statements)

Let us now return to the problem stated at the beginning of this lesson.

Read a list of numbers; compute the average of the set; then determine how far from the average (above or below) each element in the list lies.

Using a subscript will enable us to save the numbers in the list. The values will be read into an array A. If there are ten numbers to be averaged, they can be stored in ten locations labeled A(1), A(2), A(3), . . . , A(10). The loop to input the list might look like this.

```
10 FØR I = 1 TØ 10
20   READ A(I)
30 NEXT I
```

But, as before, we seek a method to process a list of any size. 9999 can again be used as an end-of-list sentinel. We now have this loop.

```
10 FØR I = 1 TØ 100
20   READ A(I)
30   IF A(I) = 9999 THEN 50
40 NEXT I
50 ...
```

The "100" in line 10 is an intentional overestimate and can be revised if necessary to fit different DATA sets. We must remember that when execution of this loop is complete and control transfers to line 50, 9999 has been entered as the last element of array A. Actually there are only I − 1 numbers in the list to be averaged.

As in Programs 5-1 to 5-3 summation of the list can be embedded in the READ loop. With this idea in mind we complete the program as follows.

Program 5-5

```
10 DIM A(100)
15 FØR I = 1 TØ 100
20   READ A(I)
30   IF A(I) = 9999 THEN 50
35     LET S = S + A(I)
40 NEXT I
50 LET X = S/(I-1)
60 FØR N = 1 TØ I-1
70   PRINT A(N), A(N)-X
80 NEXT N
90 DATA 71,67,73,84,52,58,64,80,68,71,9999
95 END
```

This statement will be explained in the next lesson. (line 10)

This loop uses N *as the counter-index. A new variable is necessary because* I − 1 *must remain fixed as the number of elements in the array.* (lines 60–80)

EXERCISES 5-2

A Write a BASIC subscripted variable for each of the following mathematical variables.

1. x_3 **2.** t_i **3.** z_{j+1}
4. R_0 **5.** q_{2x} **6.** z_{m+n}

Write *Yes* or *No* to show whether each of the following is a legal BASIC subscripted variable.

7. Z(0) **8.** J **9.** X(−3)
10. K*(I) **11.** K(A+B+C) **12.** V(L)
13. X1(17) **14.** M(1E6) **15.** Z(INT(X/Y))

Let the array a be [8 −4 16 −12 2 11] with indexing beginning at one. Give the value of each of the following.

16. a_2 **17.** a_{3-1} **18.** $a_3 - 1$ **19.** $2a_4$
20. a_1^2 **21.** a_{a_5} **22.** $6 + a_6$ **23.** $a_3 - a_4$

24. Write each expression in Exercises 16 through 23 in BASIC, if it is possible to do so.

For the array a given for Exercises 16 through 23, state which member of each pair has the larger value.

25. a_2, a_1 **26.** a_{2+1}, $a_2 + 1$ **27.** a_{1+3}, $a_1 + a_3$

Let $i = 2$ and $j = 3$. Then for the array a given for Exercises 16 through 23, find the value of each of the following.

28. $a_i \cdot a_j$ **29.** $a_{i \cdot j}$ **30.** a_{i+j} **31.** $a_i + a_j$
32. $2a_i$ **33.** a_{2i} **34.** a_{j+1} **35.** a_{i-1}

36. Write the BASIC equivalent of each expression in Exercises 28 through 35.

37. Write a READ loop and DATA statement to input the array a given for Exercises 16 through 23.

For each mathematical expression write a corresponding BASIC expression.

38. $x_1 + x_2$ **39.** $\dfrac{y_2 - y_1}{x_2 - x_1}$
40. $a_1x^n + a_2x^{n-1}$ **41.** $\sqrt{s_1^2 + s_2^2 + s_3^2}$
42. $a_3x^3 + a_2x^2 + a_1x + a_0$ **43.** $c_1d_1 + c_2d_2 - c_3d_3 - c_4d_4$
44. $|2t_1 - t_2|$ **45.** $\cos(y_1 + y_2)/\sin(y_1 - y_2)$
46. $b_1^2 + c_1^2$ **47.** $(x_1 - x_2)^2 + (y_1 - y_2)^2$

48. A travelling salesman deals in five items having fixed prices. (In practice the number of items would be much larger.) Suppose the five items are priced respectively at \$1.10, \$2.20, \$.80, \$3.40, and \$1.90. The salesman would like a program written so that when he receives an order, he can enter as DATA the number ordered of each item and the computer will print the total price of the order. Use two lists (and therefore two subscripted variables): a P-list containing the prices of the items and an N-list consisting of the number ordered of each item.

49. Exercise 2 on page 186 stated: "Input a number X and then a list of twenty numbers. Determine the number of times X occurs in the list." Switch the input so that the list of twenty numbers comes first, followed by X. Now write a program to determine the number of times X occurs in the list.

B Suppose that you are given ten numbers; now "push down" the list, that is, replace each element of the set by the element that follows it (move element one to position ten).

50. Write a program that uses a subscripted variable to input the list into an array A and merely prints the list in pushdown order without actually manipulating array A in memory.

51. Write a program that inputs the array A and actually repositions the elements in memory before printing the pushdown list. (Do not use a second subscripted variable.)

5-3 DIM STATEMENTS

"10 DIM A(100)" was the first line of Program 5-5 on page 191. DIM is short for "DIMENSION." BASIC automatically assigns storage space for any list in the program, with subscripts 0 through 10 or 1 through 10, depending on the system. But if longer lists are desired, a DIM statement is needed. The instruction DIM A(100) saves 101 memory locations for the values of an array named A: A(0), A(1), A(2), . . . , A(100). (If the system does not use zero subscripts, then 100 locations are reserved: A(1) through A(100).) Any computer possesses only a finite storage capacity and there is a limit to the number and length of the lists a program might require. However, the programs considered in this text should not exceed this limit.

The DIM statement notifies the compiler how many locations to reserve for a subscripted list. No harm results if more locations are reserved than are actually needed (provided the total capacity of the machine is not exceeded). Therefore when the programmer is uncertain of the length of an array, he should set his dimension at a value that is larger than the number of entries expected in the array.

One DIM statement may include more than one array.

Example:

```
10 DIM A(50), X(100), K(15)
```

SUMMARY OF RULES GOVERNING DIM STATEMENTS

1. If a subscripted variable is used in a program but the subscript will not take on a value greater than ten, no DIM statement is needed for that array. (Note: This rule may not hold on some systems.)

2. Whenever a program contains a subscripted variable whose subscript will take on a value greater than ten, that variable must be listed in a DIM statement with a number in parentheses behind it to indicate the maximum size of the index. When in doubt indicate a larger dimension than you expect to use.

3. Since a DIM statement is not executed, it may be entered into the program on any line before END; it is convenient and customary, however, to place DIM statements at the beginning of the program.

A common error involving DIM statements is illustrated by this program.

```
10 DIM I(50)
20 FØR I = 1 TØ 50
30   READ X(I)
40   IF X(I) = 9999 THEN 70
50     LET S = S + X(I)
60 NEXT I
70 PRINT "SUM ØF THE ARRAY IS " S
80 DATA 67,-14,81,40,75,86,104.9,9999
90 END
```

The error lies in line 10. The programmer has confused the variable naming the array (X), with the index for the array (I). Line 10 should read as follows.

```
10 DIM X(50)
```

Some systems allow variables as subscripts in DIM statements.

```
10 READ N
20 DIM A(N)
30 FØR I = 1 TØ N
40   READ A(I)
50   LET S = S + A(I)
60 NEXT I
70 PRINT "THE SUM ØF THE ARRAY IS" S
80 DATA 6,841,732,904,897,684,831
90 END
```

EXERCISES 5-3

A Write the DIM statement that is needed before each of these arrays can be read into the computer.

1. $[x_1 \quad x_2 \quad x_3 \quad \ldots \quad x_{50}]$ **2.** $[t_j]$ where $j = 1, 2, 3, \ldots, 37$

3. $[r_{10} \quad r_{20} \quad r_{30} \quad r_{40}]$ **4.** $[z_{51} \quad z_{52} \quad z_{53} \quad \ldots \quad z_{79}]$

5. B = [87 92 61 78 94 87 91 83 75 62 99]

Correct any errors in the following programs.

6.
```
10DIM X(20)
20 LET X + 1 = X
30 READ B(X)
40 LET S = S + B(X)
50 IF B(X) = 9999 THEN 70
60 GØ TØ 10
70 LET A = S/X
80 PRINT "AVERAGE ØF THE SET IS " A
90 DATA 20,5,2,7,3,8,1,9,11,3,15,20,4,0,10,2,16,9999
100 END
```

7.
```
5 DIM I = 1 TØ 40
10 LET I = 0
20 READ K(I+1)
30 IF K(I+1) > 0 THEN 70
40 LET N = N + K(I+1)
50 GØ TØ 30
70 LET P = P + K(I+1)
80 GØ TØ 30
90 PRINT "SUM ØF THE PØSITIVES IS " P
100 PRINT "SUM ØF THE NEGATIVES IS " N
110 DATA 10,-60,20,17,-3,90,4,-5,-120,-17.8
120 END
```

B In Exercises 8 and 9 consider an array A.

8. Without actually manipulating the array in memory, print A in reverse order. For example, if A = [8 10 3 5] print 5,3,10,8.
9. Create an array B such that the elements of B are the elements of A in reverse order. Print A and B.

5-4 POLYNOMIALS

In programming, polynomials are handled by means of subscripted variables. The general form of a polynomial (in ascending order of powers of the variable x) is

$$a_0 + a_1x + a_2x^2 + a_3x^3 + \cdots + a_{n-1}x^{n-1} + a_nx^n$$

where n is a nonnegative integer called the *degree* of the polynomial and each a_i $(0 \leq i \leq n)$ is a real number constant called the *coefficient* of its term. a_0 is called the *constant term.* We can think of the polynomial as an array

$$[a_0 \quad a_1 \quad a_2 \quad \ldots \quad a_{n-1} \quad a_n]$$

containing the coefficients in ascending powers of x. Note that the x^i's need not be stored because the subscript of each coefficient is the power of x for that term. Of course the variable in the polynomial may be any nonsubscripted variable. Here are examples.

Polynomial	**Corresponding Array**
$5 + 7x - 6x^2 + x^3$	[5 7 −6 1]
$-7 + .5y^3 + y^5$	[−7 0 0 .5 0 1]
$11c - 7.3c^2 + 3c^4$	[0 11 −7.3 0 3]
$r^2 - 8r^4 + 6r - 3r^3 - 4$	[−4 6 1 −3 −8]
82	[82]

Notice in the second and third examples that 0's are used in the array for missing powers of the variable.

To input the arrays on page 195, the DATA statements at the right can be used. The first numeral in the DATA list of each line is the degree of the corresponding polynomial.

```
740 DATA 3,5,7,-6,1
750 DATA 5,-7,0,0,.5,0,1
760 DATA 4,0,11,-7.3,0,3
770 DATA 4,-4,6,1,-3,-8
780 DATA 0,82
```

If the system allows zero subscripts, the READ loop to input the polynomials will appear as shown at the right. N is the degree.

```
130 READ N
170 FØR I = 0 TØ N
180   READ A(I)
190 NEXT I
```

If zero subscripts are not available, line 170 would be written as follows.

```
170 FØR I = 1 TØ N + 1
```

Unfortunately, this approach makes operations with polynomials awkward since the programmer must remember that for a polynomial of degree N, N + 1 is the index of the last coefficient and the subscript of a coefficient is one more than the power of the variable in that term.

$$a_1 + a_2x + a_3x^2 + \cdots + a_nx^{n-1} + a_{n+1}x^n$$

Printing a polynomial is a tricky procedure. One approach to the problem is to print the terms with the loop shown below. (Assume that zero subscripts may be used.)

```
560 FØR I = 0 TØ N
570   PRINT A(I)"X↑"I;
580 NEXT I
590 PRINT
```

This loop would produce isolated terms such as the following (using the first two polynomials from the DATA steps listed earlier).

```
 5X↑0   7X↑1  -6X↑2   1X↑3
-7X↑0   0X↑1   0X↑2  .5X↑3   0X↑4   1X↑5
```

There are several objections to the form of the above polynomials.

1. There are no addition or subtraction signs between terms.
2. The terms 0x ↑ 1, 0x ↑ 2, and 0x ↑ 4 should not appear.
3. The terms 5x ↑ 0 and −7x ↑ 0 should be 5 and −7, respectively.
4. The term 7x ↑ 1 should be 7x.
5. The terms 1x ↑ 3 and 1x ↑ 5 should be x ↑ 3 and x ↑ 5, respectively.

The correct form of the polynomials is as follows.

```
 5 + 7X - 6X↑2 + X↑3
-7 + .5X↑3 + X↑5
```

The following program prints the polynomial as "neatly" as possible.

Program 5-6

```
100  REM READ AND PRINT A PØLYNØMIAL.
110  REM THE PRØGRAM ASSUMES ZERØ SUBSCRIPTS ARE LEGAL.
120
130  READ N
140
150  REM    N IS THE DEGREE ØF THE PØLYNØMIAL TØ BE READ.
160
170   FØR I = 0 TØ N
180    READ A(I)
190   NEXT I
200   IF N = 0 THEN 710
210
220  REM    LINES 240-250 HANDLE THE CØNSTANT TERM.
230
240   IF A(0) = 0 THEN 290
250    PRINT A(0);
260
270  REM    LINES 290-490 PRINT THE X TERM.
280
290   IF A(1) = 0 THEN 560
300    IF A(1) < 0 THEN 410
310     IF A(1) = 1 THEN 440
320
330  REM    IF A CØEFFICIENT IS PØSITIVE, PRINT A + SIGN
340  REM    IN FRØNT ØF IT. (SEE LINES 370, 450, AND 600.)
350
360   IF A(0) = 0 THEN 390
370    PRINT "+"  A(1)"X  ";
380    GØ TØ 560
390   PRINT A(1)"X  ";
400   GØ TØ 560
410   IF A(1) = -1 THEN 490
420    PRINT "-"ABS(A(1))"X";
430    GØ TØ 560
440   IF A(0) = 0 THEN 470
450    PRINT "+ X  ";
460    GØ TØ 560
470   PRINT "X  ";
480   GØ TØ 560
490   PRINT "-  X  ";
500
510  REM    LINES 560-680 ØF
520  REM    THE PRØGRAM WILL
530  REM    PRINT THE REMAIN-
540  REM    ING TERMS.
550
560   FØR I = 2 TØ N
570    IF A(I) = 0 THEN 680
580     IF A(I) < 0 THEN 620
590      IF A(I) = 1 THEN 650
600       PRINT "+"A(I)"X↑"I;
610       GØ TØ 680
620    IF A(I) = -1 THEN 670
630     PRINT"-"ABS(A(I))"X↑"I;
640     GØ TØ 680
650    PRINT "+ X↑"I;
660    GØ TØ 680
670    PRINT "- X↑"I;
680  NEXT I
690  PRINT
700  GØ TØ 130
710  PRINT A(0)
720  GØ TØ 130
730
740  DATA 3,5,7,-6,1
750  DATA 5,-7,0,0,.5,0,1
760  DATA 4,0,11,-7.3,0,3
770  DATA 4,-4,6,1,-3,-8
780  DATA 0,82
790
800  END
```

EXERCISES 5-4

A Show the array of coefficients (ascending order of powers) for these polynomials.

1. $7 + 3x + 4x^2$
2. $11x - x^2 + 5x^4$
3. $.5z^3 - \frac{1}{4}z^2 + 113z - 61.23$
4. $6x - 5$
5. 13
6. $t + 3t^3 - 2t^2 - 16 + 5t^4$

7. Write the DATA statements for Program 5-6 on page 197 to input the polynomials in Exercises 1 through 6. Number the lines 740 to 790.

Write *Yes* or *No* to show whether each of the following expressions is a polynomial.

8. $\frac{1}{2}$ **9.** $-8y^{100}$ **10.** $\dfrac{1}{q}$ **11.** $\sqrt{t+1}$

12. $4m^{-2} - 3m^{-1}$ **13.** $|b^3 - 5b + 6|$ **14.** $\dfrac{c^2 - 1}{c + 1}$ **15.** a^n

B List the line numbers of the print section of Program 5-6 in the order in which the statements would be executed after each of these polynomials is entered as input.

Example: $7 - x + 3x^2$
Answer: 200,240,250,290,300,410,490,560,
570,580,590,600,610,680,690,700

16. $2x$ **17.** -6.75 **18.** $8 + x$ **19.** $-17 + 8x^2$ **20.** $-x - 5x^2 - x^3$

5-5 CREATING A SORT ALGORITHM

Frequently, in programming, you will need to sort a set of numbers into either ascending or descending order. Usually the sort algorithm is part of a larger program. For example, the monthly sales are computed for each salesman of an organization and then printed in ranked order.

Diagrams will help you understand the sort algorithm. Imagine that we have seven numbers in an array x.

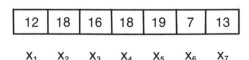

12	18	16	18	19	7	13
x_1	x_2	x_3	x_4	x_5	x_6	x_7

Suppose we must sort this array into descending order. In sorting, you would probably scan the array from left-to-right to determine the largest value, 19. Then you would scan again to decide the second largest, 18. (18 is also the third highest.) You would continue this process until you had completely ordered the array.

The computer, however, cannot "see" the values. It must instead follow a more detailed algorithm. It begins like this: compare the first number to the second; if the first is larger, leave the numbers as they are; if the second element is greater, swap the positions of the two numbers. (If they are equal, leave them as they are.)

Now compare the current first element to element three. If one is greater than or equal to three, retain their present positions; if three is larger, reverse them. Now compare element one to element four in a similar fashion, either leaving them alone or swapping, depending on which is the larger. This compare-swap routine is called one *pass* through the array. After it has been executed one complete time (1-2, 1-3, 1-4, 1-5, 1-6, and 1-7), the element that has finished in the first position is definitely the largest in the array. (There may be another element equal to it but certainly none greater.)

Return to element two and compare it to three, either leaving it in position two (if it is greater or equal) or swapping it with three (if it is smaller). Then make a similar decision for two and four, two and five, two and six, and two and seven. When this second pass is complete, the number in position two is definitely the second largest in the array. Continue the algorithm for positions three through six, at which time the array will be in descending order.

Let us apply the algorithm to the array introduced on page 198.

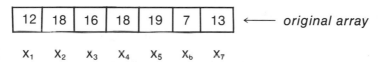

12	18	16	18	19	7	13
X_1	X_2	X_3	X_4	X_5	X_6	X_7

← *original array*

The execution of the algorithm would involve these steps (the steps are numbered in a way that emphasizes the cyclic nature of the algorithm).

1-1 Compare x_1 to x_2. Since $12 < 18$, reverse their positions. The array stands as shown at the right.

18	12	16	18	19	7	13
X_1	X_2	X_3	X_4	X_5	X_6	X_7

1-2 Compare x_1 (which is now 18) to x_3. Since $18 > 16$, leave these two elements as they are.

1-3 Compare x_1 to x_4. Both presently equal 18; it makes no difference whether we swap or not. To save work, leave them as they are.

1-4 Compare x_1 to x_5. Since $18 < 19$, reverse positions. The array stands as shown at the right.

19	12	16	18	18	7	13
X_1	X_2	X_3	X_4	X_5	X_6	X_7

(We can see that the largest element is now first and that further comparisons will cause no change. But the machine cannot make a judgment like this and must continue the algorithm.)

1-5 Compare x_1 to x_6. Since x_1 is greater, make no change.

1-6 Compare x_1 to x_7. Since x_1 is greater, make no change.

We can now guarantee that element x_1 is the largest in the array. Consequently we can forget about element one and begin cycle two of the algorithm.

2-1 Compare x_2 to x_3. Since $12 < 16$, reverse their positions. The array thus takes this form.

19	16	12	18	18	7	13
x_1	x_2	x_3	x_4	x_5	x_6	x_7

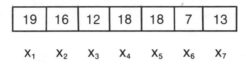

2-2 Compare x_2 (16) to x_4 (18). Since x_4 is greater, swap again, producing this array.

19	18	12	16	18	7	13
x_1	x_2	x_3	x_4	x_5	x_6	x_7

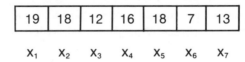

2-3 Compare x_2 to x_5. Since $18 = 18$, leave them as they are.

2-4 Compare x_2 to x_6. Since $18 > 7$, make no change.

2-5 Compare x_2 to x_7. $18 > 13$, again no change.

Location x_2 now contains the second largest element of the array. The algorithm is working and, if followed to completion, will put all elements in their correct order as shown below.

final array →

19	18	18	16	13	12	7
x_1	x_2	x_3	x_4	x_5	x_6	x_7

EXERCISES 5-5

A

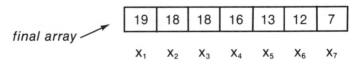

1. As in the lesson, list the steps of the algorithm for putting the following array into descending order: 71, 89, 84, 103, 97. Each time a change is made, show the new version of the array.
2. What change(s) must be made in the algorithm if the array is to be put into ascending order?
3. As in the lesson, list the steps for putting this array into *ascending* order: 70, 6, 121, −8, 10, −14.

B

4. Write a program for the flowchart in Exercise 23 on page 18.

5. Here is an explanation of a sorting method different from the one in the lesson. The method is shown through an example.

Example: Sort A = [6 5 9 2 8] into descending order.
Solution:

(i) Make pairwise comparisons of consecutive elements (1-2, 2-3, 3-4, 4-5). Switch their positions when a smaller precedes a larger. Thus A undergoes these changes on the first pass.

```
original list ──→ 6 5 9 2 8 ┐
                  6 9 5 2 8 ├ 1st pass
                  6 9 5 8 2 ┘
```

(ii) Repeat (i) until a pass finds no switches necessary.

```
list after 1st pass ──→ 6 9 5 8 2 ┐
                        9 6 5 8 2 ├ 2nd pass
                        9 6 8 5 2 ┘
list after 2nd pass ──→ 9 6 8 5 2 ┐
                        9 8 6 5 2 ┘ 3rd pass
```

A fourth pass makes no switches and the process ends. Apply this technique to the following list, showing all switches on each pass as above. B = [4 1 7 2 3 5]

6. Here is a revision of the sorting technique explained in Exercise 5. Again use the array A = [6 5 9 2 8].

(i) 6 > 5? Yes, so continue comparing consecutive elements until a smaller precedes a larger.
(ii) 5 > 9? No, so swap their positions. The array now looks like this. A = [6 9 5 2 8].
(iii) Start over (here is where the change occurs in the previous algorithm). 6 > 9? No, so swap and start over.

As the process continues, the array changes like this.

```
list after step iii ──→ 9 6 5 2 8
                        9 6 5 8 2
                        9 6 8 5 2
                        9 8 6 5 2
```

On the next pass, since no swaps are made, the algorithm stops. Apply this technique to the array B given in Exercise 5, showing the array after each swap.
NOTE: This technique is called "bubble" sorting, probably because the larger numbers "bubble" to the front of the array as the process is repeated.

Computers in Banking

Banks were among the earliest users of computers. In a typical bank today, when a customer wants to cash a check from his or her account, the teller turns to a terminal in the booth.

The dialogue between the teller and the computer might be as follows.

```
ACCØUNT NUMBER?  ←——— The computer types these two lines.
438920080  ← The teller types this number.
AMØUNT IN ACCØUNT IS $ 182.43.  ←┘
```

The computer types these two lines.

The teller types this number. → 438920080

If the amount in the account is more than the amount of the check, the teller cashes the check.

PROBLEM: Plan a program that will imitate, on a small scale, the teller-computer dialogue above.

Program Outline

1. Use subscripted variables to store the account numbers and amounts of the customers. The key line would be

```
130 READ N(I), A(I)
```

where N is the array of account numbers and A is the list of the corresponding amounts.

2. Use an INPUT statement to allow the teller to enter an account number.

```
180 INPUT "ACCØUNT NUMBER"; X
```

3. Search the N array for account number X. If X is found, print the appropriate element of the A array. If X is not found among the account numbers on file, print an appropriate error message. (Perhaps the teller typed the number wrong.) All this can be done by the following statements, where P is the number of account numbers on file.

```
200 FØR I = 1 TØ P
210   IF X = N(I) THEN 250
220 NEXT I
230 PRINT X " NØT FØUND AMØNG ACCØUNT NUMBERS ØN FILE."
240 GØ TØ 180
250 PRINT "AMØUNT IN ACCØUNT IS" A(I)
260 GØ TØ 180
```

Notice especially lines 210 and 250. When X is found at location N(I), then A(I) (same subscript) is the current amount for that customer.

Projects

1. Write the complete program for the example given in the lesson. Enter about 20 "customers."

2. Modify the program in Project 1. Because of privacy considerations, a bank does not want the teller to know the amount in the customer's account. So now, after the account numbers and amounts have been stored, the teller enters an account number and the amount of the check. The computer simply prints whether the amount on hand will cover the check.

3. Add the following feature to the program in Project 2. To prevent unauthorized access to the computer system, the bank assigns each of the six tellers a code number. To use the computer the teller first enters his or her code number. If the number matches one of the numbers in the stored list of authorized users, the computer allows the teller to proceed with entering the account number and the amount of the check.

4. Add to the program in Project 1 as follows. After the teller obtains the current amount in the account and cashes the check, he or she then enters the amount of the check. The computer then subtracts that amount from the customer's total in the A file.

5-6 THE SORT ALGORITHM IN BASIC

We are now ready to program the Sort Algorithm in BASIC. The READ portion of the program can be quickly written as shown below.

```
130  DIM X(100)
140  READ N
180  FØR I = 1 TØ N
190    READ X(I)
200  NEXT I
     ...
320  DATA ...
```

We can now concentrate on the sort portion of the program.

Recall the pattern of comparisons.

↓ X_1 to X_2	↓ X_2 to X_3	↓ X_3 to X_4	. . .	X_{n-1} to X_n
X_1 to X_3	X_2 to X_4	. . .		
X_1 to X_4	. . .	X_3 to X_n		
. . .	X_2 to X_n			
X_1 to X_n				

We need two indices: one (I) to mark the position of the first number being compared and the second (J) to indicate the position of the second. I will run from 1 to $N - 1$; J runs from $I + 1$ to N. Thus the sort requires a nested loop.

```
220  FØR I = 1 TØ N-1
230    FØR J = I+1 TØ N
         . . .
280    NEXT J
300  NEXT I
```

Once we set the indices, we write the statement for comparison.

```
240  IF X(I) >= X(J) THEN 280
```

If the answer is "no" to the question of the IF clause, we must swap X(I) and X(J). It would seem that this operation would require only these two statements.

```
260  LET X(J) = X(I)
270  LET X(I) = X(J)
```

But careful analysis proves otherwise. Suppose X(I) is 10 and X(J) is 14. Then, since X(I) < X(J), the two elements must be reversed. After the machine executes 260 LET X(J) = X(I), X(J) equals 10.

10	14	⟶	10	10
X(I)	X(J)		X(I)	X(J)

The '14' has been lost. Consequently when 270 LET X(I) = X(J) is executed, the swap is not effected and instead both X(I) and X(J) end up equal to 10.

To avoid this difficulty, a "dummy" third location is needed. Call it Z. Both diagrams below will illustrate what must be done.

Version 1

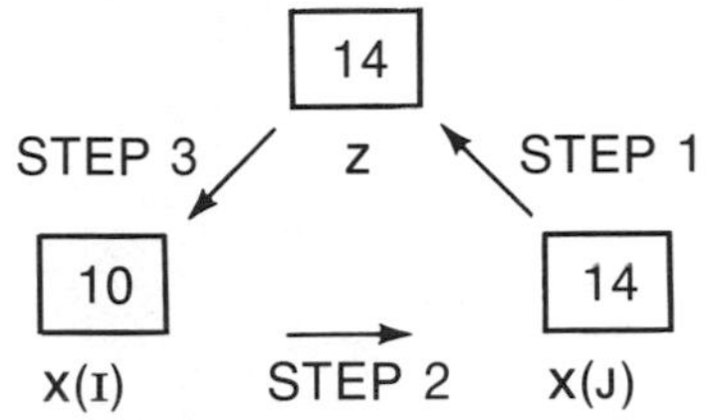

Version 2

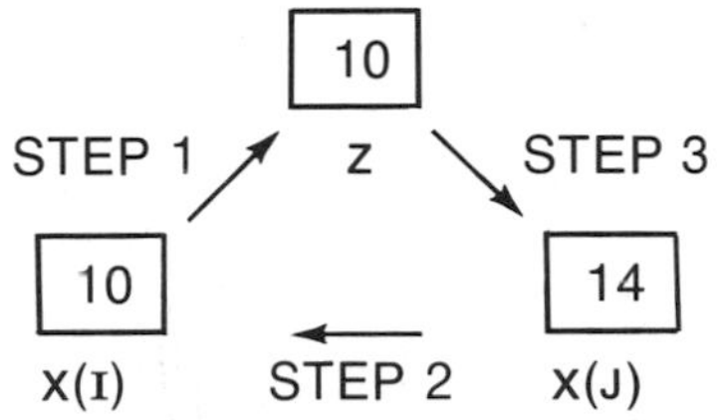

The corresponding BASIC steps for each method are shown below.

```
250 LET Z = X(J)              250 LET Z = X(I)
260 LET X(J) = X(I)           260 LET X(I) = X(J)
270 LET X(I) = Z              270 LET X(J) = Z
```

Choose either version. Then a sort sequence can be written.

```
220 FØR I = 1 TØ N-1
230   FØR J = I+1 TØ N
240     IF X(I) >= X(J) THEN 280
250       LET Z = X(J)
260       LET X(J) = X(I)
270       LET X(I) = Z
280   NEXT J
300 NEXT 1
```

NOTE: The completed sort sequence uses Version 1. Version 2 would also work.

The PRINT segment of the program can be accomplished in either of two ways. The most obvious is with a separate loop.

```
310 FØR I = 1 TØ N
320   PRINT X(I);
330 NEXT I
340 PRINT
```

The second method capitalizes on the fact that each time the J-loop is completed, one more element of the array has fallen into its proper position and consequently can be printed immediately before NEXT I is executed.

```
280 NEXT J
290 PRINT X(I);
300 NEXT I
```

So that the last element will be printed, line 220 must be changed to

```
220 FØR I = 1 TØ N
```

This shorter method is used in the complete program (next page).

Program 5-7

```
110   REM      SØRT AN ARRAY INTØ DESCENDING ØRDER.
120
130            DIM X(100)
140            READ N
150
160   REM      N IS THE NØ. ØF ELEMENTS IN THE ARRAY.
170
180            FØR I = 1 TØ N
190              READ X(I)
200            NEXT I
210
220            FØR I = 1 TØ N
230              FØR J = I+1 TØ N
240                IF X(I) >= X(J) THEN 280
250                  LET Z = X(J)
260                  LET X(J) = X(I)
270                  LET X(I) = Z
280              NEXT J
290              PRINT X(I);
300            NEXT I
310
320            DATA 7,12,18,16,18,19,7,13
330
340            END
```

EXERCISES 5-6

A

1. What changes must be made in Program 5-7 if the array must be sorted into ascending order?
2. Modify Program 5-7 so that it prints the original array, skips a line, and then prints the array in descending order.
3. What would be the output of Program 5-7 if line 220 were left as it was originally written using N − 1 rather than N?

For the DATA in line 320 of Program 5-7, how many times will each of the following statements be executed?

4. 140 5. 190 6. 280 7. 290 8. 300

B

9. Write a program to find the largest element in an array A. Use the following algorithm. First, set up a "dummy" location X. Then let X = A(1). Next compare X to A(2). If X < A(2), put A(2) in X. If X ≥ A(2), compare X to A(3), and so on. After one pass through A, X will contain the largest element.
10. Program the sort algorithm in Exercise 5 on page 201.
11. Program the sort algorithm in Exercise 6 on page 201.

5-7 "GØSUB," "RETURN," and "STØP" STATEMENTS

It is often possible to save programming time by using one or more subroutines.

Example:

Big Brain Computer Corporation has ten salespersons, each of whom has an employee number. Knowing the latest month's sales for each salesperson, the sales manager wants a listing of the ten sales totals in order of the employee numbers (which is the way the DATA will be entered) and also a listing of the sales totals in descending order.

In writing the program for the sales manager, a programmer will use two arrays. The employee numbers will be stored in array N and the corresponding sales totals will go into array S, as shown below.

Employee Number	5	12	13	. . .	43
Monthly Sales	$8367.21	$7102.63	$9186.14	. . .	$6825.25

Then the arrays N and S will look like the following.

N	5	12	13	. . .	43
	N(1)	N(2)	N(3)		N(10)
S	8367.21	7102.63	9186.14	. . .	6825.25
	S(1)	S(2)	S(3)		S(10)

In the DATA lines of the program, the employee numbers and sales totals will alternate as shown below.

```
580    DATA 5, 8367.21, 12, 7102.63, . . .
```

With this setup the algorithm for the program can be summarized in the following manner.

1. In a loop, read the N(I), S(I) pairs.
2. Print the N and S arrays in two columns.
3. Sort the S array into descending order. While doing so, whenever elements of S are swapped, also swap the corresponding elements of N.
4. Print the (sorted) N and S arrays in two columns.
5. Stop.

Notice the repetition in steps 2 and 4. The fact that the same task (printing the N and S arrays) must be done at two different times makes this program a good example of the use of a subroutine. The advantages of subroutines are explained on the following pages.

In BASIC, a **subroutine** (also called a "subprogram" or "procedure" in other computer languages) is a self-contained algorithm that is inserted in a main program, preferably at the end. In the case of the program for Big Brain Corporation, the subroutine will contain the statements for printing arrays N and S. A GØSUB statement in the main program will tell the computer when to jump to the subroutine. After the subroutine has been finished, a RETURN statement will send the computer back to the main program to continue from where it left off. The advantage of a subroutine is that it allows a programmer to write *just once* an algorithm that is to be used two or more times in the complete program. The following diagram will show the overall setup for the program being planned for Big Brain.

```
100          . . . . . . . . . .
             . . . . . . . . . .
300          GØSUB 700
             . . . . . . . . . .    main program
550          GØSUB 700
560          STØP
700          . . . . . . . . . .
             . . . . . . . . . .    subroutine to print
780          RETURN                 arrays N and S
990          END
```

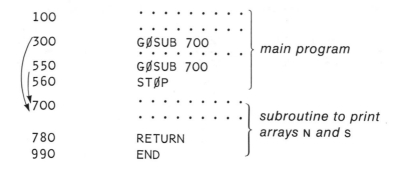

Here is the complete program, with explanatory REMarks.

Program 5-8

```
110
120   REM     PRINT MØNTHLY SALES IN ØRDER ØF EMPLØYEE
130   REM     NUMBER AND THEN IN DESCENDING ØRDER.
140
150   REM     VARIABLES:    N = ARRAY ØF EMPLØYEE NUMBERS
160   REM                   S = ARRAY ØF SALES TØTALS
170   REM                I, J = INDICES
180   REM                   Z = DUMMY VARIABLE USED IN
190   REM                       SØRT ALGØRITHM
200
210       DIM N(10), S(10)
220
230       FØR I = 1 TØ 10
240         READ N(I), S(I)
250       NEXT I
260
270       PRINT
```

```
280       PRINT "MØNTHLY SALES IN ØRDER ØF EMPLØYEE NØ."
290       PRINT
300       GØSUB 700
310
320   REM    LINES 400-500 SØRT S INTØ DESCENDING ØRDER.
330   REM    NØTE THAT WHEN ELEMENTS ØF S ARE SWAPPED
340   REM    (LINES 430-450), THE CØRRESPØNDING ELEMENTS
350   REM    ØF N ARE ALSØ SWAPPED (460-480).
360
400       FØR I = 1 TØ 9
410         FØR J = I + 1 TØ 10
420           IF S(I) >= S(J) THEN 490
430             LET Z = S(J)
440             LET S(J) = S(I)
450             LET S(I) = Z
460             LET Z = N(J)
470             LET N(J) = N(I)
480             LET N(I) = Z
490         NEXT J
500       NEXT I
510
520       PRINT
530       PRINT "MØNTHLY SALES IN DESCENDING ØRDER"
540       PRINT
550       GØSUB 700
560       STØP
570
580       DATA 5, 8367.21, 12, 7102.63, 13, 9186.14,
590       DATA 19, 8741.60, 21, 7861.92, 23, 4932.67,
600       DATA 27, 8005.04, 32, 9980.23, 35, 7813.00,
610       DATA 43, 6825.25
620
680   REM    THE SUBRØUTINE BELØW PRINTS N AND S.
690
700       PRINT "EMPLØYEE NUMBER", "SALES TØTAL"
710       PRINT
720
730       FØR I = 1 TØ 10
740         PRINT N(I), S(I)
750       NEXT I
760
770       PRINT
780       RETURN
790
990       END
```

Tracing Program 5-8 shows that the sections of the program would be executed in the following order.

1. Main program: 230-300
2. Subroutine: 700-780
3. Main program: 400-550
4. Subroutine: 700-780
5. Main program: 560

The purpose of `560 STØP` is to halt execution. Otherwise the computer would continue in sequence past the DATA and REM statements (570-690) and begin executing the subroutine at 700 as if it were part of the main program. `560 GØ TØ 990` would accomplish the same result as `560 STØP`. The END statement is used after the subroutine to tell the compiler that there are no more lines in the total program.

A subroutine always ends with the RETURN statement. This rule must be remembered when a subroutine involves a decision. For example, consider the following lines from a program.

```
. . . . . . . . . . . . . . . . . . . . .
130         GØSUB 710
. . . . . . . . . . . . . . . . . . . . .
710         IF A = B THEN 750
720           IF A > B THEN 770
730             PRINT A " < " B
740             GØ TØ 780
750         PRINT A " = " B
760         GØ TØ 780
770           PRINT A " > " B
780         RETURN
. . . . . . . . . . . . . . . . . . . . .
```

Notice lines 740 and 760. As with the end of a loop, all branches of a subroutine must jump to the RETURN statement in order to exit correctly to the main program. For many systems, it would be *wrong* in the above subroutine to have `740 RETURN` and `760 RETURN`
For such systems a subroutine may have only one RETURN statement and it must be the last statement of the subroutine.

A subroutine does not have to be at the end of a main program. It could occur in the middle of the main program accompanied by appropriate statements that will jump the computer over the subroutine when it is executing the main program. This situation is illustrated in the following program fragment.

```
100   (Start main program.)          }
. . . . . . . . . . . . . .          }  first part of the
19Ø   GØSUB 300                      }  main program
. . . . . . . . . . . . . .          }
260   GØ TØ 460
300   (Begin subroutine.)            }
. . . . . . . . . . . . . .          }  subroutine
410   RETURN                         }
460   (Continue main program.)       }  second part of the
. . . . . . . . . . . . . .          }  main program
990   END                            }
```

However, this is not a recommended programming technique. In fact, in languages such as FØRTRAN or Pascal it would not be allowed.

A program may have two or more subroutines. On most systems one subroutine may even jump the computer to another subroutine. This is called "nesting" the subroutines. In such cases the rule to remember is that a RETURN statement always sends the computer back to the next executable statement after the *latest* GØSUB that it has executed (this might be in another subroutine).

EXERCISES 5-7

A **1.** Show the output of the following program.

```
100   READ A, B, C
110   GØSUB 500
120   IF L = 1 THEN 160
130     LET R = A*B/2
140     PRINT "AREA = " R; " PERIMETER = " A+B+C
150     GØ TØ 100
160   PRINT "NØT A RIGHT TRIANGLE"
170   GØ TØ 100
180   DATA 3, 4, 5, 0, 1, 1, 2, 2, 2, 12, 5, 13
190
500   LET L = 0
510   IF A + B <= C THEN 550
520     IF A + C <= B THEN 550
530       IF B + C <= A THEN 550
540         IF A↑2 + B↑2 = C↑2 THEN 560
550   LET L = 1
560   RETURN
570
990   END
```

2. Explain the function of the variable L in the program of Exercise 1. Such a variable is often called a "flag."

3. Revise Program 5-8 so that it handles X salespersons and not just 10. Write only the lines that must be added or changed.

4. Expand Program 5-8 as follows. No longer assume that the DATA are entered in order of the employee numbers. Thus, even before the first required listing can be printed, array N (and S with it) must be sorted into *descending* order. Now, since sorting must be done twice in the program, you will need to write a general subroutine to sort an array X while also swapping the corresponding elements of an array Y. Before going to this subroutine the first time, copy array N into X and array S into Y. Then later, before going to the subroutine the second time, copy S into X and N into Y. Revise the printing subroutine of Program 5-8 to print X and Y rather than N and S.

5. Write a program that will print a sorted list of the January-February sales for the Big Brain sales manager. First, read into array S the ten January sales totals (without employee numbers). In a subroutine, copy S into array A. In another subroutine, sort A into descending order. In a third subroutine, print A preceded by an appropriate heading printed by the main program. Finally, read the February sales for each person (adding them to array S) and repeat the three subroutines.

B 6. The number of permutations of n things taken r at a time ($n \geq r$) is denoted by ${}_nP_r$. The formula is ${}_nP_r = \dfrac{n!}{(n-r)!}$ where $n!$ ("n factorial") means $n \cdot (n-1) \cdot (n-2) \cdot \cdots \cdot 2 \cdot 1$. Write a program that, given n and r, computes ${}_nP_r$. Since two factorials are needed, use a subroutine that computes $x!$ for any whole number value of x that has been set in the main program.

7. Calculate ${}_nC_r\left(=\dfrac{n!}{r!\,(n-r)!}\right)$, the number of *combinations* of n things taken r at a time. (See Exercise 6.)

C 8. Use the factorial subroutine of Exercise 6 in a program to compute the number of permutations of n things taken n at a time, where s_1 of the objects are the same type, s_2 are the same, s_3 are the same, and so on.

9. Assume that in n experiments, the probability of success for any one experiment is p. Compute the probability p' of i successes using the formula $p' = \dfrac{n!}{i!(n-i)!}(1-p)^{n-i}p^i$. Include in the program the factorial subroutine of Exercise 6.

CHAPTER SUMMARY

There are two common methods for detecting the end of a data list in a program. In the first method, a preliminary number is entered in the DATA, giving the number of remaining items in the DATA list. In the second method, a *sentinel* such as 9999 is inserted at the end of the list.

When a list of numbers must be stored simultaneously, a *subscripted variable* is used. Thus, if the variable is A(2), then A names the *array* (or *vector*) and 2 is the *index*. The *dimension* of an array is its length (number of items) and if the length exceeds ten values, a DIM statement is needed at the beginning of the program. Subscripted variables may be used in READ, INPUT, LET, PRINT, and IF . . . THEN statements.

Polynomials are handled by storing the coefficients in an array, preferably in order of ascending powers of the variable.

There are several algorithms for sorting arrays into ascending or descending order. A key section of most sort algorithms is a set of three LET statements that swap two numbers in memory, using a dummy third location.

One or more *subroutines* can be inserted into a *main program.* A GØSUB statement is used in order to jump the computer from the main program to the subroutine. The subroutine ends with a RETURN statement, which sends the computer back to the point in the main program where it left off execution.

Often a STØP statement is placed at the end of the main program to halt execution.

CHAPTER OBJECTIVES AND REVIEW

Objective: To write a program using either of the two methods for detecting the end of a data list (preliminary count or sentinel). *(Section 5-1)*

1. Write a program to read a list of real numbers and print the sum of the positive numbers and the sum of the negative numbers.

Objective: To decide whether a given expression is a valid subscripted variable in your system. *(Section 5-2)*

Write *Yes* or *No* to show whether each of the following is a BASIC subscripted variable for your system.

2. Z4(J)	**3.** M(X + 1)	**4.** N(−1)	**5.** M(0)
6. J*(T)	**7.** A(A)	**8.** X(3/2)	**9.** R(1E2)

Objective: For a given mathematical expression, to write a BASIC expression that contains one or more subscripted variables. *(Section 5-2)*

For each mathematical expression write a BASIC expression.

10. $a_2y^2 + a_1y + a_0$ **11.** $\frac{1}{s_1s_2} + \frac{1}{s_3}$ **12.** m_{i+j} **13.** b_{2n}

14. $\sqrt{x_2{}^2 - x_1{}^2}$ **15.** $a|2r_1 + r_2|$ **16.** x^{a_j} **17.** $d_2{}^2$

Objective: To write a program involving at least one subscripted variable in order to solve a given problem. *(Section 5-2)*

In Exercises 18 and 19, write a program to input an array X and two additional numbers A and B (A < B). Then print the following.

18. all elements of X that are greater than A and less than B
19. all elements of X that are less than A or greater than B

Objective: To write the DIM statement needed to input an array. *(Section 5-3)*

Write the DIM statement needed to input each of the arrays shown below.

20. $[y_1 \quad y_2 \quad y_3 \quad \ldots \quad y_{100}]$ **21.** $[a_i]$ where $i = 1, 2, 3, \ldots, 20$

Objective: To write the BASIC statements needed to input a polynomial. *(Section 5-4)*

Write DATA statements to input these polynomials to Program 5-6.

22. $134 - 91x - 5x^2$ **23.** $8 + m^3$
24. $17x$ **25.** $9y^4 - 15y^2 + y$
26. $-1812 + \frac{1}{2}k$ **27.** -9.7

Objective: To use an algorithm to sort a set of numbers into ascending or descending order. *(Sections 5-5 and 5-6)*

28. Apply the Sort Algorithm of Section 5-5 to put the following list into descending order. R = [6 14 20 3 15 12]. Each time a change is made, show the new version of the array.

Objective: To write a program involving at least one subroutine in order to solve a given problem. *(Section 5-7)*

29. For a set of n triangles, read the lengths of the sides of each triangle. In a subroutine compute the perimeter of the triangle and store it in an array P. After all n perimeters have been computed, use another subroutine to determine the largest element in P. End the main program by printing the largest perimeter and the number of the triangle that has it.

ROUND FIVE: *PROGRAMS FOR STUDENT ASSIGNMENT*

GENERAL INSTRUCTION:

In each exercise on pages 215 through 225, write and run a program that will do what is specified in the exercise.

ALGEBRA ONE

In Exercises 1 and 2, accept a list of numbers and print every other number (second, fourth, sixth, and so forth).

1. Write the program using a subscripted variable.

2. Write the program without using a subscripted variable.

In Exercises 3 through 10, input sets A and B by first reading M, the number of elements in A, and then the elements, stored as A(1), A(2), . . . , A(M). Then read N, the number of elements of B, then B(1), B(2), . . . , B(N). (If M = 0, A = ∅; if N = 0, B = ∅.) For each program print A and B.

3. Determine whether A and B are equivalent.

4. Determine whether A and B are equal.

5. Decide whether either set is a subset of the other.

6. Print $A \cup B$. In choosing DATA, include these possibilities: **(a)** $A \subseteq B$, **(b)** $B \subseteq A$, **(c)** $A = B$, **(d)** $A \cap B = \emptyset$, **(e)** $A = \emptyset$, and **(f)** $B = \emptyset$.

7. Print $A \cap B$. Include the same possibilities as Exercise 6.

8. Consider A to be the universal set and B, one of its subsets. Print the complement of B with respect to A.

9. Define a "set subtraction" as follows. Print $A - B$ and $B - A$.
$A - B = \{x \mid x \in A \text{ and } x \notin B\}$

10. Print $A \times B$, the "Cartesian" or "cross product" of A and B, and $B \times A$.

11. Change a repeating decimal to the ratio (in lowest terms) of two integers. For example, for $.\overline{45}$ (.454545 . . .) print 5 / 11. Input the repeating decimal with three DATA items: **(a)** the number of decimal places before the repeating block, **(b)** the number of digits in the repeating block, and **(c)** the decimal up to the place where repeating begins. For example, the DATA for $.12\overline{345}$ would be 2, 3, .12345. For $.\overline{45}$ use 0, 2, .45.

12. Factor over the integers, if possible, quadratic polynomials of the form $x^2 + Bx + C$ (B and C integers).

13. Factor over the integers (if possible) quadratic polynomials of the form $Ax^2 + Bx + C$ (A, B, and C integers with $A \neq 0$).

14. Multiply a one-variable polynomial by a constant.

15. Add pairs of one-variable polynomials. Assume that the variable is the same in both polynomials but do not assume that the polynomials are of the same degree.

16. A Latin square is an $n \times n$ array of n numbers such that each number appears in every row and every column. See the example at the right. Write a program to print all Latin squares of order n for $n = 2, 3, \ldots, 9$.

1	2	3	4	5
2	3	4	5	1
3	4	5	1	2
4	5	1	2	3
5	1	2	3	4

17. Implement the Olympics high-diving scoring. There are seven judges and each records a score on a ten-point scale. The lowest and highest scores are discarded. The final score is the average of the remaining five scores.

18. Read a list of numbers. Place the positive numbers sequentially (as they occur in the input list) into array P and the negative numbers into array N. Then print P and N.

19. Input a list of numbers in which an element may occur more than once. Print the list with duplications eliminated.

In Exercises 20-23, you are given a golfer's scores in each of the four rounds of twelve tournaments in which she played. (For Exercises 22 and 23, see Ex. 9, p. 206.)

20. Print her average score for each tournament.

21. Print her average for all forty-eight rounds this year.

22. Print her lowest and highest rounds of the year.

23. Print her lowest and highest tournament averages.

GEOMETRY

Input the coordinates of the vertices of an n-gon (polygon with n sides) in the Cartesian plane. If the vertices are $(x_1, y_1), (x_2, y_2), \ldots, (x_n, y_n)$, then store the coordinates in two arrays, X and Y.

24. Find the perimeter. **25.** Decide whether the n-gon is equilateral.

For two n-gons (polygons with n sides) read N, the number of sides, the lengths of the sides of the first polygon, and the lengths of the corresponding sides of the second.

26. Decide whether the n-gons have congruent sides.

27. Decide whether the n-gons have a common ratio between the sides of the first and the corresponding sides of the second.

28. Do Exercises 26 and 27 with the n-gons in the coordinate plane. Instead of accepting the lengths of the sides of the polygons, input the coordinates of the vertices. Store the x-coordinates in an X-array and the y-coordinates in a Y-array.

In Exercises 29 through 31, read N, the number of sides of a polygon. Then input the measures of N − 1 angles.

29. Compute the measure of the Nth angle.

30. Decide whether the polygon is equiangular.

31. Also read the measures of N − 1 corresponding angles of a second N-gon. Decide whether the polygons are similar.

ALGEBRA TWO

32. Accept an array X(1), X(2), . . . , X(20). Print the array with the following elements swapped: X(1) and X(20), X(2) and X(19), X(3) and X(18), . . . , X(10) and X(11).

33. Given ten National Merit composite scores, print that score of the ten which is nearest to the average of the set. (See Ex. 9, p. 206.)

Find the point(s) of intersection (if any) of the circle $x^2 + y^2 = r^2$ and the conic section with each of the following equations.

34. $y = ax^2 + bx + c$

35. $(x - h)^2 + (y - k)^2 = r_1^2$

36. $\frac{x^2}{a^2} + \frac{y^2}{b^2} = 1$

37. $\frac{x^2}{a^2} - \frac{y^2}{b^2} = 1$

38. Given the number of pins he knocked down with each ball in each frame, compute a bowler's score.

39. Input a table of common logarithms for the integers 1 to 20, inclusive. That is, L(1) = $\log_{10}1$, L(2) = $\log_{10}2$, . . . , L(20) = $\log_{10}20$. Use the table to perform calculations with these integers. Invent a code for the operations of multiplication, division, and exponentiation (taking roots can be handled as exponentiation). For example, if the computation to be performed is 2×3^2, list as DATA 3, 2, 23, 2, 21, 99, where '23' means exponentiation, '21' denotes multiplication, and '99' is an end-of-problem sentinel. Remember that the answer to every problem must be an integer from 1 to 20—otherwise the computer cannot find the antilogarithm.

40. In an array of twelve numbers, find the longest sequence of nondecreasing numbers. For example, for the list 17, 31, 40, 5, 6, 10, 46, 37, 53, 12, 9, 86, the longest string of nondecreasing numbers is 5, 6, 10, 46. If two or more sequences tie for longest, print all of them. Thus for 17, 31, 40, 5, 6, 10, 3, 37, 53, 12, 9, 86, print 17, 31, 40 and 5, 6, 10 and 3, 37, 53

41. Accept a sequence of numbers. Print the first, second, and third differences of consecutive terms.

Example:

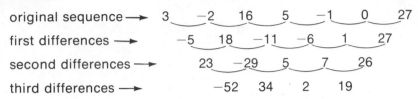

original sequence →	3		−2		16		5		−1		0		27
first differences →		−5		18		−11		−6		1		27	
second differences →			23		−29		5		7		26		
third differences →				−52		34		2		19			

42. The Factor Theorem states that $(x - a)$ is a factor of a polynomial $P(x)$ if and only if a is a root of the equation $P(x) = 0$. Use the Factor Theorem to determine whether a given binomial of the form $x - a$ is a factor of a given polynomial.

43. Every computer (and calculator) has a built-in limit for the number of significant digits it can handle. For example, 123456 × 987654 might be given as 1.21932E11. To get all the digits of a long product, the digits of the factors must be entered into two arrays and operated on digit-by-digit, the result going into a third array. Use this approach to multiply positive integers. For the example above, enter the DATA like this: 6, 1,2,3,4,5,6 6, 9,8,7,6,5,4 . That is, give the number of digits in the factor and then the digits themselves separated by commas.

44. Play on the computer the game of "Reverse." To win, a player must arrange a list of numbers (1 through 9) in ascending order from left to right. To move, the player tells the computer how many numbers (counting from the left) to reverse. Another player first enters the nine numbers in any order, and the second player tries to put them in order with the least number of reversals. For example, if the starting list is 2 3 4 5 1 6 7 8 9 and a player reverses four, the result is 5 4 3 2 1 6 7 8 9
Now, if five are reversed, the list is in order.

ADVANCED MATHEMATICS

In Exercises 45 and 46, input a vector A of dimension D.

45. Read N(N ≤ D) and assign zero to (**a**) A_N, (**b**) the first N elements of A, and (**c**) the last N elements of A.

46. Find the maximum of the absolute values of the components of A. Print the component with largest absolute value and its position in the vector. For example, if A = (13, −21, 0, 17), print −21 2 . (See Ex. 9 , p. 206.)

In Exercises 47 and 48, use Descartes' Rule of Signs, which establishes a connection between the number of sign changes between consecutive terms of a polynomial P and the number of possible real roots of $P = 0$. Input the degree and coefficients of a polynomial. (See Ex. 73-74, p. 171.)

47. Count the number of sign changes and print the number of possible positive real roots the equation may have. For example, for $2 - 3x + x^2 + 7x^3 - 5x^4 + x^5 = 0$ there are 4, 2, or 0 positive real roots.

48. Decide the number of possible negative real roots.

In Exercises 49 through 51, a polynomial P is given.

49. A function f is *even* if, for each x in the domain, $f(x) = f(-x)$. A function f is *odd* if $f(x) = -f(-x)$ for each x in the domain. Decide whether the function determined by P is even, odd, or neither. (You may want to use the DEF statement explained in Section 7-1.)

50. Print the first derivative of the function determined by P.

51. Print the second derivative.

52. For a quadratic polynomial function, use the first and second derivatives to find the critical point and whether this critical point is a relative maximum or a relative minimum.

53. For a cubic polynomial function, find the critical point(s), if any, and determine whether each is a relative maximum or relative minimum.

54. Expand Exercise 53 to find inflection points.

55. Locate the maximum and minimum points of a function over a specified domain. The user specifies the domain by entering the endpoints of the x-interval and the increment between values. (You may wish to use the DEF statement explained in Section 7-1.)

56. Consider the sequence 1, 2, 3, 6, 18, 78, 438, . . . , where the average of the first n terms is the $(n-1)$st term for $n > 2$. Find the kth term.

57. Print the quotient and the remainder when polynomial P is divided by polynomial Q. Assume the variable is the same in both polynomials but do not presume that the degree of P is greater than the degree of Q.

58. Use Newton's Method to approximate an irrational zero of a polynomial function, given the two consecutive integers between which the root lies. Newton's Method is based on the iteration formula $x_{n+1} = x_n - \dfrac{f(x_n)}{f'(x_n)}$ for $n = 1, 2, 3, \ldots$, where $f'(x_n)$ is the first derivative of f at x_n.

NUMBER THEORY

The Fibonacci Sequence begins 1, 1, 2, 3, 5, 8, 13, . . . , and each term from the third on is the sum of the two preceding terms.

59. Read N and print the first N terms of the Fibonacci Sequence.

60. Given A and B, print all terms of the Fibonacci Sequence that lie between A and B.

61. Find N such that the sum of the first N Fibonacci numbers exceeds 10^8.

62. What happens to the ratio of consecutive Fibonacci numbers as the number of terms becomes very large?

63. For the Fibonacci Sequence the *n*th term is $\dfrac{(1+\sqrt{5})^n-(1-\sqrt{5})^n}{\sqrt{5}\cdot 2^n}$.

Verify this relationship for a reasonable number of terms.

In Exercises 64 and 65, you are to consider a set of Lucas numbers. These are similar to Fibonacci numbers, but the sequence begins as follows:

1, 3, 4, 7, 11, 18, 29, 47, · · · .

64. Accept N and print the first N Lucas numbers.

65. Which of the first fifty Lucas numbers are divisible by five?

In Exercises 66-71, use the fact that a number expressed in base ten can be shown as a numeral in another base and vice-versa.

66. Given the base ten numeral for a whole number, convert it to a base-*n* numeral (*n* is a whole number such that $2 \leq n < 10$).

67. Count to thirty-one in base two.

68. Given an octal (base eight) numeral for a whole number, print the same number in binary form.

69. Given the binary representation of a whole number, convert to octal.

70. Add pairs of binary whole numbers. Do not convert to base ten.

71. Add pairs of base-*n* whole numbers (*n* is a whole number such that $2 \leq n < 10$). Do not convert to base ten.

72. Print the first fifty primes. As the primes are found, store them in an array so that they may be used to test later integers. Also gain efficiency by immediately printing 2 as the first prime (and storing it as the first element of the array) and then testing only odd numbers greater than two. (See Ex. 100, p. 173.)

73. Another method of finding primes is the Sieve of Eratosthenes.

Simulate the Sieve for the integers 1 to 100. Print 0's in place of the composite numbers (and in place of one).

74. Print a table giving the number and per cent of primes in the intervals 2–100, 101–200, 201–300, . . . , 901–1000.

75. Fermat proposed that all numbers of the form $2^{2^n} + 1$ ($n = 0,1,2,$ $3, \ldots$) are primes. Show that the statement is true for $n = 0,1,2,3,4$ but not for $n = 5$.

76. Mersenne primes are of the form $2^p - 1$ where p is a prime. For every Mersenne prime there is a corresponding perfect number $2^{p-1}(2^p - 1)$. Find three Mersenne primes and the corresponding perfect numbers.

77. A rich man wants to give away a sum of money by dividing the sum equally among a number of needy families. (The sum is below $10,000 and he will calculate the equal division to pennies.) If he kept a penny, he could divide it equally among 31 families; if he kept a nickel, he could divide it among 32 families; if he kept a dime, he could divide it among 33 families; and if he kept a quarter, he could divide it equally among 35 families. How much money does he have to give away? (Use a trial-and-error method.)

78. Use Zeller's Congruence Law to determine the day of the week for a given date from the past or future. (You may wish to use an ØN statement, as explained in Section 7-6.)

79. Find the *LCM* and *GCF* for a set of N positive integers.

80. Decide whether a set of N positive integers are relatively prime.

81. Program the computer to play the game of "Buzz." That is, count from 1 to 100 but for any number containing the digit 7 or any number divisible by 7, say "Buzz" instead of saying the number. For numbers that contain the digit 7 and are also divisible by 7, say "Buzz-Buzz."

82. Divide pairs of base-ten whole numbers by repeated subtraction, giving the quotient and the remainder. For example, for 73 and 6, print a quotient of 12 and remainder 1.

STATISTICS

83. The **median** of a list of numbers is that element such that when the numbers are arranged in either ascending or descending order, half the elements lie above it and half below. This can happen only when there are an odd number of elements in the list. If the array contains an even number of items, the median is the average of the two numbers in the middle. Input an array and print the median.

84. The **mode** of a list of numbers is that value which occurs most often. An array may have more than one mode. Write a program to accept an array and print the mode(s) and the number of times each mode occurs.

85. A set of data (for example, test results) can be summarized by a *frequency distribution chart.* For example, if the list is 90, 85, 100, 85, 70, 80, 80, 95, 80, 75, 70, 95, 80, 65, 80, 75, 80, 75, the frequency distribution chart looks like the one at the right. Write a program to input the raw scores and print the frequency distribution chart.

Value	*Frequency*
100	1
95	2
90	1
85	2
80	6
75	3
70	2
65	1

86. The *standard deviation* of a list of data measures how "spread out" or "scattered" the data is. Specifically, to find the standard deviation do the following:

(a) compute the mean;

(b) subtract each item in the list from the mean and square this difference;

(c) sum the squared differences of (**b**);

(d) divide this sum by *n*, the number of values in the list;

(e) take the square root of the quotient from (**d**).

Write a program to accept a list of data and print the standard deviation.

When you take a standardized test, your score is reported by *percentile* rank. If you rank at the 90th percentile, then your score on the test was equal to or better than 90% of the students who took the test.

87. Accept a list of test scores and the number of students who made each score and print the percentile table for the test.

88. Given the raw scores from a test, output the percentile table. Now the program must organize the data before percentiles can be computed.

89. The mean and standard deviation of a list of raw scores are used to convert the scores to "*z*-scores" (also called "*t*-scores" or "standard scores"). Reducing data to standard scores allows results of different tests to be compared because an array of *z*-scores has a mean of zero and standard deviation of one. A standard score in effect tells how many standard deviation units above or below the mean a given raw score lies. (For national tests *z*-scores are often further converted by multiplying by ten and adding fifty. This creates a scale where 50 is the mean and the standard deviation is ten; no score is negative.) Convert raw scores to *z*-scores.

90. The *relative error* of a measurement is the ratio $\frac{\text{maximum error}}{\text{measurement}}$.
For example, a measurement of .26 has a maximum error of .005. Hence the relative error of the measurement is

$$\frac{.005}{.26} = \frac{5}{260} = \frac{1}{52} \approx .0192 \approx 1.92\%$$

Given a measurement and the unit of measurement, compute the relative error and percent of error. For example, for .26 input .26, .01. For 93,000,000 miles input 93E6, 1E6.

91. Write a test-correcting program for multiple-choice tests. Assume there are twenty questions with five possible answers for each question. Count the number of questions each student gets right, the number wrong, and the number he does not answer.

92. Print histograms with (**a**) vertical bars (**b**) horizontal bars.

93. Pearson's Correlation Coefficient is a value between −1 and 1 that indicates the extent to which a linear relationship exists between two sets of data. Given N pairs of data items (X, Y), compute the correlation coefficient using the formula

$$R = \frac{N\,\Sigma XY - \Sigma X\,\Sigma Y}{\sqrt{[N\,\Sigma X^2 - (\Sigma X)^2][N\,\Sigma Y^2 - (\Sigma Y)^2]}}.$$

94. Given the same input as in Exercise 93, use the "method of least squares" to determine the "equation of best fit." Use the equation to predict values of Y for given values of X.

BUSINESS

In Exercises 95 and 96, a chain of service stations is sponsoring a lucky number drawing in your city with tickets numbered 1 to 1000.

95. Given a ticket number, check the list of ten lucky numbers to see whether the ticket is a winner of one of the ten $100 prizes.

96. Three kinds of prizes are awarded. Given a ticket number, decide whether it is a $100 winner, a $10 winner, a $1 winner, or none of these. There are only five $100 winners, ten $10 winners, and twenty $1 winners, and no number can win in more than one category.

97. At Tiger Electric Company, the overtime rate for any hours over eight in a day is double the worker's regular rate. Input into an array the worker's employee number and regular pay rate and then the number of hours worked during each of the five weekdays. Compute the employee's gross weekly pay.

98. Calculate the number of days between two dates that fall within the term of a loan. Leap years must be taken into account. Assume that there is one day between today and tomorrow. Then there are two days between, for example, March 1 and March 3 of the same year.

99. Input an array that gives the number of each item in stock at a toy store at the beginning of the month. Then enter a second array listing the number of each item sold during the month. Print an updated inventory report listing the number of each item on hand at the end of the month.

100. Store in two arrays the base monthly salary and the commission rate of each of ten salespersons for Colonel Motors Corporation. Then, given the salesperson's employee number and monthly total sales, print the commission and gross pay for the month. Also print the total commission and total pay for all ten salespeople.

101. In Exercise 100 assume now that there is a quota plan. Set up a third array that lists each salesperson's monthly sales quota. Then, given the same entries as in Exercise 100, pay the commission only if the monthly sales exceeds the quota. If the sales are less than the quota, pay only the base salary. Again print the total commission and total pay for all ten salespeople.

PHYSICAL SCIENCES

102. Write a metric-U.S. conversion program. Store in an array the various conversion constants. Then offer the user a coded "menu" of conversions to choose from. Examples: 1 = INCHES TØ CENTIMETERS, 2 = FEET TØ METERS, 3 = KILØMETERS TØ MILES, 4 = NEWTØNS TØ PØUNDS and so on. Then, depending on the desired conversion, the user enters the number of the original units and the computer prints the number of units after conversion. If, for example, the user picks choice 2, then the output should be in the form

XXX FEET = XXX METERS.

103. Store in an array the surface gravity constants of planets.

No.	Planet	Surface Gravity
1	Mercury	0.39
2	Venus	0.91
3	Earth	1.00
4	Mars	0.38
5	Jupiter	2.64
6	Saturn	1.13
7	Uranus	1.07
8	Neptune	1.41

Input the number of a planet, the weight of an object on that planet, and the number of another planet. Print the weight of that same object on the second planet.

104. Here are the masses of some nuclides in atomic mass units.

No.	Nuclide	Mass
1	Polonium 218	218.0089
2	Radon 222	222.0175
3	Radium 228	228.0303
4	Uranium 235	235.0439
5	Uranium 238	238.0508
6	Plutonium 239	239.0522

Store these masses in an array. Then allow the user to specify which nuclide is to be used in Einstein's equation $E = mc^2$ to determine the amount of energy produced by the fission of an atom of that nuclide. Note: One atomic mass unit $= 1.66043 \times 10^{-27}$ kg.

105. Store the table below in an array. Then compute the critical angle for each substance. Use air as the other, optically less dense, medium (the index of refraction of air is 1.00).

Substance	Diamond	Water	Plexiglass	Crown glass	Gasoline
Index of Refraction	2.42	1.33	1.50	1.53	1.38

106. Apply the laws of heredity to follow one trait of plants or animals through two generations of offspring. Use a code of 1 for the dominant gene (e.g., tall) and 0 for the recessive gene (e.g., short). The user enters into an array P the four code numbers for the genes of the parents. The program then transfers all possible combinations of these genes to an array F, which is then analyzed to determine the probabilities of tall and short offspring for the first generation. Then all possible combinations from F are transferred to an array S, from which the probabilities of tall and short offspring in the second generation are computed. A possible output might be as shown at the right.

```
P1: 1 TALL AND 1 SHØRT

F1: 100% PRØBABILITY TALL
    0% PRØBABILITY SHØRT

F2: 75% PRØBABILITY TALL
    25% PRØBABILITY SHØRT
```

107. Enter into an array the atomic weights of at least six gases. Then given a temperature, a pressure and the masses of each gas sample, find the volume of each gas.

6

MATRICES

6-1 WHAT IS A MATRIX?

Tables (rectangular arrays of numbers) often arise in business, science, and everyday life.

Example 1:

Table 6-1 lists the distances between certain cities.

Table 6-1 Distances Between Cities (in miles)

	New Orleans	New York	Miami	Denver	St. Paul	Los Angeles
New Orleans	0	1325	875	1282	1241	1901
New York	1325	0	1330	1851	1253	2915
Miami	875	1330	0	2046	1770	2712
Denver	1282	1851	2046	0	841	1134
St. Paul	1241	1253	1770	841	0	1940
Los Angeles	1901	2915	2712	1134	1940	0

Example 2:

Hiram orders an inventory of his clothing store. Table 6-2 summarizes the number of pairs of men's pants of each size and color.

Table 6-2 Hiram's Clothing Store: Inventory of Men's Pants

	Blue	Gray	Black	Red	White	Brown
small	27	15	22	4	6	32
medium	46	21	39	11	12	49
large	33	16	37	7	15	37

A rectangular array of numbers is called a **matrix**. In mathematical work the elements of a matrix are displayed between brackets. (Some texts enclose matrices in parentheses.) For example, Table 6-1 on page 226 includes the following matrix.

$$\mathbf{A} = \begin{bmatrix} 0 & 1325 & 875 & 1282 & 1241 & 1901 \\ 1325 & 0 & 1330 & 1851 & 1253 & 2915 \\ 875 & 1330 & 0 & 2046 & 1770 & 2712 \\ 1282 & 1851 & 2046 & 0 & 841 & 1134 \\ 1241 & 1253 & 1770 & 841 & 0 & 1940 \\ 1901 & 2915 & 2712 & 1134 & 1940 & 0 \end{bmatrix}$$

A matrix is named by a variable, say **A**. Matrix **A** above is a 6×6 matrix; that is, **A** has six **rows** (horizontal) and six **columns** (vertical). The number of rows and the number of columns (in that order) are the **dimensions** of the matrix. A particular element is specified by a double subscript. The first subscript names the row; the second subscript gives the column. For example, in the matrix above,

$A_{1,1} = 0$ (row 1, column 1) $\quad A_{3,2} = 1330$ (row 3, column 2) $\quad A_{6,2} = 2915.$ (row 6, column 2)

In general, an element of matrix **A** can be referred to as $A_{i,j}$ where i denotes the row and j, the column.

A matrix such as the 6×6 matrix above is called a **square matrix** because the number of rows equals the number of columns. For an $n \times n$ matrix, n is called the *order* of the matrix. Thus the order of **A** is six.

A square matrix has a *main diagonal* consisting of the elements $A_{i,i}$. In Table 6-1 the main diagonal contains all zeros, each representing the distance from a city to itself.

A square matrix may be **symmetric**, like matrix **A**, in which case each element $A_{i,j}$ equals $A_{j,i}$. This is illustrated in the following diagram.

$$\begin{bmatrix} 0 & \boxed{1325} & 875 & 1282 & 1241 & 1901 \\ \boxed{1325} & 0 & 1330 & 1851 & 1253 & \boxed{2915} \\ 875 & 1330 & 0 & 2046 & 1770 & 2712 \\ 1282 & 1851 & 2046 & 0 & 841 & 1134 \\ 1241 & 1253 & 1770 & 841 & 0 & 1940 \\ 1901 & \boxed{2915} & 2712 & 1134 & 1940 & 0 \end{bmatrix}$$

In a symmetric matrix row i equals column i.

A matrix does not have to be square (see Example 2 on page 226). Here are other examples of matrices, with the dimensions of each.

(a) $\begin{bmatrix} 4 & 6 & 0 \\ -3 & 2 & 1 \end{bmatrix}$ 2×3

(b) $\begin{bmatrix} 8 & 61 & 14 & -7 \end{bmatrix}$ 1×4

(c) $\begin{bmatrix} 4 & -3 \\ 6 & 2 \\ 0 & 1 \end{bmatrix}$ 3×2

(d) $\begin{bmatrix} 0 \\ 4 \\ -2 \\ 5 \end{bmatrix}$ 4×1

Example **b** shows that the concept of "matrix" includes the idea of an "array" or "list" studied in the last chapter. A matrix that has exactly one row or one column is often called a **vector.** A distinction is made between a "row vector" or "row matrix" (see Example **b**), and a "column vector" or "column matrix" (Example **d**).

The matrix of Example **c** is the *transpose* of the matrix of Example **a**. The **transpose** of a matrix **A**, represented by $\mathbf{A}^T$, is the matrix formed by interchanging the rows and columns of **A**: the first row of **A** becomes the first column of $\mathbf{A}^T$, the second row becomes the second column, and so forth.

EXERCISES 6-1

A Which of the following are mathematically accepted ways of denoting matrices?

1. 6, 8, −3 **2.** {6, 8, −3} **3.** $\begin{bmatrix} 6 & 8 & -3 \end{bmatrix}$

4. $\begin{bmatrix} 6 \\ 8 \\ -3 \end{bmatrix}$ **5.** $\begin{bmatrix} 1 & 0 \\ 0 & 1 \end{bmatrix}$ **6.** $\emptyset$

Give the dimensions of each matrix.

7. $\begin{bmatrix} 3 & 2 \end{bmatrix}$ **8.** $\begin{bmatrix} 7 \\ 10 \end{bmatrix}$ **9.** $\begin{bmatrix} 4 & 6 \\ 9 & 1 \end{bmatrix}$ **10.** $\begin{bmatrix} 6 & -2 & -1 \\ 3 & -2 & 7 \end{bmatrix}$

11. Which matrices in Exercises 7-10, if any, are row vectors? Which are column vectors? Which are square matrices?

Let **B** be the matrix of Table 6-2. Give the number named by each of the following.

12. $B_{1,2}$ **13.** $B_{3,5}$ **14.** $B_{2,1}$ **15.** $B_{2+1,3-1}$

B Exercises 16-19 refer to a square matrix **X** of order *n*.

16. Name all the elements on the main diagonal.
17. Name all the elements on the other diagonal.
18. Name all the elements in row $r (r \leq n)$.
19. Name all the elements in column $c (c \leq n)$.

6-2 MATRIX INPUT-OUTPUT

In BASIC, as in mathematics, two subscripts are used to name an element of a matrix. The subscripts are written inside parentheses behind the letter naming the matrix. The first subscript gives the row; the second designates the column.

As an example, let $\mathbf{A} = \begin{bmatrix} 4 & 6 & 0 \\ -3 & 2 & 1 \end{bmatrix}$. Then in BASIC

A(1,2) = 6 (row, column)   A(2,1) = −3 (row, column)   A(1,3) = 0. (row, column)

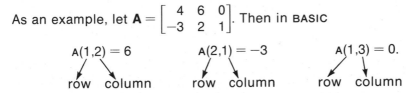

The DIM statement for this array would be 10 DIM A(2,3) . As with one-dimensional arrays, however, if neither of the subscripts exceeds ten, the DIM statement for that array may be omitted on most systems.

Usually, a matrix name must be a single letter. For example, X, Y, and Z are valid names for matrices but A1, B7, and M4 are not.

A matrix is read and stored by means of a nested loop.

```
10    DIM A(2,3)
20    FØR I = 1 TØ 2
30      FØR J = 1 TØ 3
40        READ A(I,J)
50      NEXT J
60    NEXT I
70    DATA 4,6,0,-3,2,1
              . . .
```

Matrix **A**, above, is used as DATA. Note that elements are listed by rows since J, the column subscript, is nested and varies faster than the row subscript, I.

For larger matrices, such as the one in Table 6-1 on page 226, it is a good idea to list each row in a separate DATA statement.

```
100 DATA 0,1325,875,1282,1241,1901
101 DATA 1325,0,1330,1851,1253,2915
102 DATA 875,1330,0,2046,1770,2712
103 DATA 1282,1851,2046,0,841,1134
104 DATA 1241,1253,1770,841,0,1940
105 DATA 1901,2915,2712,1134,1940,0
```

The READ loop above handles only 2 × 3 matrices. It can be generalized by first reading R and C, which give the number of rows and the number of columns, respectively, of the matrix that follows in the DATA. The loop is shown at the top of the next page.

```
100           DIM A(20,20)
110           READ R, C
120
130    REM       R = NUMBER ØF RØWS ØF MATRIX A
140    REM       C = NUMBER ØF CØLUMNS ØF MATRIX A
150
160           FØR I = 1 TØ R
170             FØR J = 1 TØ C
180               READ A(I,J)
190             NEXT J
200           NEXT I
210           DATA 2,3
220           DATA 4,6,0
230           DATA -3,2,1
                    ...
```

As mentioned for one-dimensional arrays, some systems allow variable subscripts in DIM statements, as in the following program.

```
110    READ R, C
120    DIM A(R,C)
130    FØR I = 1 TØ R
140      FØR J = 1 TØ C
150        READ A (I,J)
160      NEXT J
170    NEXT I
             ...
```

A nested loop is also used to print a matrix, as is shown below.

```
            ...
200    FØR I = 1 TØ R
210      FØR J = 1 TØ C
220        PRINT A(I,J),
230      NEXT J
240      PRINT
250    NEXT I
            ...
```

The comma at the end of line 220 above keeps the printer on the same line while a row of the matrix is being printed. Line 240 then moves the printer off that line before the next row (line 250) is printed. The comma at the end of line 220 outputs the elements in aligned columns but correctly prints only matrices with five columns or fewer. The TAB function can be used to print the matrix in correctly aligned columns even when the number of columns is six or more. A PRINT loop using the TAB function might look like the following.

```
200    FØR I = 1 TØ R
210      FØR J = 1 TØ C
220        PRINT A(I,J); TAB(J*W/C);
230      NEXT J
240      PRINT
250    NEXT I
```

In line 220 above, you should replace W with the number of spaces on a line of your printer or screen.

EXERCISES 6-2

A Let $\mathbf{S} = \begin{bmatrix} 7 & -3 & 2 \\ 0 & 4 & 16 \\ -5 & 9 & -1 \end{bmatrix}$. Use a BASIC subscripted variable to name each of these elements of the matrix.

Example: 0 **Answer:** S(2,1)

1. −3 **2.** 4 **3.** 16 **4.** −5 **5.** −1

Write a BASIC subscripted variable for each of these mathematical variables.

Example: $a_{i,j}$ **Answer:** A(I,J)

6. $x_{1,4}$ **7.** $y_{i+1,j}$ **8.** $b_{2x,2y}$ **9.** $k_{r,c}$
10. $m_{1,d}$ **11.** $g_{i,i}$ **12.** $a_{r-1,c+1}$ **13.** $d_{10,6}$

14. To read the matrix on the right, a programmer writes the loop shown below.

$$\begin{bmatrix} 8 & 3 & 1 & 2 \\ -1 & 7 & 4 & 0 \\ 10 & -6 & 3 & 5 \end{bmatrix}$$

```
100    DIM M(3,4)
110    FØR J = 1 TØ 4
120      FØR I = 1 TØ 3
130        READ M(I,J)
140      NEXT I
150    NEXT J
```

Write the DATA line(s) she needs in order to input the matrix properly with the loop.

15. Write a program to read the matrix on the right and print the matrix that results when all the elements are multiplied by two.

$$\begin{bmatrix} 9 & .3 & -1 & 7 \\ 2 & 0 & 4 & 3 \\ -.1 & 7 & 2 & 11 \end{bmatrix}$$

16. Will the READ loop and DATA lines below properly input the matrix at the right? If not, show why.

$$\begin{bmatrix} 7 & 13 & 6 \\ -4 & 21 & -2 \\ 0 & 10 & 9 \end{bmatrix}$$

```
10 DIM B(5,5)
20 FØR I = 1 TØ 3
30   READ B(I,1),B(I,2),B(I,3)
40 NEXT I
50 DATA 7, 13, 6, -4, 21, -2, 0, 10, 9
   . . .
90 END
```

Consider the partial program at the right. Show the output when each of the following sets of statements is inserted into this partial program.

```
10 DIM X(3,4)
20 FØR I = 1 TØ 3
30   FØR J = 1 TØ 4
40     READ X(I,J)
60   NEXT J
70 NEXT I
80 DATA 71,-18,24,6
82 DATA 121,62,-5
84 DATA 141,.08,1.2
86 DATA 7.35,-1.5
   . . .
```

17. `50 PRINT X(I,J),`

18. `50 PRINT X(I,J); TAB(8*J);`
`65 PRINT`

19. `50 PRINT X(I,J),`
`65 PRINT`

20. As mentioned in Section 6-1, the transpose of matrix **A**, represented by $\mathbf{A}^T$, is the matrix formed by interchanging the rows and columns: the first row becomes the first column, the second row becomes the second column, and so forth. Write a program to read a matrix and print its transpose.

B **21.** Prepare a flowchart for the loop at the top of page 230.

22. Prepare a flowchart for the third loop on page 230.

23. Rewrite the loop in Exercise 22 to output the matrix double-spaced.

24. $r \times c$ matrices **A** and **B** are equal if and only if all corresponding elements are equal: A(1,1) = B(1,1), A(1,2) = B(1,2), . . . , A(R,C) = B(R,C). Write a program to decide whether two $r \times c$ matrices are equal.

25. Write a program that, given an $r \times c$ matrix, swaps row L and row M (L and M read from DATA or INPUT) and prints the resulting matrix.

26. Repeat Exercise 25 but swap column L and column M.

6-3 ADDING MATRICES

Table 6-2 on page 226 listed the inventory of men's pants at Hiram's Clothing Store. Let us suppose that Hiram orders a new supply. Table 6-3 summarizes his new order.

Table 6-3 Hiram's Order for Men's Pants

	Blue	Grey	Black	Red	White	Brown
small	12	9	10	2	6	20
medium	12	15	16	0	12	11
large	24	8	5	2	15	13

After the new shipment arrives, what is Hiram's total inventory by size and color?

The answer is found by performing *matrix addition.*

$$\begin{bmatrix} \boxed{27} & 15 & 22 & 4 & 6 & 32 \\ 46 & 21 & 39 & 11 & 12 & \boxed{49} \\ 33 & 16 & 37 & 7 & 15 & 37 \end{bmatrix} + \begin{bmatrix} \boxed{12} & 9 & 10 & 2 & 6 & 20 \\ 12 & 15 & 16 & 0 & 12 & \boxed{11} \\ 24 & 8 & 5 & 2 & 15 & 13 \end{bmatrix} = \begin{bmatrix} \boxed{39} & 24 & 32 & 6 & 12 & 52 \\ 58 & 36 & 55 & 11 & 24 & \boxed{60} \\ 57 & 24 & 42 & 9 & 30 & 50 \end{bmatrix}$$

previous inventory + new shipment = updated inventory

The boxed elements shown in the matrix addition above are examples of the following rule.

RULE FOR ADDING MATRICES

Two matrices with the same dimensions are added by adding corresponding elements. Matrices with different dimensions cannot be added.

This rule fits Hiram's problem perfectly since corresponding elements of the two matrices represent the same size and color pants.

Here are further examples of matrix addition.

1. $\begin{bmatrix} 6 & 2 & 3 \\ 4 & -1 & -5 \end{bmatrix} + \begin{bmatrix} 10 & -6 & 4 \\ 3 & 2 & 7 \end{bmatrix} = \begin{bmatrix} 16 & -4 & 7 \\ 7 & 1 & 2 \end{bmatrix}$

2. $\begin{bmatrix} 3 & 0 \\ 1 & -5 \end{bmatrix} + \begin{bmatrix} 7 & -3 \\ 4 & 0 \end{bmatrix} = \begin{bmatrix} 10 & -3 \\ 5 & -5 \end{bmatrix}$

3. $\begin{bmatrix} 6 & 2 & 3 \\ 4 & -1 & -5 \end{bmatrix}$ and $\begin{bmatrix} 3 & 0 \\ 1 & -5 \end{bmatrix}$ cannot be added.

For any set of $r \times c$ matrices, the additive identity matrix or **zero matrix**, is the $r \times c$ matrix each of whose elements is 0. Examples are shown below.

4. The 2×2 zero matrix is $\begin{bmatrix} 0 & 0 \\ 0 & 0 \end{bmatrix}$. Thus, $\begin{bmatrix} 3 & 0 \\ 1 & -5 \end{bmatrix} + \begin{bmatrix} 0 & 0 \\ 0 & 0 \end{bmatrix} = \begin{bmatrix} 3 & 0 \\ 1 & -5 \end{bmatrix}$.

5. The 1×5 zero matrix is $[0 \quad 0 \quad 0 \quad 0 \quad 0]$.

To program matrix addition, we logically need these steps.

1. Read the elements of matrix **A** (dimensions $r \times c$).
2. Read the elements of matrix **B** (also $r \times c$).
3. Add the elements of matrices **A** and **B**.
4. Print the sum.
5. Return to step 1 for new DATA.

The computer can begin adding the elements of the matrices as soon as it has read the latest element of Matrix **B**. Hence the loops for reading **B**, adding **A** and **B**, and printing the sum can be combined. Here is a program for the algorithm above applied to Examples 1 and 2 on page 233.

Program 6-1: Adding Two $r \times c$ Matrices

```
120     DIM A(5,5), B(5,5)
130     READ R, C
140     FØR I = 1 TØ R
150       FØR J = 1 TØ C
160         READ A(I,J)
170       NEXT J
180     NEXT I
190
200     FØR I = 1 TØ R
210       FØR J = 1 TØ C
220         READ B(I,J)
230         PRINT A(I,J) + B(I,J);TAB(W*J/C);
240       NEXT J
250       PRINT
260     NEXT I
270     PRINT
280     GØ TØ 130
290
300     DATA 2,3,6,2,3,4,-1,-5,10,-6,4,3
310     DATA 2,7,2,2,3,0,1,-5,7,-3,4,0
320
330     END
```

Replace W *with the number of spaces on a line of your own printer or screen.* (arrow pointing to W in line 230)

EXERCISES 6-3

A Add, if possible, the following matrices.

1. $\begin{bmatrix} 1 \\ -2 \end{bmatrix}, \begin{bmatrix} 5 \\ 6 \end{bmatrix}$

2. $\begin{bmatrix} 2 & -1 \\ 3 & 4 \end{bmatrix}, \begin{bmatrix} 0 & 6 \\ -8 & -12 \end{bmatrix}$

3. $\begin{bmatrix} 0 & 2 & 1 \\ -1 & 3 & 5 \end{bmatrix}, \begin{bmatrix} 7 & 9 \\ -8 & 11 \\ 30 & -10 \end{bmatrix}$

4. $\begin{bmatrix} 5 & -.04 & 13 \\ 21 & 11 & -2 \end{bmatrix}, \begin{bmatrix} 10 & -.01 & -5 \\ .5 & -3 & 9 \end{bmatrix}$

5. Show the output of Program 6-1.
6. Would Program 6-1 yield the same results if line 230 were changed from "PRINT A(I,J) + B(I,J);" to "PRINT B(I,J) + A(I,J);"? What property of matrix addition applies here?
7. Change Program 6-1 so that it prints matrix **A**, skips a line, prints matrix **B**, skips a line, and then prints their sum.
8. Modify Program 6-1 to handle the situation where the two matrices to be read do not necessarily have the same dimensions. Have the computer print the two matrices, followed by their sum, or by the message CANNØT BE ADDED.
9. Write a program to read two $r \times 2$ matrices, print them *side-by-side,* skip a line, and then print their sum.

B 10. Prepare a flowchart for Program 6-1.
11. Prepare a flowchart for the program of Exercise 8 above.
12. Write a program to add three matrices. Allow the possibility that the matrices cannot be added. (See Ex. 8.)
13. Write a program to add N $r \times c$ matrices, where N is read from DATA.

C 14. Addition of real numbers is closed, commutative, associative, and has identity and inverse elements. Which of these properties does addition of matrices of the same dimensions possess? If the identity property holds, what is the additive identity for $r \times c$ matrices? If the inverse property holds, what is the additive inverse of a particular $r \times c$ matrix?

6-4 SCALAR MULTIPLICATION; MATRIX SUBTRACTION

Let us change the example of the last lesson. Suppose that Hiram wishes to double his inventory of men's pants. This idea corresponds to **scalar multiplication** of the matrix of Table 6-2 on page 226. A **scalar** is any real number. In this case the scalar is two.

$$2\begin{bmatrix} 27 & 15 & 22 & 4 & 6 & 32 \\ 46 & 21 & 39 & 11 & 12 & 49 \\ 33 & 16 & 37 & 7 & 15 & 37 \end{bmatrix} = \begin{bmatrix} 54 & 30 & 44 & 8 & 12 & 64 \\ 92 & 42 & 78 & 22 & 24 & 98 \\ 66 & 32 & 74 & 14 & 30 & 74 \end{bmatrix}$$

RULE FOR SCALAR MULTIPLICATION

To multiply a matrix by a scalar k, multiply each element of the matrix by k.

Here are some more examples.

1. $-3\begin{bmatrix} 3 & -1 & 4 \\ -2 & 0 & 7 \end{bmatrix} = \begin{bmatrix} -9 & 3 & -12 \\ 6 & 0 & -21 \end{bmatrix}$

2. $.5\begin{bmatrix} 4 & 0 \\ 3 & 1 \\ -2 & 5 \end{bmatrix} = \begin{bmatrix} 2 & 0 \\ 1.5 & .5 \\ -1 & 2.5 \end{bmatrix}$

3. $-5[6 \quad -1 \quad 4 \quad .8] = [-30 \quad 5 \quad -20 \quad -4.0]$

We can now define **matrix subtraction** by using the scalar −1. If **A** and **B** are $r \times c$ matrices, then

$$\mathbf{A} - \mathbf{B} = \mathbf{A} + (-1)\mathbf{B}.$$

Examples:

1. If $\mathbf{A} = \begin{bmatrix} 8 & 2 \\ 0 & -5 \end{bmatrix}$ and $\mathbf{B} = \begin{bmatrix} 12 & 0 \\ 1 & 13 \end{bmatrix}$, then $\mathbf{A} - \mathbf{B} = \mathbf{A} + (-1)\mathbf{B} =$

$$\begin{bmatrix} 8 & 2 \\ 0 & -5 \end{bmatrix} + (-1)\begin{bmatrix} 12 & 0 \\ 1 & 13 \end{bmatrix} = \begin{bmatrix} 8 & 2 \\ 0 & -5 \end{bmatrix} + \begin{bmatrix} -12 & 0 \\ -1 & -13 \end{bmatrix} = \begin{bmatrix} -4 & 2 \\ -1 & -18 \end{bmatrix}$$

2. Hiram's inventory of men's pants at the beginning of a month is shown below.

	blue	grey	black	red	white	brown
small	39	24	32	6	12	52
medium	58	36	55	11	24	60
large	57	24	42	9	30	50

The sales for the month are given by this table.

	blue	grey	black	red	white	brown
small	8	6	5	1	3	15
medium	12	6	14	3	10	13
large	10	4	7	0	9	8

Then the inventory at the end of the month can be found by matrix subtraction.

$$\begin{bmatrix} 39 & 24 & 32 & 6 & 12 & 52 \\ 58 & 36 & 55 & 11 & 24 & 60 \\ 57 & 24 & 42 & 9 & 30 & 50 \end{bmatrix} - \begin{bmatrix} 8 & 6 & 5 & 1 & 3 & 15 \\ 12 & 6 & 14 & 3 & 10 & 13 \\ 10 & 4 & 7 & 0 & 9 & 8 \end{bmatrix} =$$

$$\begin{bmatrix} 31 & 18 & 27 & 5 & 9 & 37 \\ 46 & 30 & 41 & 8 & 14 & 47 \\ 47 & 20 & 35 & 9 & 21 & 42 \end{bmatrix}$$

The matrix $(-1)\mathbf{B}$ can also be written as $-\mathbf{B}$ and is the **additive inverse** of **B** since the sum of **B** and $-\mathbf{B}$ is the $r \times c$ zero matrix.

$$\mathbf{B} + (-\mathbf{B}) = \begin{bmatrix} 12 & 0 \\ 1 & 13 \end{bmatrix} + \begin{bmatrix} -12 & 0 \\ -1 & -13 \end{bmatrix} = \begin{bmatrix} 0 & 0 \\ 0 & 0 \end{bmatrix}$$

In a similar fashion the additive inverse of **L** is $-\mathbf{L}$.

$$\mathbf{L} = \begin{bmatrix} 6 & -1 & 0 \\ -7 & 5 & .5 \end{bmatrix} \qquad -\mathbf{L} = \begin{bmatrix} -6 & 1 & 0 \\ 7 & -5 & -.5 \end{bmatrix}$$

EXERCISES 6-4

A Let $\mathbf{A} = \begin{bmatrix} 2 & 0 \\ -1 & 3 \end{bmatrix}$, $\mathbf{B} = \begin{bmatrix} 1 & 5 \\ 0 & -6 \end{bmatrix}$, and $\mathbf{C} = \begin{bmatrix} -2 & 0 \\ -4 & 7 \end{bmatrix}$. Compute each of the following.

1. $2\mathbf{A}$
2. $-4\mathbf{B}$
3. $-\mathbf{C}$
4. $\mathbf{A} - \mathbf{C}$
5. $\mathbf{B} + \mathbf{C} - \mathbf{A}$
6. $2\mathbf{A} - 4\mathbf{B}$
7. $\mathbf{C} - 3\mathbf{A}$
8. $\mathbf{B} + (-1)\mathbf{B}$
9. $2\mathbf{C} - (\mathbf{A} + \mathbf{B})$
10. $\frac{1}{2}(\mathbf{C} - \mathbf{B})$
11. $2(3\mathbf{A})$
12. $(2 \cdot 3)\mathbf{A}$
13. $3(\mathbf{A}^T)$
14. $(3\mathbf{A})^T$
15. $\mathbf{A}^T + \mathbf{B}^T$
16. $(\mathbf{A} + \mathbf{B})^T$
17. $\mathbf{B}^T - \mathbf{C}^T$
18. $(\mathbf{B} - \mathbf{C})^T$

19. This table represents the prices of a pair of each type of pants at Hiram's Clothing Store.

	blue	grey	black	red	white	brown
small	8.98	9.50	8.98	8.98	9.98	8.98
medium	7.98	9.00	7.98	9.50	9.50	7.98
large	8.98	9.50	8.98	9.98	9.98	8.98

Hiram plans a sale. The price reduction for each size and color pants is given by this table.

	blue	grey	black	red	white	brown
small	1.00	1.50	1.00	1.50	1.50	1.00
medium	1.00	1.00	1.00	1.50	1.00	1.00
large	1.00	1.50	1.00	1.50	1.50	1.00

Give the table showing Hiram's net pants prices for the sale.

20. Write a program to multiply any given matrix by any given scalar.

B

21. Is matrix subtraction a commutative operation? associative?
22. Write a program to input a matrix and print its additive inverse.
23. Write a program to input $r \times c$ matrices **A** and **B** and print $\mathbf{A} - \mathbf{B}$.
24. Write a program to input *and print* $r \times c$ matrices **A** and **B** and then print $\mathbf{A} - \mathbf{B}$.

C Which of the following properties hold in a system of $r \times c$ matrices? (**A** and **B** are $r \times c$ matrices and m and n are scalars.)

25. $m(n\mathbf{A}) = (mn)\mathbf{A}$
26. $m(\mathbf{A} + \mathbf{B}) = m\mathbf{A} + m\mathbf{B}$
27. $m(\mathbf{A} - \mathbf{B}) = m\mathbf{A} - m\mathbf{B}$
28. $(m + n)\mathbf{A} = m\mathbf{A} + n\mathbf{A}$

6-5 INNER PRODUCT OF VECTORS

Example 1:

A customer at Hiram's Clothing Store buys five pairs of medium-size pants: two blue pairs @ \$7.98 each, one grey pair @ \$9.00, and two white @ \$9.50 each. The customer's total bill (before tax) can be computed by taking the inner product of two vectors. Let the order be expressed as the row vector $[2\quad 1\quad 2]$ and list the prices (per pair) in a column vector: $\begin{bmatrix} 7.98 \\ 9.00 \\ 9.50 \end{bmatrix}$. Then the *inner product* is a scalar which is computed as follows.

$$[2\quad 1\quad 2]\begin{bmatrix} 7.98 \\ 9.00 \\ 9.50 \end{bmatrix} = \begin{matrix} 2(7.98) + 1(9.00) + 2(9.50) = \\ 15.96 + 9.00 + 19.00 = \$43.96 \end{matrix}$$

The **inner product** of a $1 \times r$ matrix (row vector) and an $r \times 1$ matrix (column vector) equals the sum of the products of the corresponding elements of the matrices. Using letters to express general formulas, we have the following.

$r = 1$: $\quad [a][b] = ab$

$r = 2$: $\quad [a\quad b]\begin{bmatrix} c \\ d \end{bmatrix} = ac + bd$

$r = 3$: $\quad [a\quad b\quad c]\begin{bmatrix} d \\ e \\ f \end{bmatrix} = ad + be + cf$

$r = 4$: $\quad [a\quad b\quad c\quad d]\begin{bmatrix} e \\ f \\ g \\ h \end{bmatrix} = ae + bf + cg + dh$

Here are some other instances of inner products.

(a) $[6\quad -4]\begin{bmatrix} 3 \\ 5 \end{bmatrix} = 18 - 20 = -2$

(b) $[5\quad 3\quad 10]\begin{bmatrix} 2.00 \\ 1.00 \\ 2.00 \end{bmatrix} = 10.00 + 3.00 + 20.00 = 33.00$

(c) $[0\quad 0\quad 0]\begin{bmatrix} 871 \\ -43 \\ 61.5 \end{bmatrix} = 0 + 0 + 0 = 0$

The "inner product of $[6\quad -4]$ and $\begin{bmatrix} 13 \\ -11 \\ 10 \end{bmatrix}$" cannot be taken.

Example 2:

In baseball the total bases produced by a hitter is expressed as follows.

$$1 \times \binom{\text{Number of}}{\text{singles}} + 2 \times \binom{\text{Number of}}{\text{doubles}} + 3 \times \binom{\text{Number of}}{\text{triples}} + 4 \times \binom{\text{Number of}}{\text{home runs}}$$

This formula can be expressed as the inner product of the vector [1 2 3 4], which gives the number of bases for each type of hit, with a column vector which gives the number of singles, doubles, triples, and homers of a player (in that order). For example, if a player has hit 23 singles, 8 doubles, 2 triples, and 5 home runs, his total bases are as shown below.

$$\begin{bmatrix} 1 & 2 & 3 & 4 \end{bmatrix} \begin{bmatrix} 23 \\ 8 \\ 2 \\ 5 \end{bmatrix} = 23 + 16 + 6 + 20 = 65$$

To program the inner product operation, first input a $1 \times r$ vector **A** and an $r \times 1$ vector **B**. Then, since a sum must be accumulated, initialize to 0 a location S. In a FØR-NEXT loop compute the products of corresponding elements of the vectors and add these products to S.

Program 6-2: Compute Inner Product of Vectors

```
100  DIM A(1,20),B(20,1)
110  READ R
120  FØR I = 1 TØ R
130    READ A(1,I)
140  NEXT I
150  FØR I = 1 TØ R
160    READ B(I,1)
170  NEXT I
180  LET S = 0
190  FØR I = 1 TØ R
200    LET S = S + A(1,I) * B(I,1)
210  NEXT I
220  PRINT "INNER PRØDUCT = " S
230  GØ TØ 110
240  DATA ...
250  END
```

EXERCISES 6-5

A Give the inner product of [2 −3 4] and each of the following.

1. $\begin{bmatrix} 8 \\ -10 \\ -6 \end{bmatrix}$ **2.** $\begin{bmatrix} 1 \\ 0 \\ 1 \end{bmatrix}$ **3.** $\begin{bmatrix} 7 \\ -1 \\ 2 \end{bmatrix}$ **4.** $\begin{bmatrix} 2 & -3 & 4 \end{bmatrix}^T$

Give the inner product, if possible, for each pair of vectors.

5. $\begin{bmatrix} 6 & 5 \end{bmatrix}\begin{bmatrix} 20 \\ 30 \end{bmatrix}$

6. $\begin{bmatrix} 13 & 31 & 29 \end{bmatrix}\begin{bmatrix} 7 \\ 11 \\ -9 \\ 23 \end{bmatrix}$

7. $\begin{bmatrix} 1 & 0 & 3 & 2 \end{bmatrix}\begin{bmatrix} -16 \\ 42 \\ -5 \\ 6 \end{bmatrix}$

B

8. A customer in a grocery buys 2 quarts of milk @ 64¢/quart, 3 boxes of cereal @ 24¢/box, 2 dozen eggs @ 65¢/dozen, and a jar of mayonnaise @ 57¢/jar. Use the inner product of two vectors to compute the customer's total charge (without tax).
9. Use the inner product of two vectors to calculate the total bases of a baseball hitter with 10 singles, 4 doubles, 1 triple, and 2 home runs.
10. A steel company makes three alloys. 1.5% of alloy A is iron ore, 1.7% of alloy B is iron ore, and 2% of alloy C is iron ore. Use an inner product to calculate the total amount of iron ore needed to produce 500 tons of alloy A, 200 tons of alloy B, and 350 tons of alloy C.
11. Prepare a flowchart for Program 6-2.
12. Revise Program 6-2 so that it handles A and B as one-dimensional arrays, that is, with one subscript instead of two.

6-6 MULTIPLYING MATRICES

We introduce matrix multiplication by means of several examples.

Example 1:

Big Brain Computer Corporation maintains an armada of automobiles and trucks for its sales and maintenance forces. Table 6-4 gives the operating costs per vehicle per year.

Table 6-4 Annual Operating Costs Per Vehicle

	Automobiles	*Trucks*
Depreciation	$500	$900
Taxes	50	95
Maintenance	800	650

Table 6-5 lists the number of each type of vehicle owned by BBCC for four years.

Table 6-5 Number of Motor Vehicles Owned by BBCC

	1980	*1981*	*1982*	*1983*
Automobiles	20	25	35	50
Trucks	5	10	15	25

Here are some questions about Big Brain's vehicle costs.

Question 1: How much did automobile depreciation cost in 1980?

$$\text{Answer: } \begin{pmatrix}\text{Amount of}\\\text{depreciation}\end{pmatrix} \times \begin{pmatrix}\text{Number of}\\\text{cars in 1980}\end{pmatrix} = \$500(20) = \$10{,}000$$

Question 2: What was the amount of taxes on trucks in 1982?

$$\text{Answer: } \begin{pmatrix}\text{Taxes per}\\\text{truck}\end{pmatrix} \times \begin{pmatrix}\text{Number of}\\\text{trucks in 1982}\end{pmatrix} = \$95(15) = \$1425$$

Question 3: What was the total maintenance cost for both automobiles and trucks in 1983?

$$\text{Answer: } \underset{\begin{pmatrix}\text{Maintenance}\\\text{per car}\end{pmatrix}}{\$800} \times \underset{\begin{pmatrix}\text{Number of}\\\text{cars in 1983}\end{pmatrix}}{50} + \underset{\begin{pmatrix}\text{Maintenance}\\\text{per truck}\end{pmatrix}}{\$650} \times \underset{\begin{pmatrix}\text{Number of}\\\text{trucks in 1983}\end{pmatrix}}{25} =$$

$$\underset{\begin{pmatrix}\text{Total auto}\\\text{maintenance}\end{pmatrix}}{\$40000} + \underset{\begin{pmatrix}\text{Total truck}\\\text{maintenance}\end{pmatrix}}{\$16250} = \underset{\begin{pmatrix}\text{Total maintenance}\\\text{in 1983}\end{pmatrix}}{\$56250}$$

This last calculation is the inner product $[800 \quad 650]\begin{bmatrix}50\\25\end{bmatrix}$.

These questions and others like them can all be answered easiest from a table summarizing vehicle costs over the four year period. This table results from matrix multiplication. Let **C** = the cost matrix of Table 6-4 and **N** = the number-of-vehicles matrix from Table 6-5.

$$\mathbf{C} = \begin{bmatrix}500 & 900\\50 & 95\\800 & 650\end{bmatrix} \qquad \mathbf{N} = \begin{bmatrix}20 & 25 & 35 & 50\\5 & 10 & 15 & 25\end{bmatrix}$$

The product **C** × **N** is calculated as follows.

$$\mathbf{C} \times \mathbf{N} = \begin{bmatrix}500 & 900\\50 & 95\\800 & 650\end{bmatrix} \times \begin{bmatrix}20 & 25 & 35 & 50\\5 & 10 & 15 & 25\end{bmatrix} =$$

$$\begin{bmatrix}500(20)+900(5) & 500(25)+900(10) & 500(35)+900(15) & 500(50)+900(25)\\50(20)+\ 95(5) & 50(25)+\ 95(10) & 50(35)+\ 95(15) & 50(50)+\ 95(25)\\800(20)+650(5) & 800(25)+650(10) & 800(35)+650(15) & 800(50)+650(25)\end{bmatrix}$$

$$= \begin{bmatrix}14500 & 21500 & 31000 & 47500\\1475 & 2200 & 3175 & 4875\\19250 & 26500 & 37750 & 56250\end{bmatrix}$$

Matrix multiplication consists of a sequence of inner products, with each inner product (a scalar) forming an entry in the product matrix. Each row of matrix **C** is a vector and each column of **N** is a vector. To multiply **C** times **N**, take each row of **C** and compute its inner product with each column of **N**. For example, the inner product of the *second* row of **C** with the *third* column of **N** gives the element in the second row, third column of the product matrix (3175). The answer to Question 3 earlier is found in the third row, fourth column of **C** × **N**.

$$\begin{bmatrix} 500 & 900 \\ 50 & 95 \\ \boxed{800 \quad 650} \end{bmatrix} \times \begin{bmatrix} 20 & 25 & 35 & \boxed{50} \\ 5 & 10 & 15 & \boxed{25} \end{bmatrix} = \begin{bmatrix} 14500 & 21500 & 31000 & 47500 \\ 1475 & 2200 & 3175 & 4875 \\ 19250 & 26500 & 37750 & \boxed{56250} \end{bmatrix}$$

The product **C** × **N** can be displayed in tabular form with rows and columns labeled.

Table 6-6 Total Vehicle Costs for BBCC (1980–83)

	1980	*1981*	*1982*	*1983*
Total depreciation	$14500	$21500	$31000	$47500
Total taxes	1475	2200	3175	4875
Total maintenance	19250	26500	37750	56250

The multiplication process requires that the number of columns of the first matrix equal the number of rows of the second matrix. Otherwise the matrices cannot be multiplied. Thus, in Example 1 on page 241 **C** × **N** is possible but **N** × **C** is not.

RULE FOR MULTIPLICATION OF MATRICES

If matrix **A** has dimensions $m \times n$ and matrix **B** has dimensions $p \times q$, then **A** and **B** can be multiplied if and only if $n = p$. The product will have dimensions $m \times q$.

If $n = p$, the matrices are said to be **conformable** or **compatible**.

Check the dimensions of the matrices in Example 1 to see that the rule holds.

$$\begin{bmatrix} 500 & 900 \\ 50 & 95 \\ 800 & 650 \end{bmatrix} \times \begin{bmatrix} 20 & 25 & 35 & 50 \\ 5 & 10 & 15 & 25 \end{bmatrix} = \begin{bmatrix} 14500 & 21500 & 31000 & 47500 \\ 1475 & 2200 & 3175 & 4875 \\ 19250 & 26500 & 37750 & 56250 \end{bmatrix}$$

3×2 (m, n) — 2×4 (p, q) — 3×4 (m, q)

These must be equal. (n and p)

Multiplication of polynomials can be accomplished by matrix multiplication. Compare the "long multiplication" of algebra with matrix multiplication.

Example 2: $(4x^3 - 6x^2 + x + 3) \cdot (x^2 + 2x - 1)$

Solution: "Long Multiplication"

$$\begin{array}{rrrrrr}
4x^3 & -\,6x^2 & +\ x & +\,3 & & \\
x^2 & +\,2x & -\ 1 & & & \\
\hline
4x^5 - 6x^4 & +\ x^3 & +\ 3x^2 & & & \\
8x^4 & -\,12x^3 & +\ 2x^2 & +\,6x & & \\
 & -\ 4x^3 & +\ 6x^2 & -\ x & -\,3 & \\
\hline
4x^5 + 2x^4 & -\,15x^3 & +\,11x^2 & +\,5x & -\,3 &
\end{array}$$

Matrix Multiplication

$$[1\ \ 2\ \ -1]\begin{bmatrix} 4 & -6 & 1 & 3 & 0 & 0 \\ 0 & 4 & -6 & 1 & 3 & 0 \\ 0 & 0 & 4 & -6 & 1 & 3 \end{bmatrix} = [4\ \ 2\ \ -15\ \ 11\ \ 5\ \ -3]$$

Matrix for	"Staggered" matrix for	Matrix for
$x^2 + 2x - 1$	$4x^3 - 6x^2 + x + 3$	$4x^5 + 2x^4 - 15x^3 + 11x^2 + 5x - 3$
(1×3)	(3×6)	(1×6)

A closer examination of the two methods reveals why they yield the same result. Examine closely the third column of terms in the "long multiplication" and the inner product of the row vector and third column of the "staggered" matrix in the matrix multiplication.

$$\begin{array}{rrrrrr}
4x^3 & -\,6x^2 & +\ x & +\,3 & & \\
x^2 & +\,2x & -\ 1 & & & \\
\hline
4x^5 - 6x^4 & \boxed{+\ x^3} & +\ 3x^2 & & & \\
8x^4 & \boxed{-\,12x^3} & +\ 2x^2 & +\,6x & & \\
 & \boxed{-\ 4x^3} & +\ 6x^2 & -\ x & -\,3 & \\
\hline
4x^5 + 2x^4 & \boxed{-\,15x^3} & +\,11x^2 & +\,5x & -\,3 &
\end{array}$$

$$[1\ \ 2\ \ -1]\begin{bmatrix} 4 & -6 & \boxed{1} & 3 & 0 & 0 \\ 0 & 4 & \boxed{-6} & 1 & 3 & 0 \\ 0 & 0 & \boxed{4} & -6 & 1 & 3 \end{bmatrix} = [4\ \ 2\ \ \underbrace{1+(-12)+(-4)}\ \ 11\ \ 5\ \ -3]$$

same coefficients being added

For 2×2 matrices, since there are so few terms, multiplication can be reduced to a formula.

$$\begin{bmatrix} a & b \\ c & d \end{bmatrix} \times \begin{bmatrix} e & f \\ g & h \end{bmatrix} = \begin{bmatrix} ae + bg & af + bh \\ ce + dg & cf + dh \end{bmatrix}$$

In general, matrix multiplication is not commutative. For the 2×2 case just given,

$$\begin{bmatrix} e & f \\ g & h \end{bmatrix} \times \begin{bmatrix} a & b \\ c & d \end{bmatrix} = \begin{bmatrix} ea + fc & eb + fd \\ ga + hc & gb + hd \end{bmatrix} \neq \begin{bmatrix} a & b \\ c & d \end{bmatrix} \times \begin{bmatrix} e & f \\ g & h \end{bmatrix}.$$

In other instances the fact that matrix multiplication is not commutative is even more obvious because matrices conformable in one order cannot even be multiplied when reversed. For example,

$$\begin{bmatrix} 2 & -3 \\ 4 & 0 \end{bmatrix} \times \begin{bmatrix} 8 & 7 & 0 \\ -2 & 1 & 4 \end{bmatrix} = \begin{bmatrix} 22 & 11 & -12 \\ 32 & 28 & 0 \end{bmatrix} \quad \text{but}$$

$$\begin{bmatrix} 8 & 7 & 0 \\ -2 & 1 & 4 \end{bmatrix} \times \begin{bmatrix} 2 & -3 \\ 4 & 0 \end{bmatrix} \quad \text{cannot be multiplied.}$$

An odd fact, offered here without explanation, is that, although matrix multiplication is not commutative, it is associative, that is if **A**, **B**, and **C** are matrices and if $(\mathbf{A} \times \mathbf{B}) \times \mathbf{C}$ exists, then $(\mathbf{A} \times \mathbf{B}) \times \mathbf{C} = \mathbf{A} \times (\mathbf{B} \times \mathbf{C})$.

Like real numbers, square matrices can be raised to powers. For example, if $\mathbf{A} = \begin{bmatrix} 1 & 3 \\ -1 & 2 \end{bmatrix}$, then

$$\mathbf{A}^2 = \mathbf{A} \times \mathbf{A} = \begin{bmatrix} 1 & 3 \\ -1 & 2 \end{bmatrix} \times \begin{bmatrix} 1 & 3 \\ -1 & 2 \end{bmatrix} = \begin{bmatrix} -2 & 9 \\ -3 & 1 \end{bmatrix}$$

$$\mathbf{A}^3 = \mathbf{A}^2 \times \mathbf{A} = \begin{bmatrix} -2 & 9 \\ -3 & 1 \end{bmatrix} \times \begin{bmatrix} 1 & 3 \\ -1 & 2 \end{bmatrix} = \begin{bmatrix} -11 & 12 \\ -4 & -7 \end{bmatrix}$$

$$\mathbf{A}^4 = \mathbf{A}^3 \times \mathbf{A} = \begin{bmatrix} -11 & 12 \\ -4 & -7 \end{bmatrix} \times \begin{bmatrix} 1 & 3 \\ -1 & 2 \end{bmatrix} = \begin{bmatrix} -23 & -9 \\ 3 & -26 \end{bmatrix} \text{ and so forth.}$$

We have already seen that a set of $r \times c$ matrices possesses an additive identity element, namely the $r \times c$ zero matrix. It is natural to ask whether a class of matrices can have a *multiplicative* identity element playing a role similar to the number one.

The answer is that only a set of square matrices has a multiplicative identity. The identity for each order n consists of 1's on the main diagonal and 0's everywhere else. Thus $\begin{bmatrix} 1 & 0 \\ 0 & 1 \end{bmatrix}$ is the 2×2 identity; $\begin{bmatrix} 1 & 0 & 0 \\ 0 & 1 & 0 \\ 0 & 0 & 1 \end{bmatrix}$ is the order-3 identity; $\begin{bmatrix} 1 & 0 & 0 & 0 \\ 0 & 1 & 0 & 0 \\ 0 & 0 & 1 & 0 \\ 0 & 0 & 0 & 1 \end{bmatrix}$ is the 4×4 identity, and so forth.

Examples:

$$\begin{bmatrix} 6 & -10 \\ -5 & 7 \end{bmatrix} \times \begin{bmatrix} 1 & 0 \\ 0 & 1 \end{bmatrix} = \begin{bmatrix} 1 & 0 \\ 0 & 1 \end{bmatrix} \times \begin{bmatrix} 6 & -10 \\ -5 & 7 \end{bmatrix} = \begin{bmatrix} 6 & -10 \\ -5 & 7 \end{bmatrix}$$

$$\begin{bmatrix} 1 & 0 & 0 \\ 0 & 1 & 0 \\ 0 & 0 & 1 \end{bmatrix} \times \begin{bmatrix} 11 & 0 & -3 \\ 5 & 9 & -1 \\ -2 & 1 & 7 \end{bmatrix} = \begin{bmatrix} 11 & 0 & -3 \\ 5 & 9 & -1 \\ -2 & 1 & 7 \end{bmatrix} \times \begin{bmatrix} 1 & 0 & 0 \\ 0 & 1 & 0 \\ 0 & 0 & 1 \end{bmatrix} = \begin{bmatrix} 11 & 0 & -3 \\ 5 & 9 & -1 \\ -2 & 1 & 7 \end{bmatrix}$$

EXERCISES 6-6

A Multiply, if possible, each of the following pairs of matrices in the order shown.

1. $\begin{bmatrix} 1 & 6 \\ -6 & 1 \end{bmatrix}, \begin{bmatrix} 3 & -2 \\ 2 & 3 \end{bmatrix}$ **2.** $\begin{bmatrix} 5 & 1 & -7 \\ 0 & -3 & 6 \end{bmatrix}, \begin{bmatrix} 2 & 1 \\ 0 & -6 \end{bmatrix}$

3. $\begin{bmatrix} 2 & 1 \\ 0 & -6 \end{bmatrix}, \begin{bmatrix} 5 & 1 & -7 \\ 0 & -3 & 6 \end{bmatrix}$ **4.** $\begin{bmatrix} 61 & -47 & 92 \\ 113 & 27 & -18 \\ -9 & 86 & 59 \end{bmatrix}, \begin{bmatrix} 1 & 0 & 0 \\ 0 & 1 & 0 \\ 0 & 0 & 1 \end{bmatrix}$

5. $\begin{bmatrix} 16 & -4 & 0 \end{bmatrix}, \begin{bmatrix} 0 & 2 \\ -3 & 5 \end{bmatrix}$ **6.** $\begin{bmatrix} 2 & -4 & 6 \\ 0 & 1 & -3 \end{bmatrix}, \begin{bmatrix} -5 \\ 1 \\ 7 \end{bmatrix}$

7. $\begin{bmatrix} -3 & 5 \\ 1 & -2 \end{bmatrix}, \begin{bmatrix} -2 & -5 \\ -1 & -3 \end{bmatrix}$ **8.** $\begin{bmatrix} 2 & -1 \\ 2 & -1 \end{bmatrix}, \begin{bmatrix} 3 & 4 \\ 6 & 8 \end{bmatrix}$

9. $\begin{bmatrix} 2 & -1 \\ 3 & 4 \end{bmatrix}, \begin{bmatrix} 2 & -1 \\ 3 & 4 \end{bmatrix}^T$ **10.** $\begin{bmatrix} 5 & -9 & 23 \\ 16 & -7 & 91 \end{bmatrix}, \begin{bmatrix} 0 & 0 \\ 0 & 0 \\ 0 & 0 \end{bmatrix}$

Let $\mathbf{A} = \begin{bmatrix} 2 & 0 \\ -1 & 3 \end{bmatrix}$, $\mathbf{B} = \begin{bmatrix} 1 & 5 \\ 0 & -6 \end{bmatrix}$, and $\mathbf{C} = \begin{bmatrix} -2 & 0 \\ -4 & 7 \end{bmatrix}$. Compute, if possible, each of the following. Note: As with real numbers, multiplication is done before addition or subtraction.

11. $\mathbf{AB}$ **12.** $\mathbf{BC}$ **13.** $\mathbf{AC}$
14. $\mathbf{A}(\mathbf{B} + \mathbf{C})$ **15.** $\mathbf{AB} + \mathbf{AC}$ **16.** $\mathbf{B}(\mathbf{A} + \mathbf{C})$
17. $\mathbf{C}(\mathbf{B} - \mathbf{A})$ **18.** $\mathbf{AB} + \mathbf{C}$ **19.** $(\mathbf{AB})\mathbf{C}$
20. $\mathbf{A}(\mathbf{BC})$ **21.** $\mathbf{B} + \mathbf{A}$ **22.** $\mathbf{A}^2$
23. $\mathbf{B}^2 + 2\mathbf{C}$ **24.** $3\mathbf{A} - \mathbf{C}^2$ **25.** $\mathbf{A}^2 - \mathbf{C}^2$
26. $\mathbf{A}^3$ **27.** $\mathbf{A}^2\mathbf{B}$ **28.** $\mathbf{B}^2\mathbf{C}^2$

Let $\mathbf{L} = \begin{bmatrix} 0 & 2 & -1 \\ 3 & 1 & 5 \end{bmatrix}$, $\mathbf{M} = \begin{bmatrix} 4 & 0 \\ 6 & 4 \\ -2 & 7 \end{bmatrix}$, $\mathbf{N} = \begin{bmatrix} 10 & 8 & -3 \\ -5 & 0 & 1 \end{bmatrix}$. Compute, if possible, the following.

29. $\mathbf{LM}$ **30.** $\mathbf{MN}$ **31.** $\mathbf{LN}$ **32.** $\mathbf{L}^2$
33. $4\mathbf{L} + \mathbf{N}$ **34.** $2(\mathbf{LM})$ **35.** $\mathbf{L}(2\mathbf{M})$ **36.** $(2\mathbf{L})\mathbf{M}$
37. $\mathbf{L}^T + \mathbf{M}$ **38.** $\mathbf{L}^T\mathbf{M}^T$ **39.** $(\mathbf{LM})^T$ **40.** $(\mathbf{ML})^T$

Compute these powers.

41. $\begin{bmatrix} 1 & 1 \\ -1 & -1 \end{bmatrix}^2$ **42.** $\begin{bmatrix} \frac{1}{3} & \frac{1}{3} & \frac{1}{3} \\ \frac{1}{3} & \frac{1}{3} & \frac{1}{3} \\ \frac{1}{3} & \frac{1}{3} & \frac{1}{3} \end{bmatrix}^3$ **43.** $\begin{bmatrix} 1 & 0 \\ 2 & -1 \end{bmatrix}^2$

44. $\begin{bmatrix} 1 & 0 \\ 0 & 1 \end{bmatrix}^5$ **45.** $\begin{bmatrix} -1 & 0 \\ 0 & -1 \end{bmatrix}^4$ **46.** $\begin{bmatrix} -1 & 0 \\ 0 & 1 \end{bmatrix}^2$ **47.** $\begin{bmatrix} 1 & 0 \\ 0 & -1 \end{bmatrix}^2$

B **48.** Hiram's Clothing Store deals with a company that makes three types of women's coats. The materials needed (in square inches) for each style are shown at the right.

	Coat A	Coat B	Coat C
Dacron	30	35	15
Cotton	10	20	10
Wool	40	15	50

Hiram orders 20 of coat A, 15 coat B, and 12 coat C. Use matrix multiplication to determine how much dacron, cotton, and wool the company will need to fill Hiram's order.

49. This table gives the percentage of each element used to produce three different alloys of steel.

	Iron ore	Scrap	Manganese	Limestone	Coke
Alloy A	1.5	0.3	0.7	2.1	1.3
Alloy B	1.7	0	0.5	2.4	2.7
Alloy C	2.0	0.2	0	2.5	1.7

This next table gives the production schedule for each alloy over the next three weeks.

	Alloy (in tons)		
	A	B	C
Week 1	250	150	50
Week 2	200	200	150
Week 3	350	250	0

Use matrix multiplication to produce a matrix that gives the number of units of each component that will be needed each week. Label the rows and columns to complete the table. (Note: A process using matrix multiplication that determines the needed amounts of component parts is called an "explosion" process.)

Use matrices to multiply these polynomials.

50. $(2x - 1)(3x + 5)$
51. $(x^2 - 2x + 3)(x - 1)$
52. $(2x^3 - 2x^2 + 5x - 4)(x + 1)$
53. $(2x^3 - 4x^2 + 5)(x^2 + 3x + 2)$

6-7 MATRIX MULTIPLICATION IN BASIC

Study the pattern of matrix multiplication shown below.

$$\underset{\mathbf{A}\ (m \times n)}{\begin{bmatrix} A(1,1) & A(1,2) & \ldots & A(1,N) \\ A(2,1) & A(2,2) & \ldots & A(2,N) \\ \cdot & & & \cdot \\ \cdot & & & \cdot \\ \cdot & & & \cdot \\ A(M,1) & A(M,2) & \ldots & A(M,N) \end{bmatrix}} \times \underset{\mathbf{B}\ (n \times q)}{\begin{bmatrix} B(1,1) & B(1,2) & \ldots & B(1,Q) \\ B(2,1) & B(2,2) & \ldots & B(2,Q) \\ \cdot & & & \cdot \\ \cdot & & & \cdot \\ \cdot & & & \cdot \\ B(N,1) & B(N,2) & \ldots & B(N,Q) \end{bmatrix}} =$$

$$\underset{\mathbf{C}\ (m \times q)}{\begin{bmatrix} C(1,1) & C(1,2) & \ldots & C(1,Q) \\ C(2,1) & C(2,2) & \ldots & C(2,Q) \\ \cdot & & & \cdot \\ \cdot & & & \cdot \\ \cdot & & & \cdot \\ C(M,1) & C(M,2) & \ldots & C(M,Q) \end{bmatrix}}$$

where

$$\begin{array}{l}
C(1,1) = A(1,1) \cdot B(1,1) + A(1,2) \cdot B(2,1) + \ldots + A(1,N) \cdot B(N,1) \\
C(1,2) = A(1,1) \cdot B(1,2) + A(1,2) \cdot B(2,2) + \ldots + A(1,N) \cdot B(N,2) \\
\ldots \quad \ldots \quad \ldots \quad \ldots \quad \ldots \quad \ldots \quad \ldots \quad \ldots \\
C(1,Q) = A(1,1) \cdot B(1,Q) + A(1,2) \cdot B(2,Q) + \ldots + A(1,N) \cdot B(N,Q) \\
C(2,1) = A(2,1) \cdot B(1,1) + A(2,2) \cdot B(2,1) + \ldots + A(2,N) \cdot B(N,1) \\
C(2,2) = A(2,1) \cdot B(1,2) + A(2,2) \cdot B(2,2) + \ldots + A(2,N) \cdot B(N,2) \\
\ldots \quad \ldots \quad \ldots \quad \ldots \quad \ldots \quad \ldots \quad \ldots \quad \ldots \\
C(2,Q) = A(2,1) \cdot B(1,Q) + A(2,2) \cdot B(2,Q) + \ldots + A(2,N) \cdot B(N,Q) \\
\ldots \quad \ldots \quad \ldots \quad \ldots \quad \ldots \quad \ldots \quad \ldots \quad \ldots \\
C(M,1) = A(M,1) \cdot B(1,1) + A(M,2) \cdot B(2,1) + \ldots + A(M,N) \cdot B(N,1) \\
C(M,2) = A(M,1) \cdot B(1,2) + A(M,2) \cdot B(2,2) + \ldots + A(M,N) \cdot B(N,2) \\
\ldots \quad \ldots \quad \ldots \quad \ldots \quad \ldots \quad \ldots \quad \ldots \quad \ldots \\
C(M,Q) = A(M,1) \cdot B(1,Q) + A(M,2) \cdot B(2,Q) + \ldots + A(M,N) \cdot B(N,Q)
\end{array}$$

To program this procedure, these steps must be generalized. Each C(I, J) is a sum and hence the LET statement to compute each entry of the product will take this form.

```
LET C(I,J) = C(I,J) + A(?,?)*B(?,?)
```

The step at the bottom of the previous page will be embedded in nested FØR-NEXT loops.

```
FØR I = 1 TØ M
  FØR J = 1 TØ Q
      .
      .
      .

  NEXT J
NEXT I
```

Return to the steps on page 247 for computing C(1,1),C(2,1), . . . , and note that in each term the *second* subscript of the A-factor matches the *first* subscript of the B-factor. We need a third index, say K, to occupy these two positions. The complete multiplication loop thus is as shown below.

```
300    FØR I = 1 TØ M
310      FØR J = 1 TØ Q
320        LET C(I,J) = 0
330          FØR K = 1 TØ N
340            LET C(I,J) = C(I,J) + A(I,K)*B(K,J)
350          NEXT K
360        PRINT C(I,J);TAB(W*J/Q);
370      NEXT J
380      PRINT
390    NEXT I
```

Recall the dimensions.
A: $m \times n$
B: $n \times q$
The product **C:** $m \times q$

Line 320 is included so that when the program loops back to read the elements of the next two matrices in the DATA, the C-sums are cleared to zero.

The heart of the multiplication program has now been written. Adding the read loops and the DIM, DATA, and END statements gives the complete program. This is shown as Program 6-3 below.

Program 6-3: Multiplication of Conformable Matrices

```
120    REM       MATRIX A (M X N) IS MULTIPLIED TIMES MATRIX
130    REM       B (N X Q) TØ GIVE MATRIX C (M X Q).
140
150          DIM A(10,10), B(10,10), C(10,10)
160          READ M, N, Q
170
180          FØR I = 1 TØ M
190            FØR J = 1 TØ N
200              READ A(I,J)
210            NEXT J
```

```
220         NEXT I
230
240         FØR I = 1 TØ N
250           FØR J = 1 TØ Q
260             READ B(I,J)
270           NEXT J
280         NEXT I
290
300         FØR I = 1 TØ M
310           FØR J = 1 TØ Q
320             LET C(I,J) = 0
330               FØR K = 1 TØ N
340                 LET C(I,J) = C(I,J) + A(I,K)*B(K,J)
350               NEXT K
360             PRINT C(I,J);TAB(W*J/Q);
370           NEXT J
380           PRINT
390         NEXT I
400         PRINT
410         GØ TØ 160
420
430         DATA ...
990         END
```

Replace W *with the number of spaces on a line of your own printer or screen.*

EXERCISES 6-7

A

1. Expand Program 6-3 so that it reads matrix **A** ($m \times n$) and matrix **B** ($p \times q$), then tests whether **A** and **B** are conformable. If they are not, print a suitable message. If they are conformable, print the product **AB**.
2. Write a program to read conformable matrices **A** and **B** and print **A** and **B** and their product in this form: skip a line, print "A =", skip a line, print A, skip a line, print "B =", skip a line, print B, skip a line, print "A × B =", skip a line, and print A × B. Assume that neither **A** nor **B** has more than five columns.

B

3. Write a program to test whether multiplication of conformable square matrices is commutative. (See Ex. 24, p. 232.)
4. Write a program to test whether multiplication of conformable square matrices is associative. (See Ex. 24, p. 232.)
5. Write a program to verify that $(\mathbf{AV})^T = \mathbf{V}^T\mathbf{A}^T$, where **A** and **V** are square matrices of order n.
6. Write a program that reads a scalar k and conformable matrices **A** and **B** and tests whether $(k\mathbf{A})\mathbf{B} = k(\mathbf{AB})$.

C

7. Write a program to multiply polynomials using the matrix method of Example 2 on page 243.

Computers in Sports

Nancy Lopez watches the flight of the ball after teeing off.

At every tournament of the Professional Golfers Association (PGA), a computer-based information network serves as backup scoring system and offers statistics on the progress of the contest. A CRT terminal is used to enter the scores into the computer, which can then be used to produce an analysis of the scores. The analysis may include such items as a list of the top 15 golfers.

PROBLEM: Plan a program to update a display of golf scores.

A typical display might be as shown below. The scores are shown for each of the 18 holes and for the entire round.

```
                    1   2   3   4   . . .        18   TØTAL

1. BARKEMEYER       4   5   3                           12
2. FLØTTE           4   4                                8
3. KUHN             4   5   4                           13
4. LITWINØWICZ      5                                    5
5. PRENDERGAST      4   4                                8
6. REINE            4   4   3   4                       15
7. RESØ             5                                    5
8. RØCSKAY          3   4   4   4                       15
```

The program constantly updates the hole-by-hole matrix, giving each golfer's current total in the final column. To enter new data, the user types the number of the golfer and his or her score on the latest hole. At any point the user may request a printout of the current matrix.

A program that incorporates some of the features just explained might start by presenting the user a "menu" of choices.

```
(1)   ENTER NEW DATA AND UPDATE SCØREBØARD.
(2)   PRINT UP-TØ-DATE SCØREBØARD.
(3)   CØRRECT AN ERRØNEØUS ENTRY.
```

The lines that print the menu could be followed by these lines.

```
250  INPUT X
260  ØN X GØSUB 500,600,800
```

Depending on which choice the user selects, the program branches to one of three subroutines. The subroutine starting at 500 accepts new data and updates the "scoreboard" (the matrix **M**).

```
500   INPUT "ENTER GØLFER'S NØ., HØLE NØ. AND SCØRE";N,H,S
510   M(N,H) = S
520   M(N,19) = M(N,19) + S
530   RETURN
```

The subroutine starting at 600 prints the current scoreboard. In the lines that follow, G is the number of golfers competing.

```
600   FØR I = 1 TØ G
610     PRINT I;
620     FØR J = TØ 19
630       IF M(I,J) = 0 THEN 660
640        PRINT M(I,J);
650        GØ TØ 670
660       PRINT "";
670     NEXT J
680     PRINT
690   NEXT I
700   RETURN
```

Lines 640 and 660 are written for a terminal with 75 print positions per line.

Projects

1. Write the complete program that keeps the golfing matrix shown in the lesson up-to-date.

2. Extend the program in Project 1 to add a row to the matrix so that each time the matrix is printed, the average score for each hole is printed as the last row.

3. Revise the program in Project 1 as follows. Store in an array the **par** score for each hole. ("Par" is the number of strokes required to play a hole when the hole is skillfully played.) Then as a golfer's total for a hole is entered, the computer converts it to a positive or negative score depending on the par for each hole. A golfer's printout might look like this.

	1	2	3	4	5	. . .	18	TØTAL
KUHN	0	1	-1	0	1			1

4. Revise the program in Project 1 so that the user can first enter each golfer's cumulative total for the previous round(s) of the tournament. Then on the scoreboard the TØTAL in the last column is the current cumulative total for the entire tournament.

6-8 "MAT" COMMANDS

Matrix operations occur so frequently in programming that the creators of BASIC developed a special set of thirteen instructions for such computations. They all start with "MAT" and are summarized below.

`MAT READ A,B,C,...`	Read matrices **A**, **B**, **C**, ... All elements of **A** are read from DATA first, in row-wise sequence, then all elements of **B**, then **C**, ...
`MAT INPUT A,B,C,...`	Similar to MAT READ except that the elements are entered using the keyboard.
`MAT PRINT A,B;C...`	Print the matrices **A**, **B**, **C**, . . . with **A** and **C** in regular format (one entry per zone per line) but matrix **B** closely packed.
`MAT C = (K)*A`	Multiply matrix **A** by scalar k; store the result as matrix **C**. K (any valid arithmetic expression) must be in parentheses.
`MAT B = A`	Set the matrix **B** equal to the matrix **A**. (On some systems this command is not allowed. However, the same result can be achieved by the statement MAT B = (1)*A.)
`MAT C = A + B`	Add the matrices **A** and **B** and store the result as matrix **C**. **A** and **B** must have the same dimensions.
`MAT C = A - B`	Subtract matrix **B** from matrix **A** and store the result as matrix **C**. **A** and **B** must have the same dimensions.
`MAT C = A * B`	Multiply the matrix **A** times the matrix **B** and store the result as matrix **C**. **A** and **B** must be conformable.
`MAT C = IDN`	Set **C** equal to the multiplicative identity matrix. **C** must be a square matrix.
`MAT C = TRN(A)`	Transpose the matrix **A** and store the resulting matrix in **C**. If **A** is an $r \times c$ matrix, **C** must be a $c \times r$ matrix.
`MAT C = INV(A)`	Form the multiplicative inverse of the square matrix **A** (if it exists) and store it as **C**.
`MAT C = ZER`	Set each element of matrix **C** to zero.
`MAT C = CØN`	Set each element of matrix **C** to one. ("CON" means "constant.")

Many BASIC compilers have in storage a library of routines similar to those we have written in this chapter: a routine to read a matrix, a routine to add matrices, a routine to print a matrix, and so forth. When a program contains one of the "shorthand" MAT commands, the compiler pulls the necessary statements from the library and inserts them into the program before translating to machine language and executing.

Depending on the system, there are several ways of stating the dimensions of matrices involved in MAT commands.

1. DIM statement(s)
2. Putting dimensions in the MAT READ, ZER, CØN, and IDN statements
3. Both **1** and **2** above

A difficulty with all of these methods is that some BASIC compilers begin the row and column subscripts with zero, while other versions start numbering rows and columns with ones. Consult your manual and run experimental programs to determine the rules your system follows. To compare the possibilities, suppose a 3×5 matrix **A** is to be read. If your system begins rows and columns at zero, you must use the statement 10 DIM A(2,4) . But if the system starts rows and columns at one, use 10 DIM A(3,5) .

Matrices may also be dimensioned in the MAT READ or MAT INPUT statement itself.

Examples:

```
10 MAT READ A(2,4)          30 MAT READ B(2,6)
20 MAT READ M(1,5)          15 MAT INPUT C(3,3)
```

(Note that the statement 10 MAT READ A(2,4) does *not* mean that only the element in the second row, fourth column is read.) For this method of dimensioning a matrix, as for the DIM statement, some systems begin subscripts at zero and others start at one.

Other MAT statements may contain dimensions, as in these examples.

```
20 MAT C = ZER(4,3)      30 MAT C = CØN(5,6)
           50 MAT C = IDN(10,10)
```

On some systems, variables may be used to dimension matrices, as in this program segment.

```
10 READ R,C
20 MAT READ A(R,C)
30 MAT B = IDN(R,R)
40 MAT D = ZER(R,C)
. . . . . . . . . .

100 DATA
110 END
```

Some systems require that all matrices used in a program be listed in a DIM statement even if dimensions are also stated in the MAT statements themselves. For such systems the above program segment would need this statement.

```
15 DIM A(R,C), B(R,R), D(R,C)
```

If a DIM statement is used and dimensions are listed in a MAT statement later in the program, the MAT dimensions may not exceed the number of locations reserved by the DIM statement. Here are examples.

Incorrect Combination	Correct Combination
`10 DIM A(3,3)`	`10 DIM A(10,10)`
`20 MAT READ A(5,4)`	`20 MAT READ A(5,5)`

Another error to be avoided is putting dimensions to the left of the equal sign in a MAT calculation. All these statements are *incorrect*.

```
30 MAT C(5,5) = A + B
40 MAT R(2,2) = IDN
50 MAT X(R,C) = A * B
```

It is also erroneous to combine more than one MAT operation in a computation step.

Incorrect

```
20 MAT C = A + B - X
40 MAT Y = R * S + T
```

These calculations must be broken into several steps.

`20 MAT C = A + B - X`	becomes	`20 MAT D = A + B` `25 MAT C = D - X`
`40 MAT Y = R * S + T`	becomes	`40 MAT Z = R * S` `45 MAT Y = Z + T`

"D" and "Z" were introduced for temporary storage of intermediate results. Remember that D and Z must be DIMensioned.

A MAT READ or MAT INPUT may read more than one matrix.

Examples:

```
20 MAT READ A(R,C), B(R,C)
40 MAT READ M,N,R
50 MAT INPUT X(2,3), Y(3,4)
```

There is no question here of alternating values of the matrices being read. The statement 20 MAT READ A,B will go to the DATA lists and first read the entire matrix **A** and then read the entire matrix **B**.

Matrices may be printed in various ways. Consider the 3 × 3 matrix at the right.

$$\mathbf{A} = \begin{bmatrix} 197 & 106 & 15 \\ 361 & 27 & 192 \\ 0 & 1 & 10 \end{bmatrix}$$

50 MAT PRINT A would produce this result.

```
 197              106              15
 361              27               192
 0                1                10
```

Thus 50 MAT PRINT A is equivalent to 50 MAT PRINT A,

On the other hand, 50 MAT PRINT A; would output matrix **A** like this.

```
 107   106   15
 361   27   192
 0   1   10
```

NOTE: Some systems double-space the rows of the matrix.

More than one matrix may be printed. If $\mathbf{X} = \begin{bmatrix} 71 & -13 & 4 & 19 \\ 10 & 0 & 1 & -5 \end{bmatrix}$ and $\mathbf{Y} = \begin{bmatrix} 11 & 0 & 10 \\ 3 & 14 & 9 \\ -1 & -7 & 4 \end{bmatrix}$, then 50 MAT PRINT X,Y would produce this result.

```
 71               -13               4                 19
 10                0                1                -5

 11                0                10
 3                 14               9
-1                -7                4
```

50 MAT PRINT X;Y would cause this output.

```
71 -13   4   19
10   0   1  -5

 11               0                10
 3                14               9
-1               -7                4
```

50 MAT PRINT X;Y; would yield the following output.

```
 71 -13   4   19
 10   0   1  -5

 11   0   10
 3   14   9
-1  -7   4
```

Note that the commands 50 MAT PRINT X,Y or 50 MAT PRINT X;Y do *not* mean that X and Y will be printed side-by-side.

In the list of MAT commands at the beginning of this lesson the explanation for "MAT C = (K)*A" says that scalar K may be either a number or an expression. The examples below clarify this point.

```
10 MAT F = (2)*G        50 MAT Q = (2.89+M)*Q
              75 MAT B = (N)*A
```

On most systems the same matrix may occur on both sides of a MAT assignment in case of addition, subtraction, or scalar multiplication but not in any of the other instructions. Thus the following examples are all legal on some systems.

```
MAT A = A + B      MAT A = (K)*A
         MAT A = B - A
```

However, the following are usually illegal.

```
MAT A = B * A      MAT A = INV(A)
         MAT A = TRN(A)
```

Row vectors and column vectors are permissible in MAT instructions. As with all other matrices, the dimensions are explicitly stated prior to their use in a MAT command. Row vectors are considered to be $1 \times n$ matrices and column vectors are considered to be $n \times 1$ matrices.

Example:

```
10 DIM A(1,5),B(5,1)
20 MAT READ A,B
30 MAT C = A*B
  . . .
```

EXERCISES 6-8

A Classify each of these MAT statements as legal or illegal for your BASIC system.

1. 40 MAT D = C
2. 10 MAT READ A
3. 30 MAT READ A(3,5)
4. 20 MAT C = ZER(2,2)
5. 15 MAT READ C(0,4)
6. 30 MAT B = IDN(N,N)
7. 50 MAT C = A + B - D
8. 15 MAT PRINT A,B
9. 65 MAT PRINT A;B
10. 95 MAT C = CØN(N,N-1)
11. 80 MAT F = (A+B)*Y
12. 90 MAT X = X * Y
13. 60 MAT X1 = X + Y
14. 35 MAT R = INV(R)
15. 50 MAT PRINT X;
16. 91 MAT A = A + X
17. 60 MAT C=MAT A - MAT B
18. 72 MAT L(2,3) = CØN
19. 50 MAT M = C * (2*L+1)
20. 90 MAT B = A + A

Use MAT commands in writing the programs for Exercises 21-34.

21. Add two matrices.
22. Multiply two matrices.

23. Multiply any given matrix by any given scalar.
24. Multiply a matrix by its transpose.
25. Multiply a square matrix by its inverse.
26. Multiply an order-n square matrix by the order-n multiplicative identity.
27. Multiply a $p \times q$ matrix by the $q \times p$ constant matrix.

B 28. Test matrix addition for the commutative property. Assume that the matrices to be added have the same dimensions.
29. Test matrix addition for the associative property. Assume that the matrices to be added have the same dimensions.
30. Test matrix multiplication for the commutative property. Assume that the matrices are all of order n.
31. Test matrix multiplication for the associative property. Assume that the matrices are all of order n.
32. Test the distributive law of multiplication over addition for square matrices; that is, if **A**, **B**, and **C** are $n \times n$ matrices, is "$\mathbf{A}(\mathbf{B} + \mathbf{C}) = \mathbf{AB} + \mathbf{AC}$" true?
33. If **A** and **B** are $n \times n$ matrices, which of the following equations is true: "$(\mathbf{AB})^T = \mathbf{A}^T\mathbf{B}^T$" or "$(\mathbf{AB})^T = \mathbf{B}^T\mathbf{A}^T$"?
34. **J** is an $n \times n$ matrix that contains only 1's and **I** is the $n \times n$ identity matrix. Is "$\mathbf{J}(\mathbf{I} - \mathbf{J}) = (\mathbf{I} - \mathbf{J})\mathbf{J}$" true?

CHAPTER SUMMARY

A *matrix* is a rectangular array of numbers. The number of rows and columns of a matrix are called its *dimensions.* A matrix with only one row or only one column is called a *vector.*

In BASIC an element of a matrix is named by a double-subscripted variable such as A(I,J). Nested loops are used to read and print matrices.

Matrices with the same dimensions are added by adding corresponding elements: C(I,J) = A(I,J) + B(I,J).

A matrix can be multiplied by a *scalar* (a real number). To multiply matrix **A** by scalar k, multiply each element $A_{i,j}$ by k.

The *inner product* of a $1 \times c$ row vector with a $c \times 1$ column vector is the scalar found by multiplying corresponding elements of the vectors and adding the products. Multiplying matrices **A** and **B** consists of forming the inner product of each row of **A** with each column of **B**. However, if the number of columns of **A** does not equal the number of rows of **B**, then **A** and **B** are not *conformable* and cannot be multiplied. In a program to multiply matrices, the key statement is

```
LET C(I,J) = C(I,J) + A(I,K)*B(K,J).
```

Many BASIC systems include a set of MAT commands to read, print, add, subtract, scalar multiply, invert, and transpose matrices.

CHAPTER OBJECTIVES AND REVIEW

Objective: To write a BASIC variable with two subscripts for a given mathematical variable with two subscripts. *(Sections 6-1 and 6-2)*

Write a BASIC subscripted variable corresponding to each of these mathematical variables.

1. $y_{2,3}$ **2.** $m_{r,c}$ **3.** $b_{i+1,j-1}$ **4.** $a_{k,k}$ **5.** $s_{m+n,p}$

Objective: Where possible, to add, subtract, scalar multiply, multiply, or transpose given matrices. *(Sections 6-3 through 6-6)*

Let $\mathbf{R} = \begin{bmatrix} 4 & 1 & 0 \\ -3 & 2 & 1 \end{bmatrix}$, $\mathbf{S} = \begin{bmatrix} 0 & 6 \\ -2 & 4 \\ 1 & -3 \end{bmatrix}$, and $\mathbf{U} = \begin{bmatrix} -4 & 1 & 2 \\ 2 & -5 & 0 \end{bmatrix}$. Give, if possible, each of the following matrices.

6. $\mathbf{RS}$ **7.** $\mathbf{SR}$ **8.** $\mathbf{R} + \mathbf{U}$ **9.** $\mathbf{U} - \mathbf{R}$
10. $\mathbf{S} + \mathbf{U}$ **11.** $3\mathbf{R}$ **12.** $-7\mathbf{S}$ **13.** $\mathbf{R}^2$
14. $(\mathbf{RS})^2$ **15.** $\mathbf{R}^T$ **16.** $\mathbf{R}(\mathbf{U}^T)$ **17.** $\mathbf{R}^T\mathbf{U}$

Objective: To write a program to input matrices and (if possible) to add, subtract, scalar multiply, multiply, or transpose the matrices and print the results. *(Sections 6-2, 6-3, 6-4, and 6-7)*

18. Write the DATA steps so that the matrix below will be properly read by this program segment at the right.

$$\mathbf{A} = \begin{bmatrix} 61 & -9 & 17 & 0 \\ -6 & -1 & 0 & 14 \\ 83 & 13 & 9 & -2 \\ -4 & 1 & 8 & -1 \end{bmatrix}$$

```
10 DIM A(10, 10)
20 READ M, N
30 FØR K = 1 TØ M
40   FØR L = 1 TØ N
50     READ A(K, L)
60   NEXT L
70 NEXT K
80 DATA ...
   ...
```

19. Write a program that accepts three $r \times c$ matrices **A**, **B**, and **C**, and computes (if possible) $\mathbf{AB} + \mathbf{C}$. Do not use any MAT commands.

Objective: To use MAT commands in writing a program to solve a given problem. *(Section 6-8)*

Use MAT commands in writing the following programs.

20. Read an $r \times c$ matrix **A**, multiply it by its transpose, and then find and print the inverse of this product.

21. Read $n \times n$ matrices **P**, **Q**, and **R**, and compute $\mathbf{PQ} - \mathbf{R}$.

ROUND SIX: *PROGRAMS FOR STUDENT ASSIGNMENT*

Matrices are not studied in most mathematics classes, especially in the earlier years. For this reason, the programs of this round are directed mainly to students who are studying Algebra Two or Advanced Mathematics. As usual, some exercises require familiarity with specific mathematical knowledge, such as Pascal's Triangle, truth tables, or analytic geometry. However, most programs can be written using information found in the chapter or in the problem itself.

GENERAL INSTRUCTION:

In each exercise on pages 259 through 271, write and run a program that will do what is specified in each exercise. Do not use any MAT commands unless your teacher specifically allows them.

ALGEBRA TWO AND ADVANCED MATHEMATICS

1. Given a matrix, add each column and print the results as a one-dimensional array.

   For example, for the matrix $\begin{bmatrix} 6 & -4 & 3 \\ 7 & 0 & -9 \\ -11 & 13 & 2 \end{bmatrix}$ print 2 9 −4 .

2. Given a matrix, find the sum of each row and print the results as a one-dimensional array.

3. Search a given matrix for its largest value. Print that value together with its row and column indices.

A finite relation can be stored as a set of n ordered pairs in an $n \times 2$ matrix where the first column holds the x-values and the second column holds the corresponding y-values.

4. Determine whether a given relation is a function.

5. Functions f and g are equal if they have the same domain and if $f(x) = g(x)$ for each x in the domain. Given the ordered pairs of two functions, decide whether they are equal.
   Note: The functions $\{(1, 2), (3, 4), (5, 6)\}$ and $\{(3, 4), (5, 6), (1, 2)\}$ are equal even though the pairs are in different sequences.

In Exercises 6 and 7, build Pascal's Triangle to to the tenth row. Print in the fashion at the right.

```
1
1  1
1  2  1
1  3  3  1
   . . .
```

6. Use an $r \times c$ matrix with $r > 1$ and $c > 1$.

7. Use a $1 \times c$ matrix.

8. Read 30 numbers fed five per line for six DATA lines. Print the values five per line in the reverse order from which they were read.

In Exercises 9 through 11, input a matrix.

9. Compute the average of all elements of the matrix.

10. Compute the average of all elements in row L (L read from DATA).

11. Compute the average of all elements in column M.

12. Using 1 for true and 0 for false, build truth tables for $p \wedge q$ (p and q) and $p \vee q$ (p or q) and prove tautologies.

13. Extend Exercise 12 to three variables, p, q, and r.

14. In a branch of mathematics called "game theory," a matrix is said to have a *saddle point* if one of its elements is both (**a**) the smallest value in its row and (**b**) the largest value in its column. Read an $r \times c$ matrix and determine whether it has a saddle point. If it does, print the value and its indices.

15. Print the first ten rows of a table according to the following rules.

(a) The table has four columns called N, A, B, C.
(b) The values in the first row are 0, 1, 1, 1.
(c) In any row the value of N is one greater than its value in the preceding row.
(d) In any row the value of A is one greater than its value in the preceding row.
(e) In any row the value of B is one greater than the sum of the values of A to and including the preceding row.
(f) In any row the value of C is one greater than the sum of the values of B to and including the preceding row.

16. A square matrix is *stochastic* if (**a**) each element is nonnegative and (**b**) the sum of every row equals one. Input a square matrix and decide whether it is stochastic.

In Exercises 17–19 let the set G consist of the following matrices.

$$\begin{bmatrix}1&0&0\\0&1&0\\0&0&1\end{bmatrix} \quad \begin{bmatrix}1&0&0\\0&0&1\\0&1&0\end{bmatrix} \quad \begin{bmatrix}0&1&0\\0&0&1\\1&0&0\end{bmatrix} \quad \begin{bmatrix}0&1&0\\1&0&0\\0&0&1\end{bmatrix} \quad \begin{bmatrix}0&0&1\\1&0&0\\0&1&0\end{bmatrix} \quad \begin{bmatrix}0&0&1\\0&1&0\\1&0&0\end{bmatrix}$$

All three exercises can be solved by producing the multiplication table for G. Give letter names to each matrix.
(Note that all the matrices in G have 0 and 1 entries such that there is exactly one 1 in each row and in each column. Such matrices are called *permutation matrices*.)

17. Show that G is closed under multiplication.

18. Show that G has an identity element for multiplication.

19. Show that each element of G has a multiplicative inverse in G.

20. Given a matrix, add row L to row M and print the resulting matrix.

21. Given a matrix, add to row L two times row M and print the resulting matrix.

22. Given a matrix, find the entry X in row L having the largest absolute value; if X $\neq$ 0, divide every element in this row by X and print the resulting matrix.

In Exercises 23 and 24, read N, a positive integer greater than 1.

23. Create and print an order N square matrix having 0's in the main diagonals and 1's everywhere else.

24. Print the unit matrix (multiplicative identity matrix) of order N.

25. A square matrix **A** is *upper triangular* if $A_{i,j} = 0$ for $i > j$ and *lower triangular* if $A_{i,j} = 0$ for $i < j$. Read the order of a square matrix and a code number that determines whether the matrix is upper or lower triangular. Then input the nonzero elements and print the complete matrix.

26. Input a square matrix. Find and print the largest element on each diagonal.

In Exercises 27-29 you are to consider the sum of the elements of the main diagonal in a square matrix. This sum is called the *trace* of the matrix. The trace of matrix **X** is symbolized by tr(**X**). Input square matrices **A** and **B** and verify each of the following.

27. $\text{tr}(\mathbf{A} + \mathbf{B}) = \text{tr}(\mathbf{A}) + \text{tr}(\mathbf{B})$

28. $\text{tr}(\mathbf{AB}) = \text{tr}(\mathbf{BA})$

29. $\text{tr}(k\mathbf{A}) = k\,\text{tr}(\mathbf{A})$ where k is a scalar.

30. Input a square matrix **A** and print $\mathbf{A}$, $\mathbf{A}^2$, $\mathbf{A}^3$, and $\mathbf{A}^4$.

31. Matrix **A** is *idempotent* if $\mathbf{A}^2 = \mathbf{A}$. Input a square matrix **A** and decide whether it is idempotent. (The biggest challenge is to find DATA that yield an idempotent matrix. Do research or use trial-and-error.)

32. A square matrix **A** of order n is *nilpotent* if there exists a positive integer k such that $\mathbf{A}^k = \overline{0}$ (where $\overline{0}$ is the zero matrix of order n). Input a matrix and test whether it is nilpotent. Since this could be an infinite process, limit the search to $k \leq 5$. Two nilpotent matrices are shown below.

$$\begin{bmatrix} 1 & 1 & 1 \\ -1 & -1 & -1 \\ 1 & 1 & 0 \end{bmatrix} \qquad \begin{bmatrix} 1 & 1 \\ -1 & -1 \end{bmatrix}$$

33. Let **A** be an $n \times n$ matrix of the following form.

$$\mathbf{A} = \begin{bmatrix} 0 & 1 & 0 & 0 & \dots & 0 & 0 \\ 0 & 0 & 1 & 0 & \dots & 0 & 0 \\ 0 & 0 & 0 & 1 & \dots & 0 & 0 \\ . & . & . & . & \dots & . & . \\ \\ 0 & 0 & 0 & 0 & \dots & 0 & 1 \\ 0 & 0 & 0 & 0 & \dots & 0 & 0 \end{bmatrix}$$

That is, **A**'s entries are all zero except on the "super-diagonal." For various values of n, show that $\mathbf{A}^n = \overline{0}$ but $\mathbf{A}^{n-1} \neq \overline{0}$ (where $\overline{0}$ is the $n \times n$ zero matrix). **A** will thus be proved nilpotent (see Ex. 32, p. 261). n is called the "index of nilpotence."

34. If an order n matrix **A** is triangular (see Ex. 25, p. 261) and all entries in the main diagonal are 0, show that $\mathbf{A}^n = \overline{0}$.

In Exercises 35-37, consider a *diagonal matrix,* that is, a matrix with all elements equal to zero except those on the main diagonal.

35. Given the order n of a diagonal matrix, read just the entries on the main diagonal and print the complete matrix.

36. Input and print an order n square matrix and decide whether it is a diagonal matrix.

37. By a *scalar matrix* is meant any diagonal matrix having equal diagonal entries. Given an order n square matrix, decide whether it is a scalar matrix.

38. If a matrix has an even number of rows and an even number of columns, it can be subdivided into four matrices of equal size. Here is an example.

$$\left[\begin{array}{rrr|rrr} 2 & 8 & 17 & -5 & 23 & 81 \\ -1 & .2 & 0 & 16 & 4 & -92 \\ \hline 0 & -4 & 8 & 12 & 11 & -101 \\ 5 & -2 & 9 & -4 & 15 & 16 \end{array}\right]$$

Given a matrix, decide whether it can be subdivided. If it can, print the subdivisions as four separate matrices.

In Exercises 39-41, recall that $\mathbf{A}^T$ represents the *transpose of* **A**.

39. A matrix **A** is said to be *symmetric* if $\mathbf{A}^T = \mathbf{A}$ and *skew-symmetric* if $\mathbf{A}^T = -\mathbf{A}$. Input a square matrix **A** (do you see why a nonsquare matrix can be neither symmetric nor skew-symmetric?) and decide

whether it is symmetric, skew-symmetric, or neither.
(Note: If a matrix is skew-symmetric, the entries on its main diagonal are zero.)

40. Show that $(\mathbf{A} + \mathbf{B})^T = \mathbf{A}^T + \mathbf{B}^T$.

41. Show that $(k\mathbf{A})^T = k\mathbf{A}^T$ where k is a scalar.

The *determinant* of a square matrix is a number computed from the elements of the matrix in a special way. For example, for a 2×2 matrix $\begin{bmatrix} a & b \\ c & d \end{bmatrix}$ the determinant is $ad - bc$. The determinant is often symbolized by showing the elements of the matrix between vertical segments. Thus $\begin{vmatrix} a & b \\ c & d \end{vmatrix} = ad - bc$. Determinants are important in many applications of matrices, particularly in the solution of systems of linear equations, and methods have been developed to find the determinant of any given matrix of order n.

42. The easiest way to compute a 3×3 determinant is to study an example. Suppose that $\begin{vmatrix} 2 & 0 & 1 \\ -1 & 6 & -2 \\ 3 & 4 & 1 \end{vmatrix}$ must be computed.

(i) Rewrite the first two columns alongside the determinant.

$$\begin{vmatrix} 2 & 0 & 1 \\ -1 & 6 & -2 \\ 3 & 4 & 1 \end{vmatrix} \begin{matrix} 2 & 0 \\ -1 & 6 \\ 3 & 4 \end{matrix}$$

(ii) Add the products of the main diagonals: $12 + 0 + (-4) = 8$

$$\begin{vmatrix} 2 & 0 & 1 \\ -1 & 6 & -2 \\ 3 & 4 & 1 \end{vmatrix} \begin{matrix} 2 & 0 \\ -1 & 6 \\ 3 & 4 \end{matrix}$$

(iii) Add the products of the other diagonals: $0 + (-16) + 18 = 2$

$$\begin{vmatrix} 2 & 0 & 1 \\ -1 & 6 & -2 \\ 3 & 4 & 1 \end{vmatrix} \begin{matrix} 2 & 0 \\ -1 & 6 \\ 3 & 4 \end{matrix}$$

(iv) Subtract (iii) from (ii). Thus $8 - 2 = 6$

$$\begin{vmatrix} 2 & 0 & 1 \\ -1 & 6 & -2 \\ 3 & 4 & 1 \end{vmatrix} = 6$$

Simulate this procedure for any 3×3 determinant $\begin{vmatrix} A_{1,1} & A_{1,2} & A_{1,3} \\ A_{2,1} & A_{2,2} & A_{2,3} \\ A_{3,1} & A_{3,2} & A_{3,3} \end{vmatrix}$.

43. Unfortunately, computing a determinant of an order higher than 3 is very complicated. To facilitate matters a technique has been devised that involves the *minor* of an element of the matrix. The **minor** of $A_{i,j}$ is the matrix formed by deleting the *i*th row and *j*th column. For example, in $\begin{bmatrix} 2 & 0 & 1 & 10 \\ -1 & 6 & -2 & 0 \\ 3 & 4 & 1 & 8 \\ 0 & 5 & -7 & -11 \end{bmatrix}$ the minor of 6 (that is, of $A_{2,2}$) is $\begin{bmatrix} 2 & 1 & 10 \\ 3 & 1 & 8 \\ 0 & -7 & -11 \end{bmatrix}$. Input a square matrix A and I and J. Print the minor of A(I,J).

44. The algorithm for computing the determinant of a 4×4 matrix **A** is as follows. Pick a row or column.
  (i) Multiply each element $A_{i,j}$ by the determinant $D_{i,j}$ of its minor. (Notice that each minor is a 3×3 matrix whose determinant can be computed by the method of Exercise 42.)
  (ii) For each element $A_{i,j}$ if $i + j$ is odd, multiply $A_{i,j}D_{i,j}$ (the product obtained in (i)) by -1; that is, change the sign of the product; if $i + j$ is even, do not change the sign of $A_{i,j}D_{i,j}$.
  (iii) Sum the products $A_{i,j}D_{i,j}$ (half of which have had their signs changed in (ii)); this sum is the determinant of **A**.

Use a complete algorithm that computes the determinant of a 2×2 or 3×3 matrix to test the theorems about determinants in Exercises 45-54. "det **A**" is read "the determinant of **A**." (See Ex. 42-44.)

45. det (**A** + **B**) $\neq$ det **A** + det **B**

46. det (**AB**) = (det **A**)(det **B**)

47. det ($\mathbf{A}^T$) = det **A**.

48. The determinant of a diagonal matrix (see Ex. 35 through 37, p. 262) equals the product of its main diagonal elements. (What does this imply about the determinant of a scalar matrix?)

49. If any row or any column of matrix **A** consists entirely of 0's, then det **A** = 0.

50. det **I** = 1 where **I** is the order-*n* unit matrix (multiplicative identity matrix).

51. If two rows of matrix **A** are equal, det **A** = 0.

52. The determinant of a triangular matrix (see Ex. 25, p. 261) is the product of the entries in its main diagonal.

53. If two rows of a matrix are interchanged, the sign of the determinant is changed.

54. Adding a multiple of one row to another row of the matrix does not change the value of the determinant.

55. Use *Cramer's Rule* to solve a system of three linear equations in three variables. Let the system be

$$\begin{cases} a_{1,1}x_1 + a_{1,2}x_2 + a_{1,3}x_3 = b_1 \\ a_{2,1}x_1 + a_{2,2}x_2 + a_{2,3}x_3 = b_2 \\ a_{3,1}x_1 + a_{3,2}x_2 + a_{3,3}x_3 = b_3 \end{cases}$$

where the $a_{i,j}$ and b_i are real number constants and the x_i are the variables of the system.

To implement Cramer's Rule, first compute D, the "determinant of the system." If D = 0, print NØ UNIQUE SØLUTIØN.

$$D = \begin{vmatrix} a_{1,1} & a_{1,2} & a_{1,3} \\ a_{2,1} & a_{2,2} & a_{2,3} \\ a_{3,1} & a_{3,2} & a_{3,3} \end{vmatrix}$$

If $D \neq 0$, then $x_1 = \frac{D_{x_1}}{D}$, $x_2 = \frac{D_{x_2}}{D}$, and $x_3 = \frac{D_{x_3}}{D}$, where D_{x_i} is the determinant formed by replacing the *i*th column of D with $\begin{matrix} b_1 \\ b_2 \\ b_3 \end{matrix}$.

56. Given the coordinates of three points of a circle in the *xy*-plane, print an equation of the circle in the form

$$x^2 + y^2 + \text{C}x + \text{D}y + \text{E} = 0.$$

(Finding the equation involves solving a system of three linear equations. See Ex. 42 through 55.)

A square matrix does not necessarily possess a multiplicative inverse. If matrix **A** does have an inverse, it is denoted by $\mathbf{A}^{-1}$ and **A** is called *invertible* or *nonsingular*. It turns out that **A** has an inverse if and only if det $\mathbf{A} \neq 0$ (see Ex. 42 through 54).

57. Input a square matrix of order 2 or 3 and decide whether it is invertible.

58. Finding the inverse (if it exists) of a 2×2 matrix is not difficult. For $\mathbf{A} = \begin{bmatrix} a & b \\ c & d \end{bmatrix}$ where det $\mathbf{A} \neq 0$ (that is, $ad - bc \neq 0$),

$$\mathbf{A}^{-1} = \frac{1}{\det \mathbf{A}} \begin{vmatrix} d & -b \\ -c & a \end{vmatrix} = \begin{vmatrix} \frac{d}{\det \mathbf{A}} & \frac{-b}{\det \mathbf{A}} \\ \frac{-c}{\det \mathbf{A}} & \frac{a}{\det \mathbf{A}} \end{vmatrix}$$

(From this formula you can see why it is necessary that det $\mathbf{A} \neq 0$.) Given a 2×2 matrix **A**, print $\mathbf{A}^{-1}$ if it exists.

59. For higher order matrices the best method for finding the inverse can be explained using as an example, the matrix at the right. To find the inverse of **A**, place the 3 × 3 identify matrix I alongside **A**.

$$\mathbf{A} = \begin{bmatrix} 2 & 1 & 3 \\ 3 & 2 & 1 \\ 1 & -1 & 0 \end{bmatrix}$$

The strategy is to use row transformations to convert **A** into **I**. At the same time these transformations are also applied to **I**. When **A** has been changed into **I**, then **I** alongside it will have been changed into $\mathbf{A}^{-1}$. The particular steps are shown below.

$$\left[\begin{array}{ccc|ccc} 2 & 1 & 3 & 1 & 0 & 0 \\ 3 & 2 & 1 & 0 & 1 & 0 \\ 1 & -1 & 0 & 0 & 0 & 1 \end{array}\right]$$

Divide row 1 by the scalar 2 and row 2 by the scalar 3. →

$$\left[\begin{array}{ccc|ccc} 1 & \frac{1}{2} & \frac{3}{2} & \frac{1}{2} & 0 & 0 \\ 1 & \frac{2}{3} & \frac{1}{3} & 0 & \frac{1}{3} & 0 \\ 1 & -1 & 0 & 0 & 0 & 1 \end{array}\right]$$

Let row 2 = row 2 − row 3 and row 3 = row 1 − row 3. →

$$\left[\begin{array}{ccc|ccc} 1 & \frac{1}{2} & \frac{3}{2} & \frac{1}{2} & 0 & 0 \\ 0 & \frac{5}{3} & \frac{1}{3} & 0 & \frac{1}{3} & -1 \\ 0 & \frac{3}{2} & \frac{3}{2} & \frac{1}{2} & 0 & -1 \end{array}\right]$$

Let row 1 = row 1 − $\frac{1}{3}$ × row 3; divide row 2 by $\frac{5}{3}$ and row 3 by $\frac{3}{2}$. →

$$\left[\begin{array}{ccc|ccc} 1 & 0 & 1 & \frac{1}{3} & 0 & \frac{1}{3} \\ 0 & 1 & \frac{1}{5} & 0 & \frac{1}{5} & -\frac{3}{5} \\ 0 & 1 & 1 & \frac{1}{3} & 0 & -\frac{2}{3} \end{array}\right]$$

Let row 3 = row 3 − row 2. →

$$\left[\begin{array}{ccc|ccc} 1 & 0 & 1 & \frac{1}{3} & 0 & \frac{1}{3} \\ 0 & 1 & \frac{1}{5} & 0 & \frac{1}{5} & -\frac{3}{5} \\ 0 & 0 & \frac{4}{5} & \frac{1}{3} & -\frac{1}{5} & -\frac{1}{15} \end{array}\right]$$

Row 1 = row 1 − $\frac{5}{4}$ × row 3
Row 2 = row 2 − $\frac{1}{4}$ × row 3
Divide row 3 by $\frac{4}{5}$. →

$$\left[\begin{array}{ccc|ccc} 1 & 0 & 0 & -\frac{1}{12} & \frac{1}{4} & \frac{5}{12} \\ 0 & 1 & 0 & -\frac{1}{12} & \frac{1}{4} & -\frac{7}{12} \\ 0 & 0 & 1 & \frac{5}{12} & -\frac{1}{4} & -\frac{1}{12} \end{array}\right]$$

$\underbrace{\qquad}_{\mathbf{I}}$ $\underbrace{\qquad\qquad}_{\mathbf{A}^{-1}}$

Write a program that uses this method in finding the inverse of a square matrix.

Test the following statements about inverses. (See Ex. 59.)

60. $(\mathbf{A}^{-1})^{\mathrm{T}} = (\mathbf{A}^{\mathrm{T}})^{-1}$

61. $\det(\mathbf{A}^{-1}) = (\det \mathbf{A})^{-1}$ (See Ex. 42 through 54.)

62. A permutation matrix (see Ex. 17 through 19, p. 260) is invertible and its inverse is a permutation matrix.

63. If **A** is triangular (see Ex. 25, p. 261) and no entry on the main diagonal is zero, then **A** is invertible; if an entry on the main diagonal is zero, then **A** is singular.

64. If **A** is invertible, then for all matrices **B** of the same order as **A**, $\det(\mathbf{ABA}^{-1}) = \det \mathbf{B}$. (See Ex. 42 through 54.)

65. A linear equation over the real numbers takes the form $ax + b = c$ where a, b, and c are constants and x is the variable. Similarly there is the matrix equation $\mathbf{AX} + \mathbf{B} = \mathbf{C}$, where **A**, **B**, **C**, and **X** are all 2×2 matrices or all 3×3 matrices. Given **A**, **B**, and **C**, solve for **X**. Do not assume that a solution always exists. Mimic the steps used in solving $ax + b = c$.

$ax + b = c$	$\mathbf{AX} + \mathbf{B} = \mathbf{C}$
$ax = c - b$	$\mathbf{AX} = \mathbf{C} - \mathbf{B}$
$\frac{1}{a}(ax) = \frac{1}{a}(c - b)$	$\mathbf{A}^{-1}(\mathbf{AX}) = \mathbf{A}^{-1}(\mathbf{C} - \mathbf{B})$
$\left(\frac{1}{a} \cdot a\right)x = \frac{1}{a}(c - b)$	$(\mathbf{A}^{-1}\mathbf{A})\mathbf{X} = \mathbf{A}^{-1}(\mathbf{C} - \mathbf{B})$
$1 \cdot x = \frac{1}{a}(c - b)$	$\mathbf{I}\,\mathbf{X} = \mathbf{A}^{-1}(\mathbf{C} - \mathbf{B})$
$x = \frac{1}{a}(c - b)$	$\mathbf{X} = \mathbf{A}^{-1}(\mathbf{C} - \mathbf{B})$
Subtract b.	*Subtract* **B**.
Multiply by $\frac{1}{a}$ *(assuming $a \neq 0$).*	*Multiply by* $\mathbf{A}^{-1}$ *(if it exists).*

66. Each student in a computer science class has a student number, age as of last birthday, and a code for sex (1 = male, 2 = female). Enter these data into a three-column matrix. Determine how many males and females are in the group, the per cent of males and females, the average age of the class, and the number of students between 15 and 21 years of age, inclusive.

67. Read into a matrix six test scores for each of five students. Find the test average by student and by test.

BUSINESS

68. In many states the amount of state income tax a person pays is based simply on the amount of Federal income tax paid in the same year. Suppose that part of the state tax table is as follows.

If the Federal tax is:		then the state tax is:	
At Least	But Less Than	Single	Married
$ 25	$ 50	$12	$ 1
50	75	14	3
75	125	17	7
125	175	22	11
175	225	26	15
225	275	31	20
275	325	36	25
325	375	41	28
375	425	45	32
425	475	49	36

Enter the first, third, and fourth columns of the table as a 10×3 matrix. Then, given a person's Federal tax ($0 to $475) and a code number indicating his marriage status, print the state tax.

69. The records in an inventory file contain the part number, quantity sold last year, quantity sold last month, and current balance on hand. The computer is to print a reordering report by item. If the annual rate of the quantity sold last month is equal to or greater than the quantity sold last year, order an amount equal to the quantity sold last month if the latter is greater than the current balance; otherwise, order none. If the annual rate of the quantity sold last month is less than the quantity sold last year, order an amount equal to $\frac{1}{12}$ of the quantity sold last year if the latter is greater than the current balance; otherwise, order none. Depending on the user's preference, the program should print the status of all items or only those that need reordering.

70. The table below shows the sales totals over a one-week period.

	Mon	Tue	Wed	Thu	Fri	Sat
Salesperson 1	43	35	68	115	95	85
Salesperson 2	70	125	85	135	105	80
Salesperson 3	45	67	135	120	101	87
Salesperson 4	103	70	87	147	86	82

The computer is to calculate and print (**a**) the daily sales totals, (**b**) the weekly sales totals for each salesperson, (**c**) the total weekly sales, (**d**) the high salesperson for each day, and (**e**) the high salesperson for the week.

71. For payroll purposes a company has six departments. Within each department there are five pay grades. Within a 6 × 5 matrix store the pay rates for each department and grade. Then given an employee's employee number, his department, and pay grade, print the employee's pay rate.

72. Cushy Carpet Company sells four grades of carpet and each is discounted as the quantity of carpet ordered increases. Assume that the price structure is as follows.

	Price per square yard 1	2	3
Grade A	$11.00	$ 9.50	$ 8.25
Grade B	14.25	13.00	10.75
Grade C	17.00	15.00	12.25
Grade D	21.00	18.20	16.25

1: First 15 square yards.
2: Any part of the order exceeding 15 but not more than 25 square yards.
3: Anything over 25 square yards.

The user enters the number of rooms to be carpeted and then, for each room, the length and width. The computer then prints the square yards of carpet required and the cost of the order if grade A carpet is used, the cost if grade B is used, and so forth.

73. The C and S Manufacturing Company sells chairs and sofas to its distributors according to the schedule shown below.

Quantity	Chairs	Sofas
0-49	$60	$210
50-99	55	185
100-199	50	160
Over 199	45	135

Each week the company processes the orders received from its distributors and computes the amounts to be charged. The computer is to print the following information for each distributor.

(**a**) the distributor's identification number
(**b**) the number of chairs ordered
(**c**) the price of the chairs
(**d**) the number of sofas ordered
(**e**) the price of the sofas
(**f**) the price of the chairs and sofas

Also, after all distributors have been processed, print the sums of the items in **c**, **e**, and **f**.

PHYSICAL SCIENCES

74. The molar heat capacity at constant pressure of a substance is the amount of heat required to raise the temperature of one mole of the substance one Celsius degree at a fixed pressure. The molar heat capacity of a gas can be evaluated from the equation

$$C_p = a + bT + cT^2,$$

where T = the absolute temperature and a, b, and c are empirical constants that depend on the gas being considered. Here are the constants for several gases for the 300° to 1500° K range.

Gas	a	b	c
O_2	6.148	3.102×10^{-3}	-9.23×10^{-7}
N_2	6.524	1.250×10^{-3}	$-0{,}01 \times 10^{-7}$
CO_2	6.214	10.396×10^{-3}	-35.45×10^{-7}
H_2O	7.256	2.298×10^{-3}	2.83×10^{-7}

After storing the above data in a 4×3 matrix, allow the user to enter a code number for which gas and the initial and final values desired for a temperature range and the increment between temperature values. Then calculate and print the heat capacity from the initial value to the final value in the desired increments.

75. Enter into a 9×2 matrix the equatorial diameter (km) and density (g/cm^3) of each planet. Then calculate the mass of each planet and store these numbers as a third column of the matrix. Then create a fourth column that gives each planet's mass in relation to Earth's, i.e., Earth's mass = 1.00. In a fifth column compute each planet's equatorial diameter in relation to Earth's. Finally, print the entire 9×5 matrix with appropriate headings on the columns.

76. The empirical (simplest) formula of an unknown chemical compound can be found when the weight percentage of composition of each atom is known. So, given the percentage of composition by weight of each element in an unknown compound, find the ratio of atoms (by weight) in the compound. Print the input and the output as an $n \times 5$ matrix (where n = the number of elements in the compound) as in the following example (where element 1 = carbon, 2 = hydrogen, 3 = chlorine, and 4 = bromine).

ELEMENT	WEIGHT	PERCENT OF COMPOUND'S WEIGHT	ATOMIC WEIGHT RATIO	ATOM RATIOS
1	12	18.75	1.563	3
2	1	2.6	2.6	4.99
3	35.5	36.98	1.042	2
4	80	41.67	0.521	1

77. Enter into a 10 × 2 matrix the atomic numbers and atomic masses for any ten elements. For each element compute the number of neutrons and store this number in a third column of the matrix. Then print the entire 10 × 3 matrix with appropriate labels on the columns. Do not enter the atomic masses as integers. For example, for aluminum the atomic mass is 26.9815.

78. The final molarity of a solution formed from the addition of many like solutions of different concentrations and volume can be found from the relationship $M = \frac{m}{l}$, where M is the molarity, m = the number of moles of solute, and l = the number of liters of solution. So, given the molarity and volume of four different solutions of NaCl (atomic weight 58.5), find the composite molarity of the solution, the total weight of the solute, and the number of molecules of each solute. Print the input and output as one 4 × 6 matrix with appropriate column headings, as in this sample.

SOLUTION NUMBER	MOLARITY	VOLUME (L)	MOLES OF SOLUTE	WEIGHT OF SOLUTE (G)	MOLECULES OF SOLUTE
1	3	4	12	702	72E23
2	2	1.5	3	175.5	18E23
3	9	1.8	16.2	947.7	97.2E23
4	3.6	2.1	7.56	442.3	45.5E23

79. Refer to Exercise 105 on page 225. Create and print a matrix that gives the critical angle between any two substances in the table.

7

ADDITIONAL FEATURES OF BASIC

Many variations of the BASIC language have been developed by computer manufacturers and others. Each variation offers features of its own. The ones discussed in this chapter are available on most systems and are useful or necessary for certain types of programs, including some that are in Round Seven. However, before trying any of the features discussed here, consult the manual for your system.

7-1 "DEF" STATEMENTS

Functions other than the standard mathematical functions can be defined using a DEF statement. If a function will be needed often, it can be defined near the beginning of the program and used throughout.

Examples:

```
30 DEF FNA(X) = X↑3 - X↑2
100 DEF FNB(X,Y) = SQR(X↑2 + Y↑2)
```

It is possible to define up to 26 functions in a program: FNA, FNB, . . . , FNZ. Once the functions have been defined, later steps are made easier. Thus, in the examples just shown, 150 LET Y = FNA(.1) means that .1 will be substituted for X in the expression X ↑ 3 − X ↑ 2 and Y will be set equal to the result of the evaluation. Similarly, 180 LET Z = FNB(7, −4) means that 7 will be substituted for X and −4 for Y in the formula SQR(X ↑ 2 + Y ↑ 2) and the result stored in location Z. The statement 200 LET U = FNA(R) will cause the current value of the variable R to be substituted for X in the expression X ↑ 3 − X ↑ 2 and the result assigned to location U.

In these examples FNA was a function of one variable (X); FNB was a function of two variables (X and Y). On some systems a DEF function may have up to sixteen such "dummy" variables. X and Y are referred to as dummy variables because in the formula they are simply placeholders identified between parentheses on the left side of the equal sign in the DEF statement.

In the statement

```
90 DEF FNX(X,Y,Z) = A*X + B*Y - C*Z
```

X, Y, and Z are dummy variables, whereas A, B, and C are references to variables given values elsewhere in the program. Thus A, B, and C play the roles of constants. Do not confuse the dummy variable X with the X being used to name the function ("FNX").

The DEF statement may occur anywhere in the program, and the expression to the right of the equal sign may be any formula that fits on one line. It may include any combination of other functions, including ones defined by other DEF statements, and it may involve variables other than the ones denoting the arguments of the function.

Examples:

```
20 DEF FNC(X) = SIN(X)*CØS(X)/360
55 DEF FNR(A,B) = FNC(A) + FNC(B)
80 DEF FNG(R,S,T) = R*S*T/(M-N)
```

"FN" expressions may be used in LET, IF . . . THEN, and PRINT statements.

Examples:

```
40 LET Q = FNA(R) * X - Z
90 IF FNP(X) = 3.14159 THEN 180
55 PRINT X, FNA(X), FNB(X)
65 IF FNR(3.7) = FNM(2.6) THEN 10
```

EXERCISES 7-1

A Write *Yes* or *No* to show whether each of the following is a legal BASIC statement on your system.

1. `50 DEF FNA(X) = 3 * X - 7`
2. `10 DEF FN(Y) = 4/Y + Y/4`
3. `30 DEF FNZ(A) = 9 * X - 13`
4. `81 DEF FNC(R,S) = (R + 7)/3.14159`
5. `20 IF FNA(I) <FNA(I+1) THEN 40`
6. `90 PRINT "F("A") = " FNZ(A)`
7. `80 LET R = FNX(2*R)`
8. `50 DEF G(X) = X*X - X/2`
9. On some systems a defined function must fit on one line. Assume that the following function is too long for one line and break it into two or more functions in DEF statements.

$$g(x,y) = \frac{ax^3 + bx^2 + cx + d}{ex^2 + fx + g} - |y^3 + y^2 + y - 100|$$

7-2 STRINGS AND STRING VARIABLES

Many computer applications involve processing *alpha*betic and *numeric* data (abbreviated **alphanumeric** data), particularly names, addresses, categories, and so forth. As an example, consider the following table, which shows the number of attempted passes (Atts), completed passes (Comp), and other statistical information for a season of play in a regional football league.

Player, Team	Atts	Comp	Yds Gained	TD	Had Int
Wren, Smithville	197	106	1854	15	11
Litwin, Holbrook	361	185	2734	19	17
Garcia, Elm City	426	221	3302	34	25
Muller, Yarmouth	161	84	1123	4	6
Blauvelt, Deep Harbor	324	158	2253	10	11

To store the names of the players and their teams, "string variables" are used. A "string" is any sequence of alphanumeric characters (excluding certain special control characters). "LITWIN", "SMITHVILLE", and "YDS GAINED" are examples of strings, as are "1781 MADISØN AVENUE", "DR. RØSE T. CALIFANØ" and "3302".

A *string variable* is denoted by a letter followed by a "$". Up to twenty-six string variables can be used in a program: A$, B$, C$, . . . , Z$. A **string variable** names a memory location that will store alphanumeric characters.

On some systems the size of a string is limited to fifteen characters, including blanks. Longer strings must be broken into parts. Thus, for "1781 MADISØN AVENUE", A$ could store "1781 MADISØN AV" and B$ could hold "ENUE". Furthermore, some systems require that strings contain at least six characters. Blanks must be used to extend shorter strings. Thus, "WREN" must be handled as "WREN ".

String variables may appear in INPUT, LET, IF . . . THEN, and PRINT statements. Strings may occur in LET, IF . . . THEN, and PRINT statements.

An INPUT statement may contain string variables intermixed with ordinary BASIC variables.

Examples:

```
10 INPUT A$
70 INPUT C$,X,Y
```

To respond to 70 INPUT C$,X,Y the user might type (after the question mark typed by the computer)

? LITWIN,361,185 or "LITWIN",361,185

depending on the computer system used.

The quotation marks will not be stored as part of the string LITWIN but rather act as in a PRINT statement to show where the string begins and ends, since blanks and commas can be valid parts of a string. (On these systems, since double quotation marks enclose a string, only single quotation marks may be used within a string.)

Some versions of BASIC allow strings in DATA lines and therefore allow string variables in READ statements.

Example:

```
10 READ C$,X,Y
    .
    .
    .
90 DATA WREN,197,106,LITWIN,361,185
   ...
```

Other systems allow strings in DATA statements but only if each string is enclosed in double quotation marks.

Example:

```
10 READ C$,X,Y
    .
    .
    .
90 DATA "WREN   ",197,106,"LITWIN",361,185
   ...
```

On systems where strings are not allowed in DATA statements, strings are often read from and written to external data files, as will be explained in the next lesson.

Strings and string variables may appear in only two forms of the LET statement. The first is used to replace a string variable with the contents of another string variable.

Example:

```
50 LET G$ = H$
```

The second form is used to assign a string to a string variable.

Examples:

```
60 LET J$ = "YDS GAINED"
75 LET X$ = "GARCIA"
```

A string or string variable is allowed on each side of the equality symbol in the IF clause of an IF . . . THEN statement. In fact, all six of the standard relations (=, <, >, <>, <=, >=) are permitted. This is shown in the examples that appear at the top of the next page.

Examples:

```
100 IF N$ = "SMITH" THEN 105
120 IF X$ = "END ØF FILE" THEN 9999
80 IF A$ <> B$ THEN 205
300 IF "JUNE" < M$ THEN 305
40 IF D$ >= "FRIDAY" THEN 60
```

A letter is "less than" another letter if it is closer to the beginning of the alphabet. Thus "A" < "B" < "C" < "D" < . . . < "Z". When strings of different lengths are compared, the shorter string and the corresponding part of the longer string are used. Thus, "ANDERSEN" < "ATWØØD". If all letters compared are the same, the shorter string is taken to be the lesser of the two. Thus if names are being sorted into alphabetical order, "SMITH" will be placed ahead of "SMITHSØN", as desired.

PRINT statements may contain string variables and strings intermixed with ordinary BASIC variables.

Examples:

```
35 PRINT A,B$,C$;N
100 PRINT "THE WINNERS ARE" X$;Y$
```

A semicolon after a string variable in a PRINT statement causes the string to be printed and the variable following that string to be directly connected to it. Thus, in the earlier example where "1781 MADISØN AVENUE" had to be broken into two variables, A$ ("1781 MADISØN AV") and B$ ("ENUE"), the string could be printed correctly with the following statement.

```
90 PRINT A$;B$
```

The output would be 1781 MADISØN AVENUE as desired.

On many systems, strings can be set up as one-dimensional arrays only. Two- or three-dimensional string arrays are not allowed. As with numerical arrays, any string array with more than ten entries must be dimensioned. Here are examples of statements involving string variables.

```
10 DIM A(20),C$(20),A$(12),D(10,5)
20 INPUT C$(10)
5 INPUT M$,N$(I)
30 IF M$(I) = R$(J) THEN 75
100 LET X$(100) = "ØUT ØF DATA"
```

Some systems allow string arrays in MAT READ, MAT INPUT, and MAT PRINT statements. Here are some examples.

```
20 MAT READ A$,X$          15 MAT INPUT C$
10 MAT PRINT R$            90 MAT PRINT B$;
           85 MAT PRINT T$,W$
```

When using string variables, remember that X and X$ are two different variables. Location X holds a number; X$ stores a string. X(I) would be still another variable representing an element of the one-dimensional numeric array X. X$(I) might be a fourth variable representing an element of the one-dimensional string array X$. Your system may not allow X and X$ to be both subscripted and not subscripted in the same program.

Most systems have some special functions that operate on strings. (In what follows, consult the manual for your system to see whether it has the functions below or their equivalent.) One such function is LEN, which can be used to count the number of characters in a string. For example, if A$ = "CØMPUTER", then LEN(A$) = 8.

Inside any computer all data, including letters and special characters, such as "$", "+", and ".", are stored as integers. A widely used code is ASCII (American Standard Code for Information Interchange). It is sometimes handy to be able to use the numerical code for a character. On many systems the ASC function lets you do this. For example, the ASCII code for "A" is 65. So if G$ is a student's grade, the statement

```
50 IF ASC(G$) = 65 THEN 100
```

could be used to test whether the student made an "A". On some systems the function equivalent to ASC is called STR$.

The CHR functions operates in the opposite manner from ASC. For example, CHR(65) would represent "A". On some systems the CHR function may be named CHR$ or CHAR$.

Some functions manipulate the parts of a string. For example, LEFT$ (or LEFT) isolates a specific number of characters starting from the left end of a string. Thus, LEFT$(A$, 4) gives the first four characters in the string A$. Similarly RIGHT$ (or RIGHT) "picks off" characters from the right end of a string. MID$ (or MID) pulls out characters from the middle of a string. For example, MID$("CØMPUTER",4,3) gives "PUT", which are the *three* characters starting from the *fourth* character from the left end of the string "CØMPUTER".

On some computers the STRING$ function can be used to print a character many times. For example, a line of asterisks might be desirable for separating parts of an output or in the drawing of a diagram or figure. Then

```
PRINT STRING$(75,42)
```

would print 75 asterisks. (The ASCII code for "*" is 42.) Some systems would allow the statement PRINT STRING$(75,"*"), which saves the user the trouble of finding the ASCII code for the desired character.

EXERCISES 7-2

A Write *Yes* or *No* to show whether each of the following is a valid statement on your system.

1. `10 READ A$`
2. `5 DIM R$(20),X(15)`
3. `15 LET M$ = T$ + 1`
4. `53 PRINT C$,C`
5. `8 READ N$(J)`
6. `84 DIM M$(10,10)`
7. `17 INPUT J1$`
8. `15 MAT READ A$`
9. `20 MAT READ A$(10)`
10. `10 MAT INPUT X$,Y$`
11. `35 PRINT Z$;`
12. `35 MAT PRINT Z$;`
13. `35 MAT PRINT Z$`
14. `100 LET N$ = "RØY"`
15. `20 LET A = "THE END"`
16. `30 IF X$ = Y$ THEN 100`
17. `92 IF B$ = "ENDFILE" THEN 99`
18. `85 IF K$ = 9999 THEN 1000`
19. `70 PRINT D$ " IS THE WINNER"`
20. `19 LET Z$ = "CØMPLETIØNS"`
21. `100 DATA SMITH ,JØNES ,71, 87`
22. `100 DATA "SMITH ","JØNES ",71,87`
23. `100 LET M$ = "AUTENSPERGER, CHARLES"`

In Exercises 24-30, write the given program to conform to the rules of your system.

24. Read the names of ten students and their test scores. Print the list of student names and corresponding scores from the highest score to the lowest.

25. Read ten names. Print only the name that should come first in alphabetical order.

26. Given a string, print the characters of the string in reverse order without modifying the contents of the original string.

27. The names of the twelve months of the year are listed in DATA statements. Write the steps that are needed to print the proper month name when the month number is entered by means of an INPUT statement.

B **28.** Count the number of times that each vowel occurs in a sample text that you select.

29. Merge two lists, each of which is in alphabetical order, into one list that is in alphabetical order.

30. Hockey standings are based on each team's number of "points." A win is two points, a tie is one point, and a loss is no points. Write a program that prints the standings in descending point order, given the name of each team and its number of wins, ties, and losses.

7-3 FILE OPERATIONS

Thus far in this book, all data have been either taken from the program itself by means of READ and DATA statements or entered from the keyboard during the running of the program by means of INPUT statements. But on many systems data can be stored in "files," which are kept in auxiliary storage, usually some form of disk or possibly tape storage. Special commands are used to write data to and read data from such files. The following paragraphs explain some common methods for working with files. However, in this area there is great variability among systems, and you should consult the manual for your system before attempting programs involving files.

Suppose a program must be written to rank the seniors of a high school. The input file contains the code number, last name, and grade-point average (in that order) of each of the 305 seniors in the graduating class. The data file should be entered (by paper tape, cassette tape, or from the keyboard) into the computer system. This file must be given a name, say SENIØR. (Usually file names are limited to a maximum of six characters.) When the entire list has been typed, the SAVE command should be given. This causes the file to be written into auxiliary storage.

Data files usually require the following format: line number of up to five digits (some systems do not use line numbers for data files), blank, then the items separated by commas. The format is similar to DATA lines in a program except that the word DATA is not used. Thus, the file SENIØR might be entered in the following manner.

```
NEW SENIØR          Some systems use a colon here.
READY
1  1003,AARØN    ,2.63
2  1010,ARMBRUSTER  A,3.02
3  1011,ARMBRUSTER  L,2.31
4  1023,ATTWATER,1.89
5  1031,BARFIELD,3.92
      ...
303  1973,WITTINGHAM,2.47
304  1985,YEAGER,3.52
305  1992,ZINN    ,2.64
SAVE
```

Now that SENIØR has been stored, a program can read the data from the file.

A common way to do this is shown by the following program segment.

```
100          FILES SENIØR,ØUTPUT
110          DIM C(305),N$(305),G(305)
120          FØR I = 1 TØ 305
130            READ #1, C(I), N$(I), G(I)
140
150    REM       C(I)   =  STUDENT CØDE NUMBER
160    REM       N$(I)  =  STUDENT NAME
170    REM       G(I)   =  STUDENT GPA
180
190          NEXT I
200       ...
```

The FILES statement (line 100 above) lists the names of all files that are to be used in the program. Since SENIØR is the first listed, it is referred to as file #1. So in line 130 READ #1 means "read from the file SENIØR." The file ØUTPUT will be known in this program as file #2. The statement 200 WRITE #2, A$, P would write the current values of A$ and P into the file ØUTPUT. Each line written would be preceded by a line number automatically generated by the system. On the other hand, on some systems PRINT #2, A$, P would write the two items without first putting a line number.

Generally, whatever can be printed on the terminal can be printed in a file, as shown by the following sample statements.

```
160   WRITE #1, "PERIMETER = " P
185   PRINT #6, TAB(10); "STUDENT"; TAB(20); "GPA"
210   WRITE #2, I; X(I), Y(I)
```

The comma, semicolon, and TAB function operate in the WRITE *#n* and PRINT *#n* statements just as in the ordinary PRINT command.

Some systems do not use the FILES statement. Instead the name of the file is put right in the input or output command as shown below.

```
50    INPUT:SENIØR:  C(I),N$(I),G(I)
90    PRINT:ØUTPUT:  "PERIMETER = " P
```

On other systems the ØPEN command serves the same purpose as the FILES statement, as shown below.

```
100   ØPEN SENIØR, ØUTPUT
310   CLØSE SENIØR <----------
```

This statement disconnects the program from the file.

Usually systems allow the equivalent of MAT READ and MAT PRINT for file input/output, as in the following examples.

```
90    MAT READ #1, A, B       80    MAT INPUT:WAGES: X
110    MAT PRINT #2, C; D     140    MAT PRINT:CØSTS: X, Y;
```

Here are some other statements that various systems use.

Statement	*Explanation*
80 IF END #1 THEN 100 or 80 IF EØF #1 THEN 100	When the end of file #1 is reached, go to statement 100.
60 IF MØRE #1 THEN 10	If file #1 still has more data in it, return to line 10.
70 SCRATCH #1 or 70 SCRATCH:SENIØR:	Erase file #1 (SENIØR).
80 RESTØRE #1 or 80 RESTØRE 1 or 80 RESTØRE:SENIØR:	Set the "data pointer" back to the beginning of file #1 (SENIØR).

EXERCISES 7-3

A Write *Yes* or *No* to indicate whether each statement is allowed on your system.

1. `280 READ #1, A, B` **2.** `280 INPUT:DATA1: A, B`
3. `600 SCRATCH #1` **4.** `205 MAT READ #2, X, Y`
5. `600 SCRATCH:DATA1:` **6.** `205 MAT READ:DATA2: X, Y`
7. `710 RESTØRE #1` **8.** `710 RESTØRE:DATA1:`
9. `710 RESTØRE 1` **10.** `550 MAT PRINT #3, X, Y`
11. `600 CLØSE DATA1` **12.** `550 MAT PRINT:ØUTPUT: X, Y`
13. `100 FILES DATA1,DATA2,ØUTPUT`
14. `100 ØPEN DATA1,DATA2,ØUTPUT`
15. `550 WRITE #3, "GPA = " G(I)`
16. `550 PRINT #3, "GPA = " G(I)`
17. `550 PRINT:ØUTPUT:"GPA = " G(I)`
18. `680 IF END #2 THEN 800`
19. `680 IF MØRE #2 THEN 610`

20. Refer to Exercise 24 on page 278. Revise the program to read from an external file the names of 20 students and their test scores. Then scratch the file and rewrite it with the names and scores rearranged in order from highest-scoring to lowest.

B **21.** Refer to Exercise 29 on page 278. Revise the program to read the two alphabetical lists from two files. Then write the merged list into a third file.

22. Set up a file of real estate listings. Each listing contains a line number, the name and phone number of the owner, the address, the section of the city, style of house (ranch, split-level, etc.), and price. Then write a program to search the file and list any houses satisfying requirements entered by a user.

7-4 RANDOM NUMBERS AND THE "RND" FUNCTION

Random events, such as tossing a coin, rolling dice, and dealing cards, can be simulated by a computer by means of the RND function. When it is used, a value is randomly selected from the interval zero to one. That is, if LET X = RND(I) or, on some systems, LET X = RND is executed, X will be set equal to a six-digit decimal number greater than 0 and less than 1.

The exact method used to generate the random number varies from computer to computer but it can be compared to spinning a roulette wheel: the number on which the ball ultimately comes to rest depends on the number on which the ball was placed when the wheel was spun and the amount of force expended in whirling the wheel. The argument of the RND function corresponds to the position of the ball when spinning begins. If the argument is zero, the function will generate a random number. If the RND function is executed again in the program, a second number is produced and so on. However, the next time that program is run, the computer will generate the *same* sequence of numbers.

On many systems if a different starting number is desired each time the program is executed (as is usually the case for programs simulating games or sports), a negative argument must be used for RND. A negative argument causes the RND function first to produce a random number, which is then used as the starting point for producing additional random numbers. If a positive argument is used, a random number based on its value is generated. Thus, a negative argument produces the "most random" numbers. (The rule just mentioned is not universal; on some systems the argument of RND is purely a "dummy" value or variable and has no effect on the random number generation so that the same sequence of numbers is produced every time the program is run. Another possibility is the RANDØMIZE command explained on page 283.)

As an example consider this program to generate five random numbers. Two separate runs of the program are shown.

```
10     FØR I = 1 TØ 5
20       PRINT I, RND(-I)
21  REM  NØTE THE NEGATIVE ARGUMENT FØR RND IN LINE 20.
30     NEXT I
40     END
```

First Run		Second Run	
1	.897334	1	.803628
2	.673334	2	.737032
3	3.14714E-2	3	.130812
4	.114375	4	.612766
5	.157887	5	.788928

On some systems, the command RANDØMIZE (or perhaps RANDØM) can be placed at the beginning of a program to initialize the system's random number generator. The effect is to give different sets of random numbers each time the program is executed.

If A = RND(−I), then A is just as likely to be less than $\frac{1}{2}$ as greater than $\frac{1}{2}$. Hence we may simulate tossing a coin by executing RND(−I) and testing whether the result is less than $\frac{1}{2}$, as in this program segment.

```
10 IF RND(-I) < .5 THEN 50
20 PRINT "TAILS"
. . . . . . . . . . . . . .
50 PRINT  "HEADS"
. . . . . . . . . . . . . .
```

Coin-tossing could also be simulated by generating a random number, multiplying by ten, and taking the INT part of the result.

```
50 LET C = INT(10*RND(X))
```

C will thus be a member of {0, 1, 2, 3, 4, 5, 6, 7, 8, 9}. Test if C is even or odd and arbitrarily equate "even" with "heads" and "odds" with "tails" (or vice-versa). On some systems the above approach is made easy because RND(X), where X is a positive integer, will generate a random integer between 1 and X, inclusive.

Now suppose we want to examine the results of numerous rolls of a die. This means we want to generate the integers 1 to 6 at random with equal probability. To accomplish this result, divide the interval 0 to 1 into six equal parts. The table below shows one way to distribute the die faces.

Random numbers	Die faces
.000000 to .166666	1
.166667 to .333333	2
.333334 to .499999	3
.500000 to .666666	4
.666667 to .833332	5
.833333 to .999999	6

To "roll" two dice, generate two random numbers, convert to integers as above, and add the integers together.

For card games the random number generator can be used to "shuffle" the "deck." First produce a random number that converts to one of the four suits (diamonds, hearts, clubs, spades); then generate a second random number to decide the card within the suit (ace, deuce, . . . , ten, jack, queen, king). A special problem here is that a list of cards already dealt in the hand must be stored in order to avoid dealing the same card twice. After generating two random numbers giving the suit and card, the program must check the array of previously used cards. If this card has already appeared, discard it and generate another card.

Coin tossing, rolling a die, and dealing a card are experiments that are relatively easy to simulate since each outcome is equally probable. This is not the case with more complicated games such as boxing, football, and baseball simulations. A good baseball program, for example, must weight the random numbers to produce a realistic proportion of hits, walks, and outs for particular hitters against particular pitchers. A crude approach, just to illustrate this point, would be to allow ten possible numbers to be produced by the random number generator; for a .300 hitter (one who hits safely 30% of the time) seven of the numbers would represent outs and three would represent hits. Whether the hit is a single, double, triple, or home run could depend on the results of another random generation, weighted according to the hitter's power statistics collected from his past performance.

EXERCISES 7-4

A What value might be assigned to Y by the following statements?

Example: 50 LET Y = INT(10*RND(X)) **Answer:** An integer from 0 to 9, inclusive

1. `50 LET Y = INT(6*RND(X) + 1)`
2. `50 LET Y = 10*INT(RND(X))`
3. `50 LET Y = INT(6*RND(X)) + 1`
4. `50 LET Y = INT(10*RND(X)) - 2*INT(10*RND(X)/2)`

Write a LET statement involving the RND function that will assign to Y a value from each set.

5. A random number between 1 and 2.
6. A random number between 0 and 10.
7. A random even integer from 0 to 18, inclusive.

In Exercises 8-10, write programs for your system to execute the random events described.

8. Flip a coin 1000 times and count the number of heads and the number of tails. Use the first method explained in the lesson, that is, decide whether the random number is less than .5 or greater than .5.
9. Flip a coin 1000 times and count the number of heads and the number of tails. Use the second method explained in the lesson, that is, convert the random number to an integer and decide whether the integer is even or odd.

B **10.** Simulate the game of "pick a card." That is, when the program is run, the computer prints the name of a card randomly selected from a deck of 52 cards. (You may want to use the ØN statement explained on page 288.)

7-5 ADDITIONAL FUNCTIONS: EXP, LØG, SGN

Several standard mathematical functions have been defined and stored in the computer for ready use. They are sometimes called "library functions." Here are some of them.

EXP(X) Calculates e^x where "e" is the base of the natural logarithm system. ("e" is an irrational number approximately equal to 2.7183.)

LØG(X), or LØGE(X) Finds the natural (base e) logarithm of X. This expression is often written "ln x" in mathematics texts.

SGN(X) Determines the sign of a real variable or formula. If the value of the expression "X" is positive, SGN(X) = 1; if the value is negative, SGN(X) = −1; if the value is zero, SGN(X) = 0.

Here are examples of BASIC statements involving these functions.

```
10 LET Y = EXP(X↑2 - 3)
97 IF LØG(X) > 2.7183 THEN 150
65 PRINT SGN(Z*Y);LØG(ABS(Z*Y))
110 DEF FNA(X) = EXP(-X↑3)
```

EXERCISES 7-5

A **1.** Write a program to compute e^x using the following series.

$$e^x = 1 + x + \frac{x^2}{2!} + \frac{x^3}{3!} + \ldots$$

Compare the results with BASIC's EXP(X) function.

2. Write your own program to accomplish the same results as the SGN function.

3. Two functions, sinh x ("hyperbolic sine") and cosh x ("hyperbolic cosine"), are graphed below and defined as shown.

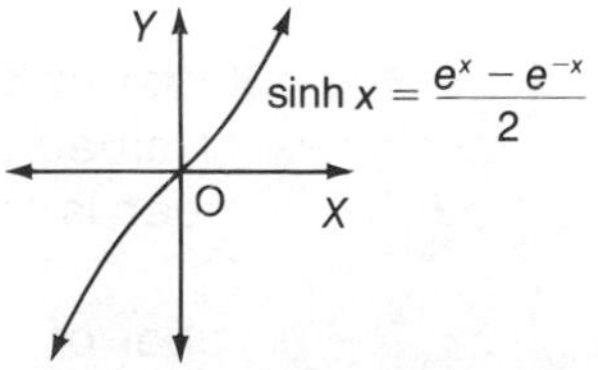

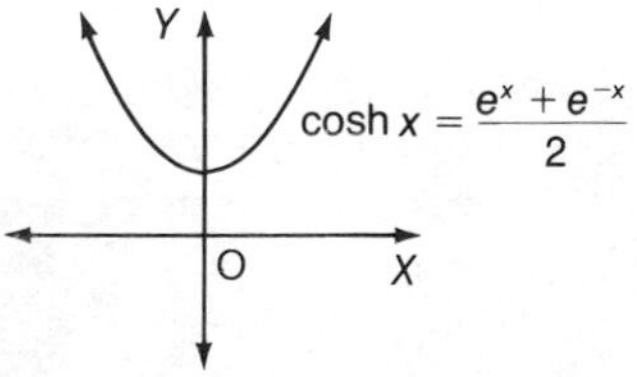

Write a program to compute sinh x and cosh x.

4. The hyperbolic sine (see Exercise 3) can be computed using the series at the right.

$$\sinh x = x + \frac{x^3}{3!} + \frac{x^5}{5!} + \ldots$$

Write a program that uses this series to evaluate sinh x. Then compare the value obtained using the series with the value obtained using the formula in Exercise 3.

Computers in Public Health

The computerized games being played in more and more homes are **simulations** (imitations) of real events. Computers enable scientists to set up and manipulate mathematical models of phenomena of interest, such as the flight of a rocket or the movement of electrons in an atom.

PROBLEM: Simulate the gradual spread of a contagious disease through a population.

Program Outline

1. Generate a population of N individuals randomly placed in "cells" on a grid, the dimensions of which depend on the size of your printer or screen. Display the individuals with, say, an asterisk (*).
2. Give the disease to one individual, either randomly or by allowing the user to specify the individual.
3. Assume that the disease is transmitted according to the following rule.

   The probability of the disease infecting an individual in a cell adjacent to an infected individual is .8.

4. During one "time period," that is, one manipulation of the matrix of individuals, focus on each diseased individual and decide, by generating random numbers, whether neighboring individuals will receive the disease. Then display the population, indicating the diseased cells by a different character, say "Ø". At the bottom of the display, print the number of diseased individuals and the number of healthy individuals.
5. Ask the user whether another time period is desired. If it is, repeat step 4. Assume that a diseased individual is sick for, say, five time periods.

One essential task of the program is keeping track of which individuals are diseased and for how many time periods. This can be done in a matrix **P**

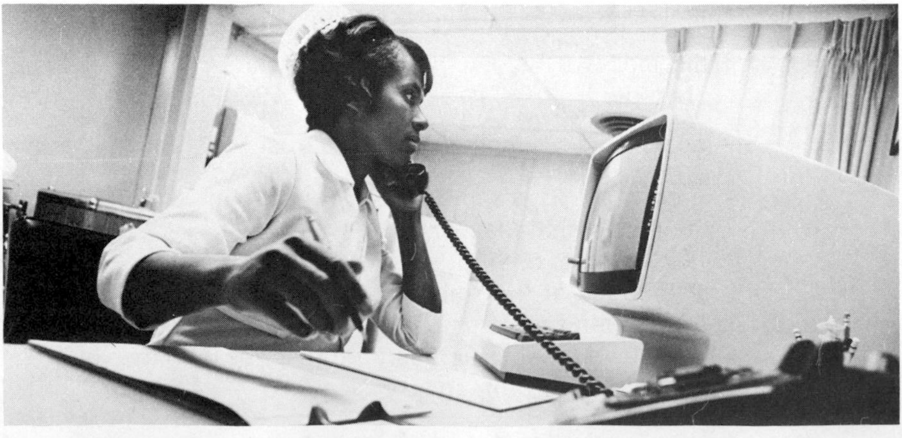

whose entries are -1, 0, 1, 2, 3, 4, or 5. A entry of -1 means that the cell is vacant. 0 indicates a healthy individual. 1, 2, 3, 4, or 5 represents an individual who has been sick for that many time periods.

Consider the section of matrix **P** on the right. Suppose the individual in cell P(I,J) is diseased. The following program segment decides which neighboring individuals, if any, will be infected.

P(I-1,J-1)	P(I-1,J)	P(I-1,J+1)
P(I,J-1)	P(I,J)	P(I,J+1)
P(I+1,J-1)	P(I+1,J)	P(I+1,J+1)

```
510  FØR K = I-1 TØ I+1
520    FØR L = J-1 TØ J+1
530      IF P(K,L) = -1 THEN 570
540       IF P(K,L) > 0 THEN 570
550        IF RND > .8 THEN 570 ←
560         LET P(K,L) = 1
570    NEXT L
580  NEXT K
```

Your system may require an argument after RND.

Line 530 means *if the cell is empty, ignore it.*
Line 540 means *if the individual is already diseased, ignore the cell.*
Line 550 means *if* RND > *.8, the disease is not transmitted.*
Line 560 means *transmit the disease.*

The following is an important point. If an individual receives the disease during one time period, he or she cannot transmit the disease until the *next* time period. This problem can be handled by first scanning matrix **P** (before statements 500-580 above are executed) and adding one to the number in each diseased cell but setting back to 0 any cell that equals 5. Then when the matrix is scanned again to find diseased individuals, only those whose number is 2 or greater are considered. At this point any "1" cell has just received the disease during this time period.

Projects

1. Write the complete program outlined above.
2. Complicate the model by allowing the individuals to move to adjacent empty cells. Let the probability of moving in a given direction be .1.
3. Add to the model the assumption that a diseased individual dies with a probability of .2.
4. Complicate the model by assuming that the disease has a **latency period** (period of time before the disease exhibits symptoms) of two time periods. During this period, the individual can transmit the disease. However, once the latency is over, the individual is *quarantined* (removed from the grid) for five time periods.

7-6 "ØN" STATEMENTS

The ØN statement provides a means of combining several equality-type IF . . . THEN statements into one. Thus the sequence of statements

```
60 IF X = 1 THEN 200
70 IF X = 2 THEN 170
80 IF X = 3 THEN 215
```

can be condensed to the following ØN statement.

```
60 ØN X GØ TØ 200, 170, 215
```

"X" may be a variable or a formula. Any number of line numbers may follow GØ TØ as long as the entire statement fits onto one line. Here is another example.

```
35 ØN A*B - C GØ TØ 100,110,60,135,10
```

Execution of this statement will proceed as follows.

1. INT(A*B − C) is computed.
2. If INT(A*B − C) = 1, execution branches to line 100.
3. If INT(A*B − C) = 2, execution branches to line 110.
4. If INT(A*B − C) = 3, execution branches to line 60.
5. If INT(A*B − C) = 4, execution branches to line 135.
6. If INT(A*B − C) = 5, execution branches to line 10.
7. If INT(A*B − C) < 1 or if INT(A*B − C) > 5, an error message is printed and execution is terminated.

The programmer must know in advance the range of possible values the formula might take so as to provide an appropriate number of transfers. Some systems allow a statement such as 50 ØN X GØSUB 700,820,950. It operates like ØN . . . GØ TØ except that it branches to the appropriate subroutine, depending on whether X = 1, 2, or 3. If X > 3, then execution continues with the statements immediately after statement 50.

EXERCISES 7-6

A Consider the following statement.

```
50 ØN X/Y GØ TØ 100, 120, 140, 10
```

To what statement will the program branch if X and Y are given as shown below?

1. X = 4 and Y = 4.
2. X = 5 and Y = 2.
3. X = 12 and Y = 3.
4. X = 1 and Y = 2.
5. Use an ØN statement in a program to generate 1000 random digits (0 to 9) and count the number of times that each occurs.

7-7 ADVANCED PRINT STATEMENTS

Sometimes output from a program should be in a special format. For example, if financial information is being printed, the figures in each column should have the decimal points in line and have two digits behind the decimal point, as in the following sample.

```
MØNTH            MØNTHLY SALES         YEAR-TØ-DATE

 JAN.             $  648.30            $  648.30
 FEB.                595.13              1243.43
 MAR.               1708.21              2951.64
 ...                 ...                  ...
```

A simple statement such as 100 PRINT M$(I), S(I), Y(I) would produce the list shown below.

```
MØNTH            MØNTHLY SALES         YEAR-TØ-DATE

 JAN.             648.3                648.3
 FEB.             595.13               1243.43
 MAR.             1708.21              2951.64
 ...              ...                  ...
```

Normally BASIC drops "trailing" 0's, as in the JAN. line above, and also "left justifies" numerals, that is, shifts them to the left end of the print zone. This causes numerals of differing numbers of digits to have their decimal points out of line, as in the second and third columns above.

Most systems have special PRINT commands that allow you to specify more exactly how you want output items printed. Below are some common methods but again your system's manual and experimentation at your keyboard must be your final guide.

The statement

```
80 PRINT USING "####.##"; X
```

would print X with two digits behind the decimal point. Each "#" represents a digit and the decimal point represents itself. A sample output from this statement might be 861.23 . Notice that, even though there are only three digits left of the decimal and the format in line 80 has four #'s left of the decimal, no 0 is printed to fill the extra space in front—which is what you want the machine to do. The statement

```
80 PRINT USING "$$####.##"; X
```

would put a $ in front of the number being printed. Notice that to get one $ printed, two $'s must be put in the *image,* which is the set of characters inside the quotes after the word USING.

Another way to accomplish these special results is shown in the following lines from a program.

```
100    LET A$ = "$$####.##"
       ...
210    PRINT USING A$; X
       ...
330    PRINT USING A$; Y
       ...
```

As you can see from these lines, an advantage of this approach is that several PRINT USING statements can use the same image (A$). On some systems a variation of the above program would look like this.

```
210    PRINT USING 300; X
       ...
300    :  $$####.##
       ...
```

Here a colon (:) immediately after a line number indicates that what follows is a print image, which can be referenced by a PRINT USING statement elsewhere in the program.

In writing large integers it is customary to put commas to separate each group of three digits, as in 1,863,417 . To achieve this effect in output, an image such as the following can be used:

150   B$ = "##,###,###" .

On some systems the same result can be created by putting one comma anywhere among the #'s of the image (except perhaps in the first two places):

150   B$ = "##,######" .

If scientific output is desired in the E-format, four exponentiation signs are used in the image. For example, if X = 861.15, then the statement

150   PRINT USING "#.## ↑ ↑ ↑ ↑"; X would print 8.61E+02 .

Usually, a form of the PRINT USING statement can be used to write in files, as in the samples shown below.

```
180    PRINT USING #1,"###.##", X
210    PRINT #1, USING "##↑↑↑↑", X
230    PRINT USING #2, A$, X  <———— A$ is the image.
320    PRINT USING #2, 150, X <———— 150 is the image line.
810    WRITE #1, USING A$, X
730    WRITE USING #3, "###.##", X
```

A final note concerning PRINT USING statements: On some systems the equivalent statement is of the form

```
PRINT IN IMAGE "###.##"; A
```

EXERCISE 7-7

A Write *Yes* or *No* to indicate whether each statement is allowed on your system.

```
 1. 170   PRINT USING A$, Z(I)
 2. 100   :####.##
 3. 170   PRINT USING 100; Z(I)
 4. 170   PRINT USING "$$###.##", Z(I)
 5. 170   WRITE USING A$, Z(I)
 6. 170   WRITE USING 100, Z(I)
 7. 170   PRINT IN IMAGE A$, Z(I)
 8. 170   PRINT IN IMAGE "##,###", A
 9. 170   PRINT USING #1, "###.##", A
10. 170   WRITE #1 USING X$, Z(I)
```

11. Given a company's monthly sales for a year, print a table showing the name of each month, the sales for that month, and the year-to-date sales at the end of that month. Use a format like the one at the beginning of Section 7-7 whereby figures are printed with decimal points in line and two digits behind each decimal point.

C **12.** A *scattergram* is a two-dimensional graph of data points, where the coordinates of the points are the values of the two variables being considered. (An example of a scattergram is shown below.) One variable defines the vertical axis and the other defines the horizontal axis. Write a program to plot scattergrams of Y vs. X values, where the data are limited to the first quadrant. Use the full width of your screen or printer page.

```
100   +                     *
      I                    *     *
      I                i     *
      I                  *     *
      I    *    *     *
 50   +      **
      I    *      *
      I
      I *
      I
  0   +----+----+----+----+----+----+
           1    2    3    4    5    6
```

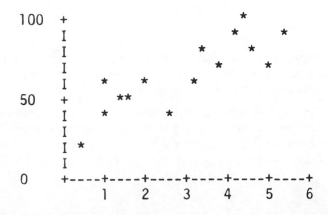

7-8 ADVANCED DECISION STATEMENTS

In Section 3-7 the IF . . . THEN statement was presented. It is amazing how much programming can be done with that simple command. But most systems allow variations of the decision statement that can save steps in programs. Here are some possibilities.

```
180    IF X = 0, THEN 300
180    IF X > 0 GØ TØ 300
180    IF X < 0 THEN GØ TØ 300
180    IF X >= 0 GØSUB 500
180    IF X2 = X1 THEN PRINT "SLØPE UNDEFINED"
180    IF X2 <= X1 LET S = 0
```

A more powerful decision statement is possible on systems that use the word ELSE to indicate what to do if the condition in the IF clause is false, as in the examples below.

```
200    IF X = 0 THEN 280 ELSE 310
200    IF X = 0 THEN PRINT "ZERØ" ELSE PRINT "NØT ZERØ"
```

Some systems even allow "chaining" or "nesting" of one decision in another. Such systems usually also allow a statement to overflow to a second line. Here is an example.

```
30    IF X > 0 THEN PRINT "PØSITIVE" ELSE IF X = 0 THEN
      PRINT "ZERØ" ELSE PRINT "NEGATIVE"
```

Another useful feature is the word "AND" as a logical connector, as in the following examples.

```
210    IF A = B AND B = C THEN 300
210    IF A = B AND B = C THEN PRINT "EQUILATERAL"
210    IF A = B AND B = C THEN PRINT "EQUILATERAL" ELSE
       GØ TØ 350
```

Following the meaning of "AND" in the logical sense, as well as in the everyday sense, the computer will not do what the THEN part says unless *both* parts of the IF clause (A = B, B = C) are true.

There is another logical connector "ØR" that is sometimes used. In logic, ØR can be used in two somewhat different senses. The computer follows the more common of the two senses by doing whatever the THEN part of the statement says unless *both* parts of the IF clause are false.

Example: `210 IF A = B ØR A = C THEN 330`

Some versions of BASIC allow several statements on a line. Usually a colon (:), a semicolon (;), or perhaps a slash (\) is used to separate the statements, as in the examples below.

```
60    PRINT "NØ SØLUTION": GØ TØ 10
70    FØR I = 1 TØ 10; READ A(I); NEXT I
90    LET Z = A(I)\LET A(I) = A(J)\LET A(J) = Z
```

This feature obviously saves lines in a program. However, care must be taken in using it. As an illustration of this caution, consider the following program segment.

```
        ....
150   FØR I = 1 TØ 10: READ A(I): IF A(I) = 9999 THEN
      180: NEXT I
180          ...
```

The problem comes from having a decision among the statements in line 150. On many systems, if A(I) ≠ 9999, then instead of "dropping through" to NEXT I, as desired by the programmer, the computer will "drop through" to the next *numbered* line, which is 180. So if multiple statements are included on a line, do not put any statement on that line after a decision. Instead rewrite the above program segment in the following manner.

```
        ...
150   FØR I = 1 TØ 10: READ A(I): IF A(I) = 9999 THEN 180
160   NEXT I
180          ...
```

Also, remember that if one statement refers to another, then that other statement must have its own line number. For example, consider the program segment below.

```
        ...
150   IF A = B THEN 180
160   PRINT "NØT EQUAL"
170   GØ TØ 190
180   PRINT "EQUAL"
190   LET C = A/B
200   PRINT C
        ...
```

Wanting to put as many statements on a line as possible, a programmer might carelessly rewrite these lines as shown below.

```
        ...
150   IF A = B THEN 180: PRINT "NØT EQUAL": GØ TØ 190
180   PRINT "EQUAL": LET C = A/B: PRINT C
        ...
```

But now the GØ TØ 190 step cannot be done by the computer because 190 LET C = A/B has lost its line number and is "hidden" in line 180. The maximum condensing of these lines is as follows.

```
      ...
150   IF A = B THEN 180
160   PRINT "NØT EQUAL": GØ TØ 190
180   PRINT "EQUAL"
190   LET C = A/B: PRINT C

      ...
```

EXERCISES 7-8

A Write *Yes* or *No* to indicate whether each statement is allowed on your system.

1. `130    IF X = Y, THEN 250`
2. `130    IF X <> Y THEN GØ TØ 250`
3. `130    IF X = Y GØ TØ 250`
4. `130    IF X = Y THEN PRINT "EQUAL"`
5. `130    IF X = Y PRINT "EQUAL"`
6. `130    IF X = Y THEN PRINT "EQUAL" ELSE PRINT "NØT EQUAL"`
7. `130    IF X >= Y GØSUB 500`
8. `130    IF X = Y AND X + Y < Z THEN 200`
9. `130    IF X = Y ØR X + Y < Z THEN LET K = K + 1`
10. `130    LET X = Y: LET Y = Z: PRINT "DØNE"`
11. `130    LET X = Y; LET Y = Z; PRINT "DØNE"`
12. `130    LET X = Y\LET Y = Z\PRINT "DØNE"`

If your system allows IF . . . THEN . . . ELSE statements, then use such a statement in rewriting and shortening each of the following programs.

13. Program 3-5 on page 97 **14.** Program 3-6 on page 99

B If your system allows more than one statement per line, then use this feature in rewriting and shortening each of the following programs.

15. Program 4-4 on page 133 **16.** Program 4-7 on page 142
17. Program 5-5 on page 191 **18.** Program 6-1 on page 234

7-9 TECHNIQUES FOR DISPLAYING GRAPHS AND DIAGRAMS

If your computer system has a video screen, it probably can display data in the form of **graphics,** that is, graphs or diagrams. On such systems, a special character called a cursor appears constantly on the screen. The **cursor,** which is used to mark your position at any point, is usually a dash (–), an underscore (__), or a solid block (■). As you type or as the computer displays information, the cursor moves across the screen from left to right.

Each screen is divided into a predetermined number of blocks. These blocks are larger or smaller depending on the amount of resolution available. A system with higher resolution allows you to "light" smaller points. The screen for one widely-used system is illustrated at the right. The positions on the screen are identified according to a coordinate system whose origin (0, 0) is the block at the upper left corner. Then the columns are numbered from left to right and the rows are numbered from top to bottom.

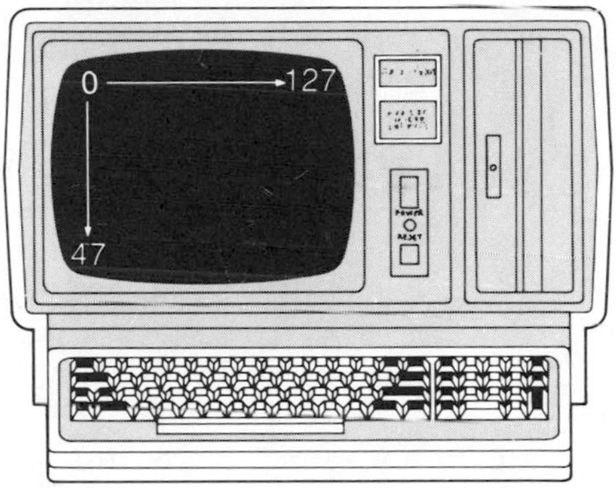

The table below illustrates how some techniques for displaying graphs and diagrams are programmed on two actual microcomputer systems. System 1 (see diagram at the right above) has 128 columns (numbered 0 to 127) and 48 rows (0 to 47). System 2 has 40 columns (0 to 39) and 40 rows (0 to 39). Thus, for System 1, $0 \leq x \leq 127$ and $0 \leq y \leq 47$. For System 2, $0 \leq x \leq 39$ and $0 \leq y \leq 39$.

Function	**System 1** (black and white)	**System 2** (16 colors)
Light a point	SET (*x*, *y*)	CØLØR = *n* ⟵ 0 ≤ *n* ≤ 15 PLØT *x*, *y*
Unlight (erase) a point	RESET (*x*, *y*)	CØLØR = 0 ⟵ 0 = *black* PLØT *x*, *y*
Draw a horizontal line	FØR X = 0 TØ 127 SET (X, *y*) NEXT X	HLIN 0,39 AT *y* ⟵ *first and last columns*
Draw a vertical line	FØR Y = 0 TØ 47 SET (*x*, Y) NEXT Y	VLIN 0,39 AT *x* ⟵ *first and last rows*

In the above table, a lower case *x*, as in SET (*x*, Y), refers to the column at which a point or line is to be drawn (or erased). A lower case *y* refers to the row at which a point or line is to be drawn. In addition to the functions just illustrated, System 1 and System 2 each has special commands or keys that permit greater flexibility in exploiting its graphics capabilities. For example, in System 1, the keys ↑, ↓, ←, and → can be used to move the cursor in a desired direction. In System 2, VTAB *n* ($1 \le n \le 24$) jumps the cursor vertically to the row (n) where the next item is to be displayed.

Each system has an instruction for clearing the screen. In System 1, the instruction is CLS; in System 2, it is GR, which is also the instruction for switching the screen to the GRaphics mode.

EXERCISES 7-9

A

1. In System 1, the instruction INKEY$ reads a character from the keyboard without waiting for the ENTER key to be pressed What is the purpose of line 210 below?

```
 . . .
200  PRINT "WHEN YØU ARE READY, PRESS ANY KEY."
210  IF INKEY$ = " " THEN 210
220  . . .
```

2. In System 2, trace the program at the right and summarize what it does.

```
100  CØLØR = 4
110  FØR X = 0 TØ 39
120    PLØT X, X
130  NEXT X
140  FØR I = 1 TØ 1E4
150  NEXT I
160  END
```

Write a program to do each of the following.

3. Let the user pick the coordinates of a point. Then make that point blink on and off.

4. "Paint" the screen from left to right and bottom to top.

5. "Paint" the screen from right to left and top to bottom.

6. "Paint" a square on the screen. Let the user specify the length of a side of the square and the coordinates of the lower left vertex. Include an error message in case the square requested does not fit on the screen.

7. Display a point in the center of the screen and let the user press the ↑, ↓, ←, or → keys to move the point. (Note: The ASCII codes are: ↑ = 91, ↓ = 92, ← = 93, → = 94.)

8. Light and unlight random points on the screen.

B

9. Draw an 8×8 checkerboard.

10. Draw a stickman.

11. Draw a stickman and make it "walk" on the screen.

CHAPTER SUMMARY

Each version of BASIC has additional commands and functions that give you greater programming power. However, consult the manual for your system to determine whether a certain feature is available.

You may define your own functions using the DEF FN statement.

Example: `20 DEF FNY(A,B) = SIN(A) - SQR(B)`

Alphanumeric data (e.g., names) are stored in *strings. String variables* are of the form A$, B$, etc., and may be used in INPUT, PRINT, LET, and IF . . . THEN statements. For manipulating strings, a system may have a special function, such as LEN, ASC, CHR, LEFT$, RIGHT$, MID$, or STRING$.

Each form of BASIC provides commands to read and write from external files, e.g., the FILES, READ *#n*, WRITE *#n*, INPUT:FILE:, PRINT:FILE:, ØPEN, CLØSE, SCRATCH, or RESTØRE statements.

Simulations and games involve the RND function, which generates a random number upon request (perhaps in conjunction with the RANDØMIZE statement).

The ØN statement combines several IF . . . THEN statements into one. For example, the statement 20 ØN X + Y GØ TØ 200, 210, 222 causes the computer to branch to line 200 if X + Y = 1, to line 210 if X + Y = 2, or to line 222 if X + Y = 3.

Some systems accept advanced statements such as PRINT USING that allow you to specify your own detailed output formats.

Certain advanced decision statements are available on many systems.

Examples:

```
50  IF X = Y PRINT "NØ SØLUTION"
60  IF X = Y AND Y = Z THEN PRINT "ALL EQUAL"
70  IF X = Y THEN PRINT "ISØSCELES" ELSE PRINT "SCALENE"
```

CHAPTER OBJECTIVES AND REVIEW

Objective: To use a DEF statement in writing a program. *(Section 7-1)*

1. Use a DEF statement to define the function $g(x) = |ax + b|$.

Objective: To use the statements available on your system to input and manipulate alphanumeric strings. *(Section 7-2)*

2. Accept a list of student names with the grade-point average (GPA) of each student. Print the list (with appropriate headings) in alphabetical order.

Objective: To use the statements available on your system to create and manipulate files. *(Section 7-3)*

3. Revise the program in Exercise 2 so that the list of names and GPA's is read from a file. In addition to printing the alphabetized list on the terminal, write the revised list into a new data file.

Objective: To use the RND function in a program to simulate chance events. *(Section 7-4)*

4. Write a program that "rolls" two dice and prints the sum of the numbers represented on the top faces. Include statements that ask the user whether he or she wishes another roll and, depending on the response, repeats the program or stops.

Objective: To use the EXP, LØG, or SGN functions in writing programs. *(Section 7-5)*

5. Write a program to produce a table of values of e^x and ln x ("natural log of x") for $x = 1, 2, 3, \ldots, 20$.

Objective: To use the ØN statement where appropriate in programs. *(Section 7-6)*

6. Write a main program that displays five options for the user. (You make up the titles of the choices.) Then, depending on which option is chosen, an ØN statement branches the computer to one of the five sections (or subroutines) of the program. (You do not have to write the subroutines.)

Objective: To use where appropriate any advanced PRINT or graphics statements available on your system. *(Sections 7-7 and 7-9)*

7. The data consist of the names of the employees of a company (in alphabetical order) and the year's sales total for each. Write a program to accept the data and print a table listing the employee's name, his or her sales total, and the sales commission (at 6%) of each employee. Print the second two columns so that the decimal points are in line and a "$" precedes the first data value in each column.

8. Write a program to draw a right triangle.

Objective: To use where appropriate in programs any advanced decision statements available on your system. *(Section 7-8)*

9. Use the AND and ELSE features in writing a program that accepts the lengths of the sides of a triangle and decides whether the triangle is equilateral, isosceles, or scalene.

ROUND SEVEN: *PROGRAMS FOR STUDENT ASSIGNMENT*

GENERAL INSTRUCTION:

In each exercise on page 299 through 308, write and run a program that will do what is specified in the exercise.

1. Devise new operations, such as $a \# b = a + b + ab$, and test the operations against the field axioms. (Note: The DEF statement is particularly useful here.)

2. Given a year (past, present, or future) print the calendar for that year.

3. The game "Twenty-three Matches" (a version of "NIM") is played as follows: Two players take turns removing matches from a pile of twenty-three matches. At each turn a player must take one, two, or three matches. He may not pass. The player who takes the last match loses. A strategy exists whereby the player who moves first can win every time. Simulate this game with the computer playing a human opponent.

4. Write a "teaching program" in which the computer provides practice problems to a student to determine his knowledge of the rules for multiplying positive and negative numbers. (This topic is only suggested; with your teacher's permission you may select another topic to teach.) The computer explains the rules and gives practice problems. It congratulates the student when he is right and corrects him when he is wrong, repeating the rule he has violated. The machine keeps track of how many problems the student answers correctly and prints his percent right at the end of the lesson.

5. Determine how many times Friday the 13th occurs in a given year.

In Exercises 6 and 7, consider an equation in two variables that is of the form $Ax^2 + Bxy + Cy^2 + Dx + Ey + F = 0$.

6. Identify the locus (straight line, circle, hyperbola, and so forth).

7. Print the equation of the image resulting from a rotation of the locus through an angle ϕ about the origin.

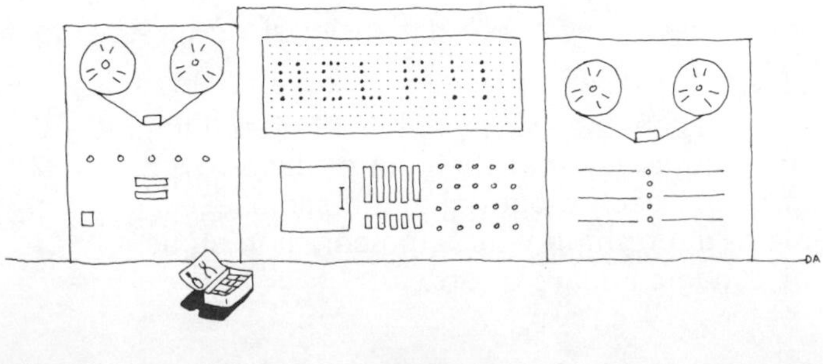

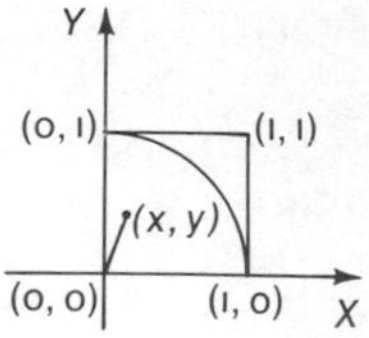

8. A "Monte Carlo" method for calculating π goes as follows: consider a unit square in the *xy*-plane with vertices at (0, 0), (1, 0), (1, 1), and (0, 1). For a circle centered at the origin with radius one (see diagram at right), one quadrant lies within the unit square. The area of this circle is π, and therefore the area of the quadrant shown is $\frac{\pi}{4}$. Imagine randomly choosing points within the square. Some of the points will lie within the circle and some will lie outside the circle. Because of the respective areas of the circle quadrant and the square, for a large number of points, approximately $\frac{\pi}{4}$:1 of the points will lie within the circle. Write a program that generates random values for the coordinates (X, Y) of a point within the square. The distance of this point from the origin is computed. If the distance is less than one, the point lies within the circle. If the distance is greater than one, the point lies outside the circle. Count the number of points within the circle. The ratio of the number of points that fall within the circle to the total number of points that are generated is an approximation of $\frac{\pi}{4}$. Four times this ratio is thus an approximation of π itself.

In Exercises 9 and 10, write a program in which the computer plays tic-tac-toe with a human opponent. Use the following numbering system for the board.

1	2	3
8	9	4
7	6	5

9. Have the computer always move first to the center square. This reduces the program strategy to offensive moves. An algorithm can be developed in which the computer either wins or ties every game.

10. Expand the program of Exercise 9 so that either the machine or the human opponent moves first (depending, say, on a RND generation). This is more difficult than the program of Exercise 9 but, here too, a nonlosing algorithm can be developed.

11. Write a program to play three-dimensional tic-tac-toe against a human opponent.

12. A magic square is an $n \times n$ array of the integers 1 to n^2 placed in such a way that the sum of each row, each column, and each diagonal is the same. (See the example at the right in which the common sum is 15.) Print a magic square of order *n*.

2	9	4
7	5	3
6	1	8

13. Eight queens can be arranged on a chessboard so that none of them is under attack from any of the others. Determine three such arrangements.

14. Generate a page of random single-digit multiplication problems. The output should appear as follows.

1. 3 $\underline{\times 4}$	2. 2 $\underline{\times 3}$	3. 6 $\underline{\times 8}$	(etc.)

15. At a certain company the mandatory retirement age is 70. Scan a file of employee's Social Security numbers, names, and birthdates. Print a list of those employees who must retire within the next year, within two years, three, four, and five years. Print the retirement lists in order of birthdays.

16. Design a questionnaire to be administered to your fellow students and a computer program to compile and analyze the results.

17. Simulate the dice game of "craps."

18. Fifty strangers are in a room. None of them was born in a leap year. What is the probability that two or more of them have the same birthday? (Consider only the day of the year, not the year of birth.) Attack the problem by generating random integers over the range 1 to 365, each integer representing a birthday for one of the strangers. Then check for identical birthdays. Repeat the algorithm many times to see how often identical birthdays occur. Print the per cent of such "successful" tries.

19. Simulate the batting of one side in a nine-inning baseball game, taking into account the batting statistics of the players. Print a batter-by-batter summary of each inning. Choose a real team and use their latest statistics to create the data file.

20. In the game of "Gunner," a human player fires a cannon at a target by entering the angle of elevation of the cannon. The computer first generates a random number that determines how many thousands of feet away the target is from the gun. When the player enters the angle of elevation, θ, the computer "fires" the gun and tells how close the shot came to the target (212 feet too short, 187 feet too long, and so forth) and invites the player to try again. Decide on some rule for destroying the target, e.g., it is destroyed if the shell lands within 50 feet of it. Also fix in the program an initial velocity v_0 for the projectile as it comes from the cannon and the acceleration, g, due to gravity. The distance that the shell travels horizontally is given by the equation $d = \dfrac{v_0^2 \sin 2\theta}{g}$.

21. Plot the graph of any function. Allow the user to input the function, the domain, and the increment between *x*-values. Here is a sample plot of a portion of $y = \sin x$. Turn it sideways to get the proper orientation.

```
FØR X:     TØP =  0  BØTTØM =  6.2832  INCREMENT =  .5
FØR Y:    LEFT = -1   RIGHT =  1  INCREMENT =  3.33333E-2

  I.........I.........I.........I.........I.........I.........I
-                               +                              -
.                                             +                .
.                                                        +     .
.                                                             +.
.                                                          +   .
.                                                 +            .
.                                   +                          .
.                    +                                         .
.        +                                                     .
.  +                                                           .
-  +                                                           -
.          +                                                   .
.                       +                                      .
  I.........I.........I.........I.........I.........I.........I
```

22. An interesting effect is created if, when graphing with a computer, you plot the spaces rather than the points. That is, where there is no point on the graph, print an asterisk, and where there is a point, leave the location on the paper (or screen) blank.

23. Plot a given function in the polar coordinate system. Thus, in the function mentioned in Exercise 21 you should plot the polar relationship $r = \sin \theta$.

24. The theory of *biorhythms*, which was developed in the late nineteenth century, speculates that each person is guided by three cycles that begin at birth. The intellectual, physical, and emotional cycles are each sine curves with amplitude one and periods of 33, 23, and 28 days, respectively. Given a person's date of birth, the day on which the chart is to begin, and the number of days the chart is to cover, print the person's biorhythm cycles.

25. Devise a program to decode messages written in a code you create. To test the program teach a friend your encoding scheme and have him or her encode a message without showing it to you. The program should decode this message correctly.

26. Teach the computer to write four-part harmony for a given melody.

27. Convert Arabic numerals to Roman numerals.

28. Convert Roman numerals to Arabic numerals.

In Exercises 29 and 30, a magazine has a file listing each subscriber's name, address, and subscription expiration date (month/year).

29. Write a program which, given a month and year, prints the names and addresses of all subscribers whose subscription expires that month.

30. Write a program which, given the current month and year, erases the names and addresses of all subscribers whose subscription expires this month. Print on the terminal the resulting condensed file and also write it back to the external file. "Condensed" means that there are no gaps: the information about the remaining subscribers have been pushed forward to fill vacated space in the array.

31. Given the names of the teams and their won-lost records, print up-to-date National or American League baseball standings. The output should list the teams in descending order of winning percentage, giving in columns the wins, losses, percentage, and games-behind. Do not assume that all teams have played the same number of games.

32. Translate dollar-cents amounts into words. Handle values up to ØNE MILLION DØLLARS AND NØ CENTS.

33. A **palindrome** is a word that is spelled the same backwards or forwards, such as "radar", "level", and "pop". Decide whether a given word is a palindrome.

34. The Rhine Test for extra-sensory perception involves a deck of 25 cards: five identical cards from each of five suits. The "deck" can be represented by 1111122222333334444455555 where the numbers refer to the suits. The deck is shuffled and the subject is asked to name the suit of each card in turn without seeing the card. Guessing at random, a person should correctly identify the suits of five of the 25 cards. If he guesses more than five, he is a candidate for having ESP. Simulate the experiment a large number of times.

35. Program the computer to "draw" a picture on the terminal.

36. Given the master file of cumulative individual statistics for past games of a basketball team and the statistics from the latest game, print the updated team and individual statistics of the team.

37. Program the computer to play blackjack against human opponents with the computer being the dealer.

38. Play the game of "Acey Ducey." The computer deals two cards face up. The player bets on whether the next card dealt will have a value between the first two.

39. Deal and analyze a poker hand. Possible outputs include "pair of eights," "full house," and "2–6 straight."

40. Simulate the trip of a mouse through a maze in search of cheese. In the diagram on the right, each intersection point of the maze has been given *x* and *y* coordinates. The mouse starts at (1, 0). At an interior intersection point such as (1, 1), assume that the probability the mouse goes in any direction is $\frac{1}{4}$. For a corner point such as (3, 0), assume that the probability is $\frac{1}{2}$ for either direction. For other border points such as (0, 2) the probability is $\frac{1}{3}$ for any direction. The mouse's trip ends when he reaches the cheese. Find the number of moves in each trip.

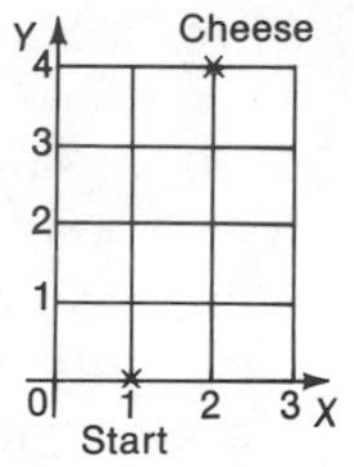

41. Determine the date of Easter in a given year.

42. Write a program that will deal a hand of bridge and that will also make an opening bid.

In Exercises 43 and 44, explanations are given of two procedures for approximating an irrational zero of a polynomial function. (There are several such methods. See, e.g., Ex. 58, p. 219.)

43. The Bisection Method: Suppose it is known (by substitution) that $P(a) < 0$ and $P(b) > 0$ (see the diagram at the right). Then *P*, being continuous, must cross the *x*-axis between *a* and *b*. To estimate the *x*-value of the crossing point, find the midpoint x_1 of the interval (a, b). If $P(x_1) > 0$, the root lies in the left half of the interval (a, b); if $P(x_1) > 0$, the root lies in the right half (for the diagram shown). In either case half the original interval can be discarded. Now bisect this new, smaller interval and repeat the analysis. By successive bisections the intervals in which the root is "trapped" become smaller and smaller and the root can be approximated to any desired accuracy.

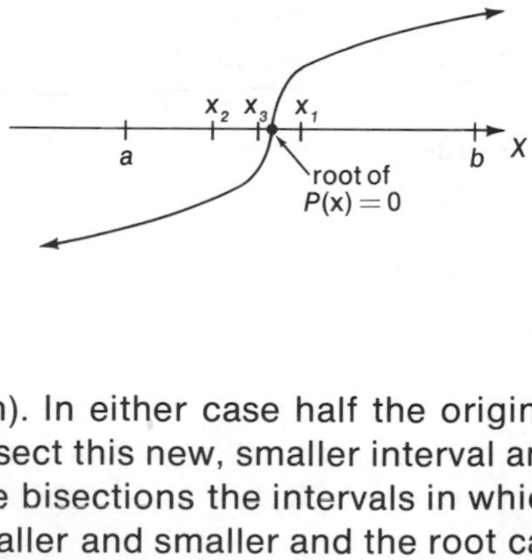

Write a program that accepts a polynomial function, finds two consecutive integers between which a real root lies, and then uses the Bisection Method to approximation the root.

44. The Method of Chords ("Method of False Position"): In the diagram at the right, chord AB crosses the x-axis "close" to the root of $P(x)$. The slope of AB is $\frac{P(x_2) - P(x_1)}{x_2 - x_1}$. By the point-slope form, the equation of AB is

$$y - P(x_1) = \frac{P(x_2) - P(x_1)}{x_2 - x_1}(x - x_1)$$

Substituting the coordinates of the point $(x_3, 0)$ into this equation and solving for x_3, we obtain

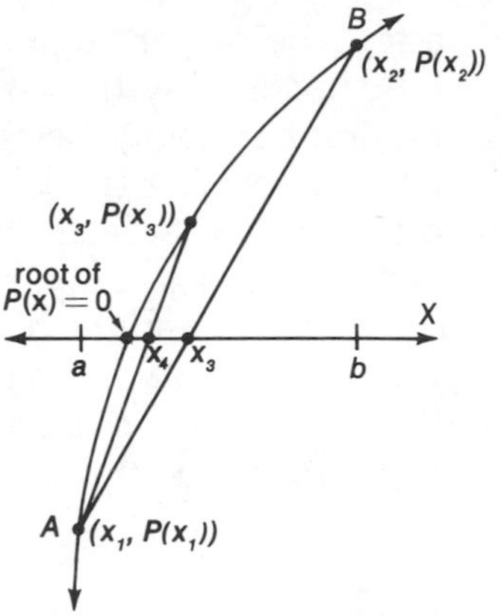

$$x_3 = x_1 + \frac{P(x_1)(x_1 - x_2)}{P(x_2) - P(x_1)}.$$

Now iterate the technique, first using the chord from $(x_1, P(x_1))$ to $(x_3, P(x_3))$ to gain a closer approximation x_4, then using the chord from $(x_1, P(x_1))$ to $(x_4, P(x_4))$ to gain a still closer approximation x_5, and so forth. Write a program that uses the Method of Chords to approximate a zero of a polynomial function.

In Exercises 45-47, the game of roulette is simulated. Two systems of betting also are considered.

45. A roulette wheel contains 38 numbers: 0–36, and 00. A player may bet on (**a**) a particular number; (**b**) even or odd; (**c**) red or black where 1, 3, 5, 7, 9, 12, 14, 16, 18, 19, 21, 23, 25, 27, 30, 32, 34, 36 are red, 2, 4, 6, 8, 10, 11, 13, 15, 17, 20, 22, 24, 26, 28, 29, 31, 33, 35 are black, and 0 and 00 are colorless; (**d**) the number falling in the first half (1–18) or the second half (19–36), and (**e**) the number falling in the low (1–12), middle (13–24), or high (25–36) range. Write a program to accept a number from 0 to 37 (37 represents 00) and print its characteristics (even-odd, red-black, 1st-2nd half, low-middle-high).

46. Under the "Martingale" betting system, a player begins with a basic bet. Then whenever he wins, he repeats the basic bet. If he loses, his next bet is double the previous amount (unless his money is insufficient, in which case he bets the remainder of his funds). A sample sequence is the following: bet \$10—win, bet \$10—lose, bet \$20—lose, bet \$40—win, bet \$10—lose, and so forth. The player continues until he either exhausts his capital or reaches a predetermined upper limit. Expand the roulette program to test this system.

47. The "progressive" system of gambling can be used for any bet that is close to even-money (such as "even-odd" or "high-low" in roulette). The player begins with a sequence of numbers, say 1, 2, 3, 4, 5. For each play he bets the sum of the first and last terms ($6 for the first bet using the sample sequence). If he wins, he crosses off the first and last terms; if he loses, he appends the amount just bet to the end of the list. Thus if the first play wins, the sample list becomes 2, 3, 4 and the next bet is $6. If he loses, the list becomes 1, 2, 3, 4, 5, 6 and the next bet is $7. The sequence should eventually disappear, at which point (theoretically) the player has won the sum of his original sequence. Write a program that will test this system for playing roulette.

In Exercises 48-51, four methods are given for finding the area under a curve, as shaded in the figure on the right. In each case write a program to compute the area of a given function over a given interval by the method explained.

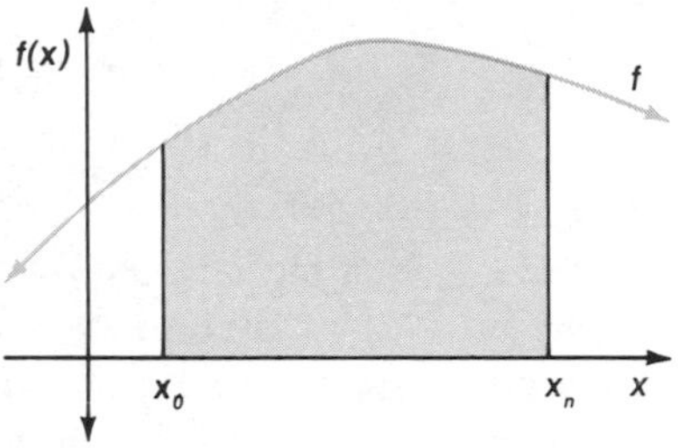

48. Rectangular Rule: Divide the interval (x_0, x_n) into n equal parts and use each interval as the base of a rectangle that has one vertex on the curve f, as in the figure on the right. The sum of the areas of the rectangles approximates the total area under the curve. To obtain a better approximation, increase (for example, by doubling) the number of rectangles.

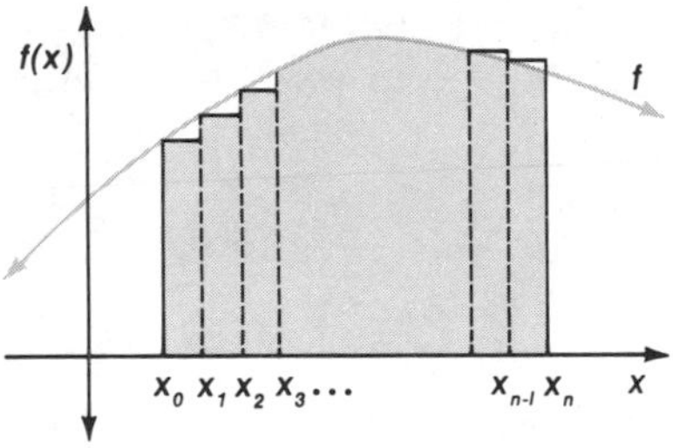

49. Trapezoidal Rule: This technique is similar to the Rectangular Rule except that trapezoids replace the rectangles (see the figure on the right). Again the approximation can be improved by increasing the number of trapezoids.

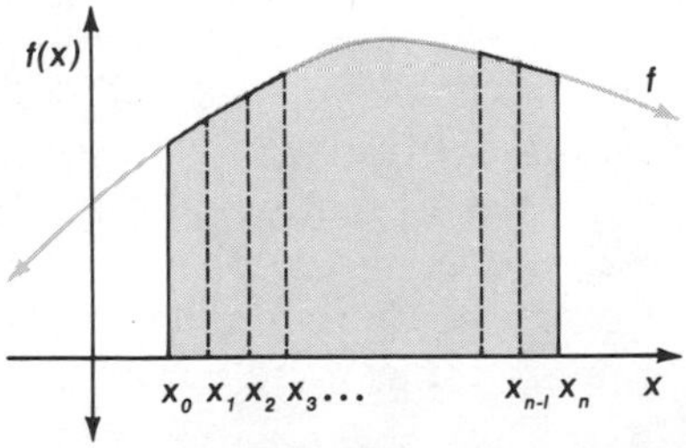

… THE OUTPUT FOR THE FOLLOWING PROGRAMS:

1.

```
10 REM FOR X = 1 TO 5
20 REM LET Y = X * 2
30 REM NEXT X
40 REM PRINT X
50 REM PRINT Y
60 END
```

OUTPUT:

READY

2.

```
10 READ X,Y,Z
20 LET A = 0
30 LET B = X - Y
40 READ A
50 PRINT B,A
60 DATA 5,7,9,11
70 END
```

OUTPUT:

-2b   b11b

3.

```
10 DATA 10,20,30,40
20 READ A,B,C,D,E
30 PRINT A;B,C;D
40 END
```

OUTPUT:

OUT OF DATA Line 20

4.

```
10 LET X = A + B
20 LET A = 13.5
30 LET B = -4.2
40 PRINT A, INT(A); SGN(A)
50 PRINT B, INT(B); SGN(B)
60 PRINT X
70 END
```

OUTPUT:

13.5   b13bb1b
-4.2   -5b-1b
Ø

5.

```
10 PRINT
20 LET A$="SAM MY"
30 PRINT A$
40 LET X =0
50 LET X= X + 10
60 IF X>20 THEN 80
70 GO TO 30
80 PRINT X
90 END
```

OUTPUT:

READY

SAM MY
SAM MY
SAM MY
INFINITE LOOP

THREE

RITE THE PROGRAM THAT GOES WITH THIS FLOWCHART:

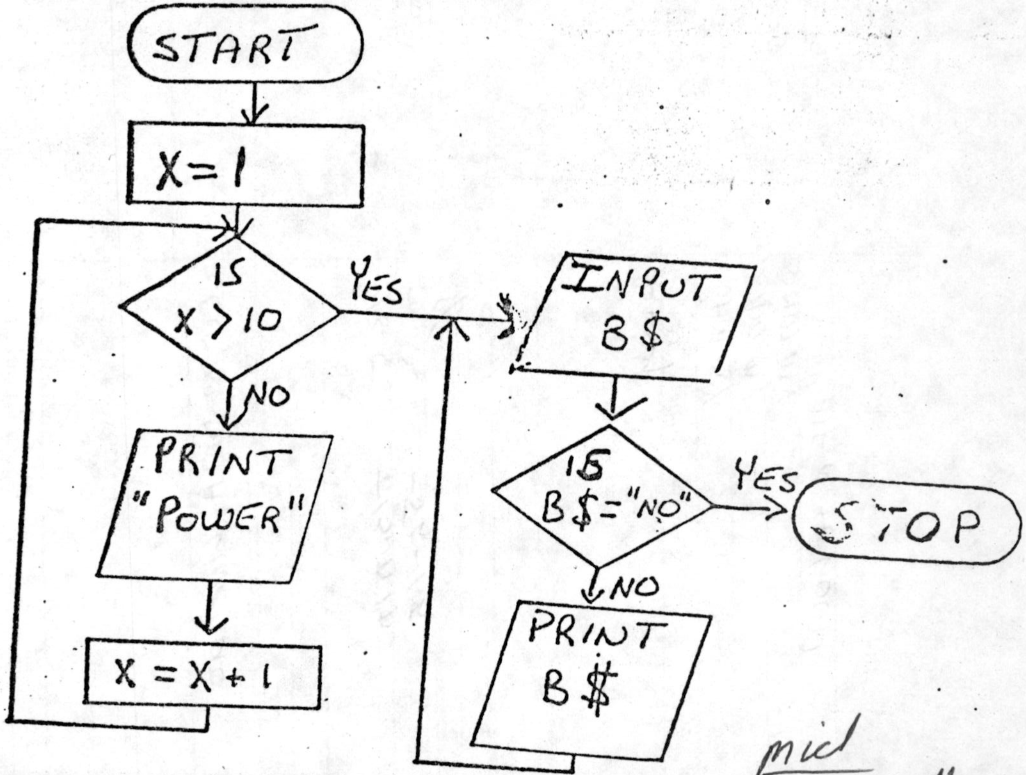

mid
62-math

```
:0 [illegible]
:0 PRINT "POWER"
:0 LET X = X+1
:0 GOTO 80
:0 INPUT B$
:0 IF B$ = "NO" THEN 100
:0 PRINT B$
:0 GOTO 60
00 END
10
20
30
```

[illegible]

ote: You need not use all the lines provided.

```
10 PRINT "MIKE"
20 LET X = 5
30 PRINT
40 LET X = X + 3
0 PRINT
0 LET X = X + 6
0 PRINT X
0 END
```

READY
MIKE
5 14 5

```
0 FOR X = 1 TO 10 STEP 2
0 PRINT TAB(X); X;"X"
0 NEXT X
0 END
```

OUTPUT:

```
0123456789012345678901234567890
 5 1 5 X
   5 3 5 X
     5 5 5 X
       5 7 5 X
         5 9 5 X
```

```
PRINT "COMPUTERS ARE GREAT"
READ A,B
IF A < B THEN 70
IF A > B THEN 60
PRINT A;"EQUALS"; B
PRINT A;"IS GREATER THAN";B
PRINT A;"IS LESS THAN";B
DATA 8,3 ,-4,2
END
```

OUTPUT:

Computers are great
8 is greater 3
8 is less than 3

```
FOR X = 1 TO 10
READ A
NEXT X
PRINT A;X.
DATA 10,20,30,40,50,60
DATA 70,80,90,100,110
END
```

OUTPUT:

5 100 5 11 5

```
EAD A$,B$
F A$= B$ THEN 99
RINT B$
RINT TAB(5);A$
O TO 10
ATA "BOB","LOU","MARY"
ATA "JOE","JOE"
END
```

OUTPUT:

```
0123456789012345678901234567890l
LOU
     BOB
JOE
     MARY
OUT OF DATA in 70
```

50. Midpoint Rule: Rectangles are used, as in Exercise 48, but the midpoint of the top side of each rectangle rests on the curve f (see the figure on the right). Note that a portion of each rectangle lies above the curve to counterbalance the small areas under the curve that are not covered by the rectangles. (This last fact helps explain why this method gives a better approximation than either the rectangle or trapezoid rules.)

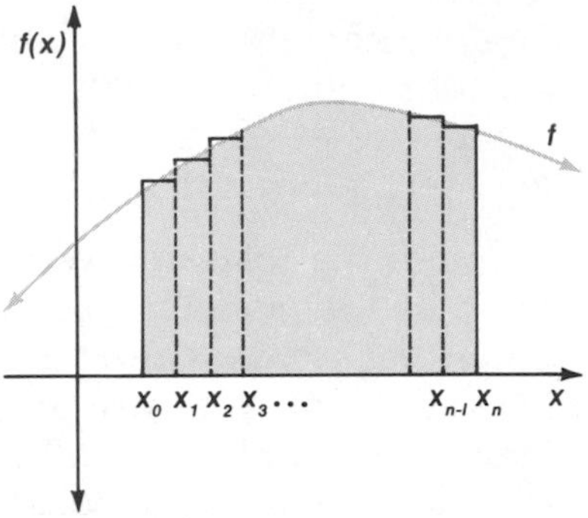

51. Simpson's Rule: This method, even more accurate than the Midpoint Rule, was invented by Thomas Simpson (1710–1761). The mathematics behind this method cannot be summarized in a diagram. Divide the interval (x_0, x_n) into an *even* number of segments and determine $y_0, y_1, y_2, \ldots, y_n$ where $y_i = f(x_i)$. Then

area $= \frac{h}{3}(y_0 + 4y_1 + 2y_2 + 4y_3 + \ldots + 2y_{n-2} + 4y_{n-1} + y_n)$, where h is the width of each interval $(x_0, x_1), (x_1, x_2), \ldots, (x_{n-1}, x_n)$. Again, a better approximation can be obtained by increasing n.

52. Generate license plate number-letter combinations. Establish a pattern, such as six characters of which the first three are alphabetic and the last three numeric. Print as many combinations as the user requests.

53. In one version of the "Mastermind" game, the computer generates a four-digit number to be guessed by the player. When the player makes a guess, the computer gives the responses indicated below.

(**a**) If a guess contains none of the digits in the number, the computer replies MISS

(**b**) If a guess contains one of the digits in the number but the position of that digit is wrong, the computer replies HIT

(**c**) If a guess contains one of the digits in the correct position in the number, the computer replies BULL'S EYE

(**d**) If a guess contains two or more digits that are hits, bull's eyes, or both, then the computer replies accordingly, but not necessarily in the order of the guessed digits.

Example: Correct number: 2795 Player's Guess: 2954
Computer reply: 2 HITS 1 BULL'S EYE

A player's score is the number of tries used to find the number.

54. Play the game of "High-Low" by having the computer generate a random integer from 1 to 100. Ask the player to guess the integer. The program then states whether the guess is too high, too low, or just right, after which the player makes another guess. Count the number of guesses and if the integer has not been guessed after ten tries, inform the player that he or she has lost.

55. Program the following version of the game of "Battleship" (there are other versions of this game). Two players (you and the computer) each have four ships: a battleship (5 units long), a cruiser (3 units long), and two destroyers (2 units long each). The ships may be placed horizontally, vertically, or diagonally and must not overlap. Your ships are located on a 10 × 10 grid and the computer's ships are located on another 10 × 10 grid. The two grids share a common boundary. The players take turns firing at one another. Only one ship may fire during a turn. Each ship is able to fire as follows: battleship—1, 2, or 3 shots; cruiser—1 or 2 shots; destroyer—1 shot. A shot is entered by giving its horizontal (X) and vertical (Y) coordinates. A ship is sunk if a shot hits any part of it. The game ends when one side has lost all of its ships.

56. A manufacturing company has a file containing a record for each part it makes. Each record contains a line number, a part number, a description, the number of hours required to make the part in each of three departments, and the number of dollars of direct labor currently needed to produce the part. Because of a pay rate increase for all employees, the company needs to know what the projected costs will be for each part. Print a list of cost projections and also produce an updated file reflecting the new costs.

57. Generate random numbers without using the computer's built-in generator.

58. Generate *n* Bingo cards (depending on the number of players) and then play Bingo.

59. Display the time of day digitally (including the seconds), starting with any time that is input.

Program the computer to play each of the following games against a human opponent.

60. Checkers **61.** Cribbage **62.** Backgammon

63. Print a maze (of any size) that includes at least one escape path.

64. Turn the computer into a slot machine.

In the two lists below, each BASIC command, statement, function, or symbol used in this book is shown, together with the page on which it was introduced.

A List of BASIC Terms

A List of BASIC Symbols

INDEX